EVERYBODY'S TALKING
ABOUT
OUT OF CONTROL!

"A TERRIFYING GLIMPSE INTO THE WORLD OF BIG MONEY, DRUGS AND DEBAUCHERY . . ."

—ALA *Booklist*

"HENDERSON EFFECTIVELY PUTS THE READER ON THE PLAYING FIELD AND RE-VEALS ALL . . ."

—*The New York Times Book Review*

"A FRIGHTENING, RIVETING TALE of how drugs can destroy a life or career. . . . must reading."

—Roger Staubach

"TOTALLY HONEST. . . . Anyone who feels there is no longer hope for a friend or loved one involved in drugs should read this book."

—Willie and Connie Nelson

"*OUT OF CONTROL* IS AN IMPORTANT DOCU-MENT FOR PEOPLE WHO ARE HAVING DRUG PROBLEMS or those who know people trying to get over drug problems. The book really spoke to me. . . . It's one book that doesn't pull any punches."

—B. J. Thomas

"COMPELLING. . . . with skillfully re-created foot-ball action, player's-view portraits of coaching legends (Landry, Ditka, Shula). . . . A HARROWING TOUR OF A RELENTLESS ADDICTION."

—*Kirkus Reviews*

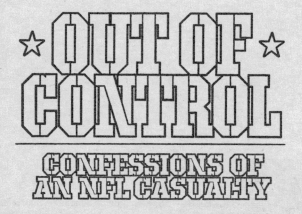

OUT OF CONTROL

CONFESSIONS OF AN NFL CASUALTY

THOMAS *Hollywood* HENDERSON
and PETER KNOBLER

POCKET BOOKS

New York   London   Toronto   Sydney   Tokyo   Singapore

POCKET BOOKS, a division of Simon & Schuster Inc.
1230 Avenue of the Americas, New York, NY 10020

ISBN: 0-671-73650-7

First Pocket Books printing September 1988

10 9 8 7 6 5 4 3 2

POCKET and colophon are registered trademarks of
Simon & Schuster Inc.

Printed in the U.S.A.

This book is dedicated to my beautiful wife, Diane Marie, and my daughter, Thomesa. Diane gave me love and understanding when I didn't feel loved or understood. Her belief in me for who I am and not who I was enabled me to love and trust again. She gave me the courage and respect that I needed to lift my head and carry on. She loves me for being Thomas and not "Hollywood." Thanks, honey.

My other girl is my child, Thomesa Holly Henderson. I dedicate to her the truth about her daddy. No man or woman can tell her anything different. I'll forever love daddy's little "stink-stink."

Last but not least I dedicate this personal inventory to athletes, alcoholics, addicts and the kids. *Know* why to say no to drugs and alcohol.

In memory of William Allen Goree and Nettie Mae Higgins.

In special memory of Len Bias, Don Rogers and Larry Bethea. They didn't have to die.

—*T.H.*

To my mother and father.

—*P.K.*

Acknowledgments

There were many people who played key roles in the creation of this book and, more important, in my sobriety. If not for sobriety the book could not have been written. I owe thanks, love and gratitude to my mother, Violet Faye Henderson Rivers Aldridge, for the special bond only a mother and son can have. James Rivers, Sr., will always be Daddy. Arnie Gold saved my life. Dr. Joseph Pursch, Dr. Mike Stone and Don Beld treated my disease and cared for me when I couldn't afford the cost of rehabilitation. These men saved my life.

Special thanks also to Phil Allen, my therapist, for his patience and care. Chuck D. and his wife, Merna, adopted me and loved me when I needed it most. P.J. gave me friendship and love at a time when we both were willing to be a friend and love unconditionally. Ted A. believed in me and was a friend, supporter and father to me through the toughest time in my life and I'm forever grateful to him.

Lifelong thanks and appreciation I extend to family and friends who, no matter what, loved me. My family in Austin, Texas, the Rivers, the Rhems, the Houstons and the Overtons.

In New York, the Gorees. In California, the Hays and the Hamptons. Also Von Holmes, Garland Lenoir, Oliver Stripling, Jr., Leroy Bradshaw and Vincent Henderson.

A man is lucky to have special friends, friends during the good times and the bad. I have had fair-weather friends but through my trials I realized that I also have real friends. Roger Staubach and Mike Murray have always been the two people I wanted to be like. I wish I could have lived like Roger Staubach and functioned like Mike Murray. They are real friends.

From my old team the Dallas Cowboys I'd like to thank Jerry Tubbs, Tom Landry, Ernie Stautner, Tex Schramm, Gene Stallings, Mike Ditka, Red Hickey, Joe Bailey, Doug Todd, Don Wilson, Buck Buchanan, Don Cochren, Ben Agajanian and Bob Ward. I'd also like to thank my favorite journalist in Texas, Frank Luksa.

My former Cowboy teammates Drew Pearson, Tony Dorsett, Tony Hill, Ed "Too Tall" Jones and Bob Breunig have continued their friendships and are still my friends. So are Charlie and Rosie Waters, Rayfield "Cat" Wright and Jethro Pugh. Thanks, fellas.

B. J. and Gloria Thomas supported and loved me and I'll always be grateful for their friendship. Willie and Connie Nelson know all about "Don't let your babies grow up to be Cowboys." I treasure them and always will.

Old friends who are still my friends: Lloyd, Biff, Corky, O'Reilly, Pam Plesko, S. R. McGruder, Bernie, Jeannie Habermehl, John Norton, Debbie Fabry, Carol Black, Laura Fuller, Nancy Brannon, Linda Hampton, Chuck Mayhew, Sharon Gabriel, Sheryl Baldridge, Bennie, Mike Harris, Barbara Horan, Steve Carbone, Jack Gilardi and my half brother Dwayne Bell. I love them all. Louise too.

Dan Reeves. Thanks for letting me serve.

I never thought the day would come when I would thank a lawyer for anything, but attorney Charles Caperton of Dallas was a tremendous counselor and has remained a friend for many years. Al Krutilek, my CPA, has gone beyond the call of duty, and of course the call of fees, and not only worked for nothing but has shown that he would help me in the good and bad times. Thanks, Al.

Thanks to Page. I appreciate her help and expertise, advice and love.

Then there are the sober folks who are just the best friends a dope addict like me could possibly hope for: P.J., Larney and Jennifer, Donahue, Tyrell, Tom V., Alice A., Peter and Veronica D., Jan G., Nolan, Bob Meehan, Frank O., Virginia H., Clarence K. and thousands of others who live one day at a time in the program. Keep it up.

I owe a debt of gratitude to Richard Pryor. Richard was there when I called. He called back and helped me when I was in prison. I love Richard Pryor.

Jay Acton took control as my literary agent and I found a professional who got the job done.

Special thanks. In March 1985 I met Frank Weimann. How lucky for me. He came to visit me in the California Men's Colony and said that he wanted to help me and be a friend. I give Frank Weimann full credit for getting my autobiography published. The man set out on a mission and succeeded. Because of his energy and persistence the book is reality. Frank is my personal agent today and my only regret is that I didn't have Frank at my side in my glory days. Thanks, Frank.

My coauthor Peter Knobler put my voice on paper. He understood exactly what I wanted to say and I was lucky to have such a talented writer to do justice to my autobiography. Thanks also to my editor Roger Scholl, Gail Olson, Neil Amdur and Ed Gallucci. If any readers would like to write to me about drug or alcohol problems and need information about the program that saved my life, and what I believe to be the best treatment facilities, you can write to me directly at P. O. Box 3828, Costa Mesa, CA 92628-3828.

There *is* life after drugs. Just don't die trying to find that life. Don't take that first drink of alcohol or use drugs. Please!

—Thomas Henderson

Acknowledgments

A NOTE TO THE ALCOHOLICS AND ADDICTS WHO STILL USE AND ABUSE.

I can't promise that the gates of Heaven will open and let you in if you quit. But I can promise that the gates of Hell will open and let you out.

Contents

Prologue

I thought I was in control. Super Bowl Sunday, 1979, I was right up there with the best-known people in America. I may have been a Dallas Cowboy but I was "Hollywood." I was on the cover of *Newsweek*—there was a little line above my photograph saying "Inside: Cambodia's Fall" with a picture of some guy with a head wound, but I took up half the page and the magazine obviously felt I was more important. Roger Staubach and Tony Dorsett didn't make the front page, I did. I took headlines away from the Shah of Iran. Joe Namath's spotlight had been shattered. It should have been the most exciting day of my life. But it wasn't, so I had brought my own excitement. Cocaine.

I was beyond snorting cocaine to get high, although I did that often. In fact, every chance I could. I needed coke for maintenance. Whether I wanted it or not I had to have cocaine near. My nose was ruined. It ran and bled like the Nile when Moses called down the plagues. I was blowing it so much that I thought one day I would look into my handkerchief and see that my whole nose had fallen off my face.

Super Bowl XIII was to be played in the Orange Bowl in Miami, a good highlife town, and the morning of the game I went to the team breakfast in a haze. I'd pampered my nose the night before and gotten so wired that I'd had to take a couple of Quaaludes to get to sleep. So I woke up groggy on game day. The first thing I usually did when I woke up was do a maintenance job on my nose, but if I didn't put something in my stomach I would suffer from dehydration and get cramps during the second half. Coke killed my appetite so I had to struggle through pancakes, steak and eggs before I lost my ability to eat completely.

I'd really mouthed off that week. I'd mastered the media circus and, fueled by my cocaine, got off as many quips and salvos as the cameras, mikes and pencils could get down. We were playing the Pittsburgh Steelers and I'd told everybody that their quarterback, Terry Bradshaw, was so dumb he couldn't spell "cat" if you spotted him the "c" and the "a." That made life hard on my teammates—the Steelers were fighting mad—but I didn't care. We could handle them. At least I could. And I knew the Steelers were out to get me.

I felt so alone that morning. I had got too famous, too popular, too cocky, too important for anybody to give a damn. My teammates were sitting at the same table all around me but they were strangers. We didn't have much to say to each other.

Win or lose, the team was going home right after the game, so I packed my kit bag with only what I'd need at the Orange Bowl and left my other luggage to get picked up by whoever did that for the Cowboys. Basically, my baggage to the Bowl was my coke. I was going to get banged around out there and my nose was going to hurt like a motherfucker. The scabs in there were sore, my eyes would water, I'd be a mess. So besides having an addiction and a real habit, I needed cocaine as medication. I had to anesthetize my face.

Throughout my football career I'd rarely played on cocaine. The drugs that I abused playing the game, and that were abused by almost everybody around me, were codeine, Percodan and amphetamines. Codeine kills pain. Percodan kills pain. People would ask me how I could take those things, didn't they make me sleepy. Well, I wasn't driving any heavy machinery, just myself, and I needed the pain killed. No matter how glamorous it may seem from the outside, football is a game of pain. Amphetamines, of course—speed—are your own personal pep rally.

I had to have my supply for the day so I packed all of them too. I had to get up. But the times I had tried cocaine in a game it had affected my breathing, affected my heartbeat, and those were the two things that you needed most, especially in the fourth quarter when the game was on the line.

But when you've got to have it you've got to have it, so I poured about a gram and a half of powder into a Vicks Inhaler, mixed it with some water to make it squeeze out easier, put it in my watch pocket and headed for the stadium.

At the Orange Bowl I went through my normal pregame routine. I tried not to blow my nose so hard that everyone would recognize what was going on. (I had started figuring out that people knew something was obviously wrong with my nose; it had to have been hard to miss, I was honking and snorting all the time.) I took a shower and then dripped over to my locker, went in my bag, pulled out my Vicks Inhaler, went back to the toilet stalls, sat down on the commode and began to medicate my nose.

I filled up pretty good, gave myself a whole series of solid jolts, then cleaned off the smudges and strode back to my locker. I was all of a sudden real fired up. It didn't take the pep squad, no cheerleaders, didn't take a lot of screaming and hollering and beating my head against the wall to get me Super Bowl prepared. The cocaine made me alive. Ready.

About an hour and a quarter before kickoff we had to go out for the pregame warm-ups. I had never taken cocaine on the field with me before, but the paranoia was beginning to get its hooks in. I was afraid Charlie Jackson of NFL Security might go on and search my locker—wouldn't put it past them—so I wasn't about to leave anything in my bag.

There's a little slot on most pants that NFL players wear where, tight as they are, there's no way that you can lose anything. I tucked my Vicks Inhaler into my uniform and headed on out to play.

I stepped on the field with amazing confidence. Nobody could touch me. I knew our team, I knew our game plan, I knew what we had to do to win.

It was the best Super Bowl ever. Usually the game doesn't live up to its hype, and I had hyped this one to the moon, but that day both teams were on fire. Even out on the field where you don't give nothing away, everybody knew this one was amazing and you had to respect the guys who were doing the job—and despise the guys who weren't.

Usually when someone gets beat for a score his teammates, even his closest friends, will turn and growl, "You sorry motherfucker," hate the guy for losing for them. When Rocky Bleier beat D. D. Lewis in the corner of the end zone for a touchdown D. D. looked like John Belushi at the New York City Ballet. Neither one of them looked worth a damn, but there was Bleier with six points and there was Lewis standing like a stooge. But when Lynn Swann leaped and caught a pass at the peak of its flight and then did a knee slide right at the back edge of the end zone to stay in for the Steeler touchdown I didn't even think about the defensive back. I thought, "What a great fucking catch."

Sometime in the middle of the second half my nose really began to hurt. It was running again and all my pregame anesthetizing had just about worn off so I decided to medicate it. Doctors use Xylocaine, Novocain and cortisone to anesthetize parts of the body that are hurting with football injuries. They're shooting you up all the time in the trainer's room to get you out there. Mine was an addiction-related nose injury. In the NFL's new drug abuse program they've got what they call the NFI, the nonfootball illness. I was having a nonfootball illness in the middle of the Super Bowl.

4

I pulled out my Vicks Inhaler. The Orange Bowl holds about eighty thousand screaming fans, plus there were about two hundred million people watching worldwide on TV, and there I was on the sideline taking a couple of major snorts in front of all of them.

We lost that day. I lost that day. I was out of control.

1

Surviving the Cut

There wasn't any man around the house when I was born. Not for some time after. Not for much time before. My mama, Violet Faye Henderson, was raised in Austin, Texas, by her older cousin Nettie Mae Higgins when Faye's daddy ran off and left her as a little baby. Nettie Mae wasn't my mother's mother, but she was the only mother my mother knew. A God-fearing, Bible-quoting lady, Nettie Mae took the Old Testament seriously. An eye for an eye. She used to beat my mama when Faye was bad, and Faye was bad often. At least that's the way my mama tells it.

Faye was a foxy little teenager. She was fair-complexioned, very pretty, about five foot five, had a big butt, real athletic. Tough, outgoing, used to run around all the time. All the boys had their eye on her.

There was an Air Force base near Austin and one summer day a young enlistee, another teenager, made contact. This military man picked up Faye and walked her home. Nettie Mae was out at a prayer meeting and the boy, Billy Goree, was just as impressive as could be. Maybe it was the uniform,

I don't know, but family history has it that Faye made love to him only once, on this big white swing chair on Nettie Mae's front porch.

Faye was still in high school when she got pregnant with me. Nettie Mae threw a fit. The girl couldn't hardly take care of herself, there wasn't no way she was going to become a mother. Not in this house. Nettie Mae filed statutory rape charges against the airman—Billy Goree was seventeen—but before anything could even begin to get to court the Air Force shipped his ass off to Korea. Then she tried to abort me. She tried to do a coat hanger program, actually brought the midwife over to perform it, but Faye ran away. Split to Louisiana and stayed with some friends. Finally she did come back, but she and Nettie Mae didn't do too much talking from then on, and at 7:05 in the morning on March 1, 1953, I was born. It says right there on the birth certificate: "Illegitimate." My mama was fifteen.

I didn't meet my daddy until twenty-one years later.

When my sister was born, two years later, she had a daddy. Mr. Rivers. Mr. Rivers was about six foot three, a good-looking man, very dark complexion, wavy jet-black hair slicked all the way to the back of his head. He and my mama got together right after I was born and Faye moved in with him. She was sixteen then and he was thirty-eight.

They did get married but it was several years later, and they had a bunch of kids. First came my sister Nettie, who I called Cookie. Then came Victoria, then James, and finally Franchot. But they were different from me. They all knew who their father was. Their last names were Rivers. Mine was Henderson. My mom wouldn't let Mr. Rivers give me his name, and even though I called him Dad she made it plain to me and my stepfather that I was not his child. "This is not your boy!" she would shout at him when he either wanted me to do something for him or was out looking to whip me. "Don't you lay a hand on that child!" So I knew this man had no jurisdiction over me, he couldn't whip me because my mother was going to be there.

At first, when there was just me and my little sister, we

lived in one room of a house at Thirteenth and Chicon. There was a blanket or a spread or something that separated Cookie and me from Mom and Mr. Rivers. There was no shower, we bathed in a galvanized aluminum number-three tub. The toilet had no handle, it had a pull chain from way up on the ceiling, and in all the corners of the room there were these bugs that had long legs and this little bitty ball for a body. I used to call them granddaddies because they looked like old fighters. The whole room was very small. If I walked in there today I could broad jump the place.

Every time the sun came up I was out in the street. The city of Austin didn't think it was really necessary to pave the streets in the ghetto so I was just rooting around in the dirt all day. There was a lot to see.

The Cut in Austin was a whole avenue of honky-tonks and bars and pool halls, a whole lot of loud talk and hot fights and beer joints open for any kind of business. There was Frank's Pool Hall and Miss Malder's Barber Shop and then a little arcade and then an alley filled with broken glass. I remember always having to run across that alleyway real fast from one curb to the other so I wouldn't cut my feet. I wasn't running around in shoes much in those days.

Across the alley was this grocery store, Miss Hattie's and Greasy Dick's. They called it Greasy Dick's because he had a hog farm and he looked like his hogs. Right past Greasy Dick's was Mr. Money. Mr. Money had a sign in the window, "We buy, sell and trade," but all he had in that little store was tires with holes in them and dusty stuff that nobody with any sense would buy. I don't know what kind of business he could've been doing.

I didn't know what kind of business the ladies who stood out in front of the next building were doing, either. I know now, but when I was four or five years old they were just some more of my playmates.

Charlie Payday looked like a black Amish. In Austin in the summertime the temperature gets up to over a hundred and cruises there for a couple of months. Well, Charlie Payday wore a black hat, black suit, white shirt, black tie and black Stacy Adams shoes every day that I ever knew him. Charlie had two brooms and a dustpan and a couple of trash cans and Charlie Payday swept the streets. I don't know who was paying him, I don't think anybody was, but every day he was out there with his brooms sweeping and cursing, all black and Texas angry. Nobody wanted to get next to him.

But I found out very quickly that everybody in the street knew Faye, or wanted to know her. By the time I was four or five years old my mama was twenty, and she was beautiful. She was a hot little mama and she would frequent the neighborhood places, the honky-tonks and beer joints where old Fats Williams would sit and play his blues.

I was good-natured, a little prankster, not breaking windows or anything like that, but I was there all the time if you came down the street. I got out in the street early in the morning. My mother and father both worked and my sister was often kept by my grandmother, who lived only two blocks away, so I was back on the streets no matter who was keeping me 'cause I had to go make me some change.

It'd be seven o'clock in the morning and I'd go find Seth and Whiskey. They were the neighborhood drunks and they were my friends. Seth wouldn't be packed discreetly in a corner, he'd be right in the middle of the sidewalk and he'd be *gone*. I'd shake him a little and bend down. "Hey, Seth, wake up!" I'd see Seth in the evening sometimes when he wasn't drunk on his ass yet, just functionally fired up, and the man talked so eloquently that even at that age I knew he was talking a different language than I was. He must've had some educational background because he'd come off as some kind of professor and I couldn't get enough of his words. In the morning he'd roll over when I'd roust him and then, when his vision cleared, say, "I am fine, sir. I simply had a few more than I should have last night. I am quite all right, thank you." It sounded to me like the king of England had come down to this alley and passed out cold.

Whiskey was a street drunk, made country sounds like plow animals would make if they could speak English and complain. His only words were, "Give me that bottle." He was a loudmouth and a complete alcoholic, kind of like a Richard Pryor character.

These two guys were my favorite characters and I knew if I went down to the street in the morning I would find them passed out somewhere. This area of Austin was not policed or patrolled too much, there was no cop walking the beat. This was its own little neighborhood with its own set of rules. Guaranteed, I could go to the alley behind Greasy Dick's and find Seth and Whiskey.

Seth and Whiskey both died on the street before I got out of high school.

I was always after trying to score something. I would sweep up at the barber shop or steal soda bottles and return them for the two-cent deposit, or go try to talk some of the guys in the pool hall out of some coin so I could go buy my cookies. Very important, those cookies.

By government standards we fell below the poverty line— way below. I mean, we didn't have any fruit bowl up on the table. But I never went hungry and I took care of my own little cookie and soda water habit (that's what we called Coke and Pepsi and RC back there, soda water). My stepfather, James Rivers, worked at a service station down in South Austin for a white man named Mr. Reedy. He pumped gas and changed tires twenty-seven years at the same station, always taking orders from white people. I worked there too, doing odd jobs for seventy-five cents every two weeks. That was a lot of money to me. After a few years I got a raise to a dollar fifty and I thought I was making a *real* lot of money then.

I often asked my mother who my real father was. I started looking around the street, in the bars and joints where my mother sometimes hung out, thinking one of these men that I knew maybe was my father. She couldn't produce a picture, she never told me who he was. I would often sit down with her and say "Mama, how did he look?" "Go look in the mirror." "Where is he?" "I don't know. I think he's in New York somewhere."

Mr. Rivers wasn't heavy on the affection and as more of his children came along I just wished they had changed my name, made this family my family. All my brothers and sisters were born at Breckenridge Hospital; I was born at Holy Cross Hospital. I just came from a different place.

When I was about ten years old my stepdad, for the first time in his life and probably the last, came with me to this little-league ballpark down on the other side of town in central Austin to watch me play ball. All the other boys had on nice baseball outfits and good sneakers, maybe even cleats. I had some kind of outfit on but I didn't have any baseball shoes, just plain old brown shoes that I'd already beat all to hell.

I stepped to the plate, this ten-year-old kid trying to hit a baseball. I could feel my stepfather behind me as I took my practice swings. I took three tremendous cuts and struck out. As I dragged my bat back to the bench I heard Mr. Rivers say in a voice only he could muster, "Boy, you sure is sorry. I ain't never seen nobody so sorry in my life."

But there were some people who liked me. My mother had a friend named Go Devil. That's all the name I ever knew for him. I never knew where he came from and I never knew his real name, but he and his wife, Miss Ruth, used to babysit for me and the other kids when my folks would go out. Go Devil was my mom's play brother, her best buddy, and he was a fun guy. He worked for a preacher, Reverend McNeese, and he had a hog farm out there by Greasy Dick's hog farm, and he kind of took care of my mother and everybody else.

Go Devil was a nappy-headed son of a gun. He had a receding hairline that went back to the middle of his head and he never combed his hair. He was into dreadlocks long before the Jamaicans! And Go Devil had this belly on him. He wore his jeans like a California gang member, a low rider, where his pockets hung down to the back of his knees. The guy was just hung low. When he walked he had a natural switch, so his ass was going one way and his jeans were going the other, and by the time his pockets caught up to his ass, his ass was going the other way. I used to love to watch him walk.

Go Devil lived out in the country, right on the east edge of Austin. He didn't have a job. What Go Devil was was a scrap metaler—copper, iron, wires, motors, batteries. You know, junk. He made a living picking up anything that wasn't nailed down. Preacher McNeese paid Go Devil a dollar a day to slop his hogs but the preacher had two hundred head so he let him have this beat-up old pickup truck all the time to do the job. Go Devil's responsibility was slopping hogs but his hustle was scrap metal.

When we'd go to stay at Go Devil's house for the weekend, or if it was holiday season or just for the afternoon, I would jump in the truck and go riding with my big pal. The floorboards smelled like a year-old trash bin but at that age it wasn't any strange odor to me. I would sit in the cab and go off to the hog pens.

That wasn't the only place we'd go. To slop hogs you've got to have some slop. Sometimes we'd head on downtown to the Commodore Perry Hotel, or the Driscoll, or a smaller restaurant called the Plantation, and Go Devil would back his truck up to the kitchen and go inside to talk to the man in charge. He'd come back out and take his fifty-five-gallon drums, he had about six of them on the back of the truck, and we would go to filling them up. I wasn't very much help but I would carry boxes of lettuce, boxes of apples and oranges and fruit that they were throwing away. Of course, the hogs never saw those items. Go Devil fed his family from the garbage of the hotels. I ate quite a few of those meals.

Back at the hog pens I watched Go Devil reach over into the fifty-five-gallon drums filled with this stinking goulash of rich people's leavings, napkins and all, and pull out a fine piece of prime beef. There was a water tank that stood up off the ground about eight feet and he would pull the truck under it and rinse off a porterhouse or a half-eaten round steak, a filet mignon that would have a couple of bites out of it, and backhand it onto a pile of meat. That stack would turn into a great stew later on that night.

In my neighborhood the typical black family was all about food and children and how to manage the two. Shopping for groceries was an event. Friday was payday so when James brought home his wages we went right ahead and turned it into bacon. We would drive way out north to this discount grocery store and buy bananas and eggs and milk and rice and macaroni and cheese, all the staples and some of the treats, and pile all the packages into the trunk. It was amazing to me. We would spend my father's salary on groceries each week, and have a big breakfast Saturday and Sunday, and by Sunday night all the extras were gone. No more Kool-Aid, no more bananas, no more eggs.

Still, my stepfather loved to barbecue. The big barbecue day of the year was "Juneteenth." That was a black Texas holiday, the biggest watermelon-selling day in the world. Every June nineteenth all the black families got together for a serious picnic. You'd get up real early and try to be the first one at the park—being black in Texas our choice of parks was limited and space was tough to find—but somehow you had to fire up something. It must've been a puzzle to the white folks: "Where's all the niggers?" I don't think they knew what the hell we were doing. I'm not sure most black people knew, they were all just down for a party. June nineteenth is the anniversary of the day in 1865 when Union General Granger proclaimed the slaves of Texas free.

Sometimes my dad would take his raggedy old Packard and we'd all go fishing fifteen, twenty miles out of town up at Lake Austin. To get out to the lake you had to get over this big dirt hill and that car didn't have no power at all. There'd be my mom and dad and maybe one of his buddies, and me and my sister sitting on soda pop crates in back, and we'd try to get up the incline and we'd never make it. Just no way. James would have to put on the brakes, put the old Packard in gear and ease it back down to the bottom. Then we'd all get out and walk and he would turn it around and go in the other direction, turn back around again, build up a good head of steam and . . . just barely . . . make it over the top. Then we'd have to walk three or four hundred yards over this dusty old hill to catch up with him.

* * *

I qualified for free milk in the morning and free lunch because of my parents' income, but that was about the best part of going to school my first year. I didn't like school. The bell would ring and I was out of there like a shot. I was six years old and a fifth grader had taken to terrorizing me—just decided that it was my ass. That first year I was chased home about every day, filled with fright.

But mostly I hung around with my friends James Sauls and Alexander. James was a juvenile delinquent from the age of six. He was the fastest kid in first grade, which was important to me, considering how fast I had to hightail it home. James and I had the same kind of schedule, going to the same school, our mothers knew each other, so we just kind of hung. More than that, we were running. I was running for nothing, just burning rubber. We'd make it home after school and then walk eight or ten blocks in different directions looking on people's back porches, picking up bottles off the street or off people's porches and returning them to Mr. Greasy Dick for the deposit, and buying cookies.

As we started to grow up, pop bottles weren't the only things we went out looking for. James was an ace bicycle rider. He could make his cycles sing. Jump up in the air, do flips, ride three blocks down these unpaved bumpy streets on one wheel—James could do all of that.

I got my first bicycle when I was about eight. It wasn't any touring model, it had solid rubber tires, we're not talking about air tires here. It was a cheap no-good-ass bike, and I tore it up pretty quickly, but I was very proud of it and very proud of my parents for getting it for me. Now, James' folks were as poor as mine, they didn't have any kind of money, but James was always coming up with these beautiful Stingrays. He had all the ornaments and extras on them, like tassels or monkey grips, he'd have a big horn, a lock. I couldn't figure it out.

Finally he let me in on his little secret. James and Alexander were going up to Chicon past Nineteenth Street about eight blocks to Manor Road. Across Manor Road were white people. Well, white kids, being the innocent kids that they

14

were, hell, they would ride their bicycles, lay them down on the front porch or on the sidewalk, and just walk away. It was like a used car lot on that side of town. We thought, well damn, if they're just going to leave them out for us . . .

So I started stealing bikes. One after another. If I got tired of one, or I just wanted another one, I'd lift it. I would steal a whole bike to get the handlebars off of it. Me and James and Alexander ended up with a garage that Mr. Schwinn would have been proud of. There was a whole gang of us— me, James, Alexander and a whole bunch of guys. We were rolling.

Meanwhile I was doing real well in school. Made all A's, learned how to read, and after the big kids stopped chasing me home I didn't have a problem in the world.

But school wasn't fun. Fun was doing what I had always been doing, hanging around the pool hall. For the first seven years of my life I lived right next door to one, and every Sunday that I can remember Frank, the owner, would be in there cleaning up from the Saturday night business. I couldn't reach the top of the table but I was messing around with the game. I knew what the stick was, what the chalk was, the balls, the game.

The best player I ever saw was Dunie Riley. He was the best player in Texas. I think Dunie could've played with Minnesota Fats or Willie Mosconi, any of those guys. Dunie was such a pool-playing fool, and worked on such a rough and dirty circuit, that twenty years later he had to have his pinky and ring fingers on his left hand amputated because of infections from pool table burns.

Dunie was the best pool player in Austin by far. Nobody could beat him. Nobody. But he never traveled with his talent. Guys would come to him to play. Mexicans, some white guys. And I would go watch him every chance I could. Dunie liked me. He had dated my mother when she was about fourteen—they were the same age. So Dunie was very fond of my mother, in fact he was still in love with her. I took a lot of good looks at him, and he at me. Dunie was good for two or three bucks instead of this quarter, nickel, dime shit I was getting from the other men.

Dunie was a big gambler but he also had a job. He worked general maintenance at Balcone's Country Club out in northwest Austin and when I was eleven years old I went out there to work with him. It was my first real up-close look at white people. Dunie would joke with them and say, "Yes, massah, okay," and "Yessir, boss," talking some jive nonsense to get a tip. He was big-time. I saw him have hundred-dollar days with his antics.

My boss at Balcone's was Mr. Williams. He liked to call me his "podnah," "Thomas, my li'l podnah." I was his "podnah" but they wouldn't let me swim in their pool. Just shine their shoes. I despised that "li'l podnah" shit but I didn't say a thing.

Back on the Cut I was haunting the pool hall and my mom was getting after me. I just didn't have anything in common with anybody in my home and I knew I didn't have to be there. The family didn't sit down together at 6:30 every night to be a family. Both Mom and Dad worked but they were responsible enough to make sure that we had dinner at night so it wasn't important for me to be there to take care of that. The kids were taken care of by babysitters or relations. I wasn't needed, didn't feel particularly wanted. I'd tell my sister Nettie, who I called Cookie, "Hey Cookie, look, I'm going to bring you some cookies back. Now here's a dime, you watch Vickie, Junior and Franchot. I'm going to the pool hall."

If you ever wanted to know where young Thomas was, you went to the pool table. Dunie was showing me how to shoot and I got pretty good. I was seriously underage but I got to be a fixture at old man Frank's pool hall, something you'd always find when you went there, like a cue stand or a rack.

Pool was ten cents a game and I'd play for a quarter a game and be sitting there, twelve years old, with four or five dollars in my pocket from beating guys older than me. Then my mother would march in.

She didn't like me staying out on the streets late, not coming home until ten o'clock every night like I was grown, and if she wasn't going to let my stepfather whip me she had no second thoughts about doing the job herself.

But it was worth risking a whipping to play some pool because I'd do just about anything to get some money. That same summer, between working for Dunie and working for Go Devil and hustling at the pool hall or running the streets, I pulled cotton. A man came by one day and said there would be a truck coming through at 3:45 in the morning and it was going to be taking some people out to Elgin and Manor to pull cotton. I said sure.

It was cool that early in the morning. I went out into this cotton field and got my instructions. I had never done this before. We were told not to put dirt and rocks in the bags and to stay on a row and finish it; not to be picking on three or four rows, but to go down one row at a time. We're talking about a damn row half a mile long. And you couldn't start in the middle of a row, you had to start at the beginning and go from one end to the other.

Well, for about fifteen minutes I was without a doubt the best **fuc**king cotton puller in the world. I was working hard and I guess I covered about a hundred yards. But the cotton bolls are still brittle when you pull on them and you can really stick yourself on your hand. I was a youngster, I had never done any hard labor and it started to bother me right quick. Now, cotton bolls are very very light, and we were being paid by weight, so after three or four hours I began throwing dirt and rocks and every little piece of whatever I saw into my sack to make up some serious poundage. It takes a lot of bolls of cotton to make any money.

By ten o'clock, with the sun all the way up in the sky, it was hot as hell. It was in the mid to high nineties, easy, when they sounded the horn for the lunch break. The wagon where you dump your cotton to get weighed is back at the beginning, at the edge of the field. I had stolen enough by then to know that I wasn't going to leave my cotton nowhere, so I dragged that sack all the way in. It was pretty fat, full of all the rocks and dirt I had thrown in there. The man weighed it. Sixty-two pounds. I think they were paying a dollar a hundredweight that day. I had about sixty-two cents coming on that load.

It was hot, a quarter to twelve, and I was surrounded by all these destitute people eating out of cans. I was just doing this for the hell of it, to get some movie money, some popcorn money, and they were serious about this. It was a life to them. I looked around and said to myself, I don't want none of this. This is not for me. I don't want to be working like my daddy, I don't want to be like Go Devil, I don't want to be like Dunie Riley. There is nobody here that I want to be.

In my neighborhood, if your daddy worked for the transit bus system that was your goal, to drive a bus; if your daddy pumped gas, you were going to pump gas; if he worked for the city you were going to too. I knew that wasn't for me. I didn't know what I was going to do, but I knew it wasn't this.

About the same time I discovered hard work I also discovered real fun. Me, Alexander, James and the guys were always out running together and we ran into this girl named Frankie who liked to make love to a bunch of guys. We never forced her, she just liked having a lot of guys around and over the course of a couple of years we obliged her quite often. We would find beds in houses where no one was home and just do it. I didn't know what I was doing but somehow I managed to get that first orgasm. From then on I was off and running.

When I was about eleven there was a man who lived cattycorner from me. He was a fisherman and he paid me a buck to go kill grasshoppers with switches for his bait, another of my many hustles. He took me out a couple of times to go fishing with him.

Well, I crossed over to his house one time and knocked on the screen door to come in, and there was him and his wife screwing on the couch like it was no big deal. The guy said, "Come in." Bright-eyed kid that I was I didn't run away, I looked and looked intensely to see what was happening. It was like he was saying, "Hey kid, you ought to try this sometime."

So I did. I started messing around with his wife. She was very receptive to me, welcomed me, showed me all kinds of things I wasn't going to learn anywhere else. I got hooked on it. At lunchtime in grammar school, while he was off at work, I was running down the street six blocks to her house to get some. And though he never said anything to me, I've got to believe the fisherman must have known what I was doing. He was a young guy. They were probably both younger than my mother.

My mom's life wasn't any picnic. She was working as a cleaning woman at the capitol building and between her paycheck and my dad's they just about managed to keep the family in food and clothing. We moved around a lot from apartment to apartment, house to house, so there wasn't anything stable about us at all. About the only fun she might have had was every Friday and Saturday night when she and my dad would go out and get drunk.

My dad was a drinker. He would come home from work every day at six o'clock, oil and grease all over him, and he'd always have a bag in his hand, and that bag always contained a bottle of whiskey or a couple of six-packs of beer. He didn't get drunk every night of the week, but you could depend on him and my mother getting drunk on Friday and Saturday nights. No question about it, they were going to be drunk, then they were going to fight, he was going to hit her, and me and my brothers and sisters were going to wake up crying.

I'm not sure what brought it on. My mother was a cute little gal and maybe she flirted when she started drinking. They were out at the honky-tonks or some parties, and guaranteed, she was going to be looking good and lots of guys were going to be looking at her. My dad, twenty-two years older and pretty well past his prime, wasn't going to stand there and let his wife make a fool of him by stepping out right in his face. He waited till they got home and then he beat her.

That went on for years. My dad would jump on my mother and beat her with his fists in front of the kids. I thought that was what being married meant, I thought it came with the territory. I hadn't lived with any other families that got along any better; this was real life.

In the spring of 1965, right after I turned twelve, all of that took a hard left turn. It was Saturday night again and I knew when I went to bed what I could expect to find when I woke up, but this time it was worse. I heard screaming, my mom was screaming. I rose up and saw my mother on the wood floor. Mr. Rivers had one of his big knees on each of her shoulders, she couldn't move and he was pummeling her. He was exploding into her face with his fists and all she could do was take it on one cheek or the other. I can hear the sound, her shrieking, her head thudding against the wood floor like rocks in sackcloth. He was beating her to a pulp, blood everywhere, she was already puffed up and swollen and he wasn't about to quit.

I took a run at him, tried to pull him off of her, but he was much too strong for me. He kept beating her as long as he wanted to and when he quit it was only because he was tired and looking to pass out. My mother was in a rage.

"Get your black motherfucking ass out of this house!" she choked at him. "I'm through with you, you motherfucker. You're not going to beat me no more! Get out!"

He'd heard that before. So had I. Mr. Rivers weaved out to his car parked in front in the street, maybe to get a bottle, maybe to grab something he'd forgot. He was coming back into the house to beat her again and then he was going to sleep. It was Saturday night.

Not this time. My mom had bought Dad a .22 rifle for Christmas and she went to the corner and got a hold of it. She obviously knew how to work it because as I watched she stood in the doorway, opened the latch and loaded the son of a gun, put the bullets in there real good, snapped it back to ready.

We were living on Seventeenth and Chicon, right in front of my elementary school, and there was my dad staggering around out by his car. My mom moved onto the porch and I went with her. The porch was about four foot high, with maybe eight steps leading up from the front yard to it. I took a couple of steps forward like I was going to protect my mom but Dad wasn't seeing me. He was about to march back into our life.

"Get the fuck away from this house," my mom told him. "Leave. Bye bye. Get out of here. You don't live here no more. You are not going to hit me no more. Get in the wind."

Well, my daddy was stupid. Drunk and stupid. He kept on walking up the stairs. I was right in the middle between them, except I was to the side, against the wall. My mom stood three feet to my left, my drunken stupid daddy three feet to my right.

My mother told him, "Don't take another step, motherfucker." Exactly like that. "Don't take another step, motherfucker." Daddy took another step and she blew his ass off the porch.

She only shot him one time and he didn't fall. He staggered back to the ground and just stood there, bleeding, with a bullet in his side. I was frozen to that wall, sweating, scared to death. I didn't know what to do. My mother had just shot a man. I saw the fire fly from the barrel of the gun. I wanted to die.

The neighbors called the police, called an ambulance. They came and got him and arrested my mom for shooting him. Held her for about two hours and then she came home. Mr. Rivers didn't press charges. He didn't die, either. They stayed together for another ten years.

2

Family Ties

My mama started to wearing a gun in her bra and I never knew but when she might start to come after me. I was out in the street, running around after hours, hanging out playing pool, and she'd want me home *now*. I took to paying kids to spot for me, watch the pool hall doors to see if she was coming and warn me, give me a head start. Lots of times I'd bust out the back door running just as she was coming in the front. I can still hear her calling as I hit the street. "Don't you run from me. Come here!" She'd be swinging an extension cord or a fly swatter or a stick, anything she could find, about to whack me across my butt right in the middle of the game, in front of everybody.

But I knew she loved me, even if she had some strange ways of showing it. I don't know what got into her but in 1965, as I was about to graduate from grammar school and enroll in seventh grade my mama told me she wanted me to go to the University Junior High School. Now, if you were black and lived on my side of town you went to Kealing. It was natural, like the sun rising in the east or boys waking up horny. You didn't think about going to McCallum or to Austin High, all of my friends were going to Kealing. Not good enough for my mom.

"I want you to get your education, ' she told me. "You've been out on these damn streets too much. I want you to go ahead and learn you something."

The school turned out to be about 30 percent white, 20 percent black and 50 percent Mexican, so it was a whole nother culture shock from the one I'd expected. All these pretty little Spanish girls walking around just about made me crazy. I didn't know that later in life they'd be eating too much flour and tortillas and getting fat, they all looked great to me.

I was doing real well in the classroom. I got all A's in math and English, got into history. I was a good enough student to study hard for three or four days and pass anybody's test. My mama was happy with my grades and that's all that mattered for her.

At University Junior High School I played organized football for the first time. Except for Little League I had never been anywhere near organized sports before; the only organized sport I knew was racking cue balls. In the neighborhood I could throw the ball, I could run, I was tough and aggressive so I played quarterback, then turned around and played defense. We were arm tackling and having a good time and I liked it. At school there was a coach named Goorley, a white man, and he put me at quarterback on the seventh-grade flag football team.

We'd practice right across the street from where Coach Darrell Royal held his University of Texas football practices and lots of times I'd walk over there and gawk. Those Longhorns looked like giants. Running through tackle drills that I thought were crazy, they were big white men in battle gear. I'd go around with the water bucket and help out, just one of those kids who's always around, maybe three days a week, carrying things and carrying on. I'd toss them the balls if they'd let me, and catch them when they'd throw one my way. I'd also steal me an elbow pad here and there, grab what I could. I even tried to walk away with a helmet but they caught me because I couldn't conceal it well enough. It was fun out there.

My own football games were fun but frustrating. We played a schedule around Austin. I had to catch a bus on Saturday morning to be over to the school at 7:30 so I could catch a ride to the game with the coach, and then here'd come seventeen or eighteen more guys in their station wagons with their moms and dads who'd stand on the sidelines and cheer for them. I would enjoy playing but I'd be there by myself, a lone warrior. I wanted to play for somebody and I wanted somebody to play for. It didn't look like it was going to be my family.

I began looking at my sisters and brothers differently. On Fridays my mama would give me five dollars and give my sister a quarter. It started to bother me that I was taking something away from them, and at the same time told me that I wasn't one of them. I started thinking of them as stepbrothers and stepsisters. Nettie, who was two years younger than I was, looked like my stepdad; Vickie, six years younger than me, looked like my mom and my stepdad. James Junior, "Red," seven years younger, had red hair and freckles. Maybe he favored my mom a little bit, but he looked like a white kid. Franchot (pronounced "fran-shot"), jet black and skinny and nine years younger than I was, looked like my stepdad had spit him out. I didn't look like anybody.

I headed back to the Cut and started hanging out more and more on Eleventh Street with Dunie Riley in all the gambling joints. Whether they were shooting dice or playing poker or any kind of cards, I'd be there. Guys in a poker game are always wanting you to run get this, run get that, and when you get through running you end up with ten or twelve bucks in tips.

My mama knew that I was okay when I was with Dunie, so it didn't matter what time I got home, and I didn't want to go home, I didn't feel good at home.

I fit into the neighborhood. I fit in with Dunie. I knew what to expect out there, at least I thought I did. One night

I was hanging in the street, just killing time. Everybody knew me. Even the junkies knew me. A couple of them, just guys I'd seen around, nobody special, were going to go do some heroin behind the drug store and they told me I ought to try some.

I got me a little swig of syrup, Robitussin AC, and I went back and watched them fix, watched them tie off, do their deal. Guy asked me, "You got any money? You've gotta try some of this." Somehow I said okay. Didn't take much coaxing.

They tied me off. I was scared of the needle but once they got the needle in there wasn't any pain.

"That didn't hurt, did it?"

"No, it was okay."

They shot me up with heroin. Right away I threw up and I puked for two hours nonstop.

The junkies split on me pretty quick and I staggered over to the card game and tried to tell Dunie what had happened. I was fucked up, coming and going, nodding in and out. I had thrown up everything in my gut, I felt weird all over, like I was made out of cold plastic and it was sweating.

Dunie took ahold of me and we went out looking for these guys. They were gone, climbed back into the backstreets for the night, but I was still there. Dunie got me home and told me to get my ass into bed. It isn't any problem going to bed when you're on heroin, you just lie there and go off into the ozone, and I nodded out with merciful speed.

The next morning, on the way out to Balcone's Country Club where I was working with him, he gave me a serious speech. "Let me tell you something, boy," he said slowly. "You're pretty smart. You're on these streets, you hustle good, you're out here. Don't let them fuck with you. What they want to do is get you hooked. They want you to be hooked like them. When they turn you out that means you're going to be coming with the bag sometimes. Don't you get in with them; you don't need that shit."

His advice was a little late. Puking told me that I wasn't going to do that stuff again, and I never did. But having Dunie there to tell me to get my life straight was real important to me and I looked into his face a whole lot of times after that to see if I could see anything familiar.

I talked my mama into letting me go back to Kealing for my eighth-grade year, 1966. Even though I had never gone there, when I hit the hallways I knew I was where I should be. Everybody knew me, all my friends were there, I didn't have to learn new life rules. It was like the street indoors, my turf.

Then Go Devil died on me.

I remember getting a phone call at Kealing early in the year. Got to the principal's office and they told me he was dead. From the time I was five years old until I was almost fifteen this man had been my friend. Everybody deviled him in town, everybody made fun of him, but I loved the floppy old fella. The guy could pick up a great piece of meat out of the garbage can, and I liked chewing on it with him.

Go Devil had a heart attack. He had about five attacks during the almost ten years I knew him but I didn't know they were heart attacks, I didn't know what a heart attack was. Sometimes we'd be driving and he'd pull over quick and straighten out in the driver's seat and get me to rub his chest. In fact he was over to my mama's house one night and had an attack, told us it was heartburn. Go Devil would eat out of the trash, he was bound to get some heartburn! Didn't think anything of it.

I cried all the way home, that hiccup kind of crying where you think and cry and can't stop and cry some more. I wanted him back. "Why you done left me, Go Devil?" He was a home I couldn't go back to anymore. He and Dunie Riley were my men. Without them I wouldn't know how to be a man, wouldn't know where to go.

I went out for the football team and made it as a running back. I was just an average player, nothing special. There were great players in the Austin high school system like Herman Alexander and Wayman Clark. Wayman Clark could play every position on the field. He played for the University of Oklahoma, always a football titan, and would have been a number-one draft choice if Austin hadn't sprung up in him. He got into some kind of trouble and never played pro ball.

My idol was a guy named John Harvey who went to Anderson High School, where I went for one year. He could run a 45.5 quarter mile, a 9.4 hundred-yard dash, he could long jump twenty-five feet. He was the greatest athlete in the history of Austin, Texas. He was better than "Night Train" Lane. He was better than me.

Harvey got drafted by the Los Angeles Rams but he ended up playing for the Memphis Southmen of the World Football League. Danny White, later the Dallas Cowboys' starting quarterback, was Harvey's teammate at Memphis, and he said that Harvey was the best all-around football player that he'd ever seen. John McVay, who coached him at Memphis and coached in the NFL, said Harvey was the best football player ever, period.

But John Harvey had the disease called Austin, Texas. He just couldn't get out of Austin, or get Austin out of him. McVay said Harvey's mother died eight times, his grandmother died seven times. He liked being in Austin, he liked being back on the corner. He had to get back to the Cut rather than pursue his career. He wasn't the only homeboy who couldn't leave home.

My mama was moving up in the world. She had stopped working for other people and opened up her own late-night chicken and chili joint: Faye's After Hours. Mama wasn't bootlegging but Mama was pouring you a drink and charging you a dollar or two for it; you couldn't get liquor after midnight in Austin. We stayed open from eleven o'clock in the evening until five in the morning and everybody who'd been drinking that hard booze and partying all night would come to my mama's place. Mama even had some employees, which was a pure switch, cooking and cleaning the place for her.

Mama got to making four or five hundred dollars a night selling chicken. And although we never saw any major development in our household or the way we lived, she did have a little extra money to spread around, and she always had spoiled me. We were very much alike when it came to dollars; we went right through them.

By the time I was fourteen I was probably one of the top five pool shooters in East Austin and my hustling was on the rise. The machines cost a quarter by then, which seemed like a million dollars for a damn pool table, but I was taking on all comers for a dollar a game and I just about became self-supporting. Still, all the money I'd pick up hustling pool would go right away, I didn't even know where. I might have eighteen dollars, or twenty-seven dollars, thirty-one dollars— I always knew to the penny what my net worth was because it was in my pockets—but it never stayed there long.

I played ball at Kealing but I was still nothing special. Nobody considered me Heisman Trophy material. Kealing didn't have any laundry facilities, all the kids had to wash their own uniforms, and every day we had to carry our equipment home with us too.

We had these thin white duffel bags with our helmets, shoulder pads, hip pads, thigh pads and everything in them, and had to walk down from school to practice. We dressed out in the middle of the football field, just took our clothes off and got dressed right on the forty-yard line. Then we'd practice for two hours and go home.

After practice it was about a two-mile walk from the field to my home. You could take the shortcut through a rock quarry, but if you really wanted to look good you could walk right down Twelfth Street. If you see a kid walking down the street in his football uniform, I mean, this guy here is a Trojan, this cat is a real warrior.

Showers were unheard of, and baths were done in the sink. I was a birdbath baby. The plumbing in our house wasn't what you'd call adequate. We had a bathtub but I wouldn't get in it because I had younger baby sisters and brothers and with Mama gone all the time they still weren't potty trained properly, there were diapers with crap in them laying in the tub.

Every Saturday or Sunday Mama would have this big laundry caravan going to the laundromat and get fifteen washers going, then come back home and throw the stuff all over the house.

By tenth grade we had moved off the Cut and I was going to Anderson High, another black school. I was in high school now and that meant something. I went out for football but I was fifteen going on sixteen, a sophomore, and I couldn't make the varsity, Coach Timmons told me I wasn't varsity material. I played on the junior varsity for Coach Jackson and really excelled for him so the next year I could play on the big team.

If I was going to be there. All my friends—James Sauls, Alexander and the guys—had dropped out and they were slowly but surely convincing me that that was the thing to do. "Fuck school," they said. "Come on with us."

We had been the boys who at eleven, twelve years old were stealing bicycles. Now these suckers were coming up with cars and I couldn't figure where the hell they were getting them. They would come up with cars that didn't look like a car . . . they looked like three or four cars. Parts from three or four cars, at least. The same thing they'd been doing with bicycles they were now doing with automobiles.

James Sauls was a serious thief. He would show up in new clothes all the time, some of which fit him. He started wearing watches and jewelry. When I woke up in the morning I went off to high school. When James woke up in the morning he went off to work, to steal something.

The one time I got arrested while I was growing up I was with James. We were all sort of bored, hanging around the Blackland section of North Austin, just fooling around looking for something to do, and we spotted this newspaper machine sitting on a telephone post about two feet high. We grabbed and dragged it down into an alley, beat at the lock until it opened.

This machine was full of money! Change fell all over the place and everybody got their hands full.

Damn it if somebody didn't call the cops.

They took me downtown and called my mom. They didn't book me, there were no fingerprints or pictures taken, they just took me out to South Austin to Juvenile Hall and threw me in there for two days.

I cried and cried. I just didn't know what to do. I was scared to death. But I knew there was one thing you don't do, you don't snitch. Don't do that, Thomas.

When my mom came to see me she was so hurt and mad. "How could you steal?!" she shouted. The small room they'd put us in got smaller the nearer she got. "There is no need to steal. I know it's that damned James Sauls. I'm going to tell on that son of a bitch."

"Mama, don't you do that," I cried. "You know I gotta go back and live over there. Don't you do that!"

They let me go the next day. Juvenile Hall was seven miles from home but they told me, "We understand you're pretty familiar with the city, we think you can make it from here."

But it takes a lot to teach me. Peer pressure's tough. James and I went to the white part of town and started breaking into houses, taking jewelry, TV sets, stereo equipment, silver.

One afternoon James and I were in these people's house gathering up whatever we thought we could sell . . . and they came home. We beat it out the back but there was no alley-way, no driveway, no way out. We had to come right around the front of the house . . . running.

I heard a flat pop and the dirt in the street kicked up beside me. These folks were shooting at us! *Goddamn!!* James could outrun me but that day when I felt the bullets flying I passed him like he was a statue. That was it for me and theft. I wasn't going to die for no portable TV.

James Sauls, on the other hand, pushed it. He didn't need me along with him on his jobs. He didn't need anybody, though he did like company. He liked having the watches and the jewelry and the cars. He liked having money and this was the only way he knew how to get it.

James was my age but by the time I was finishing tenth grade he had dropped out of school. A lot of times he would show up in the parking lot at three o'clock just to be around the guys. That's where all his friends were and just because he wasn't sitting next to us in math class didn't mean he didn't know his numbers. We'd be glad to see him when we got out. And he'd be glad to see us; he was always trying to recruit one guy or another to go with him on his burglary expeditions.

James had found a .357 Magnum in one of the houses he was robbing. None of us had any experience with guns, that wasn't our thing, but when a monster like that comes along you don't just leave it behind. James had stolen some other weapons so he was our expert and he liked to flash whatever he had to show for himself.

James was trying to recruit this boy we called Fatty. "Here, check this out," he told the kid, and handed him the Magnum. "Let's play Russian Roulette." Fatty'd never had a gun in his hand before and he was impressed. He put it in his palm and the thing went off. James Sauls was dead in my high school parking lot with a bullet in his heart.

Everybody was getting locked up. Any time anything happened they would come and rustle up all of us and send us downtown. I had begun running little crap games in the alley just like I'd seen the big guys do it when I was small, and now when they busted them up they'd let everybody go and take me to jail. They'd run me all the way down to central Austin and then let me go. I hated to weave my way home at eleven o'clock at night after another run-in, hated being on their list. They knew that if there was a crap game going on I had something to do with it. When they got to rounding up the Usual Suspects, I was one of them.

I got tired of them picking on me. It got to where the cops were saying, "This kid, Henderson, we suspect that he's involved in a lot of little crap, he's a petty thief, he's a kid to be watched for the next couple of years, so watch him." A lot of my friends were going to Gatesville Prison and I didn't want to join them but I was well on my way.

I felt a tremendous need to get straight. I would kick in half the money when my mother would buy me shoes, though we never had much to shell out. I kept looking at my brothers and sisters and they weren't even doing as well as I was because I was getting all that was available. But I was getting nowhere.

The family was having a picnic on July Fourth, 1969, when I sprang it on them. Mom, Dad and the kids were all eating chicken in the park when I told my mother. I just said, "Mama, I've got to get out of Austin. I've got to get out of here. I'm going to Oklahoma City to go live with Nettie."

I couldn't have told her anything worse. Though I didn't know it at the time, Nettie had wanted me aborted, dead before I was born, and now here I was abandoning my mother for the woman she despised most in the world.

"You ain't going no fucking place!" Mama exploded at me. "How dare you? I done took care of your black ass all them years, I brought you into this world and raised you, I gave you everything I've got. You ain't going nowhere."

"Mama," I cried, "I'm going." I was sixteen years old and I knew that if I stayed I was going to get caught up in Austin, trapped, I'd never make it past the Cut. I had already spoken with Nettie and she had told me it was all right for me to come if I got my mother's permission. "If your mama lets you come," that was the deal. But I was leaving whether I got my mama's blessing or not.

"All my friends are dying or going to prison. I'm not going to stay here in this crowded house, I'm not going to stay with four kids screaming. I don't belong here. I'm taking from my sisters and brothers and I don't want to. I'm not part of this family! I feel like I'm going to die!"

It didn't take me but three days to get gone. I had to run from my mama continually. First she cried, then she cursed me. It got past her wanting to give me a whipping or talk me out of leaving; she was going to shoot me. She said so. "I'll shoot you!" she shouted at me that night. "I love you but I'll shoot your ass!" I believed her. I packed what little I had into a small suitcase and I was out of there.

3

"Wild Man"

Nettie Mae Higgins. I called her Mama Nettie and thought of her as my grandmother, but she was really my mama's cousin. She had raised my mother and now she was about to raise me.

There were all sorts of things I didn't know about Mama Nettie. First off, she was a real entrepreneur. She worked up at the Baptist Memorial Hospital and somehow she had gathered some money and bought several of the houses around her. Now she was renting them out, a respected landlord. Across the street, around behind us, people were paying rent to my grandmother. Everybody thought she was rich, and in that community I guess she was. She rented out rooms in her own home and her tenants worshiped her.

I'd visited my grandmother the summer before and I liked it there. I liked the idea that there was a bathtub and a shower in the house. I liked the idea that I was going to have my own room for the first time in my life. I was trying so hard to live right and this looked like the right place to get it started. I threw away everything I'd brought with me the second day I was in Oklahoma City.

Within a week I had a job. Mama Nettie had a boyfriend named Frank who worked for a mail contractor, L. M. Lassiter, driving tractor trailer loads to Kansas City, Fort Worth, St. Louis, and he got me work in the truck yard. You had to be eighteen to get a driver's license in Texas but it was sixteen in Oklahoma and I got mine in a hurry. I don't think old man Lassiter thought my job deserved a salary so I was just riding in the cab with Frank and he was paying me. But I didn't know anybody in Oklahoma City so all I was doing was work, work, work, and it must have showed. I could change diesel tires, change the oil and gas up a diesel truck. I drove the tractor trailers around the yard enough to get a feel for them. I got greasy and dirty every day and finally when a real job opened up on the dock at the post office, old man Lassiter gave it to me.

I was getting five bucks an hour and I didn't mind sweating for it. I'd read the manifests and load the trucks. You had to have a U.S. Postal Service badge to go in and out of the station but in a little while I was drinking their coffee, walking by thousands of pieces of mail, a trusted employee. Nobody had ever trusted me before and every time I walked through that door I liked the feeling.

They even let me hit the road once in a while. Frank was a man of about sixty and he was tired so sometimes they'd send me to Kansas City, Dallas and Fort Worth and there I'd be, logging down the highway with ten tons of truck, Frank sitting by my side.

I was working a forty- or fifty-hour week and bringing home $190, $205 a week to my grandmother. I was saving money! I thought this was the neatest thing in the world. Who would ever have thought that two months out of Austin I'd be rolling in dough.

Not that I ever saw that much of it. I gave it to Mama Nettie and she took care of everything. I had all the cookies I could want. We were eating well. Life was great.

When I had saved seven or eight hundred dollars—more

money than my mom or dad ever held on to—my grand-mother took me to Sears Roebuck to get me some clothes. I was going to school that fall and I had to look clean. We bought me some wing-tip shoes, some shark-skin oxfords. They were big shoes, gigantic shoes, and my grandmother said, "These will last." I still have them. We bought me three suits, which I could mix and match, so I had nine outfits for school or church. Four pair of jeans, eight pair of slacks, all the socks I needed, about four sweaters. I had an overcoat. I'd never had an overcoat. I was going to kill them in high school.

I chose Douglas High School, an all-black school with a great football and basketball tradition, but I couldn't go out for football that year. In order to avoid a border war between the states they had passed a law saying that if a student moved from one state to another without his parents he couldn't play football until a full year after he'd arrived in town. I had to sit out my junior year's eligibility.

When my transcripts showed up it turned out to be a good thing I had to. I'd done okay until sophomore year when I'd let everything go. I had a whole lot of catching up to do. In fact, I had to do three years in two. My counselor, Mr. Holmes, told me, "Look, Thomas, I'm going to make you a junior, we won't hold you back, but I'll tell you right now that you have to go to night school, you have to go to Sunday school, you have to go to midafternoon school, you have to go to school school. If you want to finish high school with your class, any time there is a school open you should be in it."

I did all of that and looked good doing it. I showed up at Douglas High and thought I looked cool. Bell-bottoms were coming in but my big oxfords were sticking a mile out of my straight-leg pants and I looked a little different to these Okies. I was sharp, looked scholarly, like I was going to Yale at lunchtime. I was carrying my books and really trying to learn, doing well in class, but I was the new kid in town and took a lot of grief for the way I was carrying myself. I wasn't part of any social circle, I was too new and too busy.

I'd rush home from school and get my grandmother to drive me over to Lassiter's yard, then get driven home, do my homework, go to bed, get up and start all over. On the weekends I'd go to work Saturday, classes Saturday night, wake up and go to church and then Sunday school, and do my Tinker Field run.

Tinker Field was an Air Force base in Oklahoma City and I had to be in the post office at six Sunday morning to take a bobtail truck and go deliver their mail. Guys on the base were saluting me. I'd be barreling down the road piloting an eighteen-wheeler. If somebody honked at me, I'd pull on the air horn and go *WAAAAA! Shut up!!*

I was running my grandmother ragged, what with her having to get me everywhere. Finally she decided, "Thomas, you're gonna have to have a car." I didn't give her any argument.

We drove out to an auto dealer and got me a shiny 1966 Ford Galaxy. This was 1969. My mama in Austin was driving a '53 Chevy, my grandmother was driving a '69 Chrysler, and I was getting me a '66 Ford Galaxy 500, two-door, dark blue, navy blue interior. I think the car cost around two thousand dollars and my payments were eighty-eight dollars a month. Insurance was twenty-two dollars a month and I could carry it, no problem. I turned that sucker into a hot rod right away. I was rolling!

Right away it made school a little easier. This big-shoe-wearing guy from Texas was hitting the parking lot in his shiny new Ford, waxed down, tire black on the wheels. Yes it's me, fools. Now what do you think? Then I'd rush away and go to work.

I hadn't given up hustling but I was trying to channel it. When I worked in the garage at Lassiter's I saw that they were always in need of jack stands to hold the trucks up while they were being worked on. At Douglas I took the industrial welding class and learned how to make them. I'd buy my own pipe and sit there and heat it, weld it, drill holes in it. I made about twenty sets of four jack stands and sold them to

Mr. Lassiter. Probably made about four hundred dollars in class that year.

Mama Nettie was proud of me. I was going to school, to night school, to work, to church. In three months I was hardly the Austin street kid I had come there to escape.

I was the only person Mama Nettie allowed in her room. To everybody else it was off limits. I couldn't do this often, but when I really wanted some attention, when I really wanted to be petted, I would tell the nurse at school that I was sick, come home at lunchtime, climb into her bed and conk right out. She would get home from work and find me sleeping and she'd make me a real nice dinner. I'd wake up all groggy from sleeping during the day—I was always tired from working my jobs and hitting my books all the time—and lay there while I'd hear her tiptoeing around the house telling people, "Shh, keep quiet now. My baby's sleeping."

The one night I had free was Friday and I spent that near football. Friday night is football night in Oklahoma and if they wouldn't let me play they couldn't keep me from being on top of the game. Mr. Seward, who was the industrial welding teacher, filmed the games for Coach Burns. He took a liking to me because I worked hard in his class and he let me help out way up in the stands with him. Mr. Seward and I would take the movie cameras and the tripod to all the games. I climbed all the high school stadiums in Oklahoma City with old fat Mr. Seward, changing film for him and carting stuff around.

The best part of going to the games was watching Constance Johnson. The Douglas High majorettes were the foxiest mamas in the school and the head majorette was Miss Constance Johnson. So gorgeous. She had a taste of class around her. The band would be pounding, the drums humming, but all I could see or hear was this beautiful girl in tight spangles prancing on the grass.

I knew she was dating the drum major, a hoodlum named Glen. They were the real high school number-one couple. But I was a reformed hoodlum, I knew how he thought, what his weaknesses were, how to beat him. I heard that they were having some problems and I knew why. I was really trying to be a gentleman now, trying to be a Christian, and I saw that Constance Johnson was going to respond.

Connie knew that I had a car. I was a junior and she was a senior but she could see I was pretty good-looking and I had wheels and money. Other guys were putting together pennies and splitting malts and I would buy me a triple cheeseburger and an order of fries. In high school this was the kind of super indulgence that got you noticed.

Connie and I fell in love. Even her parents approved of me. They were impressed with how hard I was working and how full my schedule was, and that I wasn't just some bum hanging around the park like the rest of her boyfriends. Glen the drum major kind of disappeared.

I introduced Connie to my grandmother. I brought her up to the house for the true parental once-over and she passed. I took her on picnics. We were becoming a hot item in Douglas High School and my man Glen was sulking.

Sooner or later all of Douglas knew about Connie and me. We were the item. When we paraded down the halls we were what was being talked about. This big-foot Texas boy had walked off with the school's top prize.

It was Homecoming, the first really big football game, and my Connie was being crowned Miss Douglas. I loved to film the games now, all I had to do all game was train my binoculars on the number-one majorette, my sweetheart, my main squeeze. My heart was popping out of my jacket as she walked demurely in front of the band to receive the crown.

I followed her back to the sidelines, each step a road to my future. The marching band was ready to play, she was going to high-step and lead them. Glen the drum major was next to her. Drum on this one, Glen.

Then he reached over and grabbed my woman and kissed her.

They must have kissed for three hours. It may have been only two minutes, maybe just one, but it felt like I had time to cross a desert and die. Broke my heart. Just broke it.

I wanted to jump off the top of the stadium, break my body

on the ramp. I knew that everybody in the stands, everybody in the entire town, saw them. After all the clothes and all the cool cars, I was still the Texas stranger, still the fool. I was a dead man.

I waited for Connie in the parking lot after the game. I was supposed to take her home, we were going to celebrate our own personal Homecoming, but all the cars were gone and I was the only one left, looking for her, waiting for her. She never showed.

I called her and called her and called her the whole weekend but she was never home. The good boy, the Oklahoma City church-going, book-learning, hard-working sucker went out the window right then and there. "Fuck that bitch," I said. "Let her have that rotten-toothed motherfucker. Go ahead. But someday you're going to regret leaving me, Constance Johnson." I vowed never to say another word to her.

She tried to talk to me. Especially when she needed a ride home from school, because Glen the drum major could only strut home on his shoe leather, he didn't have any wheels. But I could only be fooled once. I dropped her like a bad habit.

By senior year I had learned how to play Douglas. I had made up two sophomore courses and had to complete three more or I wouldn't be allowed to graduate, but by then I knew how to get by. That summer I had met the guys who worked at Oscar's Phillips 66 service station across the street from school. Finally I had a crowd.

Oscar was Oscar Kirklin, and his brothers Mike, Melvin and Stanley were Louisiana boys who worked there. Stanley was my classmate at Douglas although we had never really met until I started hanging out. But the guy who was my favorite friend was Jerome. Everybody called him TC.

TC was about thirty-two years old. He was a little bitty fellow, about five foot six, 140 pounds, but he always wore the biggest hat in town. None of these cowboy hats for my man. Superfly hats in yellows and blues from this place called the Soul Boutique. They sold knit outfits that fit you skin-tight, and TC could afford to go and buy a new one every day. TC had his day job at Wilson's Packing House cutting slabs of meat, but that's not where he made his money. TC was a pimp, he was a gambler, he sold marijuana.

TC took a liking to me. He'd give me these little white bennies—speed—that would make my work go by like I was on fire. I'd take a couple of hits before I set out for the yard and I'd go on a tear, the terror of Lassiter's, working my ass off, rushing around the lot, smoking a lot of cigarettes. I had begun smoking when I was about five, lighting my mother's Kools because she was too pregnant and lazy to light them herself. She'd say, "Thomas, go light this on the stove."

TC turned me on to pot and a lot of other things. He couldn't drive his car or sit down anywhere without firing up a joint, so I got to smoking marijuana daily. TC was buying two or three pounds at a time, so the supply was never a problem, the real problem was finding time to do it.

I was still working and studying, though my church-going started to slack off a little. TC introduced me to the Trevas Club on Twenty-third and Eastern and the gambling shacks on Second, and I was kind of getting back into my old self.

The clubs were a revelation. I was a healthy young boy and I was growing like I was being planted and tended. Had the beginnings of a beard, a mustache coming, long hair. Good-looking seventeen-year-old kid. I started the summer at six feet even and ended at six-two and 195 pounds. It turned out that women liked me, especially older women. I was in the Trevas Club drinking Tom Collinses and taking hits of speed with TC, who knew everybody. I dressed older, looked older, tried to carry myself like a man. And every time I went in there a different woman was taking me home. My main objective in dealing with women was to see what they would give me and what I could get out of it.

I started staying at TC's house or with TC and his girl-friend, watching him buy pounds of pot and sell it off in bags or ounces. I was selling it with him, smoking it with him every day. I'd wake up in the morning and smoke a joint before I brushed my teeth. Took a little speed, every now and then did a little mescaline or LSD. And I watched as all these women gave TC their money. I figured that this was what it was all about.

Finally, my senior year I was able to play football. I'd done all this growing over the summer, and my work had filled out my body. But I had to get past Mama Nettie first and she wasn't having none of it.

"Mama," I told her. She always liked it when I called her Mama. "Mama, if I play football I can get a scholarship to college."

She said, "Boy, if you work and keep on what you're doing, you're making almost eight or nine thousand dollars a year and you're not working full-time right now. You could work and make enough money to pay your own way to college."

We talked about it and I told her, "Mama, I'm going to play football. I'll work on the weekends. I can't work every night because practice is going to run till five and I'll be tired, but I will work and I will play."

We made a compromise. I would work one night a week and Saturday and Sunday. My pay went from two hundred dollars a week to eighty or ninety, but I wasn't paying any attention. I finally got in the game.

I started out as a running back, like I'd been in Austin, but in early-season practice I changed my mind and told Coach Burns that I wanted to play defense. He put me at defensive end and I just went at it. I loved to hit, put my head in there and ram right through somebody. At defensive end I got all the action I wanted. I could manhandle any runner who dared to come in my direction, but more than that I had every opportunity to hand the quarterback his ass.

In the pros if you get twenty-three sacks, if you hit the quarterback behind the line of scrimmage, you're All-Pro. Douglas went seven and four that year and in our eleven games I had about sixty sacks. I could go all over the field and hit anything and I was loving it. By midseason they were calling me Thomas "Wild Man" Henderson and I wasn't hearing too much about my oxfords in the halls anymore.

I had my own cheering section. Between Oscar, Melvin, Mike and TC they came to every game, whether it was right across the street at Douglas or way across town. They were my boosters and they would whoop it up whenever I got in a real good shot. Stanley Kirklin was too skinny to play but he was my running buddy and the guys were family. They even put me on an incentive bonus system. "Every time you stop the quarterback," TC told me, "you'll get two dollars." I got to making fifteen bucks a game. I still don't know if they were just being nice to me or if they were betting on the games.

I started talking big stuff. I was going to go to college and be a star. I was going to play in the pros. I had never given any of this a moment's thought before; the last time I'd played ball was as a sophomore in Austin and both the concept of college and the idea of the pros had been a long long way off. Now it didn't seem so farfetched. I was "Wild Man" Henderson, haven't you heard of me?

When the postseason voting came out I had made first-team All-City, All-District, honorable mention All-State. My name was in the *Black Dispatch* and in the Oklahoma newspapers. Letters from Montana State, Boise State, other colleges I had never even heard of started coming in. I showed them to my grandmother. "Mama, I can go to college!"

She wasn't very impressed. Nettie came to my games because she loved me but she didn't approve of me playing football; it cut out time from working and my general God-praising duties. She was even less impressed when I wrote back to these colleges and sent them my transcripts and they all turned me down. My grades weren't that bad but I was still making up sophomore year and none of these schools was willing to take a chance on me. "I told you, boy," my grandmother said to me, "you should've kept working. If you had kept your job and worked like you should have you could afford to go to the University of Oklahoma now and be the doctor that I want you to be."

I was kind of mad at the University of Oklahoma myself. If you played high school ball, Norman was where you were pointing. It was the tops. If you played for the Sooners you had instant class; you were, beyond question, the best. It was a mark of honor, a matter of pride; you wanted to play for the University.

I knew that I'd just come out of the woodwork. I hadn't played my junior year, nobody had been touted on me or babysat me or even knew that I existed until I had started my "Wild Man" headhunting. I wanted to be recruited but I was a one-season wonder and now it was too late. Oklahoma's long-time successful Coach Chuck Fairbanks was leaving to go to the pros and Coach Barry Switzer was just taking over so they must not have known enough about me to make the attempt. I was also new to the idea that I was a star so I didn't expect lots of attention, but I was hurt anyhow.

When the rejection letters started coming back I wanted to do something, anything, to play some more ball. I even tried Wichita State.

Wichita State University had lost its entire football team in a tragic airplane crash that fall. Well, I figured, obviously they were going to need heartbeats, able and capable bodies to rebuild their program. I sent them a letter along with a bunch of my clippings. I was honorable mention All-State, I was just positive I'd get accepted.

They turned me down and that about killed me. If I couldn't make a team that had no players on it, how was I going to do on a team with a full squad? It didn't look like I was going to be playing any more football.

Christmas Eve, 1970, I headed back to Austin to see my buddies. I picked up the guys—C.B., Kenneth, Marlon and Harry—and we made the rounds. We hit all the spots, went to all my old favorite pool halls, smoked some weed, drank some wine, did up some syrup. Wherever people were having a ball we were there having it with them.

It was four in the morning when I headed to my mother's. Three blocks away I fell asleep at the wheel, hit a telephone pole, dragged down fifty foot of fence and flipped.

When I came to I was sitting on a curb, live wires buzzing on the ground beside me, my car sitting like a crushed blue bug on its roof. I picked my way around the electric lines and took a look. My beautiful Galaxy was a black hole now.

When I got back the insurance money from the wreck, my grandma kept it. She had made all my payments while I was playing football that fall and she told me, "Hey, you owe me this. You weren't making any money, you were playing that game. I paid the premiums, I'm keeping the check."

She was a tough old lady but I was a tough young kid. I worked up some money—actually, TC gave me seventy-five bucks and I gathered up a couple more—and bought a beat-up, run-down '56 Chevy just to have some wheels. I went from a luxury to a wreck and stayed there.

I stopped bringing my check to my grandmother. With football season over I didn't go back to full-time work, I was too busy with my nightclubbing and pot smoking and hanging out. I had developed my study habits so I could get by without hardly trying, so I was passing my courses without any trouble.

Mama Nettie couldn't figure out why I needed more money now, and why I wasn't coming home some nights till four or five in the morning, some nights not at all. She knew something was up. I wouldn't sit next to her in church anymore. It was embarrassing. I didn't want to sit there and watch her get the Holy Spirit and start screaming and hollering, totally out of control. When she'd really get the ghost I would just move four or five rows off and let the deacons deal with her.

She was a sixty-five-year-old woman and I was a seventeen-year-old boy and, as much as she loved me, she didn't have no idea about the kind of life I was living or the kind of life I wanted to live.

One day I came home from school and she was there and we got into it. She wanted to discuss my hours and what I was doing at night, and why I hadn't been to church. She didn't want to discuss it, she wanted to tell me to get it straight. I didn't want to hear about it.

"You don't run my life!" I shouted.

"Well, move out," she dared me.

"I damn sure will!"

I moved in with TC and stayed with him till the end of high school. I watched him score with women. I watched him sell his pot and take in his cash and buy his outfits. He was my man.

My mother and father and all my brothers and sisters came up to Oklahoma City for my graduation and I couldn't tell anybody I had come up one class short. I had to go to summer school and take tenth-grade biology. But for my mom's sake, my counselor Mr. Holmes set it up so that I would get my diploma and march with my class that day. I had to give the diploma right back to him, but I had spent the last two years proving to this man that I would finish and he had enough faith in me to have it printed up so that I could show it to my mom and everybody and tell them that I was the first one in my family to have finished high school. He gave me a copy of it to give to my mother, and I did pass that biology course that summer.

What I really wanted to do after high school was play football. Football had that winning combination of fun and notoriety. I had gotten a good taste of it and I wanted some more. I was going to prove to my grandmother that I was going to play football and it wasn't going to cost me any money to go to college. Besides, I had told all my friends in all the bars around Oklahoma City that I was going to play in the pros, so I started working on that again.

I just knew that Langston University, a small black college thirty-five miles north of Oklahoma City, would take me. So I just showed up there, unannounced. I just walked on the field and went up to Coach Albert Shoats and Roosevelt "Big Daddy" Nivens and told them I wanted to play football for them.

We went right inside the coach's office to talk. "I wanted to recruit you," Coach Shoats told me, "you're a hell of a football player, but I thought Oklahoma was going to get you, or Oklahoma State."

"Yeah, everybody thought everybody else was going to get me but here I am." It was more likely that Coach Shoats read the *Black Dispatch* than that Barry Switzer did. I didn't tell them that I'd never heard from Oklahoma State or Oklahoma, or that I couldn't make the body count at Wichita State.

"Well, we're glad to have you, son." Right then and there he gave me a grant-in-aid and told me to move on campus.

4

First Taste of Glory

I ran into my grandmother's house shouting. "I got financial aid, Mama, Langston is going to give me financial aid! I'm going to school, Mama, I'm going to Langston!" I was proud and she was happy that I was going to college after all.

That was on Tuesday. Wednesday I moved up there. Thursday, Langston's starting defensive end Larry Millhouse sprained his ankle. Saturday I played my first college game. I had about six quarterback sacks, five solo tackles, I blocked a punt—just about everything a defensive end could do in a game I did and I won the starting spot.

Langston was the first place I really ran into political football. Coach Shoats had been the head coach at Muskogee High School and I realized quick that he had thirty-two scholarships to dish out and thirty-one of them went to his Okies from Muskogee. Even two of the team trainers had scholarships while I was only getting financial aid. Then it turned out that the offensive line coach was Larry Millhouse's brother so that winning the job as starting defensive end was more than just playing well, I had to beat out a whole family. And I did.

The defensive coordinator was a giant of a man named "Big Daddy" Nivens. Big Daddy had been an All-American at Langston back in the sixties and he was a monster. Six foot two, about three hundred pounds, and he was not fat, he was a gorilla. He had coached at a rival high school in Oklahoma City so he knew what I could do and he was on me all the time. Big Daddy was a good Christian man, he had a wonderful wife and a couple of kids, but he also had that football side to him.

Big Daddy screamed at me from the time I set foot at Langston until the time I left. For a religious man he had a real sinner's mouth on him. "What you doin' out there, Henderson? That ain't football, man, that's fencin'. That is bullshit. You have to hit the motherfucker!" He knew what he was talking about and he could get down on the line and prove it. Football players, especially kids, respect the ability to whip your ass and Big Daddy definitely had all our respect. I saw him go just about right through guys, blow their ass right off the line when they thought they knew better than him.

I always thought I knew better. I had a lot of Austin street still in me and he and I went at it all the time. He'd growl and come on like he was going to beat me up, even jump on me sometimes, but I wouldn't back down. I'd woof at him, "Come on, motherfucker, let's go!" but I'd keep my helmet on at all times so if he did take a run at me at least I wouldn't get killed. I think he liked me. I know I liked him.

My counterpart on the other end of the defensive line was a kid named Von Holmes. He was a rough little character, looked like Fred Flintstone. About five feet nine and a half, weighed about 210 pounds, built just right, and he would hurt people. He was one of the greatest players I've ever played with, a Nick Buoniconti who never got discovered. Our running back was Ted Alexander, who got drafted in the seventeenth round by the San Francisco 49ers, only the third player in Langston history to get drafted by the pros.

Our quarterback was Prinson Poindexter. The guy had his own bizarre sense of style. He wore purple, pink and lavender. Poindexter was from Memphis, Tennessee, and he looked like he was probably hanging around Graceland—Graceland's garbage cans—picking up material left over from Elvis' suits.

Unfortunately the whole team was young and we weren't much good yet. We won two games and lost nine, but we hadn't lost badly to anyone and the talent was there. We were definitely going to be a team to be reckoned with the following season.

Langston itself was something to get used to. The school was named after the black poet Langston Hughes. It's in Langston, Oklahoma, out in the middle of the country up on a hill. The town was so small it didn't have its own post office, it used the college's. The town mayor was a teacher at the school.

Langston had eleven hundred students, mostly from Oklahoma, some from Chicago or as far away as Washington D.C., or Vallejo, California. Half male, half female. All black. It was small-town and a lot of the people there were small-town, which made my street worldly wisdom even more unique. I was making a name for myself pretty quickly.

At freshman orientation I was making time with some girl I'd just met. The lady professor at the podium called me out. "Stand up, young man," she told me. No problem doing that. I took my time standing my full six two, then just kind of hung there, real cool, like I was on the corner with the whole of street life in front of me. I think I even grabbed at my cock, smiling.

"Yeah. What's happening?"

"What's your name?" She was not amused.

"Thomas Henderson."

"Where are you from?"

"Well," I told her, "I'm from Texas but I went to high school in Oklahoma City." I wanted her to get the full information, and I got a laugh.

"And what brings you to Langston?"

There was no doubt about my answer. "I'm on the football

49

team." Might as well establish myself early. I heard an appreciative rumble.

Not from her. "I should have known," she said slowly. "Another dumb jock."

This time she got the laugh. I was left there like I'd just been juked and the quarterback was scrambling on his way for a long gain. I couldn't sit down quick enough.

I had been challenged and I was going to play it out. The professor's name was Dr. Joy Flash. I signed up for her humanities course.

Freshman Humanities was the toughest course I'd ever taken. I worked as hard as I'd ever worked, studied works I'd never heard of like *The Odyssey, Oedipus Rex, The Inferno, Don Quixote, The Canterbury Tales*, and books on the music, art and literature of the periods of history like the Renaissance. All the paintings looked the same to me, all the artists' names sounded alike, all the music put me to sleep. I didn't do that well but I kept getting the feeling that she was pushing me, jockeying this dumb animal toward a glimpse of an idea.

I took her course the next semester and got a B. She was surprised. I was amazed. Finally she showed some respect for me and I began to have some respect for myself. The class was so hard that I had to develop decent study habits just to keep up, and those habits kind of spilled over to my other academic areas as well. My grades, the last of my worries at the time, were pretty good.

But football and studies weren't the only things going for me at Langston that year. I was always trying to get some money. My mom would be good for twenty, twenty-five dollars once in a while. Even though I didn't really need it, I wanted to keep that umbilical cord stretched a little longer. My grandmother was always down for thirty-five or forty whenever I went by. But it was 1971 and most of my money I got by selling marijuana.

TC would bring me a pound, which he'd have paid seventy-five dollars for, and he'd say, "Here, man, here's something for you." He became like my sponsor, so I wouldn't have to call my grandmother. He'd been my safety net when I dropped out of her house and he knew I didn't want to go back to her.

Now you've got Maui Wowie and sinsemilla and all kinds of brands and types of pot, but the marijuana I sold on campus was just commercial dope. We didn't have no special name for it, we just called it weed. Ten dollars a bag. I was never in danger of getting caught selling the stuff because the town of Langston didn't have a police department and the campus security was a joke. The only difficulty I had was in selling it.

I was smoking while most of the people I ran with were into alcohol. I wasn't much of a drinker so I was downing my Tom Collins with them, or a little Bali Hai or Boone's Farm, while the serious folk at Langston were swilling down this Mogen David, MD 2020, and this stuff called Ariba, which was 19 or 20 percent wine, wine that makes you puke. I had seen too many guys falling down, dirty and all rotted out, to be messing with that stuff. I would often buy a guy a bottle of wine just to be sociable, have me a couple of swigs and that was it. No sir, I wasn't going to puke.

TC would sometimes leave me some speed or a couple of tabs of orange sunshine, LSD, and I would trip on that about once a week. I would be the only guy on campus walking around at three, four, five o'clock in the morning looking at the grass crawl, the trees breathe. I never really freaked. Sometimes I would go into the bathroom and peel off my face, sit there and see my skeletal system through my skin. I looked pretty ugly to myself then, like my face was melting, so I would lay back in my bed and look at the roof, watch the ceiling run, the holes in the acoustic tile take off like a big race was going around above my head. I'd close my eyes and see through my eyelids. There was nothing I didn't see.

The summer after my freshman year I was looking for a real job. I wanted to make a lot of money because I wanted a new car, I wanted some new clothes, I wanted something to impress the ladies. I heard that Kerr-McGee, a big oil company, was hiring people to do offshore work on their oil rigs so I went to check it out. They told me, "We'll give you a job but the only work we have is with our subsidiary, Trans World Drilling, in Morgan City, Louisiana."

"How much does it pay?"

"Five hundred dollars a week."

"Well, give me a map and when do you want me to be there?!"

I took the Greyhound to the Gulf.

In Morgan City it looked like they were building a hotel on pontoons. "That's an oil rig, son," they told me. "We're gonna put you on Rig Forty-five."

"Where's Rig Forty-five?" I asked, looking around.

The guy pointed out toward the water. "Forty miles that way."

It took two and a half hours in a work boat to reach the station. When I got there a crane up top swung around and dropped a little kind of rope cage that picks up personnel. It's round on the ground and turns into a loosely woven pouch when lifted by cable.

I started asking questions right off the bat. "How does this thing work?" They explained that we did workovers, worked over holes that had already been drilled. We went and plugged up holes, we drilled for new oil, and we did wildcatting. We worked all over the Gulf of Mexico. When we wanted to move we emptied the pontoons and tugboats came and took us to the next site. We worked one week on and one week off, crew changes coming in the work boats on Thursdays.

"Well, who runs this thing?"

"The tool pusher runs the boat," they told me. "And under the tool pusher is the driller, and under the driller is the motorman, and under the motorman is the derrickman, and under the derrickman are the roughnecks, and under the roughnecks are the roustabouts."

"Okay, so what am I?"

"Did you ever work in an oil field before?"

"No sir."

"You're a roustabout."

"What does a roustabout do?"

"Whatever we tell you."

My first week they had me watering down the deck, taking pipe off the work boats, painting hand rails, whatever there was to do. I was a healthy nineteen-year-old guy who knew what work was. I was also the only black guy out there.

At the end of my first week they were shorthanded, so I stayed another week and became a roughneck. This was even more real work. We tore the floor up and worked in the mud, but my main job was running the lead tongs and backup tongs, throwing the chain around the drill pipe, getting on the floor and making trips in and out of the hole.

It's really like a dance down on the oil rig floor. Everybody is in sync, everybody does a certain step at a certain time and the place just about hums. It's nasty, it's oily, but it's a wonderful sense of teamwork and a real feeling of working for your pay.

You start to looking like a man when all you do all day is lift and sweat and hone your muscles. You also make a lot of money. After three weeks at sea I came back to land with about fourteen hundred dollars. It was more money than I'd ever had in my life and I was sure that my mother and father had never had this much money in their lives.

I stayed down in Louisiana and worked that job the whole summer. I made around three or four thousand dollars and I got incredibly strong. My legs developed, my upper body got hard, my body started to cut up with real definition. By the time I started back to Langston I was a changed man.

First thing I did was buy me a new car, a white 1967 Cadillac two-door Coupe de Ville with red interior. I also bought like fifteen new shirts and fifteen pairs of pants, ten pairs of jeans, socks. I was shopping at Flagg Brothers, forgive me, yeah, those loud shoes, I had them too. So I looked sharp.

Sophomore year at Langston the team was getting good. We went 7–4 and got invited to the Cowboy Bowl at the end of the season, which was a big deal for us. I was chosen All-Conference. I was selling marijuana to pay my car notes and my insurance and I was very much my own man. I turned twenty and figured, This is my deal and I'm going to run this show. I'm going to show the world that I'm gonna make it without Mama's help and without even knowing my daddy. Everybody had told me I couldn't make it but I could, this street kid from Austin was on a roll.

That summer I went back Morgan City and worked the rigs again. I could have been the little nigger on the job but I wouldn't let it happen. Tool pushers, the bosses of the rig, recognized that in me. "You get along pretty good, don't you, boy," one said.

"Hey man," I told him back, "I'm not your boy." At six foot two, 210 pounds, and with my don't-fuck-with-me attitude, I could say it and get it heard. I could laugh and have a good time, but don't get personal with me. I was twenty, a man, and in control of my life. One driller even asked me if I wanted to go join his crew and drill oil in Saudi Arabia.

But I didn't go off to the Middle East to go wildcatting, I went back to Langston to play football. This year, 1973, I knew we would be good. Everybody was back from our 7–4 season and we were an experienced team of juniors and seniors.

Prinson Poindexter was still our quarterback. We had a wide receiver named Kenneth Payne, who would get drafted by the Green Bay Packers that next spring. On defense we had right cornerback Gerard Williams, who was going to play for the Washington Redskins and the San Francisco 49ers. We had a fullback named John Goodie who got drafted by the Baltimore Colts. Our tight end was James Thatcher, six foot four, 220 pounds, who could run as fast as he wanted to.

At defensive tackle was Raymond Bogus from Lubbock, Texas. (You could always tell a guy from West Texas because he had brown teeth. I always wondered how their teeth got brown. If you met a girl and she was real pretty and you were talking to her and she smiled and her teeth were brown you'd say, "You're from West Texas, right?") There was Chuck Harmon and Jerry Johnson and Ananias Carson. At safeties we had Leroy Jones and Alfred Nesbeth and at right defensive end stood my buddy Von Holmes, the rock man, the toughest guy on the team. And of course, anchoring the left side at defensive end there was me, Thomas "Wild Man" Henderson.

You hear a lot about the fancy patterned defenses in college ball. Well under Big Daddy Nivens at Langston we played a 5–2 Sic 'Em—five-man line, two linebackers, and everybody go after blood. And we were good. When we won our first game, and then our second, and again our third, people started to really take notice. The pro scouts had been out that spring looking at Payne and Williams . . . and me . . . and now they began to show up in force.

As a sophomore any time a scout came around, people like Vin Lindscog or Red Hickey or anybody from Quadra or one of those scouting combines, I would do front and backward flips. I would run the forty-yard dash in 4.5 seconds. They weren't asking me to run, I would always just run for them. If there was a pro scout on campus I was running, no matter if he asked me or not.

By the time I got to be a junior they had started to tell their friends. Now bird dogs from the pros were actually coming to watch me play, and I really put on a show. So did our entire team. We went 4–0, then 5–0, and our defense was tremendous. I was getting something like six sacks a game, all my tackles were behind the line of scrimmage, we were rolling over opponents.

Langston never got any kind of press in Oklahoma City. For years it was like they just never even knew we were there. Then we went down to Texas and beat Texas Southern, a team in the powerful Southwestern Athletic Conference. Now all of a sudden they were starting to catch on. "Hmmm, these Langston guys, what's happening up there?" We were just a little bitty black college with eleven hundred students and we had beat a team in the SWAC!

When we got to 9–0 the Oklahoma City film crews finally arrived and I got my first taste of talking to the press, and I liked it. Nobody expected anything out of us but here we were with the best defense in the country. No team in America had better defensive statistics than the brothers at Langston University. We were holding opponents to thirty yards a game *total yardage;* teams weren't scoring on us; we were doing just about anything we pleased out there. We were wild and slick and our 5–2 Sic 'Em was just running all over people. We were right up there with the best defenses in the history of college ball.

We ended up our regular season undefeated, 11–0, and we went into the National Association of Intercollegiate Athletics (NAIA) playoffs. We were going for the national small-college championship.

This here was a dream come true! The nation's best! I had never been in such fancy company. Langston had never come close to playing this kind of a game. We were just the boys from out of the woodwork.

Our first playoff game was in Abilene, Texas, against Abilene Christian University and they were a hell of a team. Abilene Christian had a history of playing in these games; people had heard of Abilene Christian, nobody knew nothing about Langston.

Their quarterback was a guy named Clint Longley, "The Mad Bomber." He liked to look downfield and throw the ball as far as he could see, and he had receivers who could run under it. The next year he was playing for the Dallas Cowboys. At running back was this guy who had scored something like thirty-eight touchdowns, name of Wilbert Montgomery. He went on to play about fourteen years in the NFL. Between them they put on a show.

Longley was showing off his bomb arm and Montgomery ran for four touchdowns and we hadn't seen a football team that could play like that. They were like a real football team, with an idea about what came next and why. We were out there to kick the hell out of somebody but they really took it to us.

I played as hard as I knew how. I was able to hit Longley in the backfield, then run down the line of scrimmage after he tossed the ball on an option play and catch Wilbert Montgomery after he turned the corner on the other side. I did that four times, just ran the man down coming from halfway across the other side of the field, but it was nowhere near enough.

I also took the hardest hit of my life that afternoon. I had played three years of college football and nobody had ever really hit me, I was the one doing all the hitting.

My technique of taking on a blocker was always to hit him in the head with an elbow. I knew that wherever the head went the ass followed, so I could always turn a guy whichever way I wanted just with a smashing elbow. It's an illegal blow, but who cared, that's how I learned to play and that's how we played. If you played against me for one set of downs you found out about my technique and everybody knew I was dangerous; they would duck and miss a block on purpose rather than have me slam them in the head with my elbow and risk their lives.

Well, it was a goal-line play and they put in this big old corn-fed freshman, had to be from Nebraska, six four, 265, in the backfield. A Refrigerator type. I wasn't worried, I had turned aside bigger motherfuckers than this.

So here came this guy on a slant play and I hit the sucker, tried to put the forearm and elbow to him like I had to everybody else in my career. He just ran right over me like I wasn't there. The only reason they didn't score was that the runner tripped over the pile of dead meat that was my body.

He hurt me. It was like my whole body was stunned. Just like in the cartoons, I saw the little men running around in my head. They lined up and ran the same play again. Hurt me again. Still didn't score. My guys around me were hanging tough. The third time I was ready for him. Same formation, had to be the same play. I said to myself, I'm facing a great player, I'm going to hurt this kid.

He ran over me for the third time in a row and they finally got in the end zone. I have never been hit so hard, before or since. That night at the postgame banquet we were talking about him. "Who is that guy? What is he, bionic?" He hurt me so bad I couldn't cut my own meat, they had little girls cutting my steak for me. He should've turned out to be somebody famous, but he was just another unknown small-college freshman ballplayer who could put almost any pro on his ass. I never heard of him again, and I didn't miss him.

We lost that game. Wilbert Montgomery was named Offensive Player of the Game. I was named Defensive Player of the Game and it was the first of many awards I received that winter.

I was chosen Oklahoma Defensive Player of the Year. Not some guy with a big reputation from Oklahoma University. This crazy guy from little Langston. Who would've believed it? I made All-Conference for the third straight year. Then I made NAIA All-America. We had a public relations man writing press releases nominating me for the Heisman Trophy. Forget the Lombardi Award for the nation's best collegiate lineman, he was touting me for the best player in the country. I thought it was a joke, but I loved it. What else could happen?

I made first-team Associated Press NCAA Division II Little All-America. Me, Thomas "Wild Man" Henderson, defensive end, Langston University. The other defensive end was Ed "Too Tall" Jones, Tennessee State. Also on the Little All-America team that year were Walter Payton, Gary "Big Hands" Johnson, Robert Brazile, Fred Dean. This was serious company. That spring, 1974, "Too Tall" Jones was the first player picked in the NFL draft. And I was only a junior!

Changed my life. If you're a football star in Oklahoma you're right up there with the pope and a thousand-dollar-a-night hooker; everybody wants a piece of you. The governor of Oklahoma held a Langston Day and showed up at the banquet, shaking hands, taking credit, looking for votes. Fine with me. We took pictures and got in all the papers, the governor and the best defense in the history of college football. We had arrived.

One day that spring I got a call from a Mr. Barnes, a "friend" of the university. "We think a lot of you, Thomas," he said, "and we were thinking you have a wonderful future in football and I would like to meet with you."

"Okay, Mr. Barnes," I said. "Where do I come?"

"My office is in Oklahoma City and I want you to come by. We've got something for you."

I took off to Oklahoma City that weekend to check this guy out. The address he'd given me was a big warehouse, a distributorship for one of the major soft drink companies.

"Hi, Mr. Barnes," I said after I was ushered in, "I'm Thomas Henderson."

He didn't take long to come to it. "We want to help you out throughout your senior year," he told me. "We understand you've been working in the oil fields."

"Yeah."

"Well you know, that's pretty dangerous work out there."

"Yeah, but it's a team deal and I got pretty used to it." In fact, I was planning to go back out there again that summer.

"Well, it only takes one accident and you could ruin your football career. We just want to help you out. A few people I know, plus my company, we sponsor a few players. We've been sponsoring Oklahoma and Oklahoma State, and we thought it would be fair to give you a chance."

"Oh, yeah? What'd you have in mind?"

"Thomas, we're going to set you up on a $75-a-week commission here, which means you get $150 every two weeks, $300 a month."

"What do I have to do for this?" I asked.

"Well I'll tell you what we'll do. We'll say that you're a field surveyor and we'd like for you to find some time to get our soda machines at Langston."

I never got the first machine on the Langston campus but I did get a check for three hundred dollars every month. Sometimes I'd go by to see Mr. Barnes and he'd give me envelopes with two or three hundred dollars in cash. I never got the whole story but I came to understand that some alumni from Langston were very high up in the soda company's corporate level and they set up a deal for me because they had found out that there was this same kind of kickdown going to the Oklahoma Sooners and they wanted equal time.

* * *

Pro scouts came around in a feeding frenzy, and the player agents weren't far behind. They weren't supposed to contact you before the draft, but that was more than a year away for me and they weren't about to get aced out by a faster, more persuasive talker.

Abner Haynes showed up on the Langston campus. Haynes was a great football player in his time, a quick and shifty running back who could break through the line and just go. He was no genius, though; in the AFL championship game in 1962 he won the toss and gave the other team the ball in overtime and almost cost his Dallas Texans the title. Now he was an agent and I was impressed that he'd traveled all that way to see me. I was more impressed when he gave me a ticket to Dallas and invited me to come see him to talk about representation.

I flew to Dallas to see him in the summer of '74. First he introduced me to Jim McInvale, one of the major distributors of Nautilus equipment, who took me to his new workout gym and set me loose on the machines. I had never worked out with weights a day in my life, and after I got through I couldn't even wash under my arms in the shower I was so whupped. Then I went into Haynes' office.

There was "Mean" Joe Greene, the star of the Super Bowl champion Pittsburgh Steelers. Abner's client. Oh man! There was Harvey Martin, Dallas Cowboy, Abner's client. Wow! There was Rayfield Wright, Dallas Cowboy, Abner's client. Hey, what's happenin'! And Haynes said to me, "Hey, man, you're going to be drafted next year if you just keep yourself together, and I'd like to be your agent. I'll charge you 10 percent." The going rate at the time was 3, 4 or 5 percent but I didn't know that, I didn't have anybody else to compare it to. But if these guys were with him he had to be good, so I signed with him.

First thing I did, I asked him, "Will you help me out through my senior year?" Right there he loaned me fifteen hundred dollars and I bought my mom a bedroom suite. Then every other month I'd call and be wanting one hundred dollars, two hundred dollars, and he'd get it to me. He even had me set up with a date. I was getting the treatment.

So I started my senior year with an agent and no worries. Here I had this money coming in from the soda company, I had Abner Haynes only a phone call away, my Cadillac had conked out so I had a mysterious wreck and collected insurance on it and bought a beautiful yellow 1970 Riviera.

Unfortunately the football team went 1–10. We had lost all of our seniors. Me and Von Holmes were the only two real players back and we couldn't do it alone. They even had me kicking field goals. I actually got one through the uprights but I was much better known for one that didn't come close. The first time I tried it in a game I took my four-step approach, got really far under the ball and kicked it back over my head. There was the football sailing *behind* me. I didn't think anybody could do that! It was funny but I wasn't laughing.

It was an embarrassing, frustrating season but I had to play well and I did. I made Defensive Player of the Year and All-Conference and All-America again but me and the coach were really at each other's throat. He never did give me a scholarship, just financial aid. He expected me, after leading his team for four years, to pay it all back. Meanwhile, all his Muskogee boys were on a free ride. I didn't like it and he didn't care, that's just the way he ran his program. He used to tell me, "Don't worry about it, you won't have to pay it back," like it would be taken care of. But they came after me for it. I was the best player he ever had and I wasn't on scholarship. The bottom line was that he protected his boys and nobody else, and I wasn't one of his boys.

In the middle of the season, with us losing all our games and me playing the best of anybody, he made a point of telling me in front of a whole crowd of people, "You know what, Henderson, if you make it to the pros I'll kiss an elephant's ass in downtown Chicago." Get me Barnum and Bailey!

Because of our 11–1 record the year before, Langston had been booked to play Bethune-Cookman College in Birmingham, Alabama, in the Azalea Bowl at the end of the season. Didn't matter that we had won only one game, we were going to play. Somehow they doctored the newspapers when we got down there to say that we were 7-4, but no, we were 1-10.

I called Abner Haynes before I went down. "Look, man, after this game I am through with college football and I would like to come into Dallas."

"The airplane will pick you up in Birmingham," he said.

I had had enough of Langston road trips. Our rickety old bus seated thirty-three and we would have sixty people on there. We would be hanging out of the luggage rack, little bitty school chairs in the aisle, it was pitiful. And that's the way we traveled. It didn't matter whether we were going from Oklahoma to Franklin, Kentucky, or all the way to damn Alabama, that's what we'd be in for. It wasn't quaint, it wasn't fun, it was nothing but a pain.

Bethune-Cookman kicked the crap out of us. I had two hip pointers, deep bruises that don't let you move without hurting yourself, but I played well. It was the first game I ever played at linebacker and I made a bunch of tackles and did my best.

After the game I was hurting like hell. I was glad that I had a soft seat on a plane that evening and didn't have to ride the rack back to Langston.

The soda company cut me off when the season was over. Cut me off cold. I never figured out exactly why. Then Abner Haynes cut me off. I was into him for about four thousand by then. I had stopped selling pot because all this other money had been coming in but now I was sitting there with about two dollars to my name.

I had moved off-campus my senior year and was living two miles out in the middle of nowhere with a friend of mine named David Lewis. Forget classes, college was over, I was marking time until the NFL draft.

In my junior year I'd fallen in love with my first college woman, Tawanna Myers. She was a freshman, as quiet and sweet as I was loud and boisterous. At five feet four she was very shapely, looked like Betty Boop—round face, big eyes. She was beautiful. She would come all the way out to my place and we'd fool around and everything would be all right.

The place itself was a shack, particularly when it rained,

which was often. Then it was a mud hole. I had lost my Riviera in a wreck and bought a '63 Bonneville, then a '56 Chevy. I was on a definite downward slide as far as wheels were concerned. The Chevy was yellow and black and didn't have windows on the driver's side, or on the passenger's side for that matter, and when the roads were muddy we wouldn't drive up to the house, we'd do a trick act and slide in on a four-wheel drift. I spent two months like that, high and sliding, waiting for the NFL draft to change my life.

The NFL holds its draft once each year to decide which teams have the right to sign which college players. It's a monopoly—I mean, if you don't want to play in Kansas City and they pick you, you don't have anywhere else to go—but it's the only game in town and nobody's beaten it yet. Players have no say in who picks them or who their employer will be. Still, most guys are so happy just to be in the league that they willingly go anywhere they are wanted. I was the same way. Just let me play pro ball.

Several teams were calling for information. The Rams, Cowboys, Eagles and Redskins all wanted to know where I'd be the next morning. David Lewis and I sat and talked about the pros. I wondered when the suspense would be over. The draft started in the morning and the earlier a phone call came the higher I would have been picked. I didn't know where I would go, I just hoped I wouldn't have to wait all day.

No way I could sleep. I stayed up smoking my grass and tossing and turning. That was one long night, I just wanted to get it over with but I couldn't, and when I finally fell out as the sun was coming up it wasn't so much sleep as an exhausted nod.

When the phone rang at about 10:15 on the morning of January 29, 1975, I was sprawled across my bed, a dirty taste of stale marijuana in my mouth. I had two dollars and a shoe box full of weed to my name. David picked up. Then he came in running.

"Hey, man!" He was whispering and laughing and squeaking at the same time, he was so excited. "It's the Dallas Cowboys, man.'' He shook my shoulders to wake me up. ''And it's early, man, it's early!''

David put the phone down on the table and I didn't want to pick it up. But this was my future calling. I walked over and grabbed the receiver and put it to my ear. ''Hello, this is Thomas Henderson.''

''Thomas Henderson, this is Gil Brandt of the Dallas Cowboys. How are you today?''

''Fine.''

''Thomas, we've picked you as our number-one draft choice, the eighteenth pick of the first round. How do you feel about that?''

This guy must have been looking for a testimonial, and though it didn't go with my general nature I certainly had one for him that morning. ''Hey, I'm happy. This is the happiest day of my life. This is what I've been working for. This is it!''

''Can you come to Dallas this afternoon?'' he asked me.

I may have been stunned but I wasn't dead. ''Well, let me check my schedule here.'' I was laughing but he didn't seem amused. ''Yeah, I think I can squeeze you in!''

The conversation was short. I hung up the phone and rounded out the front door of this shack in the middle of nowhere and just kept on running.

There was nothing around except acreage and I ran right out in it. Jeans, sneakers, a T-shirt—I ran and I cried and shouted and no one could hear me. I ran till I couldn't run anymore, then I walked, then kind of stumbled. It was hot, I was hot, sweating and tear-grimy and full of Oklahoma farm dirt a mile from the house, back in the woods next to this little creek. I grabbed a handful of rocks and sat there, shoes off, feet in the stream, tossing stones one by one into the water, this shit-eating grin all over my face.

I had done it. Me, all on my own, and I had made it. It took me a long time to stop laughing and crying.

5

"I'm Thomas Henderson of the Dallas Cowboys"

The press was waiting at the airport in Dallas to meet me. "Tom, how do you feel about being drafted by the Cowboys?" "Tom, we know Coach Landry picks unknown free agents but they've never taken a first-round draft choice from a school your size, how do you feel about that?" "Tom?" "Tom!"

Right from the top I began making an impression. "First of all," I told them, "my name is not Tom. My mother named me Thomas Edward Henderson. Don't call me Tom. If my sister has a little girl I don't want her growing up calling me Uncle Tom."

That kind of stopped them. I was cocky, with an edge to me. I hadn't been a Cowboy more than four or five hours and already I was stirring things up. This was going to be fun.

The team had sent a car to pick me up and on the way over to the Cowboys' offices I got my first taste of real life in the NFL. It turned out that the Cowboys had traded one of their quarterbacks, Craig Morton, to the New York Giants in exchange for the number-two pick in the draft and they had used that pick to take a guy named Randy White from the University of Maryland. White was an All-American, a big white boy, and they already had him penciled in at linebacker. He was draft pick 1A. Then they had chosen me. I was 1B. He was 1 Anglo, I was 1 Black. I didn't like that one bit. They chose me first but they didn't really choose me first.

I got off the elevator on the eleventh floor and all I saw was blue walls with Cowboy stars on them, the same stars you see on their helmets. There were two doors facing me, one to the administration offices and the other to the coaches. I headed right for the coaches.

They were busy. The draft was still going on, players were being selected as I walked on down the hall. Coach Landry, Cowboys' President Tex Schramm, General Manager Gil Brandt, all of them were making the decisions that would affect the makeup of the Cowboys for this year and several to come and none of them had time to shake my hand. Jerry Tubbs, a linebacker coach, knew who I was and introduced himself but that was it for my welcoming committee. The Cowboys had booked me a room at the Hilton and told me to come back the next day when things were less hectic.

I woke up the next morning and splashed all over the sports section was a picture of Tom Landry shaking hands with his number-one pick, Randy White. I wasn't real pleased. He didn't have the time of day for me, 1 Black, but he was more than pleased to be making the papers with his big old hunk of white boy.

And when I did get to meet him I didn't feel much better. There is a long hallway that you tramp before you reach Coach Landry. Off to the sides are small office cubicles where the assistant coaches do their paperwork and down at the end, the corner office with the windows, is Mr. Landry's. Except he didn't even invite me in. I went straight up to him and stuck out my hand. "Coach Landry, I'm Thomas Henderson." He gave me the once-over, eyeballed me, and said, "How are you doing, Thomas. Welcome."

"Fine, sir. Thank you."

"You know," he said flatly, "we took a chance on you.

You have a lot of speed and Red Hickey convinced me to draft you.'' Was this Tom Landry saying he didn't really want me, his number-one draft pick? "We took a chance on you," he repeated. "I hope it works out."

That was it. He didn't say, "Hey, go get the cameras and come in here and take a shot of me and Henderson. Hey, it's great to get you, we were afraid we weren't going to get a chance to pick you." Coach Landry just turned and went back into his office. Felt like a cold snap had blown on through.

Then I met Gil Brandt. He was going to negotiate my contract and he knew all about me, where I went to high school in Austin, in Oklahoma City, a few of the players I'd played with. Which wasn't surprising; I had filled out about seven Dallas Cowboys applications over the years. Any time they sent them over I'd fill them out. But most of what I noticed about Gil Brandt was the way he assaulted his chewing gum. I'd never seen anything like it. The guy was pretty speedy. He had no chin and his mouth was yapping and he just loved to attack that gum.

"Thomas, we have a minicamp here as of the first of April and we want you to move to Dallas at that time. You can do that, can't you?"

I had no problem with that. In fact, as excited as I was to be a pro and a Cowboy, I could have moved in that day.

"Abner Haynes is your agent, that right?" Brandt's gum was about to crack. "Abner and I are good friends. I'll be in touch and we can get together and get your contract straightened out. You don't think we'll have any problems signing it, do you?"

I knew a hustle when I heard one, this was just like pool. I told him, "I don't know, man. I just know that the number-one draft choice gets a lot of money, doesn't he?"

"Well," Mr. Brandt assured me, "you'll do okay."

I went right from there to Abner's office. There was "Mean" Joe Greene again, and Harvey Martin and Duane Thomas, and they were congratulating me. Abner had told me all along that I'd be about a fourth-round pick and here I was the Cowboys' number one. "What are we going to get?" I asked him.

"We're going to make them pay."

I needed some money. Here I was about to hit the big time and I didn't have but a couple of dollars in my pocket. "What do I owe you, about four thousand dollars?" I asked him. He was going to get 10 percent of my bonus and my contract, whatever that would be, and he knew I'd be there to get it from. "I'm going to need some cash."

"I knew that already," he told me. "What do you think you're going to need?"

"Well, I want to buy some stuff for my mama, and I want to have some money to mess around with. How about three thousand dollars?"

"Well, I have twenty-five hundred for you right here," and he reached into his breast pocket and pulled out an envelope full of cash. There were all sorts of fifties and hundreds in there. I stopped to look at them. I had seen a fifty in passing but it was always an occasion, something to stop and look at—"Hey, check this out!" Even when I was making four-fifty or five hundred dollars a week at Kerr-McGee I would get paid in tens and twenties and then convert that into a bunch of ones that would bulge out my pockets and make it seem like I was the richest guy in the world. Now here I had an envelope full of hundreds. I could get to like this real quick.

I kind of blew off the rest of my senior year. I could see my future and I didn't see where studying for finals had much to do with it. When the Cowboys' minicamp approached I packed my stuff into the fancy new double-wheeled Silverado pickup truck a local dealer had given me and headed on down to Dallas. I was flying down Route 35 doing eighty-five miles an hour when a state cop pulled me over. I told him, "I'm Thomas Henderson of the Dallas Cowboys and I'm going to training camp." The cop said, "Well hell, son, go ahead!"

You get a lot of respect for being a Cowboy from everybody except the Cowboys. I got chosen to play in the Coaches

All-America Game in Lubbock, Texas. I'd never played in front of any kind of a crowd and now all of a sudden everybody knew who I was. I went, "Well, I'll be damned!" I wore a Dallas Cowboy helmet with the star on it and I was impressed. The game was fun. It was televised and they had a camera truck roaming the sidelines getting the good angles. Right before the half I made a tackle and smashed head-on into the truck door, put a dent right in the panel. They asked me was I all right. I said, "I'm all right, check the truck."

I got back to Dallas and Gil Brandt was talking about my room accommodations. "Henderson," he said, "we're going to put you over here in the Premises Apartments. We're going to pay for it for the first six months and then you are going to have to pick up the lease on it. But we are going to put three other guys in there with you." I said, "No you are not. You're not putting nobody in the apartment I move into but me."

"But that's the only way we handle it."

"Well, look, I just won't come down here and stay then." I was getting tired real early of getting treated without respect. They had moved Randy White into a complex by himself, why was I getting the dormitory treatment?

Brandt backed down and I got an apartment all to myself, 150 yards from the Cowboys' practice field. I could roll out of bed and go to work.

The minicamp was for rookies and free agents and veterans, everyone trying to make an impression on the coaches. The veterans wanted to let the coaches know they hadn't lost anything over the off-season, that they'd kept up their conditioning and still knew the system. Free agents were trying to get someone's attention. I knew they didn't cut first-round draft choices so my job wasn't on the line but I also knew that I wanted to make the Cowboys stand up and notice me.

Tom Landry addressed the team and announced two retirements, Bob Lilly's and Walt Garrison's, so already two old Cowboys had bit the dust. I saw middle linebacker Lee Roy Jordan and offensive tackle Rayfield Wright, defensive backs Charlie Waters, Cliff Harris, Mel Renfro and Cornell Green;

tight end Billy Joe DuPree, Roger Staubach, Drew Pearson, defensive tackle Jethro Pugh, and none of them looked like they were having a good time.

I worked out with Alvin Roy, the weight coach, and the linebacker coach Jerry Tubbs. Coaches would line me up to go into a zone drop, where the linebacker had to get into his coverage area, and I would get there quick and break fast and catch the ball and run twenty or thirty yards, showing my speed, showing everything I could showcase.

I was the guy who liked to have fun. I was talking it up, clapping my hands, making more noise than everybody. I was impressing the Cowboys.

Except when it came time to pay me. I went to Abner Haynes and he told me, "I've got to talk to you about your contract one of these days."

"How about now," I said.

He seemed a little nervous. Last thing I needed was my agent, the man in charge of getting me my money, nervous about talking to me.

"They've offered you $45,000 as a bonus and a $25,000 salary."

"Hey, man, that's not a number-one draft choice's kind of money."

"I know . . ." and then he kind of mumbled something about small school or what can you expect. I could expect a lot more and I told him so. I didn't know what pro ballplayers made, how was I to know? I didn't know any of the guys personally, and it wasn't something I could just call up and find out. "Hey, O.J., what are you making this year?" Most guys won't tell you; they'd rather compare the size of their dick than the size of their contract. I had never been involved in this kind of negotiation before. I had to trust my agent to make the best deal for me, out of his experience and expertise.

The Cowboys let us stew most of the springtime. They knew I wanted to play, they knew I could play, but they were in no hurry to give me a penny more. Finally, Gil Brandt called me and Abner into his office. He offered me a $60,000 bonus and a first-year salary of $25,000 with $5,000 increases each year for four more years. He added that up and came up with a five-year total of $235,000. Abner didn't say a word.

I'd never even considered that much money in real life. I was five years removed from scraping for quarters in the pool hall. I was tired, I wanted some cash to buy the things I'd promised to my mother, I said, "I'll take the deal."

Abner never pushed for me and I don't know why. I don't know if the Cowboys or Gil Brandt had something on him. Maybe he felt that I was into him for so much cash that he better get what he could and make sure he got his commission, rather than risk pushing the Cowboys too hard, getting into a negotiating stalemate and having me take a walk on him. Years later I found out that Randy White had gotten a six-figure bonus; that Burton Lawless, who was taken in the second round that year, and Bob Breunig, a third-round choice, got more money than I did. I walked out of that office feeling like a rich man. They ripped me off and made me like it.

When I called my mama to tell her I was going to buy her a car from the bonus I was being paid she said, "I've got some news for you. I know where your daddy is."

Stopped me cold. "What, Mama?"

"I know where Billy is. Your brother Ricky told me." I was floored. I'd met Ricky when we were about five or six years old, I was about eight months older than he was. So it was true, my dad had gotten two women pregnant in Austin; Ricky's mother right about when I was being born.

"Where is he, Mama?"

"He's in New York City."

"I'm going."

She gave me a phone number and I called.

"This is Thomas . . . Henderson. Who am I speaking to?"

"Thomas, this is Gwen Goree." Had to be my father's wife or his sister. I took a guess.

"Hi, Gwen." I listened, trying to get a feeling from her voice. "I'm your nephew, Gwen."

71

"Hi, there!" Her voice warmed right up and we started talking.

"Is my daddy there?"

"Yes, Billy's here." She sounded excited.

All of a sudden I was tired, like all the air had gone out of my chest and my shoulders got rounded and I just had to sigh.

"Look here, Gwen, I want to come up there and meet him, and meet the family."

"Yeah," she said, and then gave me a quick family history. "Your uncle Phelan got killed about a year ago. You've got a grandmother up here named Myrtice and your grandpa's name is William."

"How many kids did my daddy have?" I asked her.

She said, "Thomas, I don't know."

"What do you mean you don't know?"

"Let's just say he's got about twelve."

I had a whole family and didn't know a thing about it.

"I'm coming to New York. Don't tell Billy, I want to surprise him."

The flight coming in was agony. I was a man now, a professional football player with my future on the rise, and I couldn't have felt more like a baby. I was going to meet my maker, to see where I came from, while I was full speed smashing on ahead. No free-fall could have come close to the spin I was in.

I landed at LaGuardia and Gwen was waiting at the terminal. She looked at me and burst out crying. Nobody in the family knew who the hell I was, or that I existed at all. "Boy, you look just like your daddy."

My daddy worked at Spofford House, a juvenile detention center, and Gwen drove me to him. We drove over the Triboro Bridge and I saw the city all lit up and it just plain scared me. My first impression of New York, and one I have to this day, was sheer terror. It got shown to me real quick that there was a whole lot more going on than I had ever seen in Austin.

I'd been able to handle anything Austin threw my way and I hoped I was up to New York.

My father was due to get off work at 11:30 that night. I just walked over to this ramp where Gwen told me he usually came out and I stood there and waited.

The reformatory doors gave a loud *bwonk* each time they opened. *Bwonk,* a resigned electronic bleat, as if to give the world warning about the character coming through. I was sure, after talking with my aunt, that when he walked out I'd know him.

Bwonk. A couple of men came striding through after a full day's work. I stared at them hard but they weren't my dad. *Bwonk.* Some more.

Thirty men went their own ways and I was afraid I'd missed him. I wanted a kinship I could feel, some kind of gut connection to take me in and hold me. I didn't want to be on the outside anymore. I wanted in.

The door honked in what seemed like just another false alarm and there he was. When he turned around and looked at me there was no question in either of our eyes but I had to ask.

"Billy?"

"Thomas?"

I didn't know what I was feeling. I'd been angry all my life that I didn't have a father and now I did. Here he was. My daddy wasn't some Austin street drunk like I'd been afraid, like I'd feared that my mama had been afraid to tell me. He wasn't some hustler, some farmer, some jalopy-driving mechanic. I didn't know what he was but I was glad to see him.

The hug didn't feel exactly right and I couldn't figure why. This wasn't so much emotion as relief.

First thing my daddy said to me: "I'm sorry."

We went to meet the entire family. My grandparents lived in Ossining, New York, and we drove up there that night.

At my grandparents' house I met my brother Allen. Big, good-looking, green-eyed kid. I met my old grandpa, William Goree, and my grandmother, Myrtice.

This was real! All my life I'd had half of everything: half-brothers and half-sisters, a stepdad. Now these were my *real* grandparents. I'd never had no grandparents. Everybody was all the time *kind of* my grandmother, *kind of* my grandfather, *kind of* my mother's brother; nobody was my mother's *real* mother, my mother's *real* father. Finally! Goddammit, here was my daddy's mama and my daddy's father. This was pure blood! It was all coming together for me.

I met an uncle who had been a steward on the railroad for forty-something years. My grandfather, William, had been a coal miner in Alabama. I said, "What did you do in the coal mine?" He told me, "I drove a mule."

The next day I finally got a chance to talk with my daddy alone. He took me to the cemetery where his brother was buried. His brother was a drug dealer, he told me, and somebody had beat on his head with a thirty-pound rock and crushed his skull.

I started to cry. I said, "Billy, where the fuck have you been all my goddamn life? Why did you desert me?"

Billy took a little time to get going. "I was seventeen years old, Thomas, and your mama was pretty and young. Thomas, she was fourteen and we fell in love. Nettie Mae did not approve of me seeing her so Faye and I had to start sneaking to see each other.

"When Faye came up pregnant Nettie Mae came out to the Air Force base and filed a statutory rape charge against me, she tried to get me arrested, she tried to get me a dishonorable discharge. I'm seventeen years old and this woman was after me. She scared me to death, the police scared me to death, the military scared me to death. So when they shipped me out I just ran.

"I was wrong, man. Wrong. There's nothing I can tell you to change what has happened. I have no excuse for the last twenty-one years. We can't make up for lost time. I just hope that we can start from here."

I reached into my pocket and pulled out a yellow envelope, took out some Zig-Zag papers and rolled a big old joint. We sat there, smoking and crying among the headstones.

Our first common bond was marijuana.

I stayed in New York about four days. Everybody fussed over me and I got to meet my other family.

I took a little Care package with me when I went out to my first Cowboys training camp in 1975: about an ounce of pot, three or four hits of orange sunshine acid, about twenty hits of speed. I wasn't going to do it all, but I wanted it there just in case.

Training camp was held at California Lutheran College in Thousand Oaks near Los Angeles. Sunny Southern California.

The first week of camp was only for rookies and free agents, so the coaches could see what the new talent was all about before the veterans got there and the intensive preparation for the new season got underway. My first day didn't start out great. I found out immediately that draft choices Randy White, Burton Lawless, Bob Breunig and Kyle Davis were all at the College All-Star Game in Chicago and I wasn't. It's a great honor to play in that game. The best players out of college play the current world champions at Soldier's Field, and I should have been there. The coaches of each team choose which of their rookies will play. I was a number-one pick, why were numbers two, three and five going and not me? I made a point out of going to the administrative office and asking Gil Brandt exactly that.

"Well, Tom," he told me, "we felt that you needed to come to camp. The system you played for in college was not that much of a system and we felt that you needed to be here in training camp rather than at the College All-Star Game."

I hadn't been there a half hour and I was being insulted. They'd sent the white boys. I don't know if it was intentionally discriminatory, but it was like, "Hey, these guys played at major universities, you played at Langston. We have to see if you can count to ten."

The compound itself wasn't impressive. The dorms there weren't any better than the best at Langston. Seeing a guy six foot seven, 270 pounds sleep on one of these small dormitory cots was a joke to me. There were about a hundred of us milling around when Landry took the podium for his first meeting.

"I want to welcome you guys," he started. Nothing inspirational, very businesslike. He explained the routine. We would start practicing the next day, two-a-days, which means a morning and an afternoon workout every day we were there. We would be up at 6:00 A.M. We would go to breakfast, we would go to lunch, we would go to dinner. We didn't have to eat but we had to show up for every meal. We had to be on the field, ready to go at 10:15; that means ankles taped, having run two laps and done five pull-ups. Afternoon practices, same preparations, at 3:15.

"It's going to be tough," he warned. "Make sure you put on protective wrappings, we are going to start out hitting and if you get hurt you are going to lose a lot of time. It's not good for rookies to get hurt. I've been in this business for a long time and you have to get yourself prepared, mentally and physically, to play football. You have to be tough as nails. . . ." That turned out to be one of his favorite phrases— "tough as nails"—and right there it made you think of exactly what he had in mind. Not some metaphor, some kind of hardness; I thought of nails, *nails,* and exactly how cold and tough the big ones really are.

The next morning we all lined up on the practice field in our shorts and Dallas Cowboys T-shirts. You could get the regular long ones or the ones that were cut off at the sternum that all the Southern schools seem to use. I had nice ripples in my stomach so naturally I chose the cutoffs. Anything to make an impression. I was the fastest guy in camp in the forty-yard dash. I ran a 4.5 and got people noticing. Then came the endurance test and "Landry's Hill."

The hill was tough enough, a little mountain that you almost had to bend all the way into just to keep from falling backward. I think I could have made the mountain all right, it was getting to it that was the problem. The whole thing was about a mile and a half and I had no kind of wind at all.

I knew I was no distance runner. Short bursts, that was me and my game.

The whole camp started off, coaches and everybody. I started out with everyone but that's as close as I got to winning. The fat guys passed me, the short guys passed me, the skinny guys passed me, everybody passed me. I was about halfway to the mountain when I heard this gallop behind me. Here comes Landry.

Tom Landry was a defensive back when he played for the New York Giants in the 1950s. I guess an injury ended his career because he has a gimp knee and runs like Chester on *Gunsmoke*. It's a very effective gimp, I guess, because he caught me. I was running along, my back was tightening up on me and my hips were hurting—I could run 40 yards in 4.5 seconds, I could run the 100 in 9.5, the 220 in 22 seconds flat, but I just could not do distances—and here was this lame old man about to go right by me. I could hear the pounding, not the even cadence of a cruising runner but the strange syncopation of a man with a serious limp. He pulled up by my side.

"Come on, Henderson. You're too young to be running like this. Pick it up. Pick it up!"

And he kept on going. I said to myself, "Look at this son of a gun run. He's beating me and he's crippled." I watched him pull away from me. His legs were flexed, the definition in his calves was unbelievable, his back hamstrings looked wonderful. The man looked great!

People were finishing the run in eleven minutes, twelve, fourteen. I hold the record for Landry's Hill: twenty-two minutes, eighteen seconds. If I had been a free agent from Langston they would have had a station wagon at the finish line waiting to take me back to LAX.

Out on the field they started yelling at us. Jim Myers in particular, the assistant head coach who somebody told me was once a captain in the Navy or Marines or something, was always screaming. "Let's go, Henderson, do this." "Let's go, Henderson, do that." Just berating me all the time. I'd never been treated that way, not in college or high school.

When Big Daddy yelled at me I knew he liked me anyway; here I didn't have any indication that the guy was operating on anything but anger.

Myers was the snitch and tattletale of the Cowboys, always in everybody's business but his own. He was the team enforcer, checking curfew, making sure everyone did every last pull-up he was supposed to, counting your laps around the field, making sure you lifted the right amount of weights each afternoon. He was the police, never gave anyone a break. I've never liked people who treated me like dirt and I didn't like Myers from the git-go.

The coaches I did like were Ernie Stautner, Gene Stallings and Jerry Tubbs. Coach Stautner had been a Hall of Fame lineman with the Pittsburgh Steelers back in the days when football was a no-frills, hard-ass, tough guys' game. They say he used to strap beer cans to his arms and go out and hit guys on the field. I believe that completely. He looked like a large Fred Flintstone, like he came from Bedrock; he was a rock of a man. He had back surgery once and then came back to work. I saw him pumping three hundred pounds on the bench press bar that day. He was grunting and straining, and when he got up there was blood on the bench and at the bottom of his back from where he had busted the stitches from his disc surgery. What a man. Ernie had played the game for real, and because he knew what you were going through he would usually give you a break if you needed one.

That night all the rookies, free agents and new players got introduced to two new deals: the Landry football system and Landry discipline. Neither of them was easy to take.

I'd always been an instinctive football player. Just put me out on the field and let me take someone's head off. I just wanted to hurt people, take a run at them and knock them over. At Langston we played the 5–2 Sic 'Em defense the whole game, with subtle variations like Kill 'Em, Destroy 'Em, Let's Fight This Down, that sort of thing. I played it my entire college career and I liked it. It wasn't that way with the Cowboys.

In the Cowboy system the team gets split up after the general meeting, linebackers go with the linebacker coach, quarterbacks with the quarterback coach, receivers with the receiver coach, offense with offense, defense with defense. The linebacker coach for the Cowboys was Jerry Tubbs. Tubbs had been an All-America playing both center and linebacker at the University of Oklahoma and had had a distinguished pro career. He was a gentle man, had a soft demeanor, didn't get all up in your face about anything like some other coaches did. He was quiet, spoke quietly, carried himself without any kind of I'm-the-Man swagger, but he had linebacker eyes. You could look at him and just know that somewhere inside him was a Sam Huff wildman, a raging Ray Nitschke. I had an immediate liking for the guy; he'd earned his respect and everybody knew it.

So Tubbs came into the meeting room, just some classroom on campus, and said, "Okay, gentlemen, here is your playbook and here are some pens." Trouble. These looseleaf notebooks were three inches thick, every page a defense and a diagram that I'd never seen. The 5–2 Sic 'Em would've gotten edited out of the first chapter. Here was the 31 Safety Zone, the 41–46 Man, the 41–46 Zone, the 48 Banjo Flex Strong Tiger. There were inside defenses and outside defenses and Tom Landry's famous flex weak and flex strong. And every defense had at least six variations.

I looked at 31 Safety Zone just for the hell of it. It sounded like one play, but it was really about five. It was pretty much predicated on the formation of the opponent, but it changed with the flow of the opponent, the motion of the opponent, the roll of the opponent's quarterback. A change in any of those looks changed the defense the linebacker had to play. On the page it said 31 Safety Zone, and I as a linebacker had to drop to the weak zone for pass coverage. Easy. But before I dropped to the weak zone I had to make sure that the formation, the way the other team lined up, said it was really a pass; I had to learn to recognize, when they faked a back into the line, that it was not a run, then drop into the proper zone depending on where the flow went—it could change at any time, depending on the shifting of the running backs or receivers—or whether it was a drop-back pass or a roll-out.

I turned the page. They were all like this. I was going, "You've got to be kidding me. Let me get this straight. You mean I've got to study these plays and then I've got to recognize these formations, and then I've got to recognize what the flow is and what the play is before I can drop into the zone and watch for the run and then you expect me to make a tackle, after all this thinking? In college, when the ball was snapped I made all those decisions. I don't think I like this deal. This is not going to be playing anymore, this is going to be study. This is going to be work!"

Tubbs hit the lights and put on some game films. We sat there in the dark watching the '73 and '74 Cowboys and I enjoyed seeing Lee Roy Jordan, Dave Edwards and D. D. Lewis play linebacker. I didn't have a clue what they might be thinking under their helmets but I liked watching them work. I didn't figure I'd need to learn all that, or that I could learn all that; the Austin in me said I'd have to learn just enough, then let my instincts be my guide.

The other thing I didn't appreciate was the rules. Coach Landry had told us, "I want everybody here who has a beard to cut it off. You can have a mustache but I want you to cut it at the corner of your mouth." No Fu Manchus for the coach. "I don't care what you do after your initial shave but I want all you guys to be clean-shaven by tomorrow."

Well, I had a full beard and I wasn't about to shave it off for no one. I had gotten hazed as a freshman in college and I had gone along with it because it was fun, being submissive to the juniors and seniors, because your time would come. But now I was getting paid, I was twenty-two years old, I was a man, and I wasn't having any fun anymore. People were screaming at me on the field, I couldn't just go put the pads on and hit and enjoy myself. It was regimented, like I was in the military, and I wasn't the type to get along by going along.

I said, well fuck that. My beard doesn't have one damn thing to do with playing football or being a football player.

After the evening meeting I went to Jerry Tubbs and said, "Coach, I want to talk to you. Look, I've got a black man's disease."

"What's that?" he asked. I knew that most coaches would have no answer if I started a conversation that way.

"I can't shave."

"Well sure you can shave," he said.

"No I can't. What happens when I shave is that these little hairs come out and I'm not sure if they are afraid of the world or what but they are trying to go back in and they create big mounds and sores on my face."

Tubbs sure enough didn't have an answer for this one. "I don't know what to tell you, Thomas," he said. "Everybody shaves."

The next morning everybody came downstairs looking like they'd gone through a window. Big lips that had been hidden by hair were now raw, guys who didn't know how to handle a blade had gone at themselves and made a mess of it. Everybody except me. I wasn't giving up. I went to the team trainer, Don Cochren, and ran it by him. He told me to make an appointment with a dermatologist in town for that afternoon, but to schedule it for between lunch and the evening sessions; under no circumstances could I miss a moment of practice.

When I hit the field that morning with my beard still intact there was a little buzz, but I could live with it. The first thing I noticed was that they'd given me number 90. Nineties are linemen's numbers and I didn't like it. I felt like, as a first-round draft choice, I should have been given my choice of a number as a sign of respect.

What I did like was all the new equipment and a helmet that fit. I have a very big head, about a size 7¾, and I've always had trouble finding headgear that I could get on. As a kid they called me "Squid" because my head was so big, but here they were all prepared for me.

I didn't know what kind of shoulder pads I was going to need because in college I don't think I used the same pair two weeks in a row. Langston was so poor that sometimes

I'd have to go into the caves of our locker room, which had fifty years of history to it, and sit there tying pieces of 1940s shoulder pads together to get something I could use. Here all of a sudden I could have anything I wanted.

Same thing with shoes. I made it a policy never to wear the same pair of shoes two games in a row. Always got a new pair of shoes. I found that on Astroturf, which is what the Cowboys played on at Texas Stadium and in most of our away games, a new pair of shoes would work well for me, a soft pair would get me hurt.

I didn't wear a lot of what other guys wore. I never bothered with hip pads or rib pads, they just got in the way of my natural movement, and I didn't get into elbow pads until much later. I was just a raw football player. I didn't even tape my ankles at first. Didn't think I needed it. Never did it in college, and in the pros there was always a line forty-five minutes long to get to the trainer, which took up most of your day. Tired as you were you could be napping instead, so I figured I'd try to let it slide. The Cowboys are big on conditioning and they don't want you to get hurt while you're working for them, so they fine you if you don't take care of yourself. If you sprain your ankle after you've had it wrapped, that's okay, you were just working hard and these things happen. If you sprain it without protective wrap on it that's a twenty-five-dollar fine. I got fined my first week and got myself wrapped after that.

The first thing I noticed once I got on the field was the field itself. It was the best field I'd ever played on. All my life I'd played on fields that didn't quite have enough grass on them. They were all partially bald, maybe some parts of them were clay; I had never played on real posh soft turf or artificial turf in my entire life and it was a real pleasure.

We all did five pull-ups, ran two laps around the field, went through about twenty minutes of stretching exercises to loosen the back, shoulders, hips, knees, ankles, then broke into our groups of linebackers, receivers, offensive linemen, and so forth and went through our own set of drills: drop at forty-five-degree angles and then break on the ball and get thrown a pass, hit shoulders, all the routine football mumbo jumbo. Nothing exciting. The only thing it did to me was get me winded. Forget second wind, I never had a first wind. I had never trained.

The offense had put together some plays and we had been taught how to play an inside and outside defense, so on the first morning of practice the coaches put us through a goal-line series. We weren't playing any flexes and they weren't going into motion, this was just going to be some hitting. This was what I was good at.

I stood there at the line of scrimmage and watched the offensive huddle. Coach Tubbs was running back and forth to all three linebackers telling each of us what to do, what to watch out for, how to play defense, but I didn't hear a word he was saying. I was like a hawk looking over the rats that would be his prey.

In college I'd been better than most of the guys I'd had to play. Now I was going into a new dimension of my game, playing against people of comparable size. Whether they were as good as I was I'd have to find out. Lots of times you could look into a guy's eyes and see if he was a player. You can just tell. If there's a glimmer of doubt, you know this guy can be taken . . . and you take him. It's very predatory, pro ball.

I'd sized up the rookie running backs during practice that day. The fullback was a big sucker and the halfbacks were equally big. I had to be up to it. I was the weakside linebacker, which means that I played on the side of the line that does not have the tight end. (Strongside linebacker, obviously, plays the side with the tight end.) As they came out of the huddle I saw both backs line up to my side. I knew from that formation in college that they were coming right at me. All I thought was, "Okay Henderson, relax, kick this motherfucking blocker's ass and make the tackle. You've got to make the tackle."

I was standing there talking to myself. Don't wait for something to happen, make something happen.

The slant came right at me like I knew it would. Instead of sitting at the line of scrimmage and reacting to the flow of the play I just charged. The guy who was supposed to block me found me in his face already. I bulled him aside and knocked the running back down behind the line.

I'd been taught that the perfect tackle is like a kiss. You line the ball carrier up and hit him almost mouth-to-mouth. You're looking to plant your forehead on his forehead. Nobody is going to stay up if you're flying thirty miles an hour and smack him in the head with your helmet. You can aim for the nose, the mouth, underneath the chin, the throat, they're all good, but the best is right between the eyes. Your man will go down. It's the kiss of death.

Some guys tackle with their shoulders, they put the pads to their men. But you can miss that way. You see guys running through arm tackles, getting around the side of a tackler because he's trying to grab hold of him. I didn't mess with that. I was looking to hit them head-on.

I gave this guy a good smack.

Coach Landry ran about twenty plays that practice and I made about five spectacular tackles. I made my impression. "That guy hits." I could see them tilting their heads, coach to coach along the sidelines. "That guy is a hitter."

After lunch I hustled into town to see the dermatologist. I told him I couldn't shave. Now I probably could have shaved, but it was uncomfortable for me and I did have a problem with ingrown hairs. And basically, on general principles, I didn't want to be treated like a boy when I was a man. The doctor examined me and said, yeah, I did have a skin problem. He told me its long medical name, gave his secretary a note saying that I didn't have to shave, which he then signed, and sent me back to work.

I think we lifted weights that afternoon but it went by in a blur. All I could think about was what Coach Landry was going to say that night after he got that note.

At the team meeting that night the coach was shuffling through his papers. Finally he got to mine. "We have our rule regarding shaving on the Cowboys," he announced, "but any of you players who get a notification from the doctors saying that you can't shave, I'll accept that." I waited for the word and it came. "Thomas Henderson went to the doctor today and it has been determined that he does not have to shave." That was it. He moved on to the next point, not too fast, not too slow. I didn't think he was happy about it but I had played by his rules and I had won this one. I looked around the room at all these big lips and sores and abrasions and I'm sure there were a few guys who resented me. Rough luck.

The next morning as I was warming up out on the practice field, Coach Tubbs walked over to me and said softly, "Thomas, can't you trim it down a little? You can trim those edges, can't you?"

These guys didn't quit! I wasn't quite laughing, not quite mad. "It's over, Jerry," I told him. "Leave my beard alone."

Camp was tough. I had never worked that hard in my life. I was sore all the time from both the contact and the drills. Landry had us run his famous "110s." You ran 110 yards at about 75 percent speed, in about sixteen seconds, and then walked back 110 to the original starting line. Round trip you had sixty seconds. You do ten of those and I guarantee your ass will be dragging. Mine was. I never ran wind sprints in college. For an hour and a half we'd be hitting, then we'd call it a day.

And on top of that they wanted us to study. After meetings all day and films all night and the pounding we'd be getting at the two-a-day practices, they wanted me to take that play-book back to my room and memorize it. I'd be taking on linemen 260–270 pounds, play after play after play. At Langston our biggest lineman was six foot, 250, and I didn't touch him in four years. I was hurting so bad I didn't even have the strength to brush my teeth at night, let alone study. Besides, I didn't care about their brand of football, their brand of teaching. I just wanted to play.

Everybody else there seemed scared of the coaches. Guys would be ducking behind buildings, run off and hide to take a couple of puffs of a cigarette. It was like they were playing for Bear Bryant or something. I had been smoking since I was five years old and these guys would be amazed when I would walk out of a meeting and fire me up a Kool.

Jerry Tubbs walked up to me the first time he saw me light up a cigarette and said, "Thomas, you smoke?"

"Yes, sir."

"Thomas, that's a bad habit. You ought to quit that."

I didn't. Right before the meetings, with Landry walking past me, I'd be smoking my cigarette.

When I went off and hid I'd be smoking a joint. I showed up one minute late to a meeting because I had to wait for everybody to get out of my windmosphere so I could smoke up a doobie, and I got fined fifty dollars. The way Coach Landry worked it, the meeting started when the first name was called on the roll. "Alexander . . ." and the meeting was on. I walked in at about the Cs and it cost me fifty. "When you are late to a meeting," he told the entire team, "it's a fine. The next time you are late, the fine doubles." And leave it to the Cowboys to keep good books; they never forgot about a single one.

Those first two weeks in the Dallas Cowboys' training camp I probably did more conditioning than I'd done in my entire life. My muscles were toning, my legs were strong, I was jumping and hitting and dominating all the areas I was working in. But I made a million mistakes. I was playing stupid football.

I was not a good student. In the first two weeks they expected you to learn at least one defense. I had an idea of all the defenses but I just didn't know them cold. I couldn't dissect them, I couldn't tell you what the person next to me would be doing, and that was the entire Landry teaching concept: Know what your teammate on the other side of the field is doing; see the whole picture. I didn't care to. I wouldn't conform to their system. I thought all that shit was unnecessary. Let's just line up. Bring me a couple of motherfuckers, let's play Bull in the Ring here. Let me hit somebody!

They found a place for me: the specialty teams. Reckless abandon. Just run down the field and hit the man with the ball. That was the kind of football I liked. In college the specialty teams were an insult to me, only the bodies that could afford to be broken played on them. But in the pros I found a lot of joy there. I got to the ballcarrier and made things happen. I found a way to make an immediate and significant contribution to the Dallas Cowboys.

After a couple of weeks of rookie camp all the regulars came in. I had been the most talented player in camp, the top draft choice, the loudest, the most notable. All of a sudden I died. Camp changed.

Here by my side were Lee Roy Jordan and D. D. Lewis and Dave Edwards, the Cowboy linebackers. I was watching "Too Tall" Jones and Jethro Pugh and Harvey Martin and Larry Cole work on the line. In the defensive backfield there was Mel Renfro and Cornell Green and Cliff Harris and Charlie Waters. Across the line of the offense there were these guys I'd seen on TV: Roger Staubach, Drew Pearson, Jean Fugett. At center was John Fitzgerald, next to him Blaine Nye, Ralph Neely, John Niland, Rayfield Wright. Billy Joe DuPree at tight end, running backs Robert Newhouse and Doug Dennison. I was watching like a kid for a second as they went through their paces.

The first thing I noticed was the sound. There is this very special sound when guys hit each other; it's clean and brutal, grunts and crashing as plastic hits plastic and man hits man. There's nothing like it in real life, you just don't hear this sound unless you're right down there next to it, inside it. In college I was usually the one making that sound, doling it out. Maybe once every couple of minutes I'd hear it from somebody else. The first set of downs in our first contact scrimmage I heard that sound five or six times *every play.* Somebody was either hitting or getting hit, accepting a hit or dishing it out for real. I was impressed.

I didn't get to show my stuff until a few days later. Jerry Tubbs decided to put me on a goal-line defense early that day and told me to run through this hole and hit someone. I took him at his word. I fired through the line, knocked All-Pro guard John Niland right on his ass and made the tackle. I think at that point the Cowboy team started getting the message.

I ran over tight end Billy Joe DuPree and he said, "Oh, that's the way you want to do it?" I didn't know yet about how to "brother-in-law." After you're around for a while you pick up on the "brother-in-law" clause. That's where you get up to the line of scrimmage and you give the guy across from you a wink or a little eye contact: Let's go half speed and not tell anybody; I'm not going to hurt you and you're not going to hurt me. Guys do it all the time, it's known all over the league as a way of not knocking yourself out in practice.

I didn't play that way. First off I wanted to make an impression, I didn't care if I hurt anybody, in fact I wanted to. Second, there's a lot of faith involved in pulling a brother-in-law. If the other guy decides he wants to look good, to dominate you, to run over your ass, all he has to do is go full speed and he's made you look like a chump. I didn't trust anyone with my reputation, my game, my livelihood; no way I was letting anyone get even the tiniest little chance to get one up on me. No, it was safer and all-around easier just to play my game, give no breaks and expect not to get any.

I almost got fined for sacking Roger Staubach. We were having a blitzing drill, the running backs standing in the backfield trying to protect the quarterback while the linebackers coming full-blast had to run over or around them to get to him. I liked messing with guys, especially Doug Dennison. Dennison weighed maybe 190 pounds soaking wet, but he lifted weights and pumped himself up to where he looked like he weighed 220. But he was like a balloon. We used to needle him, "If we poked a hole in you, you'd fucking take off!" So I busted my ass running and I just bulled Dennison over.

When you get to the quarterback you're supposed to stop. Not me. I went and hit him, got the coaches' attention.

Landry about fell out of his tower. "I forgot to tell you men," he called through his bullhorn. "You don't hit Roger Staubach. You don't hit the quarterback." Hell, I was disappointed.

Some of the Cowboys really impressed me. Like Lee Roy Jordan. I wasn't a football card–carrying kind of guy but I knew this sucker. I had seen him make some spectacular hits when I was a kid and when I was in college. I never dreamed that I would be sitting in the same meeting room with him every day, every night, same group, same practice, same coach. I liked that. I'd step back and say, "Goddamn. Me and Lee Roy!"

The guy I got closest to, and who had the most influence and effect on me and my game that first year, was assistant coach Mike Ditka. Ditka had been an All-Pro tight end on the Chicago Bears and then the Cowboys and now he was in charge of the specialty teams.

Mike Ditka is a maniac. He could coach choir girls and make them bloodthirsty champions. He is the Tasmanian devil of NFL coaches. He coaches like he played, fire in his eyes, an intensity that goes beyond concentration to pure obnoxious egotism, the kind of guy who just doesn't care who he hurts as long as he gets what he's after. And he only wants his kind of player on his specialty teams. He loves that good devastating hit and he hates a coward.

Ditka runs his program on fear and humiliation. If you don't play well, if you don't cut, if you don't block, if you don't tackle, if you show an ounce or a moment of cringe he will show you up. Don't want to be pusillanimous around Coach Ditka.

In football meetings the coaches show films of practice or games, shot from overhead, without sound. It's pure football. They can slow down a play, isolate individuals and situations, pinpoint good plays and mistakes. Ditka was merciless in those meetings. More than merciless, he was brutal. He liked to lay on the hit. He would slow down the film, sit in the back of the room filled with players and follow a guy with his little pointer flashlight, this little arrow on the screen.

"Look at you. Look at this cowardly shit," he would bellow. "What the fuck is this? You're getting cut tomorrow. If it was up to me you'd be leaving tonight. Pack your shit, man." He couldn't humiliate you more, and he had your life in his hands. Walk out that door and your career was over.

Ditka liked the way I played. I had the same kind of intensity he did, from the same side of the tracks but from a darker area. He became my friend and we understood each other. He knew what I liked and I knew what he wanted. I liked to hurt people, that's the way I was taught to play football. I liked to make hot blocks and spectacular tackles, I liked to strip the ball and cause fumbles, to haul ass and block punts and extra points and field goals. Ditka liked what I liked and he put me in a position to get it done.

I was the first linebacker in professional football to be split out to cover punts. Through the years they'd usually used fast guys like defensive backs, running backs or receivers. But no linebacker had ever been as fast as I was. I could get down there in a hurry and cause a lot of damage, which was the point. So I was on the kickoff team and the kickoff return team. Ditka also put me on the punt and punt return teams, the field goal team and the field goal rush team, the on-sides kick team.

I was going to play!

I still made stupid mistakes. When I was playing linebacker Jerry Tubbs would always say, in his peaceful voice, "Thomas, you went the wrong way," or "Thomas, that's not right," or "Thomas, you shouldn't have blitzed then." Well, that was my game; if I didn't know what to do, I blitzed. The first thing a linebacker does when he comes to the line of scrimmage is recognize the formation, because everything a team can do is determined by how they line up. I had done all of this instinctively and it had made me an All-American. I didn't know it but I had a lot to learn.

The Cowboys demanded that you know everything. They didn't care if you were Roger Staubach or Lee Roy Jordan, you had to study. And just when you thought you had it all down, they went and changed the game plan on you.

Every day the entire team would meet with Coach Landry. He would give the daily announcements of who got fined, how he felt about the workout, what we needed to work on.

The overview. He'd always end his meetings with, "Okay?" As if any of us was about to jump up and disagree with him. Then we'd break up into groups.

We were all carrying around these three-inch-thick school books filled with computer printouts. Page after page of diagrams and abbreviations. At our first meeting Coach Tubbs gave out four or five different colored pens. "Your blue pen is for flow weak," he told us. "Your red pen is for 'fire' or flow strong. Your green pen is for passes, you draw the routes of the backs and receivers out of the backfield." Well, damn, when you took it that way each page and each formation had five or ten different options to think about.

But these guys were writing in these books forever. Lee Roy Jordan was reading the playbook like Bible study. This man had played in the Cowboy system for twelve years and still here he was with his head in his notebook, scribbling in all kinds of colors. He knew all this, what the hell could he have been doing, writing a letter to his wife? I looked over his shoulder and he was drawing plays, defenses.

I'd look around the room and Randy White would be writing away. Bob Breunig, who was a student of the game at Arizona State, would have his pen going. He'd have an answer for every question the coaches asked him. I'd know about 30 percent.

Coach Tubbs would say, "Thomas, what do you do on a 31 Safety Zone?"

"I drop to the outside."

"Okay," he'd go on, "what do you do if they flow this way?" and he'd chalk a back's movement on the blackboard.

"I drop straight back."

"Okay." Both of those were correct. "What does the cornerback on your side do on a 31 Safety Zone?"

That was too much for me. "Wait a minute, Coach. I barely know what the hell *I'm* doing." I'd be okay some of the time on the sets themselves, but when guys started going in motion I just lost it.

"Well, you oughta know, Thomas. You've got to learn this stuff."

I'd never even seen a computer printout before. They gave me this stack of papers and said, Here are the Los Angeles Rams. There were about a hundred pages of plays, then a hundred pages of tendencies. Like it would say, "On second and five, 40 percent of the time in a Brown formation on the right hash mark, they ran Slant 34." Well I'll be damned. Do they really?

I didn't have a clue. Did people really go to these lengths to win a football game? Tom Landry did. He went to that trouble and more: tendencies, which plays they had run on first and ten, first and twenty, second and six, second and seven, second and eight . . . and what time was on the clock when these plays were run. The plays they had run on third down, fourth down; who the opposition would like to throw to on second and ten. The man was beyond thorough and into the world of the unconscious.

I thought I could play for Tom Landry on natural ability alone but that wasn't going to cut it. Camp was full of guys with great talent, wonderful athletes who could probably leap tall buildings in a single bound but who couldn't learn when to do it; they didn't know their ABCs and they were gone pretty quick. I was a number-one draft choice so they weren't about to get rid of me but I wasn't catching on real fast and I wasn't trying all that hard. I was still thinking, "This is football. I know the game, I play the game."

Out on the football field I felt more comfortable but even there I was learning. D. D. Lewis was starting at weakside linebacker and there had been some talk about him jumping to the new World Football League, which would have opened up the starting spot. But he had decided not to go and now with him in camp even that competition wasn't motivating me. I wanted to play but it didn't look like I'd get the full-time chance.

I was a contact player. If the tight end was to my side of the field I would put my shoulder or my helmet into the guy and get tied up with him while trying to make the play. One day Dave Edwards, one of the starting linebackers, took me aside. Dave had big hands, tremendous hands, and he grabbed me and told me to try to move. I was six two, 220 and I couldn't budge an inch. "What I'm trying to show you, Henderson, is you're getting in too tight to the guy, you're getting too close to him. He gets control of you, or you get caught up with him and you're not effective, you can't get off of him, you can't make the tackle. You've got to use your hands. With your long arms you should use your hands all the time."

I tried it and he was right. I don't know that without that piece of teaching I could have risen very far with the Cowboys or any other team. That was a very generous thing of Dave Edwards to do, and it was the best lesson I ever had in professional football.

Tom Landry arranged his defenses like a choreographer on Broadway. He could get down on all fours with the linemen and slide with the linebackers, make sure the bodies were all in sync. That's how he devised his flex defense; if everybody was moving in unison to cover all the holes it would be a success. But it wasn't as if real people were performing it. As much as we were recognized personally we could have been just big strong marionettes. There was nothing approachable about the man, you just didn't want to talk to him about anything. He seemed so emotionless, so untouchable, so far from the rest of us.

It might have looked like some beefy ballet to him way up on his coaching tower overlooking the entire complex, and he knew each movement of each position so well that he could get down and do it with us, but it wasn't any fun. He drafted quick linebackers who could fill vacant spots in a hurry, and even on short-yardage situations he had us down on all fours taking a quick step either way, shoulders parallel to the line of scrimmage, and then shooting up into a gap. He thought that was great. I thought it was great too, but I didn't like being told what to do. And I didn't like the way he carried himself; he was a man to be feared.

We were having a cut drill, where one running back as the lead blocker would come at the linebacker and try to cut his outside leg out from under him. Landry said, "Thomas, watch this. I want you to find a comfortable spot but keep your shoulders parallel to the line of scrimmage. Once you get in your crouch you protect your outside leg. Use your hands and chuck this guy. Give a little ground backward but never give any ground left or right. If he's going to block you high he'll block you high, but with your shoulders parallel to the line you get your gravity right and you can always take on the blocker. The guy you want to worry about is the guy who is going to cut your outside leg, which means the back is going to work off that block and run for twenty or thirty yards.

"What I want you to do," he got into the linebacker's crouch, "is get low, keep your head up, and let the guy knock you back but never sideways." Then he told a running back to come at him.

Now, nobody is going to run hard against God, so the back came in at about 50 percent speed and went for Landry's outside leg, the gimp one at that. Coach chucked the guy to the ground, stayed parallel to the line of scrimmage and was in perfect position to make a tackle. "Henderson," he said, "you have great speed, you don't have to worry about whupping this guy, you can come off the block and make a tackle. Okay?"

I felt honored that the coach would spend his valuable time on me and pissed off that he thought I needed so much work. I felt that he was teaching his system but not so much to me as to the position that I represented. I had a character that Tom Landry just wasn't set to handle. He wasn't set up to handle any kind of character except one he could create. It was a productive but confusing camp for me.

Rookies aren't taken under anybody's wing, they're usually left to fend for themselves, and I was used to that. The only guys I spent any time with were the guys in the linebackers' meetings. There were legends in the locker room but the rooks didn't gab with them.

The first time I went to chow with the veterans they made me sing for my supper. When you walked down the stairs to the chow hall there was a landing that faced the whole cafeteria. All the tables were set up in rows that ran from the landing to the other side of the room, and running along the entire back wall, perpendicular to everybody, Coach Landry sat flanked by his coaching staff. Looked like the Last Supper. I had always thought of Landry as a cold man but I would watch him listen to guys singing and he would laugh. He didn't bust a gut but he would crack a smile. (I always thought Robert Duvall would make a great Tom Landry in the movies someday.)

Maybe it used to be the old school song you were supposed to get up and do for the vets, but I sang "Ain't Too Proud To Beg" by the Temptations. Bob Breunig heard me and he played the guitar so we put together a little stage show. We could sing, and it got to be like a nightly affair. We did Sam Cooke's "A Change is Gonna Come" and "My Girl."

But even with the rookies I wasn't making any real friends. So every night after meetings I started taking little walks. I'd go out to the practice field and sit in the bleachers and smoke a joint and think, "This is nothing like Langston. This is nothing like Austin. This is nothing like I've ever seen."

I took some speed before practice one day, hoping it would improve my time in the hundred-yard dash. I had run a 9.65 the week before, and this time I thought I was flying. Checked the watch: 10.7. Didn't try that again.

The intoxicant of choice in the Cowboys preseason camp that year was beer. Ralph Neely had kegs, just big old ice chests full of brew every night. At 9:30 or 10:00 when I was out at the field smoking my weed, almost everybody else was in their cars sitting out in the parking lot drinking.

We went to the L.A. Coliseum for our first preseason game to play the Rams. The place seats 100,000 and I'd never seen anything like it in my life. You could probably seat the whole crowd at Langston in one ticket section. I was out there with a Dallas Cowboys uniform on, I had a star on my helmet, I was on top of the world. I was going to play professional football. Ain't this something!

On the opening kickoff I was going to show the world I had arrived. I busted downfield as fast as I could, first player down at the twenty-five yard line, and something hit me that felt like a railroad car. I never saw him, didn't know what his number was, but he knocked me dingy. God damn. I had never been hit that hard. This was definitely the real world.

The coaches put me out there on defense in the third quarter. I forgot about the playbook, I forgot about the computer. The formations didn't tell me anything. When they lined up all I could think about was, "Look how big these sons of bitches are!"

It was a nightmare. I was only in for eight or nine plays but I must have made eight or nine mistakes. The worst was when I ended up on the strong side lined up over a tight end named Bob Klein. I was out there as the formation laid itself out in front of me, thinking, "Dave says, 'Use your hands, extend your arms, see where the back is, get away from the tight end and make the tackle.' "

I did it just like I was taught. I got my hands on Bob Klein and I extended my arms . . . and it was as if I had skates on. The man pushed me thirty-five yards down the field. He was strong as an ox. I later learned that you don't go body to body, pound for pound with a big fucker like that, you get away from him. This first time I hung on. When it got to about twenty yards I started to get a little irritated. "Why is this motherfucker still pushing me? You've done your job, man, get off of me." I think he knew he had a fish.

By the time the ballcarrier, Lawrence McCutcheon, got through running on that play he had gained about thirty-five yards, and where he landed I was already there. Both teams fell on me.

On balance I didn't play bad for a rookie. On specialty teams I was very good at cutting people, made all my blocks, made a couple of tackles, Coach Ditka liked my intensity. But in the linebacker meeting, when they showed that play with Klein I wanted to crawl under my seat. Jerry Tubbs said, "Henderson, what were you doing, dancing with this guy?" The whole room laughed at me the whole thirty-five yards, and again when the pile fell on me. But Jerry spared me.

"This guy Klein is the best tight end in football," he announced. Good heart, Tubbs.

Coach Landry was a hard man and it took a certain type of personality to get along with him. Some players just didn't have it.

Toni Fritsch was a little Austrian field goal kicker who liked to drink and one time it caught up with him. Landry was a punter back in his day and he liked to coach the kickers. Fritsch didn't have the perfect golf-swing motion, he kicked soccer-style, punched the ball. He was very effective but at the time his delivery was unconventional. Landry wanted him to change. "Toni," he told him, "I want you to kick through the ball."

Loaded after lunch, Fritsch wasn't having any. In his Austrian accent he told the coach, "I kick the ball. You don't know how to kick the ball, Coach Landry. You don't tell me how to kick the ball. I kick the ball for one point. I kick the ball for three points."

Fritsch made his point. Landry won the game. He eventually got rid of him.

I saw Tom Landry show real emotion one time only.

It was the last week of training camp, 1975, time for the final cuts. Some guys were going to make this team and others weren't, and the decision was Coach Landry's. We still had about fifteen rookies in camp and somebody had to go.

Ken Hutchinson was a hard-hitting, jovial, fun-loving middle linebacker. Everybody liked him. Hutchinson was a member of the Fellowship of Christian Athletes, led the Cowboy player chapel services and was always trying to convert people to Christianity. He was dark black, a good man, and Tom Landry loved him.

The coaches had played Hutchinson in all the preseason games, gave him every opportunity in the world to come through and make the team. He was a hard hitter but he had a hard time, looked pretty bad in the games. I felt sorry watching his performances. He seemed to be knocked up in the air a whole lot, stumbled several times, missed tackles.

97

He was a vicious hitter but he just didn't do all the things you needed to do to make the team.

The morning of the final cut Landry strode into the meeting room. Here were the Cowboys, all forty-five of us, packed into this big classroom ready to hit the season. Landry pulled a sheet of paper off his clipboard and said, "Here are the rookies who have made the team: Randy White, Thomas Henderson, Burton Lawless, Randy Hughes, Rollie Woolsey, Scott Laidlaw, Percy Howard, Mitch Hoopes, Bob Breunig, Herb Scott, Pat Donovan, Kyle Davis, Jim Zorn."

He looked up from his list. "This is the toughest part of this business," he said slowly. "This is the only part of this business I don't really like very much. Today I had to make a decision. I had to cut a fine young man, a good friend, a good Christian. I had to let Ken Hutchinson go." And the man began to cry.

Landry tucked his chin in his chest and walked out of the room.

Everybody was going *Whoa!* Even Lee Roy Jordan, who had been around for more than a decade, hadn't seen Coach Landry do that. I'd never heard him describe anyone as a decent human being, let alone a good friend. Duane Thomas had called Landry the Plastic Man but I saw him more as the Tin Man; if that sucker cried he'd rust. He surely did bust my bubble that time.

The room kind of rumbled.

Randy White, Bob Breunig and I were standing in the corridor that led out to the practice field that afternoon when the coach walked by. He looked at us and squinted. "I hope you all were worth it."

Coach Landry decided he needed another running back to go into the season so when Preston Pearson got released by the Pittsburgh Steelers they brought him to Dallas. I was out on the practice field and I was the loudmouth with the reputation, the quickness, I'm bad. Coach Dan Reeves said, "Henderson, come here. We want you to run the forty-yard dash.'' Wanted to see how quick he was, test him against me. That's right up my alley.

I looked at Preston Pearson standing there in shorts and a T-shirt and the man was all muscle. The guy had muscles in his ass. You could hang him in the Smithsonian Institution as a perfect example of the muscle of a man but you would have to hang a sign next to him that said, ''This is a man, not a Neanderthal.'' I mean, he is one ugly guy.

There were no stopwatches, no clocks, they just put a guy in front of us to snap the ball. I had never raced by a snap, I had always started by sound not sight. Well, Pearson got off the ball one step before I did and he beat me by a step. I was busy promoting a second race because he had suckered me but they said that was fast enough. Pearson said later that Bob Hayes couldn't have beaten him that day, he was running for his job, his life.

To make room for Pearson the Cowboys traded Jim Zorn to the Seattle Seahawks for a future draft choice. That left twelve rookies on the Dallas Squad: the Dirty Dozen.

My stepdad and my mother had only seen me play one game in college so I invited them and my brothers and sisters all up from Austin for our first game of the season. We were playing the Los Angeles Rams and I really wanted to look good. I knew I wouldn't be playing on defense so I had my duties well defined on this team. I was to cover punts and kickoffs and make sure nobody ran them back for touchdowns.

That was my deal. I went for the ball. Other people had lanes to run down but Coach Ditka gave me the green light to go after the ballcarrier on kickoff and punt returns. ''You line up five yards deeper than everybody,'' he told me, ''and get yourself a good run and just make the damn tackle.''

I was the first linebacker the Cowboys ever split out wide on punt and kickoff coverage. Usually they gave that job to a sprint guy, a defensive back or receiver who could run a 4.5 forty. The whole point is to run fifty yards and arrive there the same time as the ball. That was me and that day I was on fire. If the guy caught the ball I tackled him immediately, otherwise he'd have to fair catch it. I ran over the defensive backs they put out on the flanks to block me. They were little fellas and they weren't used to having a big guy out there who could run as fast as they could; by the time I got even with them I was gone. There was no such thing as catching me and then trying to block me, they were giving away forty or fifty pounds and they'd be looking out of the ear hole of their helmets if they took me on.

The Rams didn't return any punts and we won, 18–7.

The second game of my rookie year I got my first revelation. We were playing the St. Louis Cardinals in Texas Stadium and the coaches set up a play for me. Normally on kickoff return teams I was a blocker but that week we had practiced a reverse and I was the guy who was supposed to end up with the ball. In practice it worked great, everybody running about 60 percent and me showing off going downfield full out.

Right before the half I was running down on kickoff coverage and some guy blindsided me. Planted his helmet directly into my hip. I never wore hip pads or rib pads so I took it right on the bone. I thought he'd broken me in half. They had to come on the field and help me off. I couldn't breathe or talk, I couldn't hardly blink, the pain was so bad. I just knew the hip was broken.

They walked me to the dressing room. The trainer was there with me. (The doctors waited until the last tick of the clock to come inside and look at me, but that's the way it works in pro football. If I had been Roger Staubach the whole medical establishment would've been by my side, but this was just a damn rookie.) They knew what it was but I didn't. I had never had a hip pointer like this, all I knew was that I was in pain.

Two Cowboy physicians came into the locker room. One said, "How are you feeling?"

"Well, Doc," I moaned, "right here, Doc."

He touched it and I jumped. It was already inflamed. That quick. The muscle on my hip was three times its normal size. "I'm hurt."

"Do you think you can play?"

"No, man, I can't play, man. I can't walk."

"Well, let me see what we can do."

I laid up on the trainer's table and he felt around and found the spot. "Yeah," I groaned, "that's exactly where I got hit, Doc." I couldn't stop moaning and groaning.

One doctor took this needle and shot me right there full of Xylocaine. In twenty seconds the pain went away. All the way away. Then he injected me again with more Xylocaine in the general area. It felt like from my rib cage out I had this giant piece of dead skin. There was no feeling at all.

The trainer gave me two pills. "What are these?"

"Oh, just codeine."

"Codeine?"

"Codeine IVs. We have IIIs and IVs, and we give IVs when you're hurting."

I took the two codeines and the doctor pulled out another needle. "What's happening, man?" I said. "How many times you going to shoot me up here?"

"It's just cortisone. It's all right. This is part of the treatment. This will help the area on your bone where you got hit heal more quickly."

They put a big doughnut pad on my hip for protection. It stuck out six or eight inches and I couldn't feel it but it seemed to me like two feet of me was hanging off the side. Then Coach Ditka came in the training room.

"Henderson, how are you feeling?"

"Well, I don't feel nothing." I was a little amazed.

He looked at me. "We're going to run the reverse."

I wasn't sure I was there. "I don't know if I can."

I got up off the table, bent to the left, bent to the right. I didn't feel a damn thing. No pain, no discomfort, no nothing.

Coach Tubbs came in for a look-see. He looked at Coach Ditka and at me and asked the classic football question, the only question anyone's really interested in:

"Can you go?"

That's professional football in a phrase. If you can't go, go see the doctor until you can. If you can, then let's go. A guy would rather hobble out with all kinds of stuff busted up inside than tell a coach he can't go. 'Cause if you can't go now, someone else can. And if you can't go now, maybe you can't go next game. And if you can't go then, what can you do? Why are you here? To go. So let's go.

I told Ditka, "Yeah, I think I can run that sucker."

There's a lot of politics on the football field. Each coach has control of his part of the team and they're all fighting to get the most time and attention from the head coach. It was like each assistant coach wanted a feel of the ball. They'd be huddled around Landry going, "Let's try this, I think it'll work, Coach." Ditka, as the specialty team coach, didn't have a lot of decisions to make and he was fighting to make an impression too. Plus, we were behind at halftime and we needed something to turn the game around.

The Cardinals kicked off to us to open the second half. A rookie defensive back named Rollie Woolsey from Boise State, Idaho, was back deep and St. Louis didn't have a clue. Just like we'd practiced it, I took off and looked like I was going to block somebody. Then I turned and doubled back.

But what set the play up perfectly was that Rollie Woolsey fumbled the ball. He couldn't get a hold of it, started looking for the handle. I ran toward him and finally, at the three yard line, he found the ball, handed it to me and ran the other way. I motored along the three all the way to the sideline where Randy Hughes picked up the first tackler on the picket fence and Cardinals were dropping like they'd been shot. I turned up field and Burton Lawless took somebody out, then finally Randy White sprung me—almost an all-rookie runback—and I went ninety-seven yards for the touchdown. I slam-dunked the ball over the goal post.

It came to me as I crossed the goal line: In college I wouldn't have played, in high school I wouldn't have played anymore today; but in the pros they've got these magic-assed drugs that will keep me in the game.

We won 37–31 and I got the Big Play award for the game. I got the Haggar Slacks award for Headhunter of the Week and got a whole bunch of polyester pants that I wouldn't wear outside.

No one told me that I wasn't going to be able to walk Monday or Tuesday. TC had left me some Quaaludes and a couple of Percodans from the week before and I had some pot so I tried to get by, but it wasn't easy. On Monday I couldn't even practice.

When you get hurt in the NFL the real pain comes on Wednesday. The day after the game you're basically okay, just generally sore. Tuesday you're okay. Wednesday the pain really sets in. Especially when they have anesthetized an area, because it takes that long for the cortisone and the Xylocaine to wear off. By the third day your body just refuses to be ignored anymore.

They gave me another shot of Xylocaine and another shot of cortisone and some more codeine IVs and I got hooked. By the third week of the NFL I got hooked on drugs that made me not feel. The first feelings that I knew I could anesthetize were the feelings of pain. I didn't have to feel pain when I played this game. And the drugs they didn't give me I could get on my own.

I was using marijuana and THC, the distilled active ingredient in pot, for rest and relaxation. My apartment wasn't very far away from the practice facilities so I would smoke a joint before the morning meetings, put on my sunglasses and go to work.

The first thing we would do in the linebackers meeting when we got there at 9:00 A.M. during the week was study the upcoming opponent, their plays and tendencies. We would watch films on the upcoming opponent. Then we would watch more films on the upcoming opponent. Then we would have a big meeting with the whole defense and we would decide what the game plan was going to be for the game. Then we would watch more films of the upcoming opponent, and whenever you thought you were through watching films you would watch more films of the upcoming opponent.

Most players are tired and beat-up all the time. When we're not exhausted from the workouts and the games themselves, we're whupped from whatever it was we did the night before. Football players are like that. Studying playbooks is tough enough, but sitting there in the dark listening to the drone of the film projector and the coaches is enough to put a lot of guys out. Coaches are always trying to catch you asleep, then blame the mistakes you make in the next game on the fact that you hadn't listened to what they were telling you.

My sunglasses were becoming an issue. I'd wear them indoors all the time, basically to hide the fact that I was stoned, and also to be cool. Neither would have sat well with the coaching staff. There was no rule saying that I had to take them off but all the coaches wanted me to. They couldn't tell whether I was asleep or watching the films.

Ernie Stautner was the defensive coordinator. He was a Hall of Fame defensive lineman, a beefy guy, not the most articulate man in the world but he got his points across. He ran the defensive team meetings. I was sitting in the back of the room with my head resting against the wall one morning while the films were being run. Bob Breunig and D. D. Lewis and Randy White and the rest of the guys were taking notes. Too Tall Jones and Harvey Martin weren't. Coaches were asking questions about what was being run and guys would answer real quickly.

Ernie looked at me in the back with my glasses on and told somebody to hit the lights. "Henderson."

"Yes." He thought I was asleep but I was awake and watching.

"Tell me something." I was bothering him but I hadn't broken any rules, and that was bothering him even more. "How can you see this film in this dark room wearing those sunglasses?"

I was relaxed. I knew what I had to know and I had been playing well enough when I'd been called on. Plus I was a little stoned, looser than anyone in Cowboy history. "Ernie," I said slowly, putting my feet back on the ground, "when you're cool the sun is always shining!"

Ernie Stautner wished he'd never spoken and Dave Edwards ate it up. For the rest of the year, no matter where I saw Dave—in a club, at the meetings, on the field—he would kind of amble up to me and say, "When you're cool . . . the sun is always shining!" and cackle away.

With twelve rookies on the roster this was supposed to be a rebuilding year for the Cowboys but we won our first four games and were playing well. I wasn't playing at all on defense. Dave Edwards, D. D. Lewis and Lee Roy Jordan were the starting linebackers, Calvin Peterson was going in on third down defenses and Bob Breunig was ahead of me in the depth chart. The only way I was getting in the game on defense was if there was a plane crash and I missed the flight. I'd just scribble through my playbook in different colors because the coaches would check it at the end of the week. They'd take the books and flip through them. As long as they saw some color they thought you were writing. Then they threw them away and the computer kicked out new ones every week.

In practice, as well as learning the plays and formations I was very busy working on my man-to-man coverage. Preston Pearson, who had beaten me in the dash to make the team, was the best running back I ever had to cover in my entire career. I had never come up against anyone with his skill and moves, and no one I ever covered later was as good. He embarrassed me for an entire year.

Preston would make moves on me that made me fall. Every practice, day after day, week after week, game after game, he left me on the ground. He would go up to me and stutter his feet and go one way and go the other and I would fall down. I never caught him all year long, but every time he beat me, every time he faked me out I learned something. He hid his moves well, until it became second nature not to guess with him but just to watch the motion of his body, watch where his feet were, watch what part of the field I was on when he was making a particular move.

I wasn't partying hard in my spare time my rookie season because I was so tired and pretty much alone. I had found a couple of bars to hang out in, H. P. Cassidy's and Number-Three Lift, white bars in North Dallas. North Dallas was the white section of town, South Dallas was where most of the blacks lived. Dallas was integrated legally but the social scene was anything but color-blind.

Even as a Cowboy—and Cowboys were just about walking gods in Dallas, then and now—I could count on running into some degree of prejudice every time I hit the town. I always felt a bit out of place.

The first time I went to the Number-Three Lift I was dressed sharp. I had brand new shoes on, wonderful slacks, nice shirt, leather jacket, and the guy at the door in charge of letting people in said, "There's a dress code here." I stood there wondering, What do you want me to do, put on a tuxedo, asshole? But I held my temper. I knew what was really the matter, but I said, "I'm Thomas Henderson of the Dallas Cowboys" the magic words, my passport around Dallas—and this guy couldn't get me inside quick enough.

I got into places that there was no way I would get into otherwise. I saw black people being turned away constantly for no reason other than that they were black. Even at H. P. Cassidy's, a place that ex-Cowboy Craig Morton owned a piece of, more often than not they were turned away. Several times I'd take it upon myself to go to the door when I saw a black couple or a couple of black guys being given a hard time. "Hey, I know these guys," and it worked, they'd let them in.

Black guys were the main target in North Dallas. It wasn't that white men minded drinking with them, although I'm sure they would've been just as happy if we hadn't been there, it was that they didn't want to see black guys going with white women. That drove them crazy.

I moved to a new apartment on Fair Oaks near Greenville Avenue, probably the hottest strip in Dallas. Nice one-bedroom loft, wonderful pool in the complex. I had arrived. I had just moved in a few days earlier, was getting out of my 98 Regency, and about a half a block away this beautiful brunette was coming toward me walking her Afghan hound. I don't know which was prettier, she or the dog; they were both stepping pretty nice. She had to walk right by me and I stood there and savored the view.

"Hi, I'm your neighbor here. My name is Thomas Henderson. I'm with the Dallas Cowboys." That was just part of my introduction by this point, part of who I was.

She smiled, but only a little, and moved along ahead. She was nice about it but I didn't impress her.

I figured that if she was walking her dog she'd have to come back so I ran in my apartment real quick and I was fumbling around, peeking out the window to see when she and her dog were going to make the return trip. Sure enough, here she came.

I was a little shy about approaching white women. I hadn't had any kind of experience with them, still wasn't sure of how they'd react to me. I mean, I had talked to white girls but each time was still something very new.

But this woman was so pretty, and seemed so vulnerable and at the same time carried herself with that air of Don't Bother Me, that I just had to try. I ducked out of my apartment and started walking down the sidewalk with her.

"Hi. Do you live here?" I started.

"Yes." Her voice was sweet and soft like a little girl's.

"What's your name?"

"Christie."

"Christie what?"

"Christie Blue."

"Christie Blue? That's a hell of a name for a white woman." I was saying anything that came into my head. "The only people I know named Blue are Bobby 'Blue' Bland. There was this guy in my neighborhood who was so black that they called him 'Blue.' "

A white van made the turn into the parking lot across the street. A look of horror crossed her face and I turned to see what had happened.

"Oh, God," she muttered. She was walking away already.

The van pulled up beside us and this thirty-year-old black dude got out. I'd been on the street long enough to know without a doubt that this was his woman I was talking to. I wasn't looking to cause any trouble. "Hey, man, how you doin'? I'm your new neighbor. My name is Thomas Henderson, I'm with the Dallas Cowboys. I was just admiring your beautiful lady here and this dog. Just saying hi. What's going on? What's your name?''

His name was Charles and he ran a cleaning business in South Dallas, and I could see in his eyes that he was going to give her a hard time about talking to this Cowboy. We made a bit of small-talk and I headed back to my apartment.

I came back out to get something from my trunk when I saw her running. Her place was around the corner from mine and she ran out screaming, with him in pursuit.

He caught her about halfway to my apartment, and as I was watching he grabbed her by the hair and dragged her struggling back toward their place.

Being around pimps and hustlers all my life I clued right in to what was happening: That was his woman, she was a hooker, this wasn't the first time. I also knew not to butt in. I knew how that went.

Two days later I saw her passing in her pretty Mercedes and I flagged her down. She was frightened talking to me, looking straight ahead, sometimes checking the rear view mirror. She had heavy makeup under her right eye and I could see that he had punched her. ''Hey, what's happening, Christie. I saw what happened the other day.''

''Yeah, he's crazy,'' she said to me in her soft voice, ''and he's a little jealous. I'm just so tired of it.'' She seemed to me like a desperate woman.

But my lord she was beautiful. She looked like Wonder Woman. Beautiful blue eyes, olive skin, five foot seven or eight, 130 pounds and just absolutely gorgeous. I couldn't figure how this pretty white woman ended up with this sorry black pimp. I looked at her, voluptuous, sexy, beautiful long hair with lots of curls, and said, ''You know what. I wouldn't treat you that way.''

It was the best I could do. ''Could we have dinner or lunch?'' I asked her.

''No way!''

But I knew that she liked me. I was twenty-two years old and she was twenty-five, and I'd see her around the apartment complex once in a while. A couple of weeks passed and I was playing football and coming home for lunch sometimes, and when I'd pass her place if I didn't see the white van parked outside I'd honk my horn just to let her know I was there.

I even went over one time and knocked on her door. Charles answered. "Hey, Charles, what's goin' on?" I laughed as I stood outside. I was just kicking it. "Want to smoke a joint, man?" I'd taken to smoking one joint every night and rolling one for the next day. I couldn't ever do a whole one, it would make my eyes all red and would fuck with my concentration, so if I took about four or five tokes after my shower in the morning the doobie would last me the whole day.

Christie's phone number was unlisted but I finally found it out and called her. "Look," I told her, "whenever this guy is away I want to see you. I don't care. I ain't scared of him. If you want to get away from him I'll get you away from this motherfucker."

But Christie went back to Charles and I went back to football.

Since I was only playing on special teams I took a lot of pride in running down and breaking the wedge on kickoffs, making the tackles, covering punts. Benny Barnes and I were the Mutt and Jeff tag team; if Benny didn't get the guy I did.

But it was frustrating too. I wanted to play defense but I wasn't getting the chance. In the meetings if one of the coaches tested me on a defensive alignment—"What do you do on this defense, Thomas?"—I'd look up and say, "Which one, kickoff or kickoff return?" I knew I wasn't going to play and if I wasn't playing I wasn't going to go out and learn their system.

But I had my ways of making a mark. The Cowboys had an unofficial slush fund set up for the special teams guys. If you picked up a fumble on a kickoff you got a hundred bucks. If you caused a fumble on punt coverage you got a hundred bucks. If you made a solo tackle on any of the specialty teams you got a hundred bucks. There were a bunch of ways to make a lot of incentive money and I did pretty well.

This was strictly off the books. I'm sure Landry knew about it but he looked the other way. The coaches couldn't be part of it legally, but the players could close the doors and do whatever the hell we wanted.

Roger Staubach and Lee Roy Jordan controlled the slush fund, and as straight as they were we knew the thing wasn't going to get too far out of line. The money came from our fines. If you missed meetings they fined you; if you weren't on the field on time for punt or punt coverage teams and they had to call time out because of you, they fined you. I had that happen to me a couple of times. I'd be back behind the bench somewhere drinking Gatorade or sucking on the oxygen machine and get out there late. Cost me five hundred. Still and all I'd make seven, eight hundred dollars a week on the side.

Roger and Lee Roy were the moral authority on the Cowboys. Roger the Dodger dodged everything: controversy, women, linemen. He was out there doing his job, finding a way to win. Lee Roy was a different take on the same deal. I looked at him and thought, "You're a tough old motherfucker." At first I was suspicious of the old guy. Came from Alabama, old-time hard-liner, I figured him for a super racist. Any white guys from Alabama, Georgia, Mississippi had to prove they weren't racists to me. I'd seen too much of it not to be wary. But Lee Roy never gave me any indication that he was prejudiced. All he was was tough.

At thirty-five years old Lee Roy didn't run that fast, but he still hit hard and he knew how to put his body in the right spot in the right hole at the right time. He wasn't that big, a middle linebacker at 210, but he played like 240. He'd come out of the tunnel as we were standing around before the game and say in his cracker voice, "I'm gonna outplay all of you young cocksuckers today!" Then he'd scream and take off with those bowed legs of his and go kick some ass. Got us good and fired up.

* * *

About halfway into the season I took Christie Blue out to lunch at the Fairmont Hotel in Dallas. This was a four-star spot; I enjoyed spending the money on her, having her with me. We talked for a long time and then I said, "I think I know what you do."

"What do you think I do?"

"I think you're a high-class call girl or something like that."

She wouldn't cop to anything.

"You want away from him, don't you."

She sighed. "Yeah. But he'll hurt me."

"Naw, he won't hurt you. Shit, if you really want away from that asshole you just let me know and I'll get that son of a bitch away from you." I was no badman but I was willing that afternoon to go fuck with him. I knew TC in Oklahoma City and I'd known other pimps in my lifetime, and I knew that in the pimping and hustling game if you take over somebody's turf you just have to go and take it over. Tell him, "This program is over, man. The train left the station. She don't want to be with you no more." If it comes down to war that's what happens. But it usually doesn't happen that way; somebody backs down.

I wasn't being any hero; I wanted this woman.

Christie couldn't make the move. I continued to see her around the complex and we'd chat and keep an eye out for the white van. This went on for about six weeks.

Finally, her mouth bloody, two black eyes, her ribs cracked, Christie was pounding on my door. She came in and Charles was close behind. I stood in the doorway and said, "Charles, look here, man, what's happening, man?"

He wasn't here to play. "Hey, man, this ain't none of your *business,* man."

We squared off hand-to-hand in my door. I told him, "Look, man, it's best you leave my house. This is *my* fucking house, and she is in my house right now." I slammed the door in his face.

But this thing wouldn't be over until I settled it one way or another. I walked back out to the street where he was standing by his car trying to decide what to do. "Listen, motherfucker," I raged at him, "you don't come over here fucking with me and my friends. As a matter of fact you should move your shit out of her house because this woman don't want you no motherfucking more. Come fuck with me and I'm going to beat your motherfucking head off, you woman-beating cocksucker."

Christie was in the apartment crying, hurting, all beat up. "I've got to take you to the hospital," I told her.

I was scared as hell. I had an angry pimp outside my apartment, I didn't know what he would do. I had a whore on my couch who had been beat up bad. This was the kind of life I had kind of figured on but it had been a long time since I'd had to face it for real. In fact, I had never had to face it as real as this. I walked outside with Christie holding on to my arm.

I put her into my car. I looked down the parking lot and Charles was sitting there like a vigilante in his van. I backed out. Didn't speed away. I took her to the emergency room at Baylor Hospital, wrote a check to cover her fee. I was a Dallas Cowboy, they accepted my check even though I was a black man.

When she was released from the hospital I brought her back to my apartment for a safe haven. She was too beat up to have sex, all we could do was get her some rest. Two days later she felt she had recovered enough to want to go back to her place. I went and scouted it out.

The white van was parked outside. I knocked on the door and Charles answered.

"You have a lot of fucking nerve coming over here," he growled.

"Let me tell you something, man," I snapped back. "This is what's happening: The lady don't want you in her life no more. The lady is my woman now. The lady wants you to move out of here.

"Now Charles, you have a couple of choices. We can either call the Sheriff's Department to come over here and get your ass out or you can just go ahead and move, man."

He looked at me like, Who the fuck do you think you are? But he wasn't saying a word.

"I'll give you till Monday and then we are going to call the Sheriff's Department." This was on a Thursday. "I'm going to talk to some friends at the Cowboy office too, man, to be sure that you get your ass away."

Now there was no way that anybody in the Cowboys office was going to get involved with a dispute involving a player, a hooker and a pimp, but Charles didn't know that. The guy left and didn't come back.

Christie and I developed a wonderful relationship, an understanding. She continued doing what she was doing. I often had to get up out of her bed at three or four o'clock in the morning to let a John come over; she was so beautiful, so voluptuous that she was charging five hundred to a thousand dollars a night.

Christie Blue became my best kind of friend. I had pulled her out of something that she didn't want to get back into. We made love like tigers, and for a long time she was my woman. Sometimes she'd call over one of her beautiful blonde friends and they would teach me something new, turn me out. But more than that, we could tell each other anything.

The Cowboys went 10–4 in 1975. With twelve rookies, more than the Cowboys had ever allowed to make the team before, we were inexperienced but extremely talented. Landry and the organization had thought of 1975 as a rebuilding year but we had gone way beyond anyone's expectations.

Roger Staubach was just about perfect that season. We weren't putting anybody away, most of our games were close and down to the wire. A lot of times it just blew our minds that we'd won. We had an aging defense backed up by some raging rookies. We knew that if we could hold them close till the fourth quarter with two minutes to go, Staubach would win it for us. If we needed a touchdown he got it. If we needed a field goal he'd run the ball to where the kicker, Toni Fritsch, liked it. Right hash mark? He'd put it over there.

Left hash mark? Sure. Right in the middle of the field? Sure, Toni, here it is. Now kick it.

We made the playoffs as a wild-card team and had to go up to the wilds of Minnesota for our opening-round game against the Vikings. A year before I'd been on a 1–10 team at Langston University and now I had a chance to play in the Super Bowl. This was too much. I was a Cowboy, I was on the field, I was on my way.

I'd never been to Minneapolis or St. Paul or anywhere near the entire state of Minnesota. They talk about the "quality of life" out there but I about froze my ass off. Coming out of the runway I saw that there was eight feet of snow plowed up on the side of the stadium. The field had been chopped up, frozen, thawed and rolled around in all season long. It was all mud now. For TV they painted the damn mud green and put some white stripes on it.

I was twenty-two years old. I had heard about the Purple People Eaters—Alan Page, Carl Eller, Jim Marshall and all. Prehistoric guys, as far as I was concerned. But we were underdogs and we had to dig in.

We played tough all day. It was cold and I was running up and down the field on special teams, but with seconds left on the clock we were losing 14–10. We needed a fifty-yard touchdown to keep from going home. It was over. I was sitting on the sideline shivering, thinking, "Okay, I've got to put my stuff in storage, go back to Oklahoma City . . ." No Super Bowl for us. I had given up.

Roger Staubach dropped back and slung a Hail Mary pass and Drew Pearson caught that son of a bitch under his arm and went in for the score.

I couldn't believe it.

In Minnesota, both team benches were on the same side of the field so I busted seventy yards down the field to the corner of the end zone and started celebrating. We were jumping up and down, pounding on each other. I mean, this baby was over, no way we were about to win, and suddenly it's ours. Unbelievable!

I was so damned tired from the celebration that I didn't

realize I had to cover a kickoff with seconds left on the clock. I did not want to lose this thing, and I had just seen how it could happen in a flash. I was exhausted, drained, scared. In the middle of a victory celebration I didn't want to be the one to lose it for us.

All I wanted was for this thing to be over. We kicked off and I was so tired that my peripherals weren't working. I got creamed. Some Viking just said, "Fuck you," picked a Cowboy and plastered him. I happened to be the man he picked to plaster. That's one of the other parts of pro football nobody ever seems to talk about. Even in victory there is pain. Somebody else made the tackle and the ballgame was over.

The plane ride back to Dallas was a riot. We were like death row inmates who had conned the governor and gotten reprieved. More than reprieved, we'd been pardoned. We were free!

All the guys were going crazy and I was acting the craziest. Randy Hughes gave me a Viking helmet with one horn missing and I went parading by Coach Landry, Cowboy owner Clint Murchison, Tex Schramm and all the coaches sitting up in first class with this one horn on. When we landed at Love Field in Dallas and taxied to the terminal the fans were everywhere. All the guys wanted me out of the airplane first, leading the cheers. I was ready! I charged out of the plane and the press was all over us. Lights, cameras, lots of action. I was standing there with this oddball Viking headgear and a big old grin on my face and said, "We just dehorned them suckers!"

My picture was in the newspapers, me and my one horn. I saved all the clippings. It was a first for me—I'd never been anything but a daredevil rookie hit man before—and I loved it.

Next stop was the Los Angeles Rams in the National Football Conference Championship game in L.A., and here's where I found out that Mike Ditka didn't have a heart. I knew he was a wildman, a maniac, but I didn't know until then just how cold he could be.

The Rams had a kicker named Tom Dempsey. He was born

with a withered arm and a right foot that doesn't go much beyond his ankle, but he held the record for the longest field goal in NFL history at sixty-three yards. He was a little guy with a pot belly and he pissed Ditka off. In the special teams meeting Ditka ran films of him and said, "I want you to watch this guy, Henderson."

The films showed Dempsey kick off for the Rams. He kicks it high, he kicks it hard, he kicks it long. The guy had a foot made out of lead but he ran down the field and got in the way like he wanted to make a tackle. Nobody would block him because no one wanted to mess with a cripple. He'd stand over piles of players like he wanted to get involved. Ditka wanted me to get him.

He never said so in the meetings, but all week the coach would take me aside privately and say, "I don't want this fucking guy over the ball. I don't want this guy coming down the field acting like he's going to make a tackle. I want you to knock this fucker down. I want you to knock him out. The guy has one arm and one leg but he shouldn't be on the goddamn football field if he doesn't want to get hit."

When the game began we won the toss and elected to receive the ball. They lined up to kick off and Ditka put me right in the middle of the field. I was exactly ten yards from Dempsey.

When a man kicks off from the forty yard line, keeps his head down and follows through with a perfect stride, by the time he lifts his head up he's at the forty-five. I could back up to my own forty-five, take a running start and go right through the guy.

Dempsey held up his good arm to start his teammates. He took his five steps, planted, kicked, and before he could raise his head I stuck my helmet right into his chin. He went down like he was dead and I went looking for someone else to block.

"Hey, you fucking Henderson," he yelled after me. "You fucking asshole. You're a big man, aren't you."

Made me feel bad. I was only doing what I was told to do but I felt bad about it. The next time he kicked off I lined up in front of him again. He didn't kick it very well; he was looking for me and not concentrating on the ball.

In the third quarter the Rams were stopped and had to try for a field goal. Here came Dempsey trotting out to try and score three points. I was in the gap on the outside and he was lining up his shot, and I told the guy next to me real loud, right before the snap, *"I'm gonna take Dempsey out!"*

I jumped the gap and blocked his field goal. I had him totally psyched out.

Preston Pearson had a day full of highlights and we beat the Rams 37-7. We were going to the Super Bowl.

Coach Ditka congratulated me after the game. "See that, that little fucker," he said. "He wasn't jumping on any piles today!" I wasn't very proud of what I'd done but I did think it had made a difference.

The Cowboys had already been in two Super Bowls, winning one against the Miami Dolphins and losing one against the Baltimore Colts. The veterans had Super Bowl rings, they had been there before. But this was a rebuilding year with us Dirty Dozen rookies coming out of Thousand Oaks that fall and nobody expected us to get this far. We were the first wildcard team in NFL history to make it to the Super Bowl.

Tom Landry gave us Christmas off and then we had two weeks to prepare for Super Bowl X. The first week we spent in Dallas going over all the films, plays and tendencies of our opponents, the Pittsburgh Steelers. Terry Bradshaw, Lynn Swann, Mike Webster, Mean Joe Greene, Dwight White, L. C. Greenwood, Rocky Bleier, Franco Harris—the whole lot of them. The next week we went to Florida. Super Bowl X was going to be played in the Orange Bowl in Miami, but Coach Landry called that a "hellfire town" and tucked us twenty miles away at the Galt Ocean Mile Hotel in Fort Lauderdale and slapped a 12:00 curfew on us.

Coach Landry ran through his rules and regulations for Super Bowl week and they were pretty standard: He made sure he would fuck up your whole day. From sunrise to sunset it was meetings and practice, practice and meetings. He didn't want to have to worry about you having any extra time to go run wild, he just laid out his schedule.

We jetted into Fort Lauderdale and got taken to our hotel by buses, as usual. I always hated that. Every team in the league was getting like $18 million a year from the networks, and we'd get into St. Louis or Kansas City or L.A. and they'd transport us on these dinky city buses.

In Florida the game was a really big deal. They had to break out a police escort, thirty cops in cars and on cycles, to get our buses from the hotel to the practice facilities. Now that was fun, like a presidential motorcade with sirens blaring and crowds lining the sidewalks.

I thought of myself as an impact player on special teams but I hadn't gotten in on defense hardly at all. I had played in several games in the fourth quarter with like eighteen seconds to go, "Henderson, get in there."

"Oh, okay," and by the time I'd get to the huddle the clock had run out. I figured that was what the Super Bowl would be about: Hit 'em on punts and kickoffs, punt returns and kickoff returns. With Lee Roy Jordan, Dave Edwards and D. D. Lewis in there you had thirty-some-odd years of experience.

The first day of practice in Florida, defensive coordinator Ernie Stautner pulled me aside and said, "Tonight we are going to put a defense in the game plan for you, Henderson."

"You gotta be kidding, man. Shit, I ain't played all year. What do you mean, put a defense in for me?"

But at the meeting that night, sure enough, Ernie said, "Okay, Thomas, we are going to run a Sara 33. I don't know when we are going to use it but sometime during the game we are going to run a Sara 33."

I knew that defense. On a regular 33 the weakside linebacker shot to the sideline and took away the ten-yard out pass; on the strong side, if the tight end released inside you had him man-to-man, if he released to the outside you had the running back man-to-man. On a Sara 33, when the tight end released inside you took a step with him and you blitzed;

if the tight end released outside you took a step with him, like a little delay, and then you blitzed.

They wanted me to blitz. Well, I'll be damned.

I saw the printout and there I was, "Sara 33 using Henderson." It was the first time all year my name had showed up on the game plan. I thought that was neat.

The Temptations and the Pointer Sisters were playing at Joe Namath's Bachelors III in Miami and a bunch of us went down there looking for action. Me, Too Tall, Drew Pearson, Percy Howard and a couple of other guys grabbed a cab. We had a few hours before we had to turn into pumpkins so we figured we'd go to a ball.

I met Joe Namath. I wasn't any great football fan but you didn't have to know very much about anything to know about Joe Namath. You had to be a heroin addict in a phone booth in Turkey not to know who Joe Namath was, and you had to have been there for twenty years.

I was thoroughly impressed. My heroes were Elvis Presley and Muhammad Ali, but when I looked at Namath I said to myself, It's okay, you can go ahead and be my idol too. The guy was so sure of himself, so confident and good-looking and happy, so on top of the scene, that it was like there was nothing he could do wrong. I liked that about him, I liked what it did to him, how he carried himself.

We were sitting right down front for the Pointer Sisters. Me and Percy were probably the least well-known people at the table. I was just some twenty-two-year-old rookie out of small-college Oklahoma, but I was one good-looking youngster and I knew it.

The Pointer Sisters came on and they really had me jumping. At the time they were into a lot of '40s music, "Boogie Woogie Bugle Boy of Company B" and that kind of thing, and they were cooking. Lot of energy, lot of dancing, and they were looking fine. I was sitting right at the front table and I was there looking and thinking, "Now which one of these lovely women do I want to talk to?" I pored over them for three or four songs and then picked the cutest one.

I gave her my big Houdini stare, the one that says "You can't escape from me." I think I got her attention—"This guy in the audience is staring at me"—because she started to stare back. I leaned over to my running mate, my pal, my road dog Percy, and said, "Man, is she looking at me?"

"Yeah," he said.

"I'm going to try and catch this lady."

"Good luck."

The Temptations put on a great show too and afterward we went back to talk to them. It was about 11:30 and we had to be back in our rooms by twelve or Jim Myers would rat us out to Landry, but I had to make contact. Finally the Sisters came out of their dressing room. There were four of them.

"Hi there," I said to the one I'd been staring at. I didn't know any of their names. "My name is Thomas." I think they'd been told we were from the Cowboys so I didn't have to get on with the rest of the phrase. "This is Too Tall, Percy, Drew . . ."

"Hi," she said. "This is Bonnie, June, Ruth, and I'm Anita."

"Hi, Anita." I wasn't looking at any of the others.

"Why don't you all sit down? Talk!" They were real jovial, real friendly, real loud. We sat there and started laughing and talking, bantering back and forth. A real nice little visit. We told them how great they sounded and they said how excited they were for us to be in the Super Bowl.

I put a lock on Anita. I wanted to know her, I wanted to know who she was, about her music, her family, her everything, so I just hung around. The other guys were starting to filter out but I couldn't leave just yet. I got Anita to the side and said, "Are you married?"

"No, I'm not married."

"I sure would like to get to know you."

"Oh, really?" She started kind of blushing.

"What are you doing tonight?"

"Well, I'm going back to my hotel."

"Do you want some company?"

"You sure are bold."

"You never know if you don't ask."

"Don't you all have a curfew?"

"Sure, but you know, I can get away. Where are you at?"

She told me her hotel. It was about fifteen blocks from mine, but it was on the same side of the street, along the same stretch of beach. "Let me do this," I said. "What time are you going to be there?"

"We have one more show, but I'll be there about 1:00 because the Temptations close the show and I can go early."

I loved it. I went back to the Galt Ocean Mile and got bed-checked into the room me and Too Tall were sharing and told him about it. Too Tall was impressed. This rookie had snared himself a celebrity.

I packed a little travel kit: a couple of nice fat joints of Acapulco Gold. At twelve-fifty I called her room. No answer. One-ten, no answer. One-fifteen, no answer. One-twenty she picked up the phone real quick. "Hello?"

"Hi, it's Thomas. You just getting there?"

"Yes."

"Can I still come over?"

"Come on."

"I'll be right there!"

I hit the beach like a soldier of fortune, crouched over, running through bushes, ducking and diving, trying to get out to another hotel to try and catch a taxi to get on up the street. It was a major production and all the while I was laughing at myself. I was going, This is a damn shame, a grown man sneaking around like this. The only thing missing from this wartime thriller was to paint my face black, or blacker.

The view from her suite was spectacular. You had the ocean and you had Anita in this little lounging outfit.

"You've got this room by yourself?" I asked.

"Yes."

"I thought maybe you all stayed in the same room."

She shook her head no.

"You smoke pot?" I felt like I was big-time now. "I've got some good pot, baby." I fired up a joint.

"Do you want some champagne?" she asked.

It was the first time I ever drank Dom Perignon. She busted open a bottle of 1971, with the little bubbles, and we started drinking the bubbly, laughing and talking. I told her about Austin and the Cut and she told me about growing up in Oakland, singing in church with her sisters. I told her about meeting my dad after twenty-one years and she said, "Oh, really?! That's so sad." "Yeah, I met the bum. I come from my poor background and now here I am in the Super Bowl."

"I know about all that," she said warmly. "You oughta be proud of yourself."

We got to talking and I almost got to crying. I wasn't used to sharing this with a woman. I wasn't used to sharing anything with anybody.

I stayed half the night. I woke up at quarter to five and sprang out of bed. "I've gotta go. I've gotta go to work! I really had a good time. I'd really like to see you some more. I'll call you later today. I've got to go see Deacon Landry."

My hotel was about a mile away so I took off my boots and started running down the beach trying to figure which was the Galt Ocean Mile. When I saw the pastel pink I was home. I knew somebody would be up and likely patrolling the front lobby so I ducked in the back door, slipped on down the hall, put my key in the door and walked in. Too Tall was asleep. I kicked back on the bed with a shit-eating grin on my face and said, Boy, I done stayed with one of the Pointer Sisters!

I saw Anita every night that week. I ran out of clothes. I had only packed a couple of outfits to last me the few nights I thought I'd be in circulation, but I wanted to look good for my new lady and I just ran out.

The second night I spent with her at her hotel a couple of her friends came by and they had some cocaine. Well, I'd never had any of this before. But you know me, I don't turn down nothing but my collar.

Cocaine dealers come with their own stories. Some guys like to tell you the history of their dope. This guy gave me the personal history of his Peruvian flake. This Indian man with no teeth, he told me, put it together in Peru. His grandmother brought it over here and this guy had met her at the airport. This was a special batch.

The guy was talking like a connoisseur and he laid out his lines. The stuff was shining, it almost looked like glass. Chopped up real easy. He had a gold straw. "This is a twenty-four-carat gold straw," he said. "If you never ever snort any more cocaine with a gold straw, man, you did it tonight."

I whooped it up one nostril, whooped it up the other nostril. Didn't feel anything at first. The cocaine was so clean that it wasn't until a minute later that I got that drain, that drip, that anesthetizing feeling down my throat. Then I got the smell of the coke. I don't know what it was washed with but it smelled pure, it smelled good.

Nothing tremendous happened. No fabulous rush, no frantic beating of the heart. Just, "Wow . . ." The feeling of well-being. "That's some good shit there."

And I noticed that night that I stayed up a lot longer.

Anita was a fun-loving girl, she loved to laugh, and we did a lot of that. A lot of sharing, talking, loving. Over five days we got to know each other real well. And every night I'd say, "Hey, Anita, where's that dude at?!" I was only doing about eight lines a night but he'd find me quick enough.

The Super Bowl hype was big business. Tickets to the Orange Bowl had a face value of $20 and each player got thirty-three of them. This ticket broker named Alex had stood out in the Cowboys parking lot in Dallas trying to buy the players' seats for $75 a pop and a lot of guys had been selling them. I held on to mine and waited for the price to rise. When it hit $125 I sold about twenty-five of them and came away with an extra $3,000 for the game.

I wasn't prepared for the pageantry, the intensity of the day itself. Mike Ditka had told me, "Henderson, we're going to need a big day out of you," and I'd said, "Yeah, I know." But I couldn't have known how it feels. It was crazy.

I'd been to games at Texas Stadium and Washington's JFK Stadium where you couldn't even hear yourself talk, but the

Orange Bowl was the top of that line. You didn't have fifty thousand full-blooded Cowboy fans or fifty thousand full-blooded Steeler fans, what you had was ninety thousand hybrid football fans all out for the time of their lives. The stands were full of Giants jerseys, Eagles jerseys, Rams jerseys. The tickets were hard to come by and the fans were, like, amazed to be there and letting us know it.

We were going to fight it out to see who was the top team in football, or who was lucky enough not to lose in the first round. In basketball you've got a best-four-out-of-seven tournament, in football it's whoever was best on one day. Sometimes the best teams make it to the championship game. In our case we were not the best team that year, but we had twelve rookies who hadn't woken up yet and were playing our hearts out.

We were seriously elated to be there. With twelve rookies on the squad the whole organization was really thrilled. They'd had a great scouting year, had a fine draft, made excellent decisions, and the whole scouting department was celebrating. Nobody had expected to come this far.

I sat right behind Coach Landry on the bus going to the game. I was trying to study the guy, look at him, see what was going on in his head. The man was cool. He had his little hat on, his suit. He had won an award as one of the Ten Best-Dressed Men in America that year. I had to laugh. I mean, he was wearing nice sportscoats, nice overcoats, his ties matched the rest of what he had on, but the man was wearing wrinkled pants. He looked good on TV when they shot him from the waist up but the man's pants were wrinkled. After that, Mrs. Landry started dressing him all the way down to the ground, but the man was wearing wrinkled black pants under all his jackets. Who makes those lists?

The team rule was that you had to be in the stadium two hours before kickoff. You could get there earlier if you wanted to. You could get there at 9:00 in the morning if the stadium was open, and it usually was. Guys like John Fitzgerald, Ralph Neely, Lee Roy Jordan and Bob Breunig were always there early. It took a whole case of tape to wrap Robert Newhouse's ankles, the man was on the table for an hour getting taped, so he had to show up four hours before anybody just to get started.

I went in there and got seriously taped. I had to run faster and block harder and hit tougher than I ever had in my life and I wanted to be ready for anything. I didn't usually wear elbow pads but that morning I got them taped on too. I was ready to tear people's heads off all day long.

We had started warming up, doing our stretches, going over the game plan, when Ernie Stautner came over and started drilling things into my head like I just got off the boat from Ethiopia. "Okay, Thomas, what do you do on a Sara 33?"

"I blitz."

What do you do if this happens?

"Blitz."

What do you do if that happens?

"Blitz."

"Okay, you got it."

Mike Ditka came over and said, "Henderson, we're going to run the reverse if we win the toss."

"What?!"

I went back in and got the trainer to cut all these elbow pads off. I'd had my fingers and hands taped, that all came off. Then I put stickum all over me.

At the evening meeting the night before, Landry had made me captain of the specialty teams for the Super Bowl. It was a reward for working hard and playing hard on special teams all year long. He named different special captains for each game and I had been it a couple of times during the year, but this was a big day for me. I got to go out in the middle of the field on national television while they flipped this Bicentennial coin for the kickoff.

We won the toss and I thought I would throw up on the spot. Millions of people around the world were going to see this game and I was going to be the first son of a bitch to run with the ball. I was scared, my hands were sweaty, I was cold, I was hot. I was angry. How could he do this to me?

Everything I'd ever done wrong with a ball came back to me in a flash. I felt like running back there, diving on the ball and covering up. At least then they couldn't say I fumbled and lost the game for us on the opening kickoff.

Ditka was inspiring the specialty teams. "I want you to break the son of a bitch," he growled at us. "Cram it down their motherfucking throat. Stick it up their ass!" He sent us out for blood.

Roy Gerela's kickoff was high and deep right down the middle. Preston Pearson took the ball and started straight up the field. I was twenty yards out on the wing faking like I was going to block somebody, then I did a 180-degree spin back and ran toward Preston, toward my own goal. The closer I got to him the more the fear welled up in me. "I'm gonna drop this motherfucker. I'm gonna fumble."

Preston put it in my gut at about the eight yard line and I headed up the sideline. The play was set up beautifully. Steelers were toppling like ingots as I passed them. After thirty-five yards my peripherals started kicking in. I was moving but I was looking around, Where do I go from here? I was gripping the ball so tight I about got a charley horse in my arm trying not to fuck up. I had one guy to beat and that was the kicker, who was right in my way.

My speed was to the outside. If I cut back someone might catch up to me. Gerela was a little guy, I could run right through him. He dived.

When he threw his body at me near the sideline I tried to power past him, to hurdle over him, to pull a Nehemiah, come down in stride and keep on going. If I get over him I'm coming home, I've broken the sucker, no way we can lose the game if I run this one in.

I caught my knee on his ribs and we tumbled, went down out of bounds on the Pittsburgh forty-three yard line. He definitely saved a touchdown but he cracked some ribs on the play and it affected his kicking. I wished I could've broken it but Gerela made a good play, got tangled up with me. Still I felt great, buzzing from feeling all those bodies flying by me. It was the longest kickoff return in Super Bowl history. When

I got back to the bench what I got was, "Henderson, why'd you let a damn kicker tackle you?"

Everybody remembers that game as the one where Lynn Swann made like he was Baryshnikov, catching passes all day long. Unbelievable stuff. I was standing on the sidelines watching the one catch that has made the Hall of Fame of highlight films. I knew guys in college who had great concentration, but I had never seen a guy fall and look so graceful, tripping, stumbling and still keeping the ball in his sight and finally in his hands. It made Lynn Swann famous. It didn't help Mark Washington, the Cowboy defender who was on his back.

I've got some other memories of that game. Mel Blount, the Steelers' cornerback, beat the shit out of our receiver Golden Richards all day long. Richards would come to the sidelines all bloody and intimidated, whining about getting knocked around. Finally in the fourth quarter he got himself hurt and my friend from Austin Peay College, Percy Howard, got in and caught a touchdown pass in the Super Bowl. I was really happy for Percy.

Our tight end Jean Fugett pulled a hamstring during the game and wouldn't come back in. He just refused, said he was in too much pain. That doesn't cut it with Coach Landry. I think Landry expects—in a big game—if you can't play, for you to take a dagger and stab it in your heart. Kill yourself if you can't go. Refuse to go? Get in the wind. (Fugett got traded before he played another down for Coach Landry.)

They finally put me in on defense.

In the first quarter Ernie Stautner grabbed me. "Henderson, Henderson, get over here!" Then his mind went blank and I walked back to get some Gatorade. "Don't leave me!" he shouted. "Come here, when I want you here I want you. I might want to send you in right now." Nothing. Second quarter, same thing. "Henderson, Henderson! Don't move!" Then nothing. Well, fuck this deal. I went and sat back down.

Finally in the third quarter he called me. "Okay, Thomas. Sara 33. Hit that fucker. Stick your helmet under his chin. Go get him!" I ran in the game and Dave Edwards came out.

It was supposed to be a passing situation. The tight end released to the inside and I had a dead bead on Bradshaw. He was looking the other way. But instead of passing he handed the ball to Rocky Bleier. If it hadn't been a draw play I guarantee I would've killed him, driven my helmet right into his earlobe, given him a new pair of earrings. But no pass, no blitz. I had to turn around and look for the ballcarrier. I was in on the tackle and that was my big play for the Super Bowl.

The Steelers beat us 21–17. I was on the field all day on kickoffs, kickoff returns, punt returns. . . . It was a busy day for me. I was dirty, I was tired. Afterward in the locker room Ditka came over to me and said, "Hey, I'm proud of you. I watched you the whole game. You played hard, you played good." I really appreciated it from him because Ditka wouldn't tell you that if he didn't mean it. In fact he would just as soon walk up to you and say, "Hey, you piece of pussy, I'm going to see if I can get Landry to trade your ass to Buffalo. Don't you know that Buffalo Bill was a Cowboy too?"

6

Hollywood Bound

Anita, June and Ruth picked me up in a limousine at the San Francisco airport a few days after the Super Bowl and whisked me away to Sausalito. I had told Anita, "I sure would like to spend some time with you in California," and she'd said, right away, "Come on out!" Didn't have to ask me twice. Besides, I had no home. I'd given up my apartment in Dallas, had no furniture, had nothing but the clothes I was carrying around with me and a bunch of stuff I threw into storage.

All of the sisters had their own condominiums up in the hills and I stayed with Anita. That first night we went out to a nice restaurant and I listened as they all complained about their manager. I was talking business like I was some brain when less than a year ago I had let Abner Haynes and the Cowboys run all over me. But about all I could add to the conversation was, "You want me to rough him up?" I liked the high-level music business gossip I was hearing and I liked getting paid attention to. I was a Dallas Cowboy and outside the Dallas organization that meant a lot.

Anita and I talked half that first night. She told me her

mother and ten-year-old daughter lived north of there and I could tell that her family was very special to her, even if they lived in another place. She and I were very similar; we were successful, we loved our families but we were both kind of out here on our own.

I woke up the next morning, looked out the glass door and I was in the middle of the sky. It might have been heavy fog that had rolled in but to me fog was a cloud and clouds were up there in the wild blue yonder. I walked four or five steps out onto the patio, turned around and couldn't see the house. I came from Austin where the streets were barely paved and here I was with a fabulous celebrity woman with my head in the clouds. We spent two weeks just enjoying each other. She was fun and quick and vivacious and I liked being part of this whole scene.

We went to San Francisco so I could buy some coke. I wasn't doing anything but a few lines at a time, but it was nice to have three and a half grams there if I wanted it. Mostly I just tucked the stuff away for special occasions.

"Would you like to be my date for the Grammy Awards?" Anita asked me. They were nominated for Best Country Song of the Year.

"Of course I would!" The only award I'd come close to was the Haggar Headhunter of the Week award that I kept on winning.

"Well, we've got to get you a tuxedo . . ."

"Oh, I've got something perfect." I ran back to the closet and pulled out this light blue double-knit suit. Wide dark blue lapels, dark blue stitching down the outside seam of the pants. Big bell-bottoms. The jacket came right above the waist. It looked like a short tuxedo jacket. "I'm gonna wear this!"

Too Tall Jones had introduced me to this Dallas clothier named Tim and I'd had all these suits tailor-made for me because Coach Landry had this rule about wearing suits when the team was traveling. I didn't know about gabardines or wools, I'd just picked out these polyester materials that you couldn't light a match around. From a distance they looked great, nice patterns, cool cuts, but up close they were fire hazards. I paraded around the house in them and Anita was kind enough not to tell me, "Henderson, burn that jacket with the flowers on it and your initials sewn into that cheap-ass shit." She'd just say, "It fits you well."

We went out shopping in San Francisco for a blue velvet bow tie and a white shirt with blue trimming. I already had the blue shoes to go with it.

Flew down to L.A., got picked up by another limo and taken up to Cold Water Canyon to Dennis Edwards' house. Dennis Edwards was the lead singer of the Temptations and he was dating Anita's sister Ruth. I got all decked out for the event and he said, "Man, you know that material ain't worth a fuck but that's some sharp-looking suit." I took it as a compliment.

Going to the Grammies I thought we'd have another limo but here came a Rolls-Royce. It wasn't a stretch but me and Dennis and the four Pointer sisters piled in anyhow, Anita sitting on my lap. We pulled up to this wonderful place where the awards were being held and we all piled out, dressed to kill. I walked through the doors with the cameras whirring and people taking Instamatics and professionals snapping away and had Anita on my arm and I said to myself, "You know what? I've died and went to heaven!"

Here's Marvin Gaye, Diana Ross, Stevie Wonder, Mel Torme, all the wonderful singers in the world. We were seated in the second row and in front of me was Miss Ella Fitzger ald. I couldn't believe it. Quincy Jones was there. Everybody you could think of. People whose faces I knew and didn't even know their names.

The Pointer Sisters won two Grammies that night and was proud just to stand up and cheer for them.

Later in the week when the Sisters had to go on the road for a three-day concert stand I stayed at Dennis'. Dennis used to lock himself in his room for fourteen, fifteen hours a day. If you wanted to see Dennis you had to see him in his room I was only doing a line or two a day so I didn't have caus to go in there very often. That three-day stay turned into si or seven weeks and I made a lot more use of that house than he did.

Girls have a way of dropping by at singers' houses. Dennis was always saying, "You like that one? You like that one?"

"Yeah, man, she's fine!"

One of the finer ones took a liking to the way I looked. The day the Sisters left Dennis told me she wanted to meet me, gave me her number. Soon as I found out I picked up the phone.

The fine-looking mama rushed over, didn't waste any time about it. Dennis was locked up in his room so she spent the whole day with me. We did some coke, played around, did some coke, had a little fun. Making love to some stranger in Hollywood. No big thing; this was L.A. Everywhere you looked there were beautiful women, made you want to grab one. I did.

Anita wasn't home three hours when she got this angry-sad look on her face. "How could you do this?" she said.

"What do you mean?"

"How could you have a girl over here and spend the night?"

I immediately started copping a plea. "That's Dennis' friend. She spent the night over here, yeah, but I didn't sleep with her." Lied through my teeth. She bought it.

I couldn't believe Dennis told on me. He'd set me up and then ratted on me. I guess he was in the Pointer Sisters' inner circle, he was closer to them than I was. Maybe he was trying to be a big brother and protect them: "This guy, y'all hadn't left town twenty minutes and he had some girl over here." Coming from my neighborhood I could picture that. The guy's behavior was pretty erratic.

I was walking around Hollywood with a couple of pieces of turquoise that I'd bought at the gift shop at the Galt Ocean Mile and this dumb dolphin on a silver chain around my neck. For my twenty-third birthday Anita gave me these two expensive gold chains. They must have been worth a couple of thousand dollars. I looked at Dennis and he was definitely jealous, he couldn't believe she gave them to me. I snatched off the silver and put on the gold.

There was fresh gold on my neck but something was missing. Anita was sweet and I liked her, we got along well, we talked. I knew she was special but something was not right and I couldn't quite place it.

I did like the circle she was in, though. We got invited to Richard Pryor's house for Easter Sunday.

Of course we took a limo. Anita didn't have a car, she limoed everywhere. Pryor's house was on Sunset Plaza Drive right above Sunset Boulevard and we pulled up and stood at the doorway. Right next to the doorbell was a gold-plated sign. As I remember, it read: "If you did not make an appointment to be at my home, and if you were not invited here, get your motherfucking ass off my porch."

My kind of guy.

We rang and a little black yes-man opened the door. All four Pointers bounced in and I walked right alongside them. I couldn't believe it. I was inside Richard Pryor's house! That Nigger's Crazy! What was I doing here? I was loving it!

I met the man. "Hi. I'm Thomas Henderson of the Dallas Cowboys."

It worked.

"Hey, man, how you doin'? What's happenin'?!" Pryor was friendly, like he decided on the spot that he was going to like me. And I liked him. Chicago, Austin, we came off the same streets and right from the git we both knew it. He was cracking jokes and I told him a few of my own. He looked at me like, "Stick to football." You don't mess with Richard on his own turf.

I hung by the door and this cream-colored Rolls-Royce pulled up. It had gold fenders! Gold knobs. Gold everywhere. A middle-aged woman in her mid-fifties gets out followed by this good-looking darkskinned man. It's Frankie Crocker, the former New York DJ, and his mom coming to party.

Richard Pryor's children were there playing in the pool, people were gathered in loud clusters talking and laughing.

Waiters were bringing around plates of hors d'oeuvres, you dug in and let him pass.

I had left my coke at Dennis' house, I didn't dare bring cocaine to this man's house. No way I was going to be so uncool as to get high somewhere where I didn't know the rules.

I couldn't believe it. This little yes-man who had opened the door was circulating like a busboy with a platter of cocaine. There were a couple of grams chopped up on this fancy serving plate, a bunch of lines laid out like so many pigs in a blanket. A gold snorter was sitting right next to it. Life sure was made easy around here.

I'd never been so embarrassed in my life. Here I was sitting on the couch with my new hipster's secret and here it was, all this cocaine, coming my way.

I couldn't take a whiff. Not in public. Not in front of people I didn't know.

Frankie Crocker was sitting beside me. His mellow voice rolled over my shoulder but didn't disturb the powder. "Don't worry about it, guy."

I said, "I haven't seen you take a hit, dude."

Couldn't do it.

Pryor had all these speakers set around the house. Good sound system, the guy obviously liked his music. All of a sudden Pryor's voice comes over the party like a ringmaster's. Somebody had put the *That Nigger's Crazy* album on the turntable.

Pryor burst out screaming. "Take that off!" Killed the party dead. No sound except Richard Pryor on vinyl being funny and Richard Pryor in real life yelling to get that motherfucking record off the air or he'd kill somebody. He slammed back into the kitchen.

Whoa. The edge was on. What had we done to get him so pissed? You could taste offense with the champagne.

Pryor came back out with a plate of barbecue sauce and chicken. He was looking at everybody and everybody was looking at him. Slowly, timed like a mime, he took a chicken leg, dipped it deep in some sauce and stuck it in his hair. He smeared it all in his face, under his chin, near his ears.

"Will you all forgive me for snapping at you?" He continued to baste himself with barbecue. Everybody started to laugh and the place eased. How could you not love this guy?

The party geared back up. You could hear it jump from first to second, shift easily and start to cruise in high.

A movie screen purred down the living room wall. No way you could look at anything else. At the back of the room a projector appeared. The lights dimmed, the shades were pulled.

Up on the wall Richard Pryor had a bone hard-on. Three girls were tending to him: an Oriental girl, a white girl and a black girl. For three minutes they did X-rated turns on his Johnson and Richard's face, rubbery when he's working at being funny, was flying. One girl would work him for a while and his eyes would explode. Another would take her best shot and he would give his. Onstage he does a bit about the stupid faces guys get when they're fucking; here it was in real life. The girls were trying out new material on him—I do mean they were breaking new ground—and he was trying out new material on them.

The place went nuts. That nigger *was* crazy!

It was time to head on back to Dallas. Cowboy minicamp was about to open and besides, the time was up on me and Anita. She was a celebrity, a star, and she went places I didn't know anything about. She was a wonderful lady, pure of soul, absolutely gorgeous on the inside, but I was blinded to her beauty. I hadn't finished fucking around; I was being led by my dick, not my heart.

I gave it a good workout when I got back to Texas. I moved in temporarily with a girl named Joyce Ann. Joyce Ann was a booster, a thief. She stole at Neiman-Marcus and all the better stores around Dallas. She and several other girls lived in the same apartment complex as Christie Blue. I would've lived with Christie but she had johns coming in and out of there so I couldn't. Joyce Ann did all her work at the hotels so there was a spot with her.

At the Cowboys minicamp I ran into Too Tall in the hall. I was still awed by the man. He was six foot nine, 270 pounds and didn't have an ounce of fat on him. We started talking about small schools, Tennessee State, where he came out of, and me and Langston.

"Hey, man," I told him, " 'member, we were on the same All-America team?"

"Yeah. I didn't know who you were."

"Hey, I didn't really know about you either. They called you Ed Jones. I didn't know you were 'Too Tall' until you got drafted." The NFL had made Too Tall their first pick of the first round in 1974, and me sharing the first-team Little All-America defensive end slot with him was the biggest honor I'd ever had.

So we got to talking. "What's going on with you, man?"

"Aw, man," he drawled, "I moved out of my apartment."

"I did too!" I blurted. "You want to get a spot together?"

"Yeah. All right."

We looked around and found a two-bedroom place, nothing fancy, in an apartment complex called Timber Creek down on Melody Lane. Ed had no furniture, he'd rented all of whatever he'd had in his last apartment and they'd come and taken it back. I had nothing but my clothes and my stereo system, so we needed some basic home furnishings. I did the scouting.

I looked around town, found a furniture rental company and went and walked on the showroom floor. "Hi, I'm Thomas Henderson of the Dallas Cowboys" got me the owner in a hurry, a guy named Bill Casper. He ran about eight or nine of these showrooms around Dallas and had a lot of responsibilities. I didn't want to blow my whole paycheck on some couch, I told him, I had a budget. I wanted to spend a hundred dollars a month. "Well," Casper told me, "you get a house full of furniture for that." We got two big king-size beds, a living room and dining room set, chairs, side tables, TV stand. He asked who my roommate was.

"Too Tall Jones."

"Look, Mr. Henderson," Casper said. "Don't worry about those monthly payments. I'll tell you what I'll do. You give me four season tickets and we'll just call this thing even. Even better than that," he went on. "I'll give you the furniture."

Well I'll be damned. This is the way it works.

I loved taking care of that house. I was the guy who bought the groceries, paid the bills, wrote the checks. It was fun for me to write checks and know the damn checks were good. It was fun to go buy things and know that it was okay to spend the cash, not to sweat it. I didn't have to worry about how I was going to pay for something; it was paid for already. For the first time in my life I felt like I was out of the street.

I started to get to know Ed Jones. Too Tall was an honest man of simple tastes. He liked to fuck, eat and play football. He was driving this 1974 Eldorado Cadillac. Padded roof. Purple. I mean, only Ed Jones and Isaac Hayes had one. Looked like something they threw off the back lot after *Super Fly*. I said, "Ed Jones, you are countrier than a fresh dozen brown eggs." He'd just laugh and drive it around town.

We'd drive to the practice field every day before training camp and go work out with the new conditioning coach, Bob Ward. We'd go out afterward and drink beer. Ed Jones could drink some beer. I tried to keep up with him, because beer was about the only thing I could drink, and I'd last five, maybe six bottles. Too Tall could go through a case a day, sometimes more. I had other ways of getting high. I still had my little stash of acid and my pot. Marijuana was something that I smoked every morning and sometimes during the day and I was always trying to get him to try some. I wanted to share it with him. "Come on, just try it. It's okay, try it."

"Uh, homeboy"—he called everybody "homeboy," his voice deep like he was talking in a well—"Uh, homes, I don't smoke unless it's real good." What's he saying, that my shit ain't no good? Okay, I only had a little Colombian but even when I came up with Acapulco Gold he wouldn't take a hit. That was just his way of getting rid of me. I never could understand why he didn't get high. He was drinking a case of beer a day, so it wasn't like he didn't want to lose control. Never did figure it out.

Too Tall and I did like to party. We started frequenting some black clubs in South Dallas like the Flying Fox and the Plush Pub, out on Grand Avenue down by Fair Park where the old Cotton Bowl is. The Flying Fox was about the size of Too Tall's bedroom and served the same purpose. We'd walk in and people would get on the phone calling their uncles, their sisters, their cousins and all the single women in South Dallas: "Ed Jones and Thomas Henderson are here!"

We would sit there for about an hour and a half and then we'd see flocks of women start coming through the door, two women here, three women there. Walk outside and there'd be five sets of women standing around looking like they were fresh out of the tub. "We know they're here, let's see who they pick tonight."

Too Tall and I batted a thousand from May, June, until we went off to training camp. Every time we went to South Dallas we brought two girls back to North Dallas. Foolproof. Neither one of us had a steady girl, we were always looking for action.

The Flying Fox was run by Macaroni. He liked having celebrities in his place and he was a good guy to know. Macaroni had introduced us to Walter, the pharmacist. Walter ran a very open house and one night he invited us over.

Walter lived out in South Oak Cliff, a really nice home in the middle of the ghetto. He had some acreage, some property around his house, but all around him down the road were these little shotgun homes. No new sight to me, I could've been brought up in one of them. Walter's house had bars on the windows for security.

Ed had a couple of girls with him, I had a couple with me. We parked in back and came inside.

We entered through metal doors into a giant bar area, bottles on the wall, bar stools, a reel-to-reel tape deck turning out sounds. The place looked like a high-tech speakeasy. The living room was separated from the lounge by a steel rail.

Several little couches sat undisturbed next to chairs that looked like they'd never been moved, like the plastic bags had just come off them. The room looked like it had never been sat in, like people had always skipped right over it.

Up two steps was a long hallway. On the right a door led to one bedroom. A few steps down another opened on the left, then another. Finally, down on the right, was The Room.

The Room was dominated by a huge round waterbed, with a red velvet bedspread lying over it like an open invitation. A huge aquarium bubbled away against the wall, all kinds of odd eyes on you. Rugs covered the floor. There was nowhere you could sit, stand or fall that wasn't warm and padded and soulfully comfortable.

The bathroom had this giant marble tub and a couple of huge mirrors. A hand-held Jacuzzi could push water just about anywhere you wanted it to go. Towels were tripled, laying over the towel rack. There were seven robes.

Walter had five girls there already. We were expected.

I had never come close to this. Sure, one time Christie Blue and her girlfriend attacked me in bed, but I'd never, ever, been to an orgy.

They started pulling off my clothes. I just let them, didn't even make a stab at grabbing off theirs, they did that themselves. I kicked back on the bed and they commenced to licking me from head to toe. That was it for me, I was hooked. Hooked! You don't get this one time and try to live without it.

By the time I had gotten naked, two girls had come to the door leading Ed by the hand. They brought him to the bed and the both of us got the same treatment, both ends of the Little All-America defensive line sprawled out over the red velvet. All night long. Or at least one of us lasted all night. I had taken a couple of hits of speed in the car on the way over so I was gonna keep on keeping on. Ed did his business and fell asleep.

From then on it was Monday Night Football at Walter's. He would use my name as a calling card—"Thomas Henderson of the Dallas Cowboys will be there"—but I didn't mind.

I liked the crowd it drew. I gave him my phone number and told him to call me whenever he had some action. Well, Walter had too much action; Walter called me almost every day. He'd tell me not to bring Too Tall. "The man falls asleep too quick," he said. What's it to him? I wondered. Then I found out.

Walter had a little bit of the freak in him; Walter liked to watch. He would just stand there and look at the program. Didn't bother me, I was too busy. I had never done anything like it; roll off of one girl, roll onto another. I didn't care if he memorized the moves as long as I got a chance to make them.

Plus, being a pharmacist, Walter had access to pharmaceutical cocaine. I had read somewhere that cocaine was dangerous. I did the smart thing, I quit reading.

"You like this stuff?" Walter asked me. "Yeah, sure," I told him. You could whiff the stuff and not even smell it until it had already frozen your throat. Forget impurities, this was the serious rush.

Too Tall wouldn't do anything close to drugs. He'd go, "Oh, gimme a beer, homes." But that didn't stop him from partying. He and I ran into some of the girls we'd met at Walter's and invited them up to our place in North Dallas, and in June 1976 we hosted our own first orgy.

We prepared for this better than Landry planned for the Super Bowl. First thing we did, Too Tall and I realized that the girls liked Dallas Cowboy T-shirts, gave them something to prove that they'd been there, some piece of equipment to remember us by. We went to Buck Buchanan, the Cowboys' equipment manager, and got a couple of dozen of those short-cut T-shirts. When the party started we had four of the finest young women you ever want to see walking around our house naked except for these shorty Cowboy T's.

I didn't have much else on myself. I was ripped at that time, muscles in my stomach, muscles in my butt, muscles everywhere. I was a little worried about how to start this thing off, though. I mean, I wasn't any great party-giver and this was no society ball. Or if it was a society ball it was a very strange segment of society. It took a little while to get started.

We were standing around smoking a couple of joints, drinking beer and peppermint schnapps, and I was a little apprehensive. I knew what I wanted to happen but I wasn't quite sure how to get it there. The girls were pretty frisky but there's a difference between showing up for a couple of beers and getting it on with everyone in sight.

I was kind of shy. I just took the girl I liked most at that moment—she was the one with the long legs and the flat stomach—and brought her into my bedroom. No big deal about that, nothing that hadn't been done more than a few times before. But my trick was that I didn't close the door. A lot of my friends, when they had made their move and were about to get into it, would shut the door behind them. This time I left it open in case anyone wanted to come look. I'd gotten kind of used to it. Hey, it was my party.

So she and I were getting into it. Deep into it. But, what the hell, this was supposed to be an orgy we were running here, not some private showing. I said to her, "Do you want somebody to join us?" She didn't mind. I got up, pulled on my gray Cowboy shorts and went back into the living room.

"Hey." Too Tall and the other girls turned toward me, gave me the quick once-over. No matter how hard you party it's still a surprise to see someone when they're right in the middle of fucking: a little out of breath, the hair starting to get matted, not the way you usually go out into the day or night. They looked me up and down.

"You all want to join us?"

Thought I'd never ask. In unison: "Yeah!" Everybody came into the room! We tossed the bedspread off the bed, threw the mattress on the floor and had a freefall. I've got a friend in Dallas who calls them All Skates. Like in skating: first the girls go, Girls Skate; then the boys go, Boys Skate; then everybody goes, All Skate. This was our first All Skate and they only got better.

* * *

Dave Edwards had retired before the 1976 season started. Well, not retired exactly. Tom Landry had told him, It's been fun, Dave, see you later. The Cowboys are cold when it comes time for guys to get out of the way. I think Dave would've liked to play another year, but he got pulled in way back in minicamp and told that his future was over. Calvin Peterson was the new strongside linebacker and everybody was moving up a notch.

I wanted to start. Even though I didn't know Tom Landry's system of defenses, I knew I was the most talented linebacker they had. I knew Calvin Peterson wasn't going to star for the Dallas Cowboys, but he was in line ahead of me and he knew the system. I knew that Tom Landry was not going to let me compete with D. D. Lewis for the starting job at weakside linebacker.

I couldn't really blame him for that. I was a far better athlete than D. D. but he knew the system cold. He knew where to be on the field and that made up for a lot of speed that he didn't have. D. D. Lewis was pound for pound one of the toughest football players I ever played with. He wasn't very tall, maybe six foot one, he weighed only about 205, but D. D. Lewis never backed down from nothing. He took on the best blockers and he took on the best runners. He would not make many big plays, he was not able to cover a back out of the backfield on a pass or get into a zone properly, but he was smart. And he was extremely tough. I had a lot of respect for that toughness and so did Landry.

In the second week of training camp, July 1976, Gene Stallings walked up to me and said, "Henderson, we are going to use you on third-down situations. We have seen you come around and do a good job with Preston Pearson and we think you can help us on the 4–0 nickel defense. We're gonna work with you throughout camp, we're gonna work with you during the preseason and you're gonna learn this nickel."

Maybe he expected me to get excited about that, but I really wasn't. Any real competitor wants to start. This still felt like a substitution role to me and I was never satisfied being a substitute. In fact, I started to get mad. "Why are these guys starting and all they do is play first down? At second and ten I'm on the goddamn field trying to save their ass," I said to myself. When the p.a. announcer's voice was echoing to the crowd at the beginning of the game, "Starting at right linebacker . . . from Mississippi . . . this is D. D. Lewis!" my stomach would just bind up. Every time a game started that season and the defense was introduced and I wasn't on it, I'd get mad.

But I was getting closer. I wasn't a rookie anymore. By the third week of camp I got moved over to the veterans' locker room. My locker was by the window next to where the equipment manager, Buck Buchanan, would give out new jocks, new T-shirts. We always had the best of stuff. Across from me were Cliff Harris, Charlie Waters, Ralph Neely, John Fitzgerald. Quarterbacks Roger Staubach, Clint Longley and Danny White. The whole year before I hadn't felt really a part of this team. I didn't get invited to anybody's house, wasn't really in any of the circles that friends always fall into. I was on the outside looking in. I was playing football with them but I didn't even know who liked who. I just figured not a whole lot of them liked me. This year I got a little closer.

Roger Staubach was the star, leader and calm center of the Cowboy team. On the field he could be counted on to perform at his peak when things were at their toughest. He was a killer at the two-minute offense, getting the ball up the field at the crucial times when the games were on the line. He was a devout Christian, soft-spoken, the whole deal. It wasn't just an image, that was him.

But he could be tough too. That year the Cowboys had drafted a quarterback named Danny White out of Arizona State and White and Clint Longley, the "Mad Bomber" from Abilene Christian, were battling it out for the backup quarterback slot. Only one guy was going to make it, the other would be cut. It's tough to catch on with another team once you're cut, so it could easily be good-bye to your pro career.

Clint Longley had his own set of rules to live by. On his off-days Clint would go hunt rattlesnakes by himself and then the next day bring them in to work. Didn't make him a lot of friends on the team but he didn't seem to care. He was no company man, he was an outlaw, always standing on the outside of everything, and it was no surprise that he and Roger weren't the closest of friends. He was a very different human being, and even though I was too, his program was even different from mine and we didn't have much to do with each other. It's tough to lead your team when they're wondering about you and your rattlers.

Staubach had decided to take Danny White under his wing, to make the new kid his protégé, the heir to his throne, and that pissed off Longley. At practice one morning Clint had let that be known to Roger in terms that were apparently unacceptable to Roger's sense of decorum, and Roger had invited him over to the baseball field to air their differences.

This was a private matter. There wasn't any crowd that gathered to watch, no grandstand and no grandstanding. Just a couple of Cowboys out to settle a score.

It seemed that Roger got the best of it. Reports from the front said that Roger had picked Clint up and body-slammed him. You didn't think of Staubach as a fighter, you'd figure Longley for the one with the fists, but I guess the guy just didn't like to lose.

Practices were tough and we had to run sprints at the end of them. After the sprints that morning the offense had to go to the weight cage and lift weights for twenty minutes (the defense would have to do the same thing that evening; it all evens out), so by the time the offense got back I was sitting at my locker, fresh out of a shower, in gray shorts with a towel draped around my neck. I was pretty whupped, just sitting there trying to gather myself.

The offense clattered in, cleats making the place sound like a paddock. I was still in awe of Roger Staubach and I watched him as he walked to his locker. His number 12 jersey was draped over his shoulder, one finger on his right hand was really crooked from one beating or another he'd taken out on the field; he had the nice hairline, he was a good-looking guy. This guy could be president one day if he wanted to, or at least a senator; he could be whatever he wanted.

Longley came dragging in a little later and headed for his locker, which was right next to Roger's. (I guess the Cowboys wanted to create some kind of quarterback's corner, keep the leadership in one place, because their lockers were lined up next to each other: Longley, Staubach and White, with Longley the farthest from me.) Staubach was talking to somebody about what had just happened, not like he was barking signals but more like he was dissecting a play after it's been run.

Roger wore small shoulder pads, not the huge protective ones that linemen and linebackers wore but little ones that would let him take a hit but not interfere with his throwing. He stood up and started stripping down to get into the shower, his arms in the air, pulling his pads over his head.

When Roger's head popped into his jersey Clint Longley hit him with a right cross and sent him flying into the lockers. Staubach's arms were all caught up in his equipment and Longley hit him again. Roger stumbled into this metal stand-up scale that we used to get weighed on each week. His head hit the corner of the crossbar and broke open a big gash, just missed his eye.

Longley took off. He didn't stick around to try and finish him off like any good street fighter. Didn't wait for Roger to get himself untangled and come after him. Longley wailed through the door in full uniform, shoulder pads and everything, and all of us ran and watched him take off two hundred yards up an embankment toward the dormitories.

Nobody could believe it. Guys fight all the time out on the field, but not quarterbacks, and not in the locker room.

Roger was furious. I'd never seen him like this, never would again. He wanted to kill Clint Longley. He didn't shout or scream, it was worse; he measured his words as he measured the man. "That fucking coward." He was biting off the sounds like he was spitting out brimstone. "That goddamn asshole."

Roger Staubach said *fucking!* I couldn't believe it! Roger says stuff like "hellfire" and "gosh darn it." But on this day he was a vulgar football player.

Roger bolted to the door trying to take off and get Longley

at the dorms but Jerry Tubbs wouldn't let him. Jerry stood and barred Roger's way until he cooled down some. Roger stood there raging, trying to fight Tubbs to get out the door and go settle this whole deal, but Jerry had handled quarterbacks before and this one didn't get away either.

The locker room was in an uproar. "Fuck, wasn't that a cheap shot." "Ain't that chickenshit!" Guys were walking by looking for a blow-by-blow. It all happened right in front of me so I gave it to them. Some guys cared. Some didn't. There was a live buzz going around.

Then the rumors started: Clint was embarrassed at getting whipped on the baseball and football field; Clint was a pussy; Clint was out of here.

I got dressed in a hurry. I wanted to get over to Clint's room. I wanted to be there when the shit hit the fan.

Too late. By the time I cruised out of there Clint was in a car headed out of camp. He'd been screaming in the dorm to the coaches and the press and whoever else was down there, "Trade me, you motherfuckers! I don't want to play here no goddamn more. Fuck the Cowboys!" He just took off out of there. Gone, good-bye.

Roger had to go to the hospital and get stitches over his eye. Danny White was the backup. A few years later he would become the Cowboys' starting quarterback. The Cowboys' next decade got decided by a sucker punch.

Cowboys defensive back Mel Renfro had a three-bedroom duplex out in Garland, Texas. Mel wasn't living in it, the thing was an investment for him. Too Tall and I needed a nice place to stay so near the end of the preseason Mel and I got to talking.

"Mel, do you think me and Too Tall can get that place? We'll take care of it and you know we'll pay the rent. Just come to work every week, we'll pay you."

"Okay, man. Hell, it's just sitting out there. Why don't y'all take it."

Too Tall and I made the move. We flipped a coin to see who got the master bedroom and I won. My room had mirrors everywhere, big bed, it was beautiful. Too Tall's room was a closet. We bought a giant dining room set, a big couch, a dinette set for the kitchen, we were happening homemakers in a fine part of town.

We had been the first wild-card team ever to get into the Super Bowl but in 1976 the Cowboys were still in a rebuilding phase. Coach Landry's expectations were, with the young guys growing into a team, that we should of course get back into the playoffs. The Super Bowl was a hope but not a certainty. We weren't that dominating a team, we had lost to the Steelers so they were the ones who were looked to to repeat. Still the team was ready to roll.

We thought playoffs. We didn't just think about winning individual games, we were looking at the overall picture. Coach Landry told us, "This is what it's going to take to get you back to the playoffs. You need to be 11-3."

The Dallas Cowboys negotiated your contract with the thought of playoffs. That got you extra money. They'd say to players, "Oh, don't sweat the salary, son. Just play hard and get to the playoffs." That was their idea of a bonus.

The season started and just like they said they would the Cowboys were playing me on third down as well as special teams. They had let Calvin Peterson go, which gave me the chance to start seeing some action. I was on the field a lot and feeling good playing.

Football was going through one of its changes, teams were getting into the tendencies of down and distance. Third and one or two, teams would probably run; third and five-plus they were more likely to pass. Teams were keeping tighter statistics on each other and as coaches knew what the other coaches were likely to call, they called defenses to stop them. In our case, when the other team was likely to pass we took all three linebackers—Bob Breunig, Lee Roy Jordan and D. D. Lewis—off the field and I would go into the game with Benny Barnes to cover the backs out of the backfield. It was the "nickel" defense, the "4-0."

I wasn't a starter but I started feeling good about my role. I was actually being a part of the defensive strategy now and

I liked the responsibility and the coaches' confidence in me. They'd be screaming "4-0! 4-0!" and I was the man.

Once I got going I found that playing backs man-to-man, going over the tight end, stopping the draw play, these were easy chores for me. In the season opener against Philadelphia we won 27-7 and my man didn't catch a pass. I started separating myself from everybody. Other people had their men catching passes on them but not me. I took a lot of pride in that.

We had won three in a row when we flew into Seattle to play the Seahawks.

They drove us in ratty buses to the hotel (I've got to admit it, the Cowboys did put us up in some fine hotels), and as usual I was staring out the window wondering what these streets had to offer. I didn't have to look far. Standing right outside, meeting the bus at the hotel, was this incredibly gorgeous woman in a white jumpsuit. She had a body that demanded hands, the most incredible skin, the most incredible everything I had ever seen in my whole life.

I got out of the bus and she was talking to Too Tall and Michael Hegman. There's some good luck. At least she's not with some gorilla like Harvey Martin. Mike Hegman was a linebacker out of Tennessee State, Too Tall's school, who had come to the Cowboys that year. I walked over to where they were standing and just about panted, "Hello! What is your name, baby?"

She smiled. Too Tall looked at me. "My name is Wyetta."

"Hi, Wyetta. My name is Thomas Henderson. How are you?"

"Fine."

"Look," I laughed, "why don't you come up to my room?"

She laughed back at me. "I don't go up to strangers' rooms."

"We won't be strangers long," I promised. I was just kidding around, a gleam in my eye, acting smart in front of my teammates.

Didn't work. I went on up to my room. Smitten.

When Too Tall, who was my roommate on the road, got up there I asked him, "What's happenin', man? Who was *that?*"

"Her name is Wyetta Boswell," Too Tall rumbled. "She was a majorette at Tennessee State. She dates a friend of mine."

"Who's that?"

"Guy who plays for the New York Giants. Larry Mallory. We call him Funnyhead."

"Why's that?"

"Man has a crooked head."

I really wanted to get to know her but, damn, she had an old man. I should've known.

I tried to get the story from Mike Hegman but he wasn't real easy with the details that I wanted, like where she lived, what was her phone number, how could I get in touch with her, could I fly her into Dallas. All the important stuff. Hegman wasn't helping.

Too Tall was just saying, "Hey, man, you'll meet her sometime." Nobody was giving it up.

We beat the Seahawks 28–13 and the next week we played the Giants in New York, beat them 24–14. I came out of the dressing room in another of my tailor-made polyester wonder suits with my initials on the collar, weird-colored tie. I was clowning. I walked down the tunnel to the team bus and there was this girl again. Wyetta. Turns out she was a flight attendant for Western Airlines and she could get around pretty much anywhere and any time she liked.

She had the same white jumpsuit on! She must've figured the people in Seattle won't be in New York, and the people in New York won't know what I wore last weekend. But I knew.

I got about twenty feet from the bus and I heard a voice. "Hey, Henderson!" I looked over there and it was Funnyhead. I never met the guy but this was definitely Funnyhead. He and Too Tall and Mike Hegman and Wyetta were standing over there like the Tennessee State marching band.

Funnyhead was calling me. "Hey, you can come over here, man. I heard about what you did last week. That's all right."

I looked at the little circle of friends and shouted down the concrete hall. The walls bounced my sound around. "I ain't coming over there, man. You might lose something!" I got on the bus like it was no big deal.

But out the window I was watching her. I'd made her blush.

But I didn't need Wyetta Boswell to have a good time in Dallas. Christie Blue and I were seeing each other quite often. I was going out with a girl named Rita from South Dallas. I was going to Walter's place every Monday night. He would always have a couple of freaks, some Quaaludes and some pharmaceutical cocaine, but I was off on Tuesdays and would have time to recover.

I had a friend in Oklahoma City named Artlet who would come down and sell me some pot, and one time he brought along this white guy named Art. Art wanted to start coming to some games and he had some cocaine, some good marijuana and some THC. "Tac" was some weird shit. I would snort it and it would really just bomb me. I would know what was going on but I couldn't move.

We were 5–1 when we played the Chicago Bears and Walter Payton. Payton had been drafted in the first round in 1975 and so had I, both of us from small black colleges. In 1976 the Bears were not a team to be feared but Payton was already an extraordinary back. Gene Stallings told me, "Now you know this Payton guy is a talented kid, Thomas. Watch him, he'll push off, he'll beat you."

Walter Payton is a feisty, aggressive, elusive kind of guy but he doesn't have very much speed. Payton probably ran a 4.7 or 4.8 forty, while in 1976 I was at the top of my speed. I wasn't worried that he was going to outrun me, but I was worried. I didn't want to follow Walter Payton to the end zone.

What Payton did, and still does better than anyone else, was explode on you. He would lull you to sleep running toward you very routinely, like "Oh, well, you've got me," and then all of a sudden, as the defender would relax for a routine hit, he'd lean forward another twenty degrees and accelerate. He'd be gone before you knew it. You'd just miss him. He'd do that stutter step, kick out his leg at you and be gone. He made people miss tackles because he was half a step further than you thought he'd be, because you had relaxed and he'd made you think he had too, but he hadn't. Then he'd shake you and motor on down the field. Even if you got your body on him he would get the extra three or four yards just from that last-minute explosion.

Walter Payton didn't catch any passes on me that day but he did impress me. Late in the fourth quarter the Bears got down to our one yard line but we held them three times. Because of my ability to stick my hat into a lot of holes Coach Landry had put me in the middle linebacker spot on the goalline defense. On fourth and goal Payton took the ball a couple of steps in the backfield and instead of powering into the line, dove through the air. I was ready, right there. Had the good line on him. Payton dove in the air, I dove in the air. . . . He dove a little higher. I would've stopped him but he jumped over me for the score. We still won 31–21.

The day after we beat the Bears I invited two of my teammates over to try some Tac. These were two major get-high rookies, one on offense, one on defense. White guys. We hooked up because somehow dopers know each other and none of us was very hard to spot.

I spread out this THC in nice cream-colored lines for them, all chopped and ready to go. I knew what it was going to do to them, but they said they wanted some and I was just being friendly.

They left my house after some sit-around talk, a bunch of smoking and a good set of toots. The next day the report I got was that they drove home ten miles an hour and the next morning still didn't feel right. That stuff will screw you up.

The next weekend we played the Redskins. I was living in this nice place, playing for this great team, had an All-American for a roommate and I wanted to share it and show it all off. I decided to have a party. I invited my mother and my stepdad and my brothers and sisters. My coach from college, students from Langston, all my friends from Oklahoma City, all my friends from everywhere—my house was full of people. I was host and master of ceremonies.

To get things started I went back to my room, locked my door and took me a big hit of this THC. It would give me a buzz if I got the right dosage, but getting there took more time and concentration than I had right then. The stuff was so thick it wouldn't chop up right so I put a medium-sized chip in my nose and said, Well, it won't all dissolve right now, it'll dissolve over the next three or four hours. I figured I would create my own little tiny time capsule.

This sucker dropped. I felt it go down the back of my nose into my throat and straight into my system. There was nothing I could do. I laid back on my bed and went into a trip. I was paralyzed.

My door was locked. People started looking for me, the host, the emcee. They knocked on my door. Then they pounded. After about two hours Too Tall broke my door down and found me. I was lying on the bed and all I could do was say, "I'm okay, Ed. Just tell everybody I'm okay."

Too Tall didn't have a clue what was wrong. Nobody did except Art. Everybody I knew, all my friends and relations, filed by my bed like they were at a funeral. I was lying there, seeing everything that was going on, but I couldn't move. It was like I was pinned to the mattress, like some offensive lineman was kneeling on my chest. I didn't have the strength to move and I didn't have the will.

I was embarrassed. My mother didn't know what was wrong with me; here her professional-football-playing son was paralyzed. I could talk, but barely. "I'm all right, Mama, just let me lie here for a while." By the time I got myself straight the party was over. Everybody had gone.

I got it together in time for the game. The Redskins' quarterback was Billy Kilmer and the whole week before we played them I was thinking, "This little pot-bellied, ugly-faced guy, he can't throw the ball, he can't run, he's not mobile. Why is this man the quarterback for this team?" I compared him to Roger Staubach, it was no contest.

On a third and six in the first half Kilmer did a godawful ugly rollout. I dropped to the flat and the back came out and ran a sideline route. Kilmer threw it to him.

This had to have been the worst pass in professional football history. This wasn't even a dead duck, it was as if he'd kicked the ball. Almost end-over-end. The damn thing was knuckling. And it was coming right at me. I could catch that ball 999 times out of 1,000, but that day in Texas Stadium the ball was coming at me so wobbly that I started to wobble right along with it. Dropped it like a stone. I couldn't believe his receivers had to work with that their whole careers, the poor bastards. We beat the Redskins 20–7 to run our record to 7–1.

Somebody was knocking at my door. Nine weeks into the season I didn't care who it was, I was glad to see them. Too Tall was in the shower, I was just wearing jeans and sneakers and I couldn't be bothered with "Who is it?" I just pulled the door open.

Wyetta Boswell stood in front of me like a gift. She looked at me and said, "I didn't know you had hair on your chest!"

Standing behind her was Mary Ann Hegman, my teammate's wife. I had gotten Wyetta's address finally, sent her a letter and some flowers, but that was a month ago and I hadn't gotten any kind of answer so I'd just kind of stopped. I couldn't say a word, just stood there with my mouth open looking at this totally beautiful woman.

She had a suitcase in her hand. "Aren't you going to invite me in?"

"Oh, oh, I'm sorry. Yeah. Come on in." They came through the door and all of a sudden the house looked a mess. "Let me put a shirt on." I headed away.

"No, no, please. I like you just like that."

I wasn't thinking very quickly. Creatures like this didn't just drop in. "Where are you staying?" I asked.

She wasn't shy. "I was hoping to stay with you."

I got the big lump in my throat. This is it, baby. You got it. "Yeah. Of course. You can have my bedroom." I kind of tailed off before I said something uncool like, "I'll take the couch." I mean, this whole deal was a first.

Mary Ann left and it was me and Wyetta. Why did it have to be that night? I'd been invited to the opening of this new club—that's what I had been dressing for—and I had told several girls to meet me there: Christie Blue, Rita, several of the young women I had played with over at Walter's house. Hell with that; I was going with Wyetta.

We walked in that night and the place about stopped breathing. She was so beautiful and I was so proud to have her with me. I was still wondering how I was going to get away with this; I've been to all these orgies and I have all these women at my beck and call, and everybody's thinking we're going to go back to my house and have a really big party that night, and I'm taken.

I had ordered Wyetta a cocktail and got myself a beer and was standing with my back against the bar, kind of taking the place in. It was packed with people, the music was loud, the spot was happening. Looked like I was going to spend a bunch of time here.

Well, maybe not. Wyetta leaned back against me and put her firm, round bottom right up against me . . . and kind of wriggled. I rose like a shot. I knew she could feel it. I kind of felt like everyone in the place could see it too.

Wyetta turned around and set me on fire with a passionate kiss. I mean, we were tussling. That settled it. I was sure that the whole club was sitting there going, "Did you see that broad kiss him?"

We got back home and still hadn't discussed the sleeping arrangements. I went in and turned down the bed for her, smoothed down the sheets, did everything but put a mint on her pillow. Wyetta went to the bathroom to change.

Mel Renfro, bless his heart, had put all these mirrors in the bathroom of his house and from where I was sitting I had the perfect view. She took off her top, then her bottom, and stood there for a moment before she put on her negligee. I just stayed stock still. My God. The woman was Venus with arms.

She came out wearing this little two-piece negligee, a top and see-through panties, and I said, "Well, I'm gonna sleep outside on the . . ."

"No you're not." Wyetta was calling these shots. "You're gonna sleep in here with me."

Okay.

I got into bed with her and we lay back and started to talk a little bit. I said, "Listen, Wyetta, it was a wonderful surprise for you to come. I'm glad that you're here, it's the best surprise that I've had in a long time. I want you to know that I'm not just after your body, I want to really get into your head and know who you are."

"Oh, bullshit," she laughed. "Roll over on top of me!"

We made love all night and she stayed for a week. Then, being a stewardess, she flew away again.

We had beaten the Rams 37-7 in the 1975 NFC Championship Game to get into the Super Bowl and we expected to beat them again. We had gone 11-3 just like Landry had said we had to, we'd won our division and had the home field advantage and a lot of confidence when the Rams came into Texas Stadium.

We never got going. The offense never jelled. None of our runners or receivers gained over 43 yards and we just didn't move the ball. On defense Charlie Waters blocked two punts and intercepted a pass, and Benny Barnes got two INTs but once we had the ball we couldn't do anything with it. We held the Rams pretty tight and were up 10-7 at the half but in the fourth quarter Lawrence McCutcheon scored from the one to make it 14-10 Rams.

Still, we almost pulled it out. Landry and Roger put together one of our classic last-minute drives but on fourth-and-10 from the Rams 17 Staubach passed to Billy Joe DuPree and the Rams stopped him for a nine-yard gain. We had to give the ball up. The Rams gave us a safety as the clock ran out.

Just like that our season was over. We all thought of it as a fluke day, the last thing that anyone was expecting. We were ready to play a couple of weeks more football. We were thinking World's Champions but we didn't pull it off.

The Cowboys weren't going to the Super Bowl. Too Tall and I started looking into some business ventures. Macaroni, who owned a couple of clubs, suggested a beauty supply house, a beauty salon, a bail bonding company (I knew there'd always be a need for those) and another club. I was really interested in getting into some kind of business; I was making some money now, let my money make me some money.

A club sounded good. We found a location on Knox and Henderson in Dallas and I went to my bank for a loan. Borrowed fifty thousand dollars, cosigned with Too Tall and put up a twenty-thousand dollar CD as collateral. I liked doing it. For the first time in my life I felt like I was taking care of some real big business. We bought the building and they made me president of the corporation because I had taken care of most of the situation personally. We contracted for the renovations and looked around for a name. I came up with "Playmaker," because that's what I was. We called it Playmakers Plaza. It would open in the fall when the Cowboys did.

I spent some more time with Christie Blue that summer. I knew she would do what she had to do, but that now everything she did was for her, not for some pimp. She was grateful to me and she would've given me all her money. But I didn't want her money. I made more money than she did (of course, all of hers was tax-free) but more than that, I loved her. She loved me too. I never judged her, never took her inventory. I felt free enough to ask her, "What do you want?" and "How do you feel?" and she'd tell me. And when she asked me the same things I could tell her without worrying that somehow it would come back to haunt me.

Christie felt open enough to tell me about her tricks, how she could get her johns so worked up that even before they'd got their clothes off in the hotel room they'd stained their pants. She was always telling me stuff like that, maybe to smooth it over with me, as if she wasn't really sleeping with these guys, not really in her heart. They were all technique; I was passion. Of course, we shared technique too. She'd tell me secrets and work them on me in ways I'd never even heard of before. The sex was out of this world.

For the first time in my life I took a position with a woman that, It doesn't matter what you do, whatever you do with me is what's important and I like you the way you are. Even having to get out of her bed at four in the morning because a John was coming over, I liked the fact that she trusted me enough to let me that far into her life. Nobody else ever had.

Too Tall's birthday was February 23 and we put together a nice little shindig for him. Then eight days later, March 1, 1977, I turned twenty-four and we were ready to get down again. I had two girls from Oklahoma City coming to Dallas. One had bought me a gold chain, one bought me a gold bracelet with my initials in it in diamonds. I knew we were going to party.

It was set up for one of our regular clubs and Too Tall made sure I got there late. The place looked deserted. I walked through the door and it was still pitch black. Then somebody hit the lights and every woman I've ever slept with was there grinning at me. Well, a lot of them anyway. Around thirty. Dallas women I'd slept with, girls from Austin and women from Oklahoma City. Wonderful days, nights and afternoons all in front of me. Whoever thought I'd see them all in one lit room?

I sat at the head of the table full of women only. Wasn't a man except me seated at that table nowhere. Everybody was looking at me and I was sitting there grinning. Going, "So this is what I get for having an open mind!"

And—surprise!—Too Tall had flown in, special for the occasion, Wyetta! I hadn't seen her since our midseason romance but I was happy now. Of course she took right over and took me with her. I didn't mind. She was the finest woman there. We all ate and drank and told stories and partied hard and long.

The next day Wyetta came over to the house and announced to me that she was moving to Dallas. I had no choice in the matter. I didn't know it but Wyetta had flown all her furniture, all her clothes, everything she needed to live with—all of it—into Dallas with her.

Wyetta and Christie Blue didn't get along at all. They knew about each other—I told them—but Christie didn't approve of Wyetta, and Wyetta didn't want Christie around.

A new Playboy Club was opening in Dallas and auditioning bunnies at the same time that the Dallas Cowboys cheerleaders were holding their own tryouts. Now, I knew something about the cheerleaders; I'd had an affair with one of them. Players are strictly forbidden to fraternize with the girls—management didn't want them disrupting the team, guys fighting each other over them; didn't need any paternity suits either—but I found a way. I went in to the director Suzanne Mitchell's office and told her, "I want to date this one," "I want to date that one." Suzanne would laugh and say, "Thomas, you can't do that." Then when she walked out of her office I'd copy their names and phone numbers out of her address book.

When Suzanne Mitchell first saw Wyetta at a team function she came up to me and said, "Thomas, she is beautiful. Can she dance?"

"She was a majorette at Tennessee State," I told her.

The Playboy Club was in the Dallas Cowboys office building at 6116 North Central Expressway. (Hell of a contrast: Tom Landry on the eleventh floor, the Playboy Club on the second floor.) Wyetta chose to become a Playboy bunny rather than a Cowboy cheerleader and got selected. Christie Blue auditioned at Playboy too. She wanted to do something besides what she'd been doing all her life. I thought it was a good idea. In fact, I was one of the judges. I had her penciled in.

Wyetta went to the management and told them that Christie was a hooker and that she was trying to use the Playboy Club as a base. That blew it for Christie. I probably could still have gotten her the job but she didn't want it anymore. Didn't want to live under suspicion. It wasn't going to be a clean start anymore.

I was so angry I spent the next several weeks with Christie Blue. This whole thing was turning real hard.

The Cowboys needed a running attack. We hadn't gotten to the Super Bowl and we didn't have a breakaway runner who could change a game in a moment. Then in the 1977 draft we got one. Management managed a deal that got us Tony Dorsett. Tony was a quick, tough, game-breaking running back who won the Heisman Trophy while leading the University of Pittsburgh to the NCAA national title. The Cowboys swapped first-round draft picks with Seattle and gave them three second-rounders for him. It looked like he was everything the Cowboys needed.

They gave Dorsett his college number, already had a jersey made up with his name on it when he came to town. Tom Landry had his picture taken with the new kid, which did not fail to piss me off. Landry hadn't taken a picture with me yet! They gave him a whole bunch of money and here I was, going into my third year as a Cowboy, making thirty-five thousand dollars.

Then Landry came out with his plans for the 1977 team and really cut it for me. Lee Roy Jordan had retired after the 1976 season and Dave Edwards was gone and it was time for the new generation to move on up. Landry said he expected Randy White to start at linebacker with D. D. Lewis on the other side and Bob Breunig in the middle. Nowhere did he mention Thomas Henderson.

Well, shit. I was so fucking angry I had bloodshot eyes for three days. I stayed in my house and didn't go anywhere, read the newspapers and got mad. Read that "Henderson has a ways to go but we think Randy White is ready to step in and play." That just wasn't true. If he was going to be a linebacker Randy White could only play in the middle, but even then he still wouldn't be effective. He was too big to run back there and look graceful. He had a roadrunner tattooed on his leg but he wasn't that kind of guy. He couldn't cover shit out of the backfield and he couldn't be no kind of linebacker at all.

Jerry Tubbs asked me to come to training camp early. I said, "What the fuck for?" Just like that. "Randy White is going to start so why should I show up early? I know what I'm going to do all year, I'm going to play third down. I'm going to cover the Terry Metcalfs and get you all out of trouble, but you're going to let the white boys start. It's going to be D. D. Lewis and Randy White and Bob Breunig. That's fucking right up you all's alley. When you get into trouble, though, when you got Terry Metcalf on the field, or O. J. Simpson or Chuck Foreman or Walter Payton on third down and it's a pass situation, then you'll send the nigger out there, won't you."

Tubbs was calm in my face. "Well, Thomas, that's not fair now."

"That's the fucking truth, though, ain't it, boss," I told him. "Yeah. Let it get second and fifteen and you'll pull those slow fuckers out of there. They can tackle on first down, they can line up there and tackle, but I'm talking about the overall play of a player.

"I should be a starter. I'm better than D. D. Lewis. I could play in the middle. I could play anywhere compared to them fuckers you've got on the field. I mean, Bob Breunig is smart but Bob Breunig is nobody's athlete. I thought it was a damn shame when they sent him to the Pro Bowl. I mean, he's a wonderful guy, I love him, but he's not a Pro Bowl–type player."

Jerry didn't argue with me. "Thomas," he said, "you're not being fair."

"Fair, hell. I'm a veteran. The union bargaining agreement says I don't have to be in camp until the veterans come in. I ain't coming till then. Don't wait up."

Early, with the rookies, Randy White showed up in training camp, Bob Breunig showed up in training camp, Mike Hegman showed up in training camp. I was the only linebacker who didn't show up early in training camp. Landry was out of bounds. Not he nor Tex Schramm nor anybody else could make me come in, because I was within my rights. I was coming in with the veterans because I was a veteran.

But the Cowboys have their ways. The first week of camp, before the veterans were supposed to show, a big article came out in the Dallas *Times–Herald*. Basically it said, "Randy White, Mike Hegman Out at Camp Working to Secure Starting Job at Outside Linebacker. Henderson a No-Show." And somewhere inside it said something like, "It would seem that Thomas Henderson would be out here challenging Randy White for this job."

Sure. I could do somersaults and flips and tackle everything in sight, but if they wanted to give Randy White the job—which they did—there was no way I was going to have any effect and I knew it. But they had the press in their pocket and they got me. Put the bullshit guilt trip on me. So I called Gil Brandt and said, "All right, Goddammit, I'm coming to camp." Jumped on the next plane to California.

When I got there Randy White was working out with the first-team defense. Now, Randy White is a great football player. He will probably be in the Hall of Fame. He's a great defensive tackle, but as a linebacker he was a disgrace to the position. Dropping back on a forty-five-degree angle and moving his legs up and down and then breaking on the ball, he looked like he should have been in the Special Olympics.

They called him "Manster," half-man, half-monster. He was a cross between Lou Ferrigno and Frankenstein. He was stiff, no fluidity, no grace at all. He could take a tight end and shake him like a rag doll, of course. He was effective on the run, but the important part of playing linebacker is to take the short zones away from the pass receiver and he couldn't do that at all. I could.

I don't know how it happened. I had heard about the defensive system so much and had been to so many meetings that when I got out on the field all of a sudden things were making sense to me. I had a clue to what was going on. I knew the defenses; all of a sudden I just knew them. I can't tell you how it happened, maybe it was just three years of repetition, but I knew where I was supposed to be and why. I knew the system!

I was making very few errors. Randy White was making

mistake after mistake but Jerry Tubbs was all the time saying, "That's all right, Randy. You'll get it, Randy." He'd say to me, "Thomas, you ought to know that."

Then the veterans came in and we had our first big scrimmage. I made about six tackles, intercepted a pass, did everything I was supposed to do as a linebacker. The difference between us was obvious when you saw it on the films. Randy White had all the advantages: He was white, he was strong, he was powerful, he was a great athlete. But he wasn't a linebacker!

Still, he had the upper hand on me. It would be like Too Tall playing defensive back; of course you let him play. "Wherever you want to, Big Guy!" Put him at free safety. "Go, Big Guy, until you prove us different." If a man came to training camp who was six foot seven, 250 pounds, ran a 4.5 forty and told you, "Sir, I play free safety," you'd say, "Yes, you do! Wherever you want to play, that's fine." Until he fucked up.

Finally, Landry could see the writing on the wall. It wasn't that Randy was a terrible linebacker, the point was that Bob Breunig was a terrible *outside* linebacker. But Bob Breunig was one of the two smartest players on our defense—him and Charlie Waters—and Bob Breunig was the kind of guy you liked to have in there.

So Bob Breunig had to be on the field some kind of way. Landry put Bob in the middle. But Randy White, if he was a linebacker at all, was more of a middle linebacker; neither one of them could play the strong side. So there was a problem. It's the kind of problem I guess you like to have, especially if you have a guy like me fuming on the sidelines.

Randy even said to me one day, "Fuck, I hate playing over here." It was a lot of wear and tear, a lot of running for a guy six four, 250. The way he's built he was lugging around some stuff.

We stayed in training camp for about six weeks and around the third week Tom Landry made a decision. He told the team, "We have tried Randy at strongside linebacker and he's done a good job. But we think Randy can be of more value to the team at defensive tackle. We are going to move him to defensive tackle. At strongside linebacker, Thomas Henderson and Mike Hegman will compete for that job.''

He could've hit me in the mouth with a brick. No matter what I did I wasn't going to be good enough for Tom Landry. Randy White and I had been drafted the same year, had gone through the same camps and lessons. Mike Hegman was a year behind me; he didn't know the system. Instead of saying, ''Henderson, you're going to start at strongside linebacker. Go at it,'' he said, ''Henderson and Mike Hegman are going to compete for this job and we'll see who starts the first game of the season.''

That's what's wrong with Tom Landry. He was trying to motivate me. He knew I was better than Mike Hegman; I finally knew the system, I could play with flair and precision, I was the best man for the job. Clearly. But he wouldn't tell me.

Landry was a good man, a good family man, but his policy of hands-off, no touch, no feelings for the player—the individual—worked against him. For a man who says he's a Christian he sure doesn't act like one when it comes to an injured player. He may talk to a man on Monday or Tuesday after a game, but he doesn't say a word right when the guy needs it, when he gets hurt. He doesn't come back and ask how you're doing, he's too busy with the clock, the game situation, who has the ball. I think it hurts him in the eyes of his players. It definitely did with me.

He had all the qualities of a great coach but if Tom Landry would ever once hug a player, or walk on the field when a man is down hurt, that player would probably jump up and run off the field. It'd be like Jesus walking through and healing the sick. Landry acted like he didn't care but I think deep down he really did; he just worked at being hard.

On trial again. That was all I needed. I was so damned hot I went to see General Manager Tex Schramm and said, ''I want my fucking contract renegotiated. I'm not going to play for these pennies and have to deal with all these games and these head trips and all this fucking bullshit that they're putting me through!'' I was really wailing.

Schramm said, "Thomas, go talk to Gil." Gil Brandt was the Cowboys' vice-president of player development. No problem, he was down the hall and I launched into him.

"Gil, I'm not going to take this bullshit anymore! I want to tear this fucking contract up. I'm renegotiating! All these head trips. I'm the hardest-working man on this team. I play specialty teams, I'm on kickoff, kickoff return, punt return, special on-side kick return, special kickoff return. I'm on everything! I play third-down defense. And now they're playing games with me! I'm starting and then I'm not. Randy goes on the line and I'm still competing with somebody. I don't understand. I want my contract renegotiated!" It all came out in one breath.

"Thomas," Brandt said, "settle down. We'll look at it."

"No, no, no! We're not looking at it. I want a new contract. You understand? I want a new contract or else I'm leaving out of here."

Brandt wouldn't talk money and I couldn't. I wasn't any businessman. I didn't know what the fuck to do. All I wanted to do was play football and get the respect I deserved.

I walked out of his office crying. Like a kid who just got a spanking and got sent home from school with a pink slip. I was weeping and shaking, shuddering, panting and losing my breath.

I put in a request to see Landry. By ten o'clock that night, after the team meeting, I had pulled myself a little more together. I went to the coaches' quarters and walked in. Landry was expecting me.

"What can I do for you, Thomas?"

I poured it out to him. "Coach," I began, "I don't know what kind of head trip you're trying to put on me. What's going on? Am I going to play for you? Are you going to give me a chance to start this year? You had me competing against Randy White; you put him on the line. Then you put another linebacker up here. What do I have to do to win your confidence?"

Landry was straight as a board, tough as nails. "Well first of all, Thomas," he said, "you didn't come to camp."

I couldn't believe it. Not only was I within my rights, I'd come early. "Coach, that is dead. That's over with. I mean, that was three weeks ago. I missed four days. I'm here."

"Well, Mike was here on time."

The man didn't let up. Okay. "I'm asking Mr. Brandt to renegotiate my contract. I know I can play football and I don't need no more head trips. You gave Bob Breunig a job last year and you give Randy White a job. He doesn't work out so you give him another job. I don't understand. I can't take this whole trip anymore. I want my contract renegotiated. I ain't making no money, I'm working hard and I want to renegotiate my contract."

"Why don't you talk to Gil."

That was it. Everybody sent me to everybody else and I didn't get anywhere.

I went to work. I hated to do it; they'd all just think that treating me like shit was the way to get the best out of me. But what other choice did I have? If I didn't play well I wouldn't play at all.

A friend of mine from Los Angeles came in and brought me an eighth of an ounce of cocaine and I went off by myself. I quit talking to people, quit talking to the press, but I got serious about my books. I was snorting coke at night, sitting in my dorm room with my playbook, and nobody knew. I wouldn't sit out there where anybody could see me—aha, there's Thomas studying; we broke him. This was my own little deal. I would even bring a chair into the bathroom, prop my playbook on the sink, do a couple of lines and flip through the pages. Look at the defenses, look at the flow, look at the formations. In three weeks I consumed the Dallas Cowboy system.

In practice Jerry Tubbs said, "Okay, Mike, you go in this time with the first group." I could feel the hair raise up on the back of my neck.

When the preseason began he'd go, "Okay, this week, Michael, you're starting. Thomas, you're going to play the second quarter and the fourth quarter. Mike, you're going to play the first and third." Then it was reversed. "Thomas, you start . . . Michael almost beat you out this week." Like a schoolmarm.

I've got to say about Mike Hegman, he rose to the occasion. In meetings he would make verbal mistakes but on the field he had that same kind of knack I had, a natural instinct to be where you're supposed to be.

I told Mike Ditka how I felt and he said he thought I was a valuable player. Gene Stallings, who was in charge of the 4-0 special nickel zone, thought I was a vital part of the defense. Gil Brandt wanted to get their reports. Like he didn't know. He was out there every day assaulting his gum.

I knew something was up when, right before we broke training camp, Brandt came in and offered me a new five-year contract. With incentives it came to about $650,000, average of more than $120,000 a year. First of all, I knew I deserved it. I was worth it. And I knew the suckers had just been fucking with me all along.

What I didn't know was how to negotiate. If this was what they were offering, they probably would have gone higher. But I was no businessman and I was happy to get this off my back. The money sounded good, much better than what my professional agent had been able to score for me. I had more than doubled my salary. I didn't know what everybody else was getting—that's the way management kills you, by telling you not to share that kind of information with your teammates so you all can benefit. I accepted the Cowboys' offer.

And still they drove me. We were to open the season against the Vikings and right before the big final meeting, Jerry Tubbs said to me right as I was going in, "Thomas . . ."

I said, "Let me go in there so he can tell me I'm the starter, finally."

Even then. Jerry drawled, "I don't know. . . ."

Landry announced the starting teams. He went through the whole offense, then the whole defense. He waited to do the linebackers last. "My starting linebackers are going to be

D. D. Lewis on the weak side, Bob Breunig in the middle, and Thomas Henderson.

"Okay? Okay. Let's go."

I walked out into the hall and said, "I knew it all along." Jerry Tubbs pulled me aside.

"Thomas," he confided, "it was real close."

"Oh, yeah? If it was so goddamn close why is Mike making only twenty thousand dollars?"

I don't know what it was about me that made them do me that way. They chose to keep me hopping, to keep me insecure, never to give me the satisfaction. All I was doing was working my ass off for Mike Ditka. I never knew I could talk to them that way, and I never would have until they pushed me. I was flighty, but hell, I was off the street.

Dallas' tradition had always been white linebackers: Jerry Tubbs, Chuck Howley, Lee Roy Jordan, Dave Edwards, D. D. Lewis. I was the first black linebacker to hold down that position. Rodrigo Barnes and Calvin Peterson had had quick shots but I was the first to get the position and keep it and I'm not sure that set right with them. Keep America Clean; Keep the Linebackers White. I don't know. Something was going on.

I was no saint. There were several guys running around inside me. There was a Thomas Henderson who would come to meetings late or sleep through them, a Thomas Henderson who talked back to the coaches, told them "Fuck you." I was the defiant one but I wasn't being malicious, I was having fun, and that's the part I think they missed. Always will. They just kind of missed the sense of humor and got stuck on face value, and I don't think they really valued my face. There's a lesson there somewhere: Fuck with authority and authority sure as shit will fuck with you. No reason not to do it, but it helps to know what you're doing.

I was becoming "Hollywood." I had learned about limousines from my summer with Anita Pointer and I sure enough liked them. I found this guy in Dallas named Wesley Crawford who ran a limo service. They called him Hi-Low—one leg was shorter than the other—but he was driving most of the time. I'd call Hi-Low to come get me, take me around. The guys started to get on me called me, sarcastically, "Hollywood," like I wasn't no star. "Hollywood," ha, ha, ha.

I liked that. "Hollywood" Jones didn't have no ring to it. "Hollywood" Staubach had nothing to do with reality. "Hollywood" White? "Hollywood" Breunig? Forget it. "Hollywood" Henderson—it sounded good, it felt good, it was right on target. Laugh, suckers, I'm "Hollywood" now.

My roommate that training camp was Duane Thomas. When I was a junior in college I had met the man in Abner Haynes' office and been impressed. This was a Dallas Cowboy 1972 Super Bowl hero. This was the guy who had called Tom Landry a "plastic man." I'd gone out to the park one day in the summer of 1973 and run around and caught passes with him, covered him, and I'd thought it was the greatest thing in my life. Now he was a free agent trying to catch back on with the Cowboys.

Thomas had pulled a hamstring running against Robert Newhouse in a forty-yard dash. From where I was standing it looked like Newhouse was about to dust him when Thomas pulled up like he was lame. From then on he didn't practice one day of camp. He had his own workout program. He got up at four in the morning and took his ten-speed bike out for a spin. I don't know if it worked but he was amazingly flexible, he could fold up like a cheap chair.

But Duane was a strange guy. He ate mostly fruit and he used to bring huge piles of it back to the room. I mean tons. And he used to leave it on the top of the dresser till it would spoil, rot, start to ferment. He didn't care where the stuff was lying, he'd use part of my dresser for his bouquet. One day he came in and I was throwing fruit in the trash can.

I always had the feeling that Duane Thomas had been big early; he was about six two, 205 now and I'd bet that he'd been about that size since he turned fifteen. His looks, his attitude, that look in his eye told me that he was a bully, an intimidator who had been throwing it around and always gotten away with it.

"What the fuck you doin', man? Don't touch my shit."

I wasn't about to back down. "Man," I told him, "you've got your shit all up here in my shit."

"Don't touch my stuff."

"What you wanna do here, motherfucker?" I jumped. "What's happening? What you wanna do?"

He looked at me and I think he understood. I was from the same school. I had it on me like sweat: I'm a linebacker, you're a running back; I'm supposed to kick your ass. I could see the look in his eye. It said, "This fucker ain't scared of me so let's go to Plan Two." We didn't have much to say to each other from then on. I was a talker but I went into his bag; I was real quiet when I was in that room. I wasn't too upset when the Cowboys cut him.

But training camp wasn't all two-a-day sessions and meetings. We were in Thousand Oaks, California, and if it wasn't exactly Beverly Hills it was still a whole nother country and we were ready to explore it.

Too Tall and I ran into a guy by the name of Lou. "Big Lou," we called him. Big Lou had one of these stucco places high on a hill on Wynettka Boulevard off the 101 Freeway and every Wednesday night Big Lou had swing parties. I'm not talking about Benny Goodman here, I mean swingers. Too Tall and I were running buddies, like dogs, and we fell by there one night to see if everything they said about California was true.

First off, there was a twenty-five-dollar admission charge for couples. They waived that for us and we walked in. The furnishings were sparse, mostly throw pillows that had already been thrown, a bar that looked like it had been stocked that afternoon and hors d'oeuvres that had just been unwrapped. There was a heated pool but nothing fancy.

We got there about 7:30 and our curfew on Wednesdays was midnight. Hell, the party didn't even get started until midnight except for the early arrivals who didn't know better. But sooner or later the regulars started showing up with their dates. Big Lou had a wife and daughter who were part of the arrangement and I started to witness things I just didn't know went on in front of strangers.

I thought I knew about orchestrating these sorts of deals. I was capable of getting five, six or seven women out of their clothes and into a bed, having fun, making them feel good. But most of us knew each other, or were going to from now on. Big Lou's deal was something else. This was the All Skate to end all All Skates.

It was mostly people going down on each other, but it was going down all over the room, every room. I guess you paid your money and you came for a good time. It was so out front. I mean, this was suck heaven.

But you had to ask first. This was not a party where you were guaranteed some action. You couldn't crawl onto just any pile and start your deal; people had to agree. I was very agreeable, and so, it turned out, was everybody else.

Somehow the word got out. Okay, I put the word out. The next Wednesday night a half dozen of my teammates—and those are only the guys I saw—were up there trying to get into Big Lou's. Lou gave them all one courtesy visit and then started turning them away.

Lou took a liking to me. Put his wife and daughter on me one night. He said, "Henderson, I don't mind you and Too Tall. Why don't you bring Dorsett up here with you sometime? But these other guys are too many. Plus, you're not bringing no dates." Didn't matter. Two of the guys showed up every week anyway, just to get rejected at the door.

Being a starter was exciting. I got introduced in Texas Stadium for the first time in my career and it was fantastic. The echo of the p.a. system bouncing my name all over the field, the roar of the crowd, I knew this wasn't no dream. I went out and played like a tiger.

I also learned a little more about how the game really worked. Starters hang together more because they play together more, so now I could lean over and find out what this crowd was truly into. Things I hadn't noticed, or hadn't really wanted to notice—things I hadn't even thought about—were beginning to happen around me. In the locker room of America's Team I sat there and watched a defensive back take two black capsules half an hour before game time, drop them into a hot cup of coffee and then drink it all down. A little while later the hair on the back of his neck was standing up and his high beams were on.

I began to notice teammates drop off some kind of medication, or what appeared to be medication, at each other's lockers. I figure that about 40% of the Dallas Cowboys were into pre-game drugs. I made some inquiries and pretty soon I got my first good pregame dose of speed, Percodan and codeine. It was a practice that was going on long before I found out about it and it kept on going long after I got out. I used to ask a guy on Tuesday, "Hey, you going to take care of me this weekend? You need any money? Can I give you ten bucks? Twenty? How much do those things cost?"

Pregame medication is a fact of NFL life. Speed, uppers, bennies came in capsules. The black capsules we called Black Mollies or Niggers. We'd say, "That boy's playing like a nigger today. Must have some nigger in him."

I started and we started winning. I was pleased to be a starter but at the same time I was a little nervous; I knew how critical the coaches were going to be of me. I didn't know everything out on the field. I knew some of the tendencies but nowhere near all of them. I didn't know what I should know to be out there under Landry. It was my talent, more than my knowledge, that had me out on the field. That had to be a Landry first.

We opened the season against the Vikings and I had to cover Chuck Foreman, one of the best receiving running backs in the game. But more than that, I was going up against Fran Tarkenton. I had done a good job against him in 1976 but being the quarterback that Fran Tarkenton was—smart, agile, always looking for an angle—he decided he was going to pick on me. He knew I was the new guy in there and he set out to test me.

On a third and six in the second quarter he sent Foreman out of the backfield at me. I engaged him at the line of scrimmage and we took off.

Normally, when a guy gets to the outside of you he runs

an out route, stays on the outside and looks for the ball and a long gain. I was protecting the inside because that's where you can get badly beat.

But Foreman was cagey. He was a fast man and he tried to outrun me on the outside and then turn to the inside maybe seventeen or eighteen yards down the field.

I let him go outside, tried to mirror him. He made a move to the outside as if the ball was on the sideline. I didn't go for it. Then he juked back inside and I went with him. He stopped. I stopped. I fell. If the pass had been where it should've been it would've been So Long. I looked up and the ball was about two feet off the ground, coming right at me. I caught it.

It was my first professional interception as a starter. I got up off the ground with the ball and I looked back. Tarkenton was looking at me, kind of half smiling, like, ''Goddamn, you covered that son of a bitch!'' We won that afternoon, 16–10.

We beat the Giants 41–21 and the Tampa Bay Buccaneers came to town. On a regular defense, not the nickel, their quarterback tried to slip one on the outside to the tight end. I had position, grabbed it and took off. The tight end chased me and I ran for my life. My notoriety was my speed, if I got caught from behind so early in my starting career—*ever* in my starting career—I'd never live it down. I ran seventy-nine yards for the score. It was humid that day, early in the season at Texas Stadium, you could lose as much as ten or fifteen pounds during a game, but I could feel the crowd exploding and it pumped me right up. I got to the end zone and slam-dunked the ball over the goal post. Not some finger roll, a definite jam. I'd done it in 1975 with my first touchdown and it became my trademark. We beat the Bucs 23–7.

The more I played the more natural this all got. I really started to learn my trade.

A running back on a pass route is supposed to get to a given area at a given time; the ball is released before he gets there, and if he isn't there to meet up with the ball there's no chance for a completion and a good shot at an interception. A good working linebacker will do about anything to prevent a running back from getting to the ball, and the great running backs will use all their moves to elude the linebacker and get open. Chuck Foreman was quick and sneaky, trying to get by me without being touched, but I held him up. Joe Washington was another back who was almost impossible to get a hold of but I managed.

At one time in the NFL you could hit receivers anywhere and any time before the ball was released. To open up the game offensively they created a rule that made it illegal to hit a man more than five yards down from the line of scrimmage, which made pass routes easier to run and harder to defend against. Now these backs are quick, tough guys coming at you. They line up in the backfield and by the time they reach the line they're moving fast and you're standing still. They can blow right by you. They know where they're going and you don't, you can only anticipate their moves or follow them.

I would always meet them at the line of scrimmage. The less steam they worked up the better. I'd engage them, check them, hit them head-up and not let them skip around me. You want to jam a receiver before he gets into his pass route, and you have to do that within five yards. If I could stop a guy, break his stride and make him start all over again—"Okay, I'm with you now"—I was going to win. My speed, and three years of covering Preston Pearson in practice, had given me that.

I always took away something. I took away the inside, I took away the outside; it all depended on where I had help, the positioning of the players next to and behind me. The more I played, the more I knew where my help was. That's Landry's game.

Running backs are great athletes and I have seen defensive players watch them run rather than knock their ass off. I have seen linebackers acting like spectators on the field, like they've got thirty-dollar seats and here is the great O. J. Simpson or Walter Payton throwing Hall of Fame moves that they'll tell their kids about.

O. J. in particular. He never ran over anybody, he never bloodied anybody's nose, he had such grace and sleekness that he just ran around them. I'll admit it, when the play was across the field away from me and I knew I couldn't get there, I watched him too. The art of his running, his style and stride, almost put opposing players in a hypnotic state. You wanted to watch the guy run. You damn near pulled for the son of a bitch.

But that didn't happen often. We on the Cowboys were serious about killing the guys with the ball, stopping them, stomping them. If a man had thirty-two carries we wanted to keep him to one yard each time, if that. If he got thrown the ball all night we were looking for the shutout.

Most times I didn't need any help, I could cover these guys one on one by myself. Of course, this was the big leagues and there were tricks. When I hit a back at the line I stayed on him. I'd engage a guy at the shoulder level and grab his jersey, but we were in such a clinch that the official couldn't see it. I had the back stopped, and then I let him go and stayed on him. With my 4.5 forty and 9.6 hundred speed he wasn't going to get away. If I was to the side of my man and reached out and grabbed him I'd get called for a hold; when I met him head-up there was no way anyone could tell. O.J. used to cry to the official all night about this Henderson guy, "He's holding me!" Well of course I'm holding you. Get real.

Early in the season we met up with the St. Louis Cardinals. St. Louis had Jim Hart at quarterback and coming out of the backfield absolutely the toughest guy I ever had to cover man to man, Terry Metcalf. Better than Walter Payton, O. J. Simpson, Chuck Foreman, Tony Galbreath. This guy had all the moves. He was fast, he was quick, he was strong, he had no fear in him and he was a scrapper. If a linebacker tried to nold him, Metcalf would fucking knock his arm off. He'd hurt your arm, he'd beat it off of you. Other guys would go crying to the official, Metcalf would take care of you personally.

Jerry Tubbs called Metcalf "Rabbit Man." "You can't believe this guy," he'd tell me. At some point during that season I believe Metcalf led the NFL in rushing, receiving, punt return yardage and kickoff return yardage. Every category except passing. He was the best all-around back I ever came up against. The man was intense.

The Cardinals always played us tough. While we were beating most of the rest of the league, they consistently took at least one game from us each year and all the games were hard. Mel Gray, their great wide receiver, was feared. He could bust us all by himself. The guy was a bullet. Landry would tell our defensive backs, "If Mel Gray gets even with you, you're beat."

This one game against them scared the hell out of me. We were leading 30–24, it was the fourth quarter, time was running out, the Cardinals were driving; they had to score a touchdown to win. Everybody else was getting help; we were double-covering Mel Gray and also J. V. Cain, their tight end, and their other wide receiver was getting doubled too. Gene Stallings put me man on man with Terry Metcalf.

I had never been so afraid, so vulnerable, so alone.

I met Metcalf on the other side of the line of scrimmage. I just rushed him. He was trying to get out of there and I was pushing him and holding him and scrapping with him. I just figured if he couldn't run a precision route, a timing route, then anything he might get away with would be a junk play and by the time he might catch anything I'd be getting some help. I wasn't going to let him catch a pass in stride. No way. Landry might have his tendencies but I knew my football.

The Cardinals threw to Metcalf four straight times and four times I knocked it down.

I felt like a hero! I'd faced the best and I'd beaten the best.

No one on the team said a thing about it after the game. The coaches had put all their confidence and faith in me, and I had rewarded that faith by living up to it, but they didn't say one fucking word after the game.

I played my finest football that year, the best I'd ever played. Most starters and veterans don't play on special teams, there's too high a risk of their getting hurt. The Cowboys knew I was an All-Pro special teams' player so I was starting at linebacker, playing on all the third-down situations, plus playing on the kickoff and kickoff return teams, punts and punt returns, field goal rush; I was on the on-side kick team and the "hands" team that received on-side kicks. I don't know anybody else who did that. Except for offense I was on the field almost all the time. And I was the hardest-working man on the entire squad.

We beat the Redskins, the Eagles, the Lions, the Giants again. Eight in a row to start the season. The Cowboys' owner, Clint Murchison, would fly with us to all the road games. He and his wife would sit up in first class surrounded by the coaches and management. I'm not sure whether he knew any of our names but we surely did know his. Mr. Murchison was a very rich man. He looked tiny and pink on the outside but underneath he was J. R. Ewing. He'd come down the aisle of the plane smiling at his investments and all the guys would smile back.

But after a win the ride would get pretty raucous. I don't know what Mr. Murchison did up in those executive boxes during the games but on every plane ride home, every single time, he was completely stone drunk. He would come teetering down the aisles now and I'd look at him and go, "Man, I could have some fun with all that money." Lot of times I'd ask him for it. "Mr. Murchison, let me tell you something," I'd say softly. He'd lean over to hear me. "I need a million dollars. How 'bout writing me out a check?" He'd raise up and look at me. Drunk as he was, he was a nice man, very friendly. Good thing for him he didn't travel with his checkbook.

Tony Dorsett was new to the team. Fast, strong, good-looking, he was going to take Dallas by storm. He and wide receiver Tony Hill from Stanford were rookies that year and one practice I was standing on the sidelines with them jiving. "Dor*sett*," I told him—any guy who changed the pronunciation of his name because the new way sounded cool was all

176

right with me—"I got it now. You're the Beast from the East. Tony Hill, 'Thrill' Hill, you're the Best from the West."

"What about you, man?"

"Me? I'm the Mouth from the South."

I was also the Nose from the Ghettoes. My friend Art was sending me cocaine every week from Oklahoma City by Federal Express and I was getting into it. It wasn't like I couldn't leave it alone—I could let it sit in the drawer for a day or two, I could go out and leave all the drugs in the drawer except for maybe a joint that I'd take along for the ride. But it was always there, it was part of my life.

It didn't hurt with the ladies. "You want a toot?" seemed to be the magic words that season. Women would come from far and wide for some blow.

Being a starter for the Cowboys had some real benefits in that department. On special teams, careening down the field with ten other nameless bodies doing a job, I'd had to introduce myself around as "Thomas Henderson of the Dallas Cowboys." As a starter I was introduced to the crowd before the games, I was in the papers every week making tackles and getting mentioned. I didn't need to tell people who I was; they knew.

Life was going great. I really had it in control. Too Tall and I opened our club, Playmakers Plaza, that fall and it was a bonanza. We had a party every week in honor of one or another of our teammates—"Drew Pearson Week," "Tony Dorsett Week"—and we had lines out the door trying to get in. We had a cover charge, drinks at the bar; it was just a place that my friends came to, my teammates came to, and because the Cowboys are larger than life itself down there the club was a big success.

Too Tall and I had a little office in a trailer at the back of the place and that room became like a fornication palace for the two of us. He bought a pool table for our house and after a couple of weeks it was all stained.

I don't know whether it was my good spirits, my sense of humor, the way I looked, my frankness or my general approach, but women always seemed to like me. At the Playboy

Club I got involved with five or six Bunnies; at the Playmakers Plaza I could have just about any girl I saw. It was wonderful. I was honest. I never would judge a woman. And I always wanted to make them happy.

I always liked to give a woman what she wanted. I'd ask her, "What can I do to make you happy? What do you like? What can I do?" If she didn't know, I'd be more than pleased to run down the possibilities with her and see if there was something maybe she forgot. Or hadn't tried.

I liked to talk to women and they liked to talk to me. Ladies around the country find ways of getting through to professional athletes and I was easy to find, didn't have to ask me twice.

One night I was in the Fairmont Hotel in downtown Dallas with one of the most beautiful women I'd ever met. Blonde, leggy, smooth, the kind of girl that five years before I would have been killed for talking to. My room was like a palace: black marble Jacuzzi, gold handles on the fixtures, gold towel racks, three-inch-thick carpet. We'd had Dom Perignon and caviar and a candle-lit room service dinner and the mood was just right.

I was sitting there with her, in the Jacuzzi, talking to her. We were doing cocaine, snorting lines from a neat little mirror through a gold straw, smoking some primo marijuana, and I was really getting into talking to her. She was so beautiful I didn't want to just jump into the sack, I wanted to savor the moment, just kind of relax and let this bath last forever.

"You know, baby," I said as the water gurgled around us, "I really want to please you. Whatever you want, I want you to have." I was soothed just saying the words, my muscles untightening, my whole body unwinding. "Pleasing you, turning you on, is what turns me on. Just tell me what you want—whatever you want—and I'll do my best to give it to you."

This beautiful woman stretched out in the bath and I was in long-leg heaven. She smiled as she turned to me.

"I want Tony Dorsett."

Well, maybe next week.

(I told Tony about her. That was all right. She and I had our night and it was the kind of evening you hold on to.)

I did the same thing another night and the woman told me she wanted Drew Pearson. He was married so there was a problem, but I said, "I'll work on it but first thing you got to do is give me something I can report to him."

Women often did that. They were always around looking for an entrance point to the team. Some would go through the front door, some through the side. Too Tall, Charlie Waters, Beasley Reese, Harvey Martin and I—Tony Dorsett for a year—were about the only single guys so the picking was intense. Of course the women wanted to meet Roger Staubach and Danny White and those guys, but they were almost untouchable, they had families and reputations to protect and they lived a different life. My heroes were Elvis Presley and Muhammad Ali and I emulated both of them pretty well for a while. Hugh Hefner would've been proud of me many nights.

I found that sex the night before a game took the edge off the nervousness and I'd really sleep well. I did my best to have sex before every game, and the times I didn't get any I didn't play well the next day.

A football team on the road is a real little back-street ramble. In training camp, where you're supposed to be getting mentally and physically prepared for a long and grinding season, guys would fly their wives, girlfriends and mistresses in and put them up in the Howard Johnsons, Holiday Inns or Hiltons down the road. Some players put their women forty miles away because they were afraid somebody might see them.

Training camp was prime time to be nice to the girl you'd screwed around with all year—like a vacation for a road girl—and then go home to your wife. It was funny. You'd see six or seven women at every practice for about two weeks who you knew were with somebody but you didn't know who. They weren't coming out onto the practice field, throwing their arms around the guys and saying, "Hi, darling, you coming home to dinner tonight?'' I had women fly up there and take a room in a hotel down the street, then I'd leave training camp after curfew and beat the bushes for eight or nine blocks like Kunta Kinte running in the dark. By the time I got to where I was going I'd be sweating and tired, scared, my heart beating like the drums, but it was all part of the thrill.

On the road during the season the single guys had most of the opportunities but the married guys would find all kinds of ways to get it done. Some would have a woman book a room in the same hotel that we were staying at and then sneak upstairs after curfew. Must've been a lot of fires lit under them; the fire escapes and fire stairs were in constant use. Didn't want to use the elevators; the coaches were in all of them shuttling in and out of the bars.

Cocaine turns the women out. In the NFL it doesn't matter how you look or where your belly sets, if you've got the bag you've got the broads. You will find girls who'll say, ''Hey, we need some nose candy. We'll do whatever you want to tonight, let's party!'' Well, damn, let's go to the all-night bank teller! ''I got a connection,'' they tell you. ''He's got the best!'' Then the guys start meeting drug dealers and start getting into the scene. I met a whole bunch of people that way. A lot of guys find coke with their dick.

What with the Playmakers Plaza and all I was meeting a whole lot of people. I was hanging in my regular run of bars, widening my sphere of influence, and people were wanting to get to know me. My friend Biff, who had been a bartender at H. P. Cassidy's where I'd spent a good part of my first two seasons, had opened his own place. There, Biff introduced me to a guy I'll call Sonny Vale.

Sonny was real Dallas. His family were a whole bunch of multimillionaires long before I was born and he had inherited millions of dollars and made more on his own. He was driving a two-seater Mercedes–Benz, which was parked all the time outside of Biff's, and he was the first guy I met in Dallas who was actually a cocaine connection. All my coke had been coming out of Oklahoma City. Not any more. Sonny was my age and he was both a friend and a source.

Sonny was a damn good shot. He took me to a gun club and let me shoot off this elephant gun, used bullets the size of my index finger. He was hitting everything in sight.

His living room looked like it belonged to Marlin Perkins. He had a full-grown lion stuffed and standing there. A full-grown hyena. A leopard. He had elephant feet for sitting stools. Zebra rugs and what looked like every member of the African deer family.

Sonny Vale was also a real little bigot—he refused to call Rhodesia by its new name, Zimbabwe—but at the same time he liked me; I was a Dallas Cowboy. I didn't like what he stood for. I wasn't crazy about his menagerie or his personality. What I liked best about him was that he had the best cocaine in Dallas.

I started bringing my show to the white part of town. My parties began to consist mostly of white women, the forbidden fruit of the ghetto. Sonny liked that. He was a short little guy, about five six, maybe 130 pounds, not very good-looking. But we'd be cruising the clubs and I would talk to some gals about how much money he had, and how much cocaine, and it didn't take long for me to get a party going. Before the night was over his heart would be filled, his nuts would be empty, and I'd have a nice amount of cocaine to go home with.

It became like a deal. He liked me because I could get it on. I used to call Sonny at four in the morning and say, "Hey, man, I've got a couple of hot ones . . ." and he'd say, "Bring them over, baby!"

So now I had as much cocaine as I wanted, girls at any time. I was meeting all kinds of people. I was becoming a star.

One afternoon after practice I was sitting at home with Tony Dorsett and the bell rang. Federal Express from Oklahoma City. My friend Art had figured a way to keep me supplied as well: just pouch the stuff. I opened the package and it was a half ounce of this pink cocaine. Tony was shocked and surprised that I was getting coke through the mails. Being the high-profile guy he was he didn't want to get involved. Me, I didn't care.

Tony left and I did some more snorting. And some more. Started to combine cocaine with something called crank, which was speed washed with formaldehyde. Too Tall was out of the house and as night fell I started getting very paranoid. I'd heard about this but it had never happened to me. All of a sudden I felt like the Dallas police force and the Texas DEA and the Anti-Drug Task Force and the SWAT teams—everybody was out to get me. I'd never felt anything like it. I was scared to death.

Mel Renfro's place had a big back yard and I slipped out there, me and my Doberman D'Artagnan, and dug a hole and put the rest of the half ounce of cocaine in the ground.

D'Artagnan and I went back in the house and I was peeking through the front door, creeping at the side windows. I walked out in the middle of the street and looked around. I was sure that the cars over on the middle of the freeway were on their way to my house.

I couldn't sleep. I was amped. And I was still going at it. At about 5:30 in the morning I went out and hid dope all over. Buried it all in separate holes. I hid the THC, I hid the cocaine, I hid the speed, I hid the marijuana all in the ground.

Two hours later I had to go get it. Somebody on the rooftop—I just knew it—had seen me bury my stash and was either going to call the cops or go dig it up for themselves.

So there were me and D'Artagnan out there in the backyard prospecting for dope. Neither of us could remember exactly where we'd put it. I was digging holes and he was digging holes. He'd look at me like, "Hey, maybe over here!" and I'd scramble over on all fours and help him. Sometimes I'd get the scent and he'd stick his nose and paws in and scratch on down. Once in a while I had the presence of mind to sit back and laugh but mostly I was feverish. Dirt under my nails, knees of my pants all soiled, a nasty A.M. sweat all over me, this wasn't funny anymore. Where were those drugs?!

I woke up the next morning and it looked like a pack of gophers had been out on a road test back there. The place was a regular *Caddyshack*. What was worse, I never did find the dope. I kind of laughed at myself. This cocaine shit was getting pretty weird but I wasn't about to stop.

Late in the season Mel Renfro decided he wanted to come back and live in his duplex and Too Tall and I had to leave. We found a townhouse on Timberleaf and continued our winning ways.

I met Martina Navratilova in the lobby of the Fairmont one night that fall. I introduced myself and she, being a Cowboy fan, gave me her phone number. I gave her mine. She called me one day and asked what I was doing. Nothing. Would I like to have lunch? Sure. We met and hit it off real well. She was smart, good to talk to. Her tennis-playing arm was big and developed and she had wonderful legs. We would call each other once in a while and have lunch together.

Martina came to visit me and Too Tall a couple of times. She'd pull up in front of our place in her Jaguar with the license plates X-CZECH on it and we'd go for a spin. We liked to cruise down Beltline Road, her doing 120 with me and my Mercedes on her bumper. She was a very speedy gal.

Martina was living in North Dallas and she invited me to come over and go swimming. My body was really good at that time, all my muscles were in use and rippling, and I slipped out of my jeans and my shirt and stood there in this real sexy pair of bikini briefs I had bought for the occasion. I was out at poolside flaunting it and parading around.

Martina was lying on a raft in the middle of the pool. On a raft next to her was this pretty SMU coed basketball player. "Mind if I join in?" I asked, and dove into the water. As I swam toward them the girl pushed herself to the edge, got out and wrapped herself in a towel. She kind of cut her eyes at Martina before she went into the house. Okay.

Martina and I sat there and talked for a while but there was a strong sense of distance in the air. I had kind of thought about putting the moves on Martina but I understood now

183

that that was out of the question. It was clear to me that she was gay. The feeling I was getting from her was, "Hey, guy, let's just be buddies." That was fine with me.

I told her, "Martina, come here, I want to show you something."

We went into her bedroom and I pulled out a vial of cocaine. "Would you like a toot?"

Martina didn't hesitate. "No, I don't think so."

"Do you mind if I take one?"

"No, go ahead."

I dumped some out on her dresser and made a couple of quick lines. "You sure you don't want some?" I hadn't met many people who would turn this stuff down.

"No, Thomas, and I don't think you should be doing that stuff, either."

"Do you smoke grass?"

"No."

"Well what do you *do?*"

We both laughed and that was that. It didn't strain our friendship, we're still friends today, but it did surprise me. I was thinking this cocaine was a big deal, I thought this was what was happening, and she'd told me no. I just kind of tucked that away.

The stuff worked on just about everybody else, though. I was meeting and making women in record numbers. At a club called Le Jardin I met a white girl named Joy. Nobody knew that we were having an affair and we liked it like that. Joy gave me the key to her apartment. I'd leave the club at night and go home, then I'd go over to her house and put the key in the door, go in and get in bed with her. We would get up the next morning and make some breakfast and it would be warm and nice. She was a wonderful lover and a wonderful friend.

Wyetta, who had moved all her furniture to Dallas from Seattle and who I had helped get her own apartment and settle in, had become my girlfriend. When I had somewhere important to go, some class evening or team function, she was the woman I wanted with me. She was five eleven, 140 pounds, with not an ounce of fat on her. She was gorgeous and I enjoyed having her on my arm. She could dance, she could talk, she was great to have around. I loved her, everybody knew she was my girl.

Wyetta liked the NFL Wife Syndrome: She never wanted to wear the same dress or the same pair of shoes to a football game. I bought her Charles Jourdan shoes and new dresses every week we played in Dallas. Wyetta spent two or three days a week at my house. She didn't have a car so she used my Mercedes. She took me to work in the morning and kept my car all day and picked me up at night. I gave her a key to my place and she started taking over some responsibilities for me, like paying my monthly bills and buying groceries, getting a maid over to clean my house. I liked all the women in my life—I liked to have them there, I liked making love to them, I liked them wanting me—but I also liked to belong to somebody, and to have them belong to me.

But Wyetta turned out to be a very possessive woman. And the more possessive she got, the more I fucked around. I mean, she was not about to control me. If she thought she was going to shut me down just because she wanted me for herself she could think again.

But that's exactly what she wanted. She decided I was the man she was going to have and she set out to make it happen. I don't know who told her I was looking to settle down. I wasn't. I wasn't anywhere near ready. I mean, there were hundreds of beautiful, exciting, mysterious, unknown women out there just waiting for me to find them . . . and I meant to keep up the hunt.

I told her about it and she went into a rage. Of course, if she was going to start shouting so was I. Where I came from that's what men and women did, they argued and fought. Fighting was loving. I'd never seen a peaceful couple. So I thought Wyetta had been sent to me by God.

And this girl Wyetta was amazing. Interpol, the FBI, the CIA, Sherlock Holmes—all of them would've been proud of her. She kept records on me like you wouldn't believe!

Records! A diary, my movements every night I wasn't with

her. What time I left home and what time I got back. Where I was, who I was with, and how I got to be with them. *What we did when I was there!* She could come to my house, go through my closet, pull a strand of hair off a shirt and tell me which woman it was from. "I know who dyed her hair!"

Wyetta was quick and verbal, very fast with her tongue, and many times she got me so infuriated that I was about to bust. But the game of keeping out of her way got to be fun; in spite of her catching me I was happy to stand up to her. "You know about me and other women? So what you know? I don't give a fuck. I haven't made any vows, I'm not married to you!"

A lot of times I'd come home after being with another woman and she'd be at my house. I'd be coked out of my mind at five in the morning but this was the thing about Wyetta, no matter how mad she'd be she'd make love to me; I needed that to go to sleep. When I woke up she'd make me pancakes and eggs.

Wyetta was devoted to me. We would fight all the time about my midnight prowl but she would never have another man while she was with me. For some reason that was important to me with Wyetta. Up till then, what the women I was with did with their time and lives didn't bother me at all. I thought of my relationships with women as fairly liberated— You do what you want, I'll do what I want; when we're together we'll have a good time. But I knew at some point in my life I had to have somebody special and she was that special person.

The Cowboys started off the season by winning eight in a row and some of us began to think about doing what the Miami Dolphins had done in 1972: Going undefeated. We had a shot at it. We had that good combination of youth and experience, calm and dog madness. Coach Landry was always the pessimist, but among the players we were pretty optimistic. We didn't think we could be beat.

The St. Louis Cardinals knocked us off our quest, beating us 24–17. The next week we lost to the Steelers 28–13 and it was time for a little reminder. Coach Landry gave us what he called his pep talk. "Okay, guys, you got real comfortable at 8–0. Here we've lost two games in a row. We can't afford to lose any more. Okay?"

We beat the Redskins 14–7 the next Sunday and nobody got within a touchdown of us for the rest of the season. We finished at 12–2 in the last fourteen-game NFL season and had the home field advantage all the way through the playoffs.

The Chicago Bears had made it into the playoffs some kind of way as a wild-card team, the first time they'd made it since 1963, but they weren't any match for us. In the first half Roger Staubach passed 32 yards to Tony Dorsett to set up our first score, then hit Billy Joe DuPree for our second touchdown. On offense the Bears couldn't do a thing with us. We were Doomsday Defense II and we held Walter Payton to 18 yards rushing in the first half. We were up 17–0 at intermission.

On the first play of the second half D. D. Lewis picked off a pass from Chicago quarterback Bob Avellini and ran it back 23 yards to the Bears 19. Two plays later Dorsett ran the ball in and we were up 24–0. It didn't get any better for them. I slammed into Avellini and he coughed the ball up which Bill Gregory recovered on their 11. Charlie Waters grabbed three interceptions on the day, the Bears turned the ball over seven times and we embarrassed them 37–7.

The Minnesota Vikings came in next for the NFC Championship Game. On the second offensive play, after Minnesota had fumbled the ball to us on their 40, Staubach sent Drew Pearson in motion to the left, where Golden Richards was lined up. Roger faked Newhouse into the line and then pumped toward Pearson on the left. When the Vikings' cornerback Bobby Bryant went for the fake, Richards blew past him, Roger lofted the ball and Richards went in for the score. We were up early. But that was about it for our offense. They didn't have a great day.

Fran Tarkenton was a feisty little catch-me-if-you-can quarterback who would run around all day if you let him, but he'd gotten injured and couldn't play. His replacement was

Bob Lee and we just handled him with ease. It's tough for a backup to come in and expect to win a playoff game. Too Tall racked up twelve tackles, forced two fumbles and sacked Lee once.

At the half it was only 16–6 because our offense was sputtering. But I was in top form now. We took control of the game mainly on special teams. Late in the game a Viking named Manfred Moore caught a punt and tried to put a move on me. I caught him with my helmet and knocked him back three or four yards. He fell like he was dead. The ball spurted loose and Jay Saldi recovered. Tony Dorsett went right in for the score that made it 23–6. And finally, late in the fourth quarter I iced the game with an interception. We were going back to the Super Bowl.

Super Bowl XII, January 1978. New Orleans. I'd watched them build the Superdome when I was working the oil fields for Kerr-McGee. That was only five years before. Now all my friends were calling for tickets.

We were playing the Denver Broncos, the "Orange Crush." We were looking to play the Steelers again but our ex-quarterback Craig Morton and the Broncos beat them in the AFC playoffs. Didn't matter. We were here to win.

My man Macaroni was in town along with a drug supplier named L.C. so I had a nice quantity of coke. I got to go sample Bourbon Street with them one night. They brought along this little freak named Debbie, one of the superstar recruits from our orgies. Debbie was very good at what she did; she did Dallas. I drove twenty miles an hour down Canal Street and headed out toward the airport to where we were staying, Debbie attached to my Johnson all the way.

The Cowboys were corralled at the Airport Hilton in New Orleans and it was a dump. We stayed at a better hotel in St. Louis in a nothing midseason game than we did at the previous two Super Bowls. Why not splurge, let us enjoy ourselves? We had earned it.

They also played out their morality on you. The team would pay for rooms for players' wives, but if a guy had been living with a woman for ten years and they weren't married, forget it. Landry wouldn't consider letting girlfriends fly with us, stay with us, be with us. He wanted to see that piece of paper, like a shotgun father. I got Wyetta her own room. The Cowboys couldn't stop that.

Too Tall and I were rooming together for the two weeks of practice and hype that make up the Super Bowl. He had dressed and gone out to dinner and I was sitting around the room in my underwear when there was a knock on the door. I had all sorts of friends showing up down there all week and I was into my cocaine pretty regular now. It could be anybody. I opened up.

My teammate Rayfield Wright was standing there. Behind him were former Detroit Lions defensive back Lem Barney and Marvin Gaye.

"Marvin! What's happenin'?" I had met the man and his wife Jan in Los Angeles, in a recording studio, when I was with Anita Pointer. "Come on in, man. What's goin' on?" I went back and put on some pants and pulled up some chairs.

"I told you I was going to be here," he laughed.

I couldn't believe it. This was God's own soul singer in my room, and he was bullshitting me. "Man, I ain't talked to you since '76. You didn't even know we were going to the Super Bowl, what're you talking about?" We laughed.

I looked at the other visitor. "Lem Barney," I bubbled. "I remember you when you were with Detroit. You were *tough,* man!"

We all small-talked about the game. I was glad Rayfield Wright brought these guys. Rayfield was a man I respected totally. He was eight years older than me, a veteran's veteran who I didn't hang with.

I leaned to Marvin. "Hey, man, step into my office. Excuse me, fellas!" We went into the bathroom. "You want a toot? You want a line?"

"I got my own, Hollywood." He reached in his pocket and pulled out a long vial.

I said, "Well, look, I got something that's pretty decent here too. You wanna try some of this?"

So we locked the door and were sitting there exchanging

lines of coke, saying, "That's pretty good stuff," "Yeah, that's not bad what you got there."

I got on the phone and called Wyetta. "Wyetta, get your ass down here. Marvin's here and I want you to take some pictures of us."

"Marvin Gaye?"

"Yeah, get on down here!" She couldn't get there quick enough.

A lot of guys would bring their grandpas around the hotel to meet the guys. The lobby was full of famous handshakes. Some would bring their friends by to meet me but I would just say hello at the door. But this was Marvin Gaye. "Ain't No Mountain High Enough." He got to come on in.

I started singing his songs, kidding with him. Wyetta showed up and I pulled out the camera. Me, Marvin Gaye behind me, then Lem Barney and Rayfield Wright—we stood there and held our hands out like a big man's quartet while Wyetta snapped our eight-by-ten glossy. The Temptations, the Miracles had nothing on us.

"You need any tickets, man?"

"No," Marvin said, "we're taken care of."

"You need extras?"

"Look, man," he told me, "I ain't gonna use your friendship. I don't need them, you know? I don't need nobody asking me for no tickets, so I know how it is."

Me and Marvin hit it off. He was a very good man, a lifelong friend. He got caught up in the moments of cocaine is all. Cocaine produces great moments, and we always want those moments again and again. But those moments turn into lifetimes before you know it. I was sorry to see him leave.

The Denver Broncos were a Cinderella team. They'd come from nowhere and played good football all season long, then beat the Steelers and the Raiders in the playoffs. They had these loud orange uniforms and loud orange fans who we had to shut up. They played in blizzards. Their quarterback was Craig Morton, who had been traded by the Cowboys to the Giants, been booed out of New York and had miraculously caught on and succeeded with Denver. He was a God-fearing kind of guy, not an emotional leader but one who could get the job done. It was our job to stop him.

I had an instinctive hatred for quarterbacks but Craig Morton wasn't a bad guy. In fact, in Texas Stadium one time while he was playing for the Giants I had let him off the hook. I had blitzed and he was standing there open to one of my helmet-to-the-chin devastation tackles, but I had let him go. After the season we'd found ourselves at some of the same parties through mutual friends in Dallas and he had thanked me. "Fuck, Henderson, I'm glad you didn't hit me." Yes, he said some nasty words. He may be born-again but he's been in and out of the Kingdom.

But this was the Super Bowl and I wasn't doing any brother-in-lawing here.

Craig had terrible surgical knees. We called them "Knock knees" because they were like wood. Looked like a broken mannequin. He was going to be pretty stationary. He wasn't as bad as Joe Namath but we knew we didn't have to worry about Craig Morton running anywhere except a slow lope to the sidelines. Norris Weese was the backup who would come into the game if Morton got knocked out but we wanted Craig in there; we knew where he was going to be.

There wasn't any way that we were going to lose. At 12–2 we were tied with Denver for the best record in the NFL. Two years before we'd had twelve rookies and been in the Super Bowl, now we were seasoned veterans with a whole lot more punch. We'd never had a power running back before but now Tony Dorsett had rushed for over a thousand yards in the season and was the sparkplug of our offense, tough and shifty and unstoppable. We were the best team in football. We were unbeatable. We knew it, they knew it, everybody knew it. There was no way we were letting this thing slip away.

I was starting on defense and playing on third down, but the man who had the biggest plans for me, as usual, was Mike Ditka.

Ditka is an incredible coach. He always came up with a

game plan that attacked the strength or the extreme weakness of a team. I know why his Chicago Bears play the way they play; because Ditka won't have it any other way. He demands all you've got and if you don't give it you're gone.

Right before the game Ditka pulled me aside. "Henderson," he told me, "this is what I want you to do. I'm going to take responsibility for it. Don't worry about it, I'll back you up with Landry, I'll tell him I told you to do it.

"On the first punt I want you to run down the field and I want you to hit Rick Upchurch. I don't care where the ball is, you just go get his ass."

Game plan! Rick Upchurch was the Bronco's most potent offensive threat. He'd been running back punts and kickoffs for touchdowns all year. He was fast, quick, a game-breaker who could give them both field position and the kind of emotional lift that wins Super Bowls. Ditka wanted me to take him out.

But the coach was cagey. He didn't tell me to go do it on the opening kickoff when the whole world would be watching. The first punt was early enough to make the point and not so obvious as to get us in trouble.

The first time we punted to the Broncos I lined up on the outside. I beat my man off the line, just juked him and took off down the field. The ball was nowhere near Rick Upchurch. He was looking at the ballcarrier, away from the play, didn't have a clue. I motored over him. That was a psych move. I knew that for the rest of the game he'd be looking for me, wondering, "Where's Henderson?" It's hard to concentrate on a runback when you're looking to cover your ass.

It was a flagrant foul and the referees caught it. Cost us fifteen yards.

I looked over to the sidelines and I could see Landry wince in disgust. He was not happy. He thought I was plain stupid. I didn't see Mike Ditka anywhere near him explaining that he'd told me to do it. The only backing up Ditka did was backing away from Coach Landry.

But it worked. Later in the game Rick Upchurch fumbled a punt. I had to have had something to do with it.

I wasn't letting anybody alone out there. Not only did I have pride and passion lit under me, I was full of Percodan and that by itself would have made me go out and get somebody.

I was starting as the weakside linebacker but I took whatever they put in front of me. The Broncos decided that tight end Riley Odoms was going to handle me. At six four, 250 pounds he figured to waltz with me and let the running backs get their yardage. I was giving away two inches and thirty pounds but this guy had more than he knew what to do with.

Big tight ends are like that; an explosion to the chin makes them offer you lavish gifts and free vacations off-season. At the very least, after a serious shot they want to brother-in-law the rest of the afternoon. Riley and I didn't have any problems after I set him straight a couple of times.

They couldn't beat us because we wouldn't let them. Tony Dorsett powered over them and our defense wouldn't let them into the game. I was loving the whole thing. Played well all season long and capped it off with a good day at the Super Bowl.

The Broncos were coached by Red Miller. I didn't know much about him but every time we lined up to kick off there I was out on the end of our line, in front of the Bronco bench. One time, after they had scored a touchdown or a field goal (they only got one of each), I found myself right in front of Miller. As their kicker ran up to the ball to kick off I yelled to the coach, "Hey, Red, watch this!"

Their front line of blockers came wailing down the field trying to take us down. I stood there and waited on the guy who was supposed to take me. Right in front of Miller I took a forearm, an elbow actually, and laid it to the guy's head. I mean I knocked him out.

Red went nuts. "Did you see that?! Henderson, you dirty son of a bitch! Hey, ref, did you see that?! You can't do that! Fifty-six, you can't do that!"

In the middle of the play I shouted at him, "What do you mean, I can't do that? I already did it!"

We won the game 27–10 and it wasn't that close. All the pageantry and pomp and everything was involved in the Broncos trying to do the impossible—beat us. People across the country were either rooting for America's Team or hoping that we'd get our ass handed to us. No contest.

They gave the Most Valuable Player award to the wrong guys. I'm not saying I deserved it—and I was damn sure they weren't giving it to me even if I did—but Harvey Martin and Randy White, who won the award, weren't the guys either. The man who should have been chosen MVP for Super Bowl XII was a backup safety from the University of Oklahoma by the name of Randy Hughes.

I'll admit this is a little hard for me to admit. Randy and I didn't always get along. His disposition was pretty clear; he didn't like blacks. Plus, he resented me for getting drafted ahead of him. We were both coming out of Oklahoma that year and his Sooners were the national champions. I was always on him about that. "Randy," I'd bait him, "you don't really like me, do you? You think you are better than me. You played at Oklahoma, I'm just a nigger from Langston. I had no business being drafted in front of you; don't you really feel that way, Randy?" He wouldn't deny it.

But in Super Bowl XII Randy Hughes got three turnovers, a couple of fumbles and an interception, which were the keys to our success in that game. Turnovers are almost always the deciding factors that turn a game around, and he had three of them. Hell, I had more tackles than Harvey Martin and Randy White myself. But those awards are almost always all politics. Randy and Harvey, salt and pepper, were a good symbol of the Cowboys' defense but they weren't the men that day. It was Randy Hughes. He told me so.

7

Cocaine Cowboy

In the off-season lots of guys go home or just get away from Dallas. Dallas was my home now; I wasn't going back to Austin to live, that was for certain. Too Tall and I had looked into the possibility of building our "dream house," even went so far as to pay an architect fifteen hundred dollars to draw up some plans for a three-hundred-thousand-dollar home, swimming pool and all. We bought the lot to put it on but then zoning got involved and it didn't work out. Next thing I knew, Too Tall was buying and customizing his own place.

I was pleased for him but a little bit jealous. I mean, this was a guy who couldn't handle the responsibility of buying groceries, now he was a major homeowner and I was still renting. I had bought a house for my mother in Austin and had it fixed up but it wasn't my dream home by any means; I wasn't even going to be living in it.

Tex Schramm had called me and Too Tall into his office and warned us about a co-owner of the club, "this fellow Macaroni," and what a shady character he was. I told Schramm, "You can't tell me who I can associate with. Who do you think you are? Get me out of here, I don't have to sit here and listen to this!'' Too Tall looked at me like I was crazy while I was making that scene. But Playmakers Plaza had stopped making plays so we closed it down.

My friendship with Too Tall was still solid but I think he was getting a little leery of my drug use. His agent was putting pressure on him, I'm sure, saying, ''You've got to get away from this guy,'' and finally Ed gave in. All these plans had been in preparation and I hadn't even known anything about it.

Too Tall moved into his customized condominium and it was great. Professionally decorated apartment where the carpet matched the couches; mirrors on the walls, bedroom full of mirrors, and a bed. . . . Biggest bed I ever did see. I mean, we could get eight women in that bed.

I moved into a duplex and got right back into Dallas.

I had a friend called Loosewire whose father owned a string of women's clothing stores all around Texas. Loosewire had money and Loosewire always had cocaine on him. Loosewire became my best friend.

There was a special camaraderie about the people who could afford cocaine, a high-class crowd that I liked to run with. I hung out at Biff's, like a speakeasy, and there was no shame in my game. I'd walk right into the rest room with three or four other guys and each one of us would take a turn taking a toot in the stalls. I wouldn't say, ''Hey, let's go to the car''; I wouldn't have to hide or be discreet. I enjoyed the whole process. I enjoyed the people I did it with. It was a sociable, fun thing to do. I'd stand there and have a few beers and say, ''You want another toot?'' and pass the vial down the length of the bar.

I spent a lot of time in rest rooms that winter, standing and snorting. I made a personal survey and I can tell you that most of the toilets in America are made by Standard. I developed my own Standard operating procedure.

Loosewire was dating a former Miss Texas and he and I, just like Too Tall and I and Walter and I, had our deal; ours was Quaaludes and women. Women loved to do Quaaludes and wait for the morning and go, "Oh, what happened last night? I can't remember." That must've happened fifty times that year at orgies and parties. Loosewire never could get it up, that was his major problem. Seemed like cocaine had the reverse effect on me; I couldn't get it down.

Loosewire and I decided to go to Las Vegas one time during the off-season. It was time I got out into the world! On the flight out we met a high-roller named Bob who, because we were flying in first class, thought I was a class cat. I had a couple thousand dollars on me and we played a little blackjack and damned if I didn't win some more. Then I found out that Bob was a big-time gambler. I'm sure he could've broken me if he'd wanted but he took a liking to me and when we got to Vegas they comped him half a floor. He in turn put a hundred thousand dollars cash into the cage and gambled.

Bob also traveled with a full ounce of coke and when he invited me to come visit him the next month in North Carolina where he lived, I said sure. I flew from Dallas to Atlanta where his private twin-engine plane met me. On board were Carol and Paula, two girls I'd seen with Bob in Vegas. They had an ounce of coke for me and a couple of six packs of beer.

As the plane slid down the runway and got airborne Paula asked me, "Are you a member of the Mile-High Club?"

"What do you mean?" Then it dawned on me. "Oh, no I'm not! Let's do it!"

Carol went and sat with the pilot and Paula and I made our own air pockets for the next forty minutes.

We landed on Bob's own landing strip. His own airfield? I found out very quickly that Bob was a big-time marijuana dealer with commercial pot going all over America. Big connections in Miami too; I was able to buy two ounces of cocaine for a thousand dollars. Insider's price.

I stayed for about a week. One night we were driving around the woods in his Jaguar when we heard a shotgun blast that just about blew out the tires.

"Get the fuck down!" I yelled. I'd been around enough weapons to know when it was serious.

"Oh, that's my friend," Bob drawled. "Don't worry about it. He just shoots to warn, you know, 'cause the police come up in here." He had that slow Southern kind of certainty, a man walking in his own woods.

Crackers with shotguns. I'm scared shitless. I heard the blast again.

"Don't worry about it, Thomas, he knows we're coming. He just does that."

We drove down this long path and there in the clearing, just like in the movies, was the still. They're making moonshine. This bootlegger came and was talking to Bob.

"I got a good brew I mixed up 'bout a week ago," he told him. "Might be the best yet."

Bob sauntered over and tasted the stuff. "Here, Thomas, take a shot."

It blew a hole in the inside of my stomach. I said, "Bob, I have to have some of this!" I had a specific need that it could fill.

By that time I had a ritual. Every morning I would smoke a joint, then do some heavy lines of cocaine, then blow my nose raw, then do some more lines of coke, then go out into the day and start to get loaded. This moonshine was going to take the edge off me that the cocaine was putting on.

"Bobby," I said, "I *have* to have this."

"Sure. We'll get you a gallon." He thought he was being generous.

"You don't understand," I told him. "I want ten gallons of this stuff."

I needed it; my nose was going bad on me. I had gotten into coke because of the high, I didn't know shit about how to use it or what it did. I just started to do it up. I never owned a Deering, one of those grinders that scrapes everything down to a fine powder, I just cut the dope up with the edge of a matchbook and snorted it up my nostrils. The stuff wasn't clean, it had impurities and rocks and when it lodged in the side of my nose it just stayed there and ate it away.

I had a deviated septum from all the hits I'd been delivering with my head all those years and the coke had dug right into the deviated part and developed a major-league sore. Early in 1978 my cocaine use became not only recreation—I mean, it was still fun—but also maintenance. I would wake up in the morning (or afternoon) with tears in my eyes and a frozen face from where the coke had never drained. I needed something to deal with it.

I took one gallon jug of moonshine under my arm with me and they sent the rest to my home.

At the end of my visit they flew me back from North Carolina to Atlanta where I was going to make my connection through Dallas. I introduced myself to the ticket agents and, because I was falling-down exhausted from a week's worth of fun, they preboarded me. I was sitting in first class relaxing. I watched as the plane at the next gate backed out and taxied for takeoff.

"How long is this flight to Dallas?" I asked the stewardess.

"Oh," she told me, "we're not going to Dallas. We're going to Charleston, South Carolina. It takes about forty-five minutes."

"No, no, no. This flight is going to Dallas."

"I'm sorry, sir. The flight to Dallas just left the gate."

No good. I was loaded, tweaked, wired. I had two ounces of cocaine on me, a gallon jug of moonshine. "Miss." I wasn't playing around. "You saw them board me. I want to go to Dallas. I don't want to go to Charleston, South Carolina."

"I'm sorry, sir."

"I need to see the captain."

The plane was moving. "I'm sorry, sir, we're taxiing."

I stood up and banged on the cockpit door. The stewardess knew enough not to get in my way. A man in uniform opened up.

"Sir," I explained as calmly as I could, "my name is Thomas Henderson. They preboarded me on the wrong flight.

I'm supposed to be on my way to Dallas. I do not want to go to Charleston, South Carolina."

The captain turned around in his seat and looked at me.

"Mr. Henderson! Well, damn, they sure did preboard you, didn't they! Well, look, this turnaround shouldn't take but about three hours and there's no flight from Atlanta to Dallas right now anyway. Why don't you just take a ride with us. There won't be any charge to you."

The man was friendly enough, I just wasn't buying any.

"Captain," I said, "I don't want to go with you. I want you to take me back to the gate. I don't want to go to South Carolina or anywhere else."

He lost some of his down-home charm. "I can't turn around and go back to the gate," he told me.

"You don't understand, Captain. Read my lips: I am not going to South Carolina. If I have to open this fucking door over here and jump on the fucking tarmac I am doin' it, okay?"

The people in first class were looking at me funny. Who was this nigger trying to hijack this jet to Dallas?

The captain looked at me and knew I was serious.

I said, "I'm going to get my bags and I'm getting off this plane before we take off." I saw myself jumping twenty feet to the ground from a moving jet.

The captain got on the radio and contacted the tower. I heard the tower reply, "No. Proceed to destination."

"Sir!" I shouted. "I'm not going!" It got funny to me. I couldn't believe that Delta Airlines was going to hijack *me* to South Carolina! I brought my bags up by his door. "If you're not going to take me back I'm jumping off of here." I headed toward the emergency exit.

The captain radioed the tower in a hurry. "This is the captain. I have an individual on my aircraft who I want *off*. I am returning to the gate." I guess the captain has the prerogative to discharge passengers if he feels they are a hazard to his flight. Well, good. Get me off of here.

I didn't think a thing of it until he turned that sucker around and headed back toward the terminal. Then I remembered.

"Oh, fuck," I said to myself. "I've got two ounces of coke on me. And moonshine. I done raised hell out here. This is a federal program I've been messing with, they may fucking search me." I was close to paralyzed.

When they opened the flight door it looked like all of the Atlanta police department had been in the neighborhood. I had my bags in my hands as I walked off the aircraft. All they needed to do was cuff me. Then the ticket agent, God bless him, rushed up and said, "Mr. Henderson, we are so sorry!" I about dissolved in sweat but the whole situation got taken care of. Their mistake.

The Dallas Cowboys had been invited to participate in the Super Teams SuperStars Competition in Hawaii. That was fine with me except for one thing, the Cowboys had neglected to invite Thomas Henderson. The team had invited all nine players who had been selected to the Pro Bowl plus D. D. Lewis. Another political move. I'd had the best year of my life, I'd played on all of their teams, I was sure they were going to pick me. They didn't. Well, kiss my ass. I crashed the party. Packed a bag, caught me a flight, rented a room at the same hotel and checked in. I wanted them to know I was disappointed for not being chosen.

Roger Staubach was practicing for the swimming event when I met him by the pool. "Hey, Roger," I called to him, "you want to race?" I didn't have any swimming trunks, I just stripped down to my bikini briefs and dipped my feet in the water.

Roger, an old Navy man, looked over to me. He'd graduated from the Naval Academy and had spent five years in the service before he had returned to play ball so I figured he was the man to beat.

Roger is a fierce competitor. All of a sudden he transformed from this nice happy-go-lucky guy into this maniac who was going to turn into a motorboat. The smile just washed from his face.

We hit the water, him with a racing dive, me with what I learned at the public pools. I beat him by one body length.

The Denver Broncos were there and the Los Angeles Dodgers and Kansas City Royals. Everybody brought their wives. Steve Garvey brought his and she wasn't as pretty as everybody said. It looked like somebody had dug her up.

I got a bikini made for me on the beach and I was out there on parade, made sure that all the guys knew I was making it with hula girls and beach beauties. I kept the elevators busy. Seemed like every two hours I was on my way to my room with a different gal, watching the guys watch me as I'd go.

My mother and stepfather separated. Mama had finally had enough. I had bought a house in Austin for her but I'd kept it in my name. Now my stepdad stayed in it; my mother took off with another man. My brothers and sisters were being split up through custody, my family was falling apart and I was the only one who could do anything about it. I went to my mom and stepdad and asked permission to take my two brothers.

My younger sister Victoria was eighteen and I put her through Texas Woman's University, bought her a brand new 1978 Honda. James and Franchot moved in with me.

Seemed like Austin had this giant magnet underground and my brothers' asses were full of iron. I had to get them out of that town before they'd be stuck there forever. James was seventeen and a junior in high school and Franchot was fifteen and a sophomore, and they thought it would be neat to come live with me in Dallas. I did too. I was reckless. Too Tall had moved out and I didn't have anything but my cocaine, my parties and Wyetta waiting for me. I figured I'd try to be a father to my brothers. I sent them their fare and picked them up at the airport.

James and Franchot were a little haggard when they got in, they had a lot of Austin dust on them. I sat them down in my living room and had a talk. I wanted to establish the rules.

"I'm not a disciplinarian," I told them. "I will not whip either one of you but I will kick your ass if you disrespect me. I won't use a belt, we'll just fight.

"There are certain rules here." Both of them were looking

at me with this strange combination of obedience and disregard, the same way I probably was looking at my coaches. "Look here," I said, "I'm kind of struggling with this so I want you to know that there are certain rules that are going to go on in this house and when you break them I'm going to let you know about it. I don't have any set pattern for you, I don't know how to be a parent, I just want to let you know that I'm your brother, I love you and I want you to have the best that I can give you.

"I want you to go to school. There is no missing any school, there is no hooky. Do you smoke grass?"

"Yeah."

"Do you smoke cigarettes?"

"No."

"How long you been smoking grass, James?"

"Couple of years, man."

"Franchot?"

"I don't know. About a year."

"Okay," I said firmly, "you don't buy no weed in Dallas. You don't ask nobody for any marijuana in Dallas, Texas. I'll have grass for you here. If you want marijuana, you get it from me. You don't bring friends home to smoke marijuana, you don't tell friends there is marijuana in the house, you don't take any marijuana from the house to your friends." I didn't want them getting into trouble and I didn't need people around town getting wind of my smoking habits.

"Does Mama know you smoke weed?" I asked James.

"No, Thomas." He had a real bass voice, real slow Texas way of talking and always pronounced my name like it rhymed with home-us.

"Well, I'm going to tell her."

"Don't do that, Thomas."

"Mama knows I smoke marijuana, so if you are up here she'll know about you. I'm going to tell Daddy too."

"Oh, why you doin' that, man?"

"I'm just doin' it. Trust me. How are your grades, Red?"

"Oh, they're okay."

"How are your grades, Franchot?"

203

"I make A's and B's, Thomas."

"Good. You all want to play football, you can. If you want to play basketball, you can. I'm not going to force you to do anything but I expect you to go to school every day. I expect you to do your homework and I expect you to shower every night. I know there isn't a shower at home in Austin but I expect you to be clean in my house. I don't want any musk. There is a washer and dryer in the garage, you wash your damn socks. I don't want any funk in my house. I know how it is at home, I lived there before you did, but there is no excuse for not being clean in my house."

I wanted a clean start. "Red, here is some shampoo, here is some conditioner, here is some soap, here is a towel. Go in and take a shower. Wash good." He went in and spent some time at it. Franchot went next. Then I got them both in my car and we went shopping. I bought them jeans and slacks and each of them got a suit. I bought them shoes and T-shirts and underwear, socks and athletic socks, jocks, shorts, jackets. I dressed them out so they could really look presentable. I told them I expected them to take care of their clothes and themselves.

I went and enrolled them in the neighborhood high school. Gave them each twenty-five dollars a week allowance and bought them a beat-up used car to get them to and from school each day. I felt like I was finally doing something worthwhile.

Things went real well for months. The guys respected my curfews, they were paying attention in school, hadn't gotten into any trouble. They were both playing high school football. The only thing they did was stink up my house.

I was twenty-five years old and I did not want to live in a pig sty. Maybe it's all teenage boys, I don't know, but their room smelled like a locker room after practice. I'd go, "Hey, guys, I'm not going to have it. Strip these beds and vacuum this floor, wash every damn thing in this house!" I'd go in their drawers and here was a pair of dirty socks looked like they'd worn them in a swamp. About once a month I'd go in there and do my review.

One night I got home and Franchot didn't look too good. Red was smiling so I figured something was up. Franchot said, "Thomas, I have to talk to you."

"Okay, let's talk."

"Not here." I went to the icebox and got myself a beer, sat down at the kitchen table. "What's happenin'?" I didn't like the sound of this. Franchot wasn't the type of guy to mope.

"Thomas," he looked real long in the face, "I don't know how to tell you this. . . ." What could he have done? He'd only been in town a couple of months. Robbed a liquor store? Grand theft auto?

"I have some bugs on me, man."

"Bugs? What do you mean, bugs?"

"I think they're crabs, Thomas!" Red yelled in from the other room.

"Franchot, where did you get bugs on you, man? You ain't been with a woman." I was so relieved I had to laugh, but I knew this was serious to my little brother and I didn't want to shame him.

My baby brother was faster than I thought. "Remember that night I stood out till 1:00 and you got mad at me? It was her, man."

But that was two weeks ago. "You've had these things for two weeks?"

"Yeah, man. I talked to Red and he said he had them once and they went away." Red was a good guy but he never was too bright. Crabs multiply like crazy and now they were all over his little brother.

I went to the store and got four bottles of blue ointment, then put Franchot in the middle of the tub and bathed him from head to foot. The tub was crawling. I covered the mattresses with the ointment, put it on the carpet and in their dresser drawers. I made him throw out everything in the room. "Don't take it through the house!" I warned him, so I put a big piece of plastic over the doors, quarantined him, made him go in and out through the window.

But at the same time that I was trying to play Daddy and

bring my brothers up right I was getting heavier and heavier into cocaine. I liked what it did to and for me. It made me ebullient and energetic and sexy. I could keep a hard-on forever. I wanted to be with people, I wanted to talk and laugh and do pranks and party. The stuff was fun, my life was fun. But gradually, not overnight, not even so quickly that I could feel anything happening, I started to need the stuff to get there.

I'd wake up in the morning and my nose would start to bleed. With my deviated septum I never could breathe through my right nostril, but I'd force big rocks of coke up there anyway, push them up there with my finger and hope that they would dissolve and drain me some good times. I developed a large sore in my nose from all that pressure, a serious scab from all that cocaine eating away inside me, and the only way I could anesthetize the pain from that large sore was with more coke.

It became maintenance. Every morning there would be a booger as big as my pinky lying against the top inside of my septum. I would go to the bathroom, snort some cocaine to loosen the scab, then blow my nose to try and clear it. Every two or three days this *thing* would fall out. It would be hard like a large pebble and if it'd had legs it would have crawled away. Most mornings it felt like somebody had taken a pencil and shoved it up my nose a couple of times. Some days it just wouldn't come, so I'd go on and pack more coke in there to stop the pain. Then I'd be fine and go out into the day.

I knew my nose was going all to hell and that the coke was doing it but I just figured the problem would go away. Maybe, I thought, I was doing it wrong. Maybe I needed a Deering grinder, maybe I should start doing pharmaceutical coke to cut down on the impurities, maybe I should find a way to get this stuff liquid. The idea of quitting the coke altogether never crossed my mind.

The stuff was definitely getting to me. I thought, "This stuff won't let me go." During the season, if I quit snorting at two o'clock in the morning I kind of wanted to go to sleep. I'd sit there thinking, "I need to go to bed. I have to get up in the morning, I have a long practice tomorrow.'' But it wouldn't let me. I had to take downers to cut through the buzz. Then I'd lie on the pillow and it'd be six before I dozed off, and at 8:30 when my alarm went off I let the sucker ring.

Still, I didn't want to let go. There was more right with the stuff—I just knew it—than there was wrong.

But this was the off-season and I didn't have to think about that now. My new duplex was about ten blocks from this dealer named Philip who I'd met at Biff's. Philip always had three or four ounces of coke on hand and I quickly became his best customer. I didn't want to buy dope in quantity—I figured that if I had it around I'd just use it—so I bought it from him one gram at a time. Very expensive way to buy drugs but it was my way of trying to control myself.

It didn't work too well. I ended up driving to Philip's house two or three times a day, every day, spending two or three hundred dollars a day on cocaine that summer. He tossed in some free marijuana and I was perfectly happy. From the time I got back from Hawaii until early May I was running around Dallas, staying up all night partying, seeing a few women and doing my cocaine.

I started waking up in the morning feeling worse than usual. I went through five or six bottles of Visine for my eyes and Afrin nose spray and still I'd go to the mirror and no matter how much stuff I poured into them my eyes would be yellow and red. I started just going back to bed.

Then my shit turned white. I knew something was wrong now but I didn't know what to do.

I went to the Cowboy complex for off-season training a week later. We were all supposed to keep in shape so that when we got back to serious conditioning in preseason training camp we would be just about ready to go. I walked in each morning for several days but I didn't stay long. I didn't feel good. I was tired, my side was hurting a little bit, I didn't feel right. Finally I went in to see my friend the equipment manager, Buck Buchanan. He looked me in the eye and said, ''Henderson, come here. Look at that light.'' I looked up.

"Stick out your tongue." I stuck out my tongue. He said, "You have hepatitis."

"What are you talking about?" I sneered.

"You have hepatitis. Your eyes are yellow. You got it good." He sent me in to see the trainer.

The trainer took one look at me. "Oh, God."

They called the Cowboys' doctor, Dr. Zammarano, immediately. He told me, "Report to Baylor Hospital now. Do not go home. Do not make contact with any people, you might infect them. When you get to the hospital I will already have contacted the emergency room to have you admitted."

I got in my car and drove straight to Philip's. Picked up two grams. "Don't put it in a vial," I told him, "I may have to hide it. Put it in a baggie for me."

When I checked into the hospital they took all my clothes, sounded to me like I had the plague and they were going to burn them. I palmed the baggie in a tissue and kept it in my hand. They stuck an IV in my arm, wheeled me to this isolated room and left me. I don't like needles at all. The IV was really uncomfortable, I couldn't move my body around because of all the tubes, it was making me crazy. I said, "Fuck this" and pulled it out. Blood spurted down my arm. I took some medicine but it was my own medicine; I snorted some cocaine.

They checked me in and took some blood tests. The next morning, first thing out of the doctor's mouth was, "Mr. Henderson, I don't know how you are even sitting with your eyes open. Your body is so badly infected that it could kill you. I want you to be very careful from now on." Then he looked at me closely.

"Have you shot any drugs, Mr. Henderson?" He was watching my eyes for more than their color.

"No, man, I have not."

He took a flashlight and examined my veins. He looked in my eyes, he looked at all the possible places I could shoot drugs into my body. When he was satisfied that I had not been injecting myself he asked, "Where have you been?"

"I went to Hawaii this winter."

"Did you eat seafood?"

"A whole lot of it. Sushi, clams, oysters, everything that was around."

"That's the only other way you might have contracted this," he told me. "That or sex."

"You know, that's probably the number right there," I admitted, " 'cause I have had a bunch of that."

Once I got in the hospital it seemed like I got even sicker. I couldn't eat anything. My liver was inflamed and swollen, felt like it was just hanging there. My weight had dropped from around 230 pounds to 194. I was lying in the hospital bed skinny as I'd been since high school, feeling lousy, and here came Loosewire and his girlfriend Barbara.

They looked like characters out of *Lost in Space,* all decked out in hospital-issue white robe, mask, hat, shoe covers, the whole thing. They came with two other friends and had a giant plastic sheet wrapped around all of them. They huddled in the far corner.

"We're not supposed to come any closer," Loosewire called to me. He reached into his pocket and pulled out a long bottle of cocaine and threw it over onto the bed.

"I don't want it back!" he laughed.

Later in the day the doctor continued with his bad news. He was telling me numbers that I didn't understand, but the bottom line was that I was in serious trouble. "Do you know, Mr. Henderson, that Elvis Presley's mother died of half of what you have now."

Wyetta had to get a gamma globulin shot, which is no fun, but then they let her come see me. Every day for about three weeks she'd visit. I got a private room and I told the hospital, "This damn room is a couple of hundred bucks a day. This is my wife. I don't care what the fuck you all think, she is going to spend the night up here with me." It was against all regulations but they let us do it. It was that, I told them, or I'm going home.

We made love every night and every day, all day. One night Wyetta went and entered the Miss Dallas Legs contest over at SMU. She came in third, the only black woman there, and when she got back to the hospital she still had on her hot pants. That night we barricaded the door.

I went round and round with the doctors about the IV. They had been concerned about possible needle marks in my arm but after I refused to stick this thing in me they were pretty well convinced. They said, "You need the nutrients that are coming from the IV." I said, "I don't need that fucking pain in my arm. I'm not wearing it, Doc. You put that sucker in, I'm taking it out."

When I checked out of the hospital I was down to 189. I looked like a linebacker Gandhi. The doctor told me it was going to take several months to regain my strength, that all I should do was rest, that any kind of strenuous activity could set me back severely. Four weeks away was Cowboy training camp.

Coach Landry was not very sympathetic. I'm sure when he first heard that I had hepatitis he blamed it on me, figured maybe I was using needles or somehow had brought it on myself. Whatever the reason, because I couldn't do any off-season training I was already behind where he thought I should have been when I came to camp.

I showed up at Thousand Oaks at 208 but weak. The team physical showed I still had all the traces of the disease, high blood counts, low endurance. The doctors told me they didn't want me to work out during camp, they were afraid I would collapse.

I had missed practices before but not enough to cause any big stink. I normally missed them when I was hurting, had a shoulder separation or pinched nerves in my neck, or was just not feeling well and wanted to take a day off once every three or four weeks. I saw other people doing it and it was okay, and I never had any problem with that, as long as they were doing their jobs on the field. With me, however, all of a sudden it became everybody's issue. Maybe I was too vocal, my style of living rubbed the coaches the wrong way, whatever. I knew that people were angry at me. Everybody on the team, everybody who had had any kind of contact with me, was forced to get a gamma globulin shot. Nobody was much fond of that.

When I reported to camp Landry called me in for a meeting.

Going down the hall to Landry's office was like a Doom Walk, the last mile. I knew I was in the right—I had the doctors on my side, I had a whole series of hospital tests to back me up, I'd been told by medical professionals to rest and recuperate—but I knew the coach was going to see things differently. I knew the whole speech, the whole be-prepared spiel. Landry was going to say that he knew what the doctors said but he wanted me to be out on the field, maybe work once a day if I could.

I walked into his office and the coach was all business. His flat voice was like the desert. "I had to go get one of those shots."

"I'm sorry, Coach, I didn't intend to bring none of this back with me. I guess the seafood in Hawaii was infected when I was over there." They had found out that it was the Hawaiian fish that got me sick. The only reason they believed me was that several wives of the Kansas City Royals had come down with the same thing I had. I could only hope the Cowboys didn't think I was fooling around with the Kansas City wives.

"Yes, I understand some of the wives had it over there too." It was like he was registering an alibi that, tight or not, was going to have to stand. "Let's get down to business.

"You know we are going to start camp and I need you. You had a great year last year and we expect that same kind of performance from you this year."

"Well, Coach, I intend to do the best I can."

"You know, Thomas, you have to get in condition. We cannot allow you not to be in condition when the season starts. It is critical that you get some conditioning in because right now you are not in condition at all."

This was classic Landry. If a player wasn't in condition the player was worthless. All the talent in the world wouldn't be good enough for the man, you had to be able to use it at all times.

"What are you saying, Coach?" I asked him. "The doctor doesn't want me to do anything for a while."

"Well, Thomas, I want you to work in the mornings. It is cooler then. You can take the afternoons off."

"But the doctor doesn't want me to work at all until my blood count goes down, until it's close to normal."

"Well . . ." He knew all that but he chose to plow through it like a fullback going for that extra yard. "I understand that, Thomas, but don't you feel that you can work?"

I knew what he was asking. Can you go? There was only one answer.

"Yeah. I feel I can work. I'll give it a try." I didn't want to fight him on it. I wanted to play, I wanted to be well, I didn't want to start the season with Landry on my ass.

I went to my first practice and worked out. I felt weak and out of shape but I didn't feel completely wasted so I kept on with it. Took the afternoons off, worked the mornings. It was okay. Everybody accepted the fact that I had hepatitis. The doctors checked me once a week.

My blood count wasn't dropping as fast as the doctors thought it should. My recovery was a yard ahead and two feet back. Around the third week of training camp Landry called me in again.

"I think you should start doing two-a-days now. You only have another week of camp, that's only twelve practices to get yourself ready."

I got mad. "Coach Landry, I'm not going to work no two-a-days. Last year Tony Dorsett hurt his damn knee and you kept him out for five weeks. I'm working once a day, I have hepatitis, I'm weak. The doctors say I shouldn't be out there at all and you tell me this? You do what you gotta do, I'm doing what the doctors say this time."

He couldn't argue with me. He always listened to his doctors, he put a lot of faith in them, but this time he wanted to break his own rules. I think, despite all their tests and diagnoses and treatments, he thought I was malingering. I think he just suspected me. The coaches were saying, "What's next, Henderson? You know the symptoms for every damn thing, don't you." As if I was just out to con everyone to get out of work.

Up till then I hadn't in general missed more practices than the next guy but from then on I took pride in missing all that I could. I was getting no respect and I didn't see why I should give any back. A real strain developed between me and Coach Landry. I had learned his system, I had played hard and well, I had done everything he'd wanted me to do and still I was getting the short end. I was legitimately hurt, sick, weak, and he was giving me nothing.

Plus, the cocaine—I had to have some in me every day now—wasn't helping my paranoia level. I thought they were all out to get me. I snorted once before practice but it screwed up my breathing so bad that I decided that I could wait until after practice to pack it up. I was trying to be discreet about it but in team meetings I'd be falling asleep or blowing my nose all the time. That's a telltale sign, when a guy's got a runny nose, blowing and puffing for weeks at a time. I started carrying a roll of toilet paper around with me. Nobody asked any questions.

I would blow my nose and look in the damn hankie and go, "There goes twenty dollars." Matter of fact, and I'm not proud to admit this but it's the truth, if the booger didn't look too bad I would eat the sucker and freeze my whole face again. There's the glamour of drugs for you.

I didn't have a whole lot of other places to spend my money—I was renting and didn't have any mortgage payments, furniture was free, all I had to do each month was pay off my Mercedes—so I started spending about a thousand dollars a week on coke. I went to see James and Franchot play high school football and there I was over in the high school boys' room, doing cocaine in open stalls. I learned a new trick: I would open the vial and, instead of trying to dip into it with a matchstick, just lean my head back and pour cocaine into my nostrils. I was a Dallas celebrity but I was fighting for control. That would have surprised the Cowboys; they all thought I had none.

I worked myself into good enough condition to play in the preseason games. I was still weak, couldn't pursue the way I wanted, didn't have any wind, but I could get out there and play.

I continued to run around. When my hepatitis let up I went out and found more women. Wyetta had moved in part-time with me and my brothers but I was still out there frequenting the clubs. I met a beautiful girl named Kathy. She was sweet and innocent and absolutely gorgeous. Our only problem was that her parents didn't like black people. It drew us closer. On our first date I called Harvey Martin. "Hey, Harvey, what's goin' on, man. Are you going to be home? I want to use your house one time." Harvey knew that one favor deserved another and that I would probably invite him to the next orgy so he could come and steal a girl. Harvey was funny that way, he would never get out of his clothes with us. I never understood that. He used to just hang around and steal one, take a girl off by himself to his house. She was usually the dog of the litter. They were a pair.

Harvey had a beautiful home in North Dallas. Heated indoor swimming pool right off the master bedroom. Jacuzzi. A rock waterfall that came off the top of the pool. I thought it was a romantic-looking spot to take a white girl whose parents didn't like niggers. We made love in the ninety-degree water and I fell in love with her.

She had enough guts to tell me to pick her up at her house one evening and take her to dinner. I drove out to Irvington, a middle-class neighborhood not far from Texas Stadium. I parked my Mercedes and knocked on her door. This short, squatty man opened it and gave me the intense once-over. I'm sure he thought I was either the telephone man or the gas man, maybe some solicitor. "Is your daughter home?" I asked.

The guy's face froze. He didn't invite me in. He left the door ajar and disappeared into his home. I heard voices talking. Then he came back and gave me the once-over once again. Then his face about lit up. "You're Thomas Henderson! Well, come on in here!" He started calling all his neighbors and when they started coming over he went nuts with pride. That's Dallas when you're a Cowboy; you're not white or black or yellow or brown, you're two-toned: silver and blue.

I had a woman living with me but I was in love with several women. I was always in love because as I got more notable the women got more incredible. If somebody told me that a gal was untouchable or unfuckable I would meet her and take her out on a date and touch her and fuck her. Lots of times I'd find out that somebody had said, "Don't go out with Thomas Henderson." Boy, then they really wanted to know what it was about Thomas Henderson that people were warning them about.

Wyetta would often make friends with the women I was having affairs with. That was her way of letting me know that she knew I was stepping out on her. But in no way would she react or quit me or walk away. I couldn't believe the lengths she went to find me out. She'd look in my phone book, get numbers out of my dresser drawers, go in my car and search out matchbooks. She'd give me descriptions of the locations of hotels and apartments in different sections of the cities I had been in. She would have no way of knowing but she'd know.

What was she getting out of all of this? She had "Hollywood" Henderson. She liked the whole Dallas pageantry, the Mercedes she got to drive, the clothes, the shoes. I knew she loved me but I don't think she would have loved me if I'd been broke.

I went off and did some coke with a Cowboy cheerleader and Wyetta threatened to tell Suzanne Mitchell, the cheerleader director, and get the girl fired and me in deep hot water with the team. She started screaming at me. "Keep doing it, motherfucker! Just keep fucking with them white girls and cocaine. That damn cocaine is going to ruin you, that damn cocaine and them white whores!"

I'd rather get run over by a running back or take a right cross to the jaw than take a tongue-lashing. Especially from her. I stood there and looked at the woman. "Are you crazy?!" I shouted. She wouldn't stop screaming. "Who have you been fucking, my teammates?"

I slapped her on top of the head. I slapped her again and again. "Are you crazy? Crazy?" I kept hitting her till my hand got sore. What went through my mind, right then, was, This is the way my stepdaddy hit my mother, this is heritage coming up here.

I always kept an open hand, I never hit her with my fist. But I was hitting tight ends about the head with these same open hands.

I believe that was the cocaine at work. I never hit Wyetta when I wasn't loaded. When I was, it was lucky for me and everybody around me that I didn't knock a lot more around. My moods were in a jumble, sometimes cranky, suspicious, paranoid, other times buoyant and outgoing. I crawled out of bed with a woman and went home and accused my girlfriend of having an affair. The cocaine was making me lose it.

Still Wyetta didn't quit on me. What she did was try to get a firmer grip. She moved from keeping tabs on my movements with other ladies to getting in the middle of them.

Wyetta took to calling the Cowboys' practice facility to see where I was. She started calling my teammates at their homes and talking to their wives, calling at night and saying, "Have you seen the motherfucker? I know he is probably with some white bitch doing cocaine." She was embarrassing me. I was never embarrassed out with the hip guys who had gold around their necks. I had gold around my neck too, and it was cool for me to say, "Hey, you want a toot? Let's go to the car." But she was calling me out where I was making my money. I would walk into practice and I'd get it from everybody.

"Where you been, Henderson?"

"I been home."

"You ain't been home. Wyetta said you been out all night doing cocaine." I didn't need that. I didn't need her putting my business out in the street.

Robert Newhouse, our fullback, once said to me, "I don't know what's wrong with that girl, man. She called my house and said you were out with some white bitch doing cocaine. What you doin' there?"

I was about ready to dump her when she told me she was pregnant. She was carrying my child and pretty soon everybody knew that too. I didn't want to have anything to do with her but I couldn't leave her. I couldn't do it. I couldn't pull a Billy Goree.

We shut out the Baltimore Colts in the 1978 opener, 38–0, and then went to New York to play the Giants. My eighty-year-old grandfather had black lung disease and was walking around with a tank of pure oxygen. I asked Coach Landry if it'd be okay if he came down on the field with the team during the game. Landry surprised the hell out of me by saying yes.

We always played the Giants tough, we were just better than they were and they knew it. They were in our division and we looked on that game as a win. The Big Apple is the media center of the world and we liked going in there and grabbing the headlines.

In the second quarter the Giants ran a Power 49 NGO play at me. On that play the near back blocks the linebacker, the on guard pulls and the off guard pulls. In the defense we were in my assignment was to attack and defeat the near back and make the tackle. Well, the blocking back for the Giants was Larry Csonka.

Larry Csonka was a former All-Pro, the bull who had driven the Miami Dolphins to three Super Bowls and the only undefeated season in NFL history. Where Jim Kiick had been the Dolphins' Sundance Kid, Csonka was Butch. He was a thousand-yard runner who went over defensive players rather than around them, dealing out punishment as he chewed up the yardage. Csonka was a completely hard-nosed guy who could run with a determination that approached zealotry. He liked to hit people. So did I. It was going to be a nice confrontation.

The big son of a bitch must have weighed 270 at the time.

I was fresh out of the hospital, fresh out of not working out very much in training camp, fresh out of luck. I hit Larry Csonka with my shoulder, got under him like I was supposed to, but the impact of his power ran through me like a poker. You're supposed to plant yourself but Csonka planted me. My left ankle snapped. I felt like a sniper had shot me from the stands.

They carried me off to the sidelines. The pain was incredible, even worse than the hip pointer my rookie year. Forget about it, I couldn't walk. They trotted out a dolly, one of those things they cart around tubs of Kool-Aid with on the sidelines. As they were loading me on and I was trying to hold everything together, the conditioning coach Bob Ward leaned over to me. He'd been impressed by the hit. "What a fucking explosion!"

The New York fans are savage. They started to cheer. I was lying there with my ankle ballooning as I looked at it— I mean, you could literally see the thing growing in front of you—and seventy-five thousand assholes were glad to see me hurt. Well, fuck them. Genius that I was, as they wheeled me off the field I raised up and flipped Giants Stadium the bird. The Cowboys won the game without me.

I was not on Coach Landry's A-list. Besides hepatitis here I was with an ankle as big as my head and my middle finger in the papers. I knew what he was thinking: If Henderson had worked out like I told him this would never have happened. Well, if I'd worked out like he told me I wouldn't have been on the field at all, I'd have been back in the hospital.

The ankle wasn't broken, I had only torn some ligaments. We flew home to Dallas that night and they sent me home to bed. The next morning I called in sick. I told them I couldn't get out of bed. It was the truth. My ankle was so swollen I was crying.

They didn't believe me. The trainer said, "Can you come in?" Now, normally I would have. You don't want to say you can't go. But this time it was out of the question.

"We need you to come in."

I cursed him out over the phone but I knew I had to show up. There was no way to prove an injury except to show them, and there was no way to show them but to risk further injury and come in. Cowboy logic.

I arrived late. I blew my horn long enough until I made them come out to the car to get me. When they saw my ankle everybody was stunned. I actually was hurt!

I didn't do any work all week. Just iced it and went to the meetings. The worst part of it was that I couldn't move around, couldn't get up during the ten-minute breaks and go to the washroom for some cocaine. I just suffered through the days.

I told Coach Landry that I'd be okay for the Redskins game two weekends away but not for the Rams game in L.A. that coming Sunday. He made me travel with the team anyway. Normally when a guy is hurt to the point where he can't play, Landry will leave him at home. But not Thomas Henderson. You're going, bud.

Fat old Rams' Coach Ray Malavasi had gone public and said they were going to "kick our ass." That pissed me off. I didn't think a coach should be mouthing off like that. It was okay for the players to talk, they were going to be out there backing it up, but for a coach to say something like that just wasn't right. You'd never catch Coach Landry being loud and vulgar. I thought Malavasi was totally horseshit but there was nothing I could do about it.

I showed up at the L.A. Coliseum with a full-length beaver coat and an ankle the size of a grapefruit. I was powerless to help. All I could do was root my teammates on.

The Cowboys replaced me with two men: Mike Hegman on regular defense and a defensive back on third down. I don't know if my not being in there made any difference but they beat us down. The Rams took us 27–14. They truly kicked our ass and all I could do was watch. Two weeks later we lost to the Redskins.

I missed five games because of my ankle and I was really mad. I'd never had to sit out this much time and it was no fun at all. There was nothing to do but wait for the damn thing to heal. The crutches were gone but I couldn't work out, I couldn't run, I couldn't do anything to relieve the pressure and tension that were building up inside me. About all I could do was cocaine.

It got to be, "Do I have any coke? Where will I get some today? Where will I get some tomorrow?" Everything was based on where I could get me a gram or two. I had access to eighths, quarters, ounces, even pounds, but I was too fearful of getting busted to take in any great amounts at any one time. Plus, it gave me something to do.

It got to where I couldn't start my day without snorting some cocaine. I'd go to work and be nodding in the meetings, grouchy, wanting to go home. I wanted to bring a pillow so I could lie down in the middle of the floor. I found I didn't need the meetings anymore; the coke made me concentrate better, I'd absorb the playbook in a tunnel-vision flash, then I'd have to sit there and wait while everyone else got it. The whole system had become second nature to me; I had finally become a Cowboy linebacker, in spite of myself.

As the ankle healed I could practice. I was always amazing Charlie Waters. He was the defensive genius, had a great football mind, knew where everybody was supposed to be at all times. He and I developed a nice relationship on and off the field. I used to drop by his house and sit with him under a big oak tree, just talking and playing with his dog. That was kind of nice. On the field I was the strongside linebacker and Charlie was the strong safety, he played on my hip. In front of us was Too Tall and we were a strong strongside.

Charlie could recognize an offense in a flash. He was Landry's perfect man because Landry based most of his defense on recognition, on your seeing the play before the play develops. If a tackle pulls, or the off guard, you're supposed to know that a certain play tended to be run in that situation and one of our defenses would stop it. Charlie could do that. Even when I learned the system and the tendencies I tended to do things my own way. While the ball was on the ground I was a Dallas Cowboy, trained, very businesslike, a computer-brained football player. When it was snapped I became

Thomas Henderson from Langston, Oklahoma, and to hell with the computer, I was going after the ball. Charlie would go, "Henderson, I can't believe you did that." I would be out of position, in the completely wrong place, but I would make the play. Early in the season he was still infuriated but as time went by he started appreciating my ability. He'd go, "Goddamn, you are incredible." I think that was a compliment.

My locker was with the linebackers, right across from defensive backs Charlie Waters, Cliff Harris and Randy Hughes, and during the 1978 season I started to make some enemies. Not on purpose, but my attitude or disposition just didn't seem to sit right with some of the guys. Cliff and Charlie were the Cowboys' version of Butch Cassidy and the Sundance Kid. Cliff was balding, he had pretty much lost it by then, and he'd gone in for the hair implants. I gave him a bunch of shit about it, called him "Cliff Hairless," told him I thought he went to Nebraska because they'd planted some corn all over his head—and I think he would have whipped me if he could've.

I'd get into these little bullshit arguments with Randy White. It was easy to get under his skin. The thing we used to argue about most was the fact that he could not beat me in a fight. "Hey, you can't whip me, motherfucker. You know, you are big and people have told you you are scary-looking, but you can't whip me. I can whip your white ass!" Ever since we were rookies I'd tell him that almost every day. "You can't whip me, white boy. I know you chased some niggers in your time up there in Maryland, in the back hills where you are from, but you cannot whip me, Randy White." I meant it. I was quick and fast and had good hands. I called my hands Dobermans. I told him, "I'll sic these dogs on your ass. That old wrestling shit? You ain't going to be able to wrestle me, I'm just going to turn that head of yours to the color of a beet!"

White would sit there steaming. I knew he didn't take this kind of talk well, that's why I fed it to him. He liked to pick people up and intimidate the shit out of them. That didn't work with me and I could see him trying to find some way of getting to me.

"Oh, sure, Henderson. I'm real scared. Sure, Henderson, sure." That was about as verbal as Randy White got. He was sitting there like Goliath. Nobody had ever dared to talk to him like me before and he had no way of handling it.

Randy White is a great football player. Aside from Conrad Dobler, who was a complete wild man, he was by far the toughest, most aggressive, reckless football player I've ever seen in my life. The guy is tough. He has no regard for whatever is coming at him, he will just attack it. Plus, because of his size, he's usually bigger than whatever he has to face. An offensive line trying to block him is like a swarm of Volkswagens trying to stop a diesel.

Linemen don't have the big opportunities to really hit people hard, they usually come and hit them with a shoulder pad or wrestle a guy down. A linebacker or defensive back gets a chance to work up a ten-yard head of steam and really cream somebody. Randy White was different, he could mangle you from a standing start. He could dish out punishment in a very confined area, the line of scrimmage. That's what he'd do all day; every series of plays he'd beat up the center and two guards.

Randy wasn't a bad guy, he was just getting all the attention from Landry that I wanted, that I knew I'd never get, so I found a way to get in his face. Sometimes we laughed and had a good time, but my mood swings were getting so erratic that, if he'd ever had an idea about who I was, he'd have had a hard time finding me then.

The guys who didn't have a hard time finding me were the guys with the cocaine. The biggest dealer I knew was a guy I'll call James Suite. He was from old Dallas and he was handling pounds of the stuff. With power like that he became a cool little man and everybody around him was scared of him. They worked for him, they answered the door, collected the money, ran for him. He might have been a nice guy if he didn't want it so bad. He might give you dope but he never gave an ounce of respect.

Respect means a lot to me. If you're secure you can afford to give it, and if you have a hard time giving it then something is very wrong. Suite liked power and he was in the right field for it.

The first time we met he gave me some cocaine, wouldn't even let me pay for it. The oldest trick in the book, but it worked. After that I was buying from him regularly. I hung around for the coke and he liked my company. I was this big monkey he had on a string. Or so he thought.

I was the only one who wasn't afraid of him. I mean, Suite wasn't the only connection in town, even if he was the best.

I knocked on his door one night and a guy answered with a double-barreled shotgun. I was a little scared of the weapon but I had one thing in mind, cocaine, so I walked in and pointed to the sentry. "Who's this?" I walked into the kitchen and there were three pails full of cocaine. Pails.

Three guys in rubber gloves were running their hands through the stuff, cutting it up for distribution, adding the powders that dilute the drug and raise the profit margin. There must have been three or four pounds in each pail just sitting there. I knew I should have run for my car—getting caught in a house with this much dope would have meant years in prison—but I was high and wanted to get higher. In some crazy way this was a lot of fun.

"Why don't you smell the stuff, Henderson?" Suite said. He was enjoying watching his men work. "You want to hit some of this, Hollywood?" He held this little blue popper, a little testing device that you fill with a pinch of coke and then break open. If it comes back dark blue it's 87 percent pure. I was sure this stuff was coming up navy.

There were several pretty girls sitting around. (There always seem to be several pretty girls sitting around when large quantities of cocaine are present.) They were too good an audience not to please. I stuck my whole face in one of the pails.

Came up looking like Bozo the Clown. A negative Al Jolson. I got coke in my mouth and my eyes, a whole wad up my nose. It was great shit! Everybody was laughing. Suite was sitting back like the Godfather. "Give me a baggie over there," he told one of his henchmen. He scooped up seven or eight grams of pure powder and tablespooned it in. Handed it to me. He was generous but erratic. He was using too.

Suite surrounded himself with some strange muscle. One of his goons wore a toupee and I used to give him a hard time every time I ran into him at Biff's. Finally he ran out the front door, called me a couple of Niggers, threw his coat on his car, squared off and wanted to fight. I said, "Come on over here, you want me so bad. I'm not going over there. I don't want you to run downtown tomorrow and file a lawsuit on me saying I attacked you. I want you to come over and attack me and I'm going to whup your motherfucking ass!"

The joker stood off over there and called me "nigger" this and "nigger" that, but I knew the moves. The guy didn't work for a living, he was looking for a good lucrative lawsuit to settle.

The same thing happened at Suite's one night. The same dude actually ran out the back door, jumped a fence and told me to come out to the middle of this field so we could go to it. Suite loved it; one of his goons was standing up to me.

By then I was insulting Suite so consistently in front of his friends that he didn't like me anymore. One night he called me at home and told me he wanted to talk to me. Sounded to me like a party. I drove over to his house.

When I walked in the door I knew something was different. I couldn't say what, just different. I went into Suite's den and there was a Thompson submachine gun hanging from the ceiling. Suite was sitting dead center, one goon on each side of him, each with a piece. "Sit down," he told me.

"Suite stuff, fuck you," I sneered. "Who the fuck do you think you are, man? You call me over here and tell me you want to talk to me like I'm some punk. I ain't fuckin' listening to none of you or your clowns. I don't owe you a thing I ain't one of your fucking peon punks. I spend money when I come over here. You don't own me, man." I turned my back on him and left his house.

The guy I did like spending time with was a guy I'll call

Jeff Cohen. Jeff had about twenty million bucks. Born to money. He was a land developer, very articulate, very smart and educated. I hadn't met a lot of this kind of people and I really wanted to know how they thought, how they acted, how it felt to be completely secure.

Cohen was from Highland Park, posh Dallas. He had a Rolex on his wrist, was driving a Rolls-Royce, buying new homes and selling his old ones. The man knew how to make money and how to hold on to it. A gram would last him about a week; it would last me the time I dumped it on the table. I was impressed with his restraint.

Going to Jeff's house was one of my great joys. I always got such good conversation, a thousand times better than Randy White or Too Tall or Suite or anybody I knew or had ever known. I was always meeting the upper class of Dallas society there and they liked me. This was a whole new deal. Jeff's main statements to me were, "You've got to give people what they want, Thomas," and, "Do what you say you're going to do. When you do what you say you're going to do, don't do it for another person, do it for yourself."

Jeff and I exchanged cultures. We'd swap stories that were incredible to the other; I'd tell him about growing up in the ghetto and he'd tell me about the elite of Dallas. No way either of us could relate to any of what the other had gone through, but we grew to be tight friends.

Finally my ankle started coming around. I could practice at half speed without killing myself, even though the coaches thought I was dogging it. I had to wear high-topped football shoes for support, which were ungainly to begin with, and one day I just kind of got the idea to paint them.

I felt shitty. I couldn't move the way I wanted, my body was not in the kind of shape I wanted it to be, my ankle hurt, my wind wasn't back, the cocaine was messing with whatever conditioning I had left. (I was twenty-five years old, I was in naturally great shape at all times, but football shape is something completely different, that's the ability to get pounded and keep coming back for more. That takes a lot of practice.) I looked at these awkward shoes and said, that's me.

I painted them black. I smeared paint all over them, not in neat lines or one even coat, I just slapped the shit on, tried to paint the bottoms black too. Black soles. My shoes were my personal definition: Look at those shoes and you know how I feel.

These shoes were ugly. In practice I was hobbling, I wasn't my old graceful self. On the films I looked like I was running in shit. We played the Philadelphia Eagles in Texas Stadium my first game back and I wore them, looked like I was covering kickoffs in combat boots.

After the game Landry told me, "Thomas, you can't wear those shoes anymore."

Now wait a minute. I knew that Tom Landry himself had worn black high-tops when he'd played for the Giants in the early fifties, that's what everybody wore. It had taken ten years for the players to convince him that white shoes were okay. Joe Namath had made his name wearing white shoes when black shoes were standard issue. Think of Johnny Unitas. Now Landry wouldn't let me wear my damn shoes. These people were unbelievable.

I hung them in my locker where everyone could see them. The paint was starting to come off and they were all scuffed and dirty. I took them on the road. Put them on in the locker room for the pregame and paraded around in them. I made a point of catching Landry's eye. He just shook his head in disgust. I didn't wear them in the game.

I had hoped I'd only miss two games or so but I was out for five and by the time I got back the season was almost half over. We had started out well but we lost back-to-back to the Vikings and Dolphins and with ten games played we were only 6–4. Not Cowboy numbers.

We beat the Packers 42–14 and finally we started to get into the groove. We had become "America's Team," or that's what the merchandisers had begun to call us, and we'd been in the playoffs every year except one for over a decade. It was time to turn it on.

Our next game was against the New Orleans Saints. Tony Galbreath was their big confrontation for me. He was the best in the business at catching passes out of the backfield. He ran crisp patterns, knew the field well, knew where the seams were in the zone and how to get there, catch the pass, hold on and bang for extra yardage. He was my responsibility.

We blew away the Saints like we knew we would, 27–7, but Galbreath caught three of the seven passes thrown to him and Landry felt like I'd gotten beat. "I told you it was going to be a big day and Galbreath got the best of you," he made a point of telling me after the game. Well, shit. The passes he caught were for four or five yards, nothing big, nothing spectacular. But Landry felt that I should have shut him out. The man was a pisser to please.

After the game I went down and caught Richard Pryor's show at the Dallas Fairgrounds. It was my town this time and I led his postperformance tour. We club-hopped, picking up a little business here and there. I was driving on the Central Expressway, telling him some jokes, trying to give him some material, when he said quickly, "What are you doin', man?"

I had a quarter ounce of coke and I was about to snort some. "Doin' a little toot. You want some?"

"No, thank you, that's not what I'm talking about. What the fuck are you doin' driving this car with your goddamn legs, man?"

I'd perfected the drive-by-thigh system of automotive navigation: Park my legs under the steering wheel when I'm doing like fifty or sixty miles an hour and guide my car by shifting my weight. Left my hands free to poke around in the bottle and grab myself a spoonful.

Pryor actually seemed worried. He was laughing but he wasn't too happy. "Look, motherfucker," he said in his high-pitched panic squeal, "if you're gonna hit that coke you pull off the fucking freeway and hit it. Don't fucking drive and hit that shit!" Okay. I pulled off onto the emergency stop lane, tapped my nose full of stuff and offered some to him. He didn't want any. I was surprised.

When I got back in the lineup I started playing well. I teamed with Too Tall and Charlie Waters to keep our side of the field free from anyone who tried to take it from us. My speed returned, my stamina came back to me, I was playing the Cowboys' game and my game at the same time. I felt like I had finally arrived. This was what pro football was supposed to be like. We were winning and I was playing great.

We were going to play the Redskins in Texas Stadium on Thanksgiving Day and I couldn't help myself. "Washington is in trouble," I told the reporters. "The turkeys are coming to town on Turkey Day. We're gonna pluck 'em and cook 'em!"

The guys in the press loved this kind of talk, it made their lives so simple, put them in the middle of the game, made them a factor. They could run over to the Redskins and get their comments, which would be choice, and then run back to us for the topper.

Controversy sells papers. I wasn't saying anything that wasn't true, it's just that you normally don't like to get an opponent riled up unnecessarily, particularly a real rival. But what the hell, it was partly the cocaine talking and partly the fact that this time I would be there to back it up.

I had also become increasingly aware of the exposure that the Cowboys were getting. In Dallas, whole sections of the daily newspapers were given over to us and these guys were always needing something to write about. Might as well be me. I was good-looking, flamboyant, always had a way with a phrase. I made their life easy and the notoriety helped me along with mine. The more I got into the papers and on the tube the better it was in the clubs after the game, the more attention I'd be getting around town. Me and Tony Dorsett were the only black players driving around in dealer-provided cars and mine was top-of-the-line, a Corvette, not some low-rent Nova or something. I'd driven it, physically driven it, out of the showroom. Great kick.

But while I made the sportswriters' lives easy I also made them nervous. I was cocky and they were little. I was brash and they were beholden to the Cowboys for their jobs. They were better educated than most of the players but they were getting paid less, and the envy level in the press room was pretty high. Here we were, these physically threatening man-monsters who could crush any one of them with one arm, and they had to be careful around us. Piss any one of us off and their access to the team might be changed, their working conditions made much more hazardous.

There's a lot of mixed emotions in the press corps, a lot of power struggling. The players are physically and socially powerful—I mean, who cares if some writer is sitting in a bar when there's a running back in the corner giving autographs; who are the girls going to go after? The reporters' power comes from what they say about you and the fact that thousands of people read or see and hear them. If some know-nothing decides that you're playing lousy—and, believe me, lots of people don't know good play from bad when it is rolled right in front of them—then he can broadcast it all over town and the fans, who read and pay attention to these great judges of talent, will boo or cheer according to what they've been programmed to see. The press has the power to affect the homefield advantage, to invade a player in what should be his home.

There's a lot of Cowboy loyalty at play here too. The writers depend on the team, the organization, for their livelihood, not the players. Players come and go, the team is in Dallas for the duration. Management has got these guys by the balls. Women sportswriters too.

Getting stories in the papers and on the air is the job of the team's public relations men. On the Cowboys they were Doug Todd and George Hedelson. They controlled the credentials, the passes, the access; they could point a writer toward a certain player or away from him. Doug and I got along fine, I liked him very much. Hedelson and I didn't see eye to eye. He was a real company man and I think I made the Cowboy organization as nervous as I made the writers. They were afraid I was going to embarrass them by the things I said. I surely was not a company man, I spoke my own mind. I wasn't that polished, I wasn't a prep school kid, I had so much street in me that when I talked it all came out. I was outspoken on every issue, which should have made me a writers' favorite, but it seemed like somehow they tried to stay away from me. As if I was working too hard at getting into print, using their medium instead of letting them use me. Still, I did love to talk.

Hedelson wasn't getting me any stories. In fact I kind of felt he was directing the writers away from me. "If you won't promote me," I told him, "I'll promote myself."

"Thomas," he told me, "you're not quite that good yet."

"You'll see."

This high-visibility life was working for me and I decided to really play it. Look at me, world. My antics on the field took a great leap forward. I waved to the fans in the second deck. I pursued cameras on the sidelines. I would take ten or twenty seconds right in the middle of the game, I should have been in the huddle but I was fooling around with some cameraman, saying, "Catch this next shot, guy!" I was really hogging it for the press, hogging it for the cameras.

Probably the longest-running rivalry in American history is the cowboys and the Indians and we were prepared to play the part. George Allen, who was the coach of the Redskins, said the Cowboys had a "cakewalk" each year and he was going to end it. We were both 8-4 when we woke up that Thanksgiving morning.

The Cowboys always had to get up for the Redskins. They were in our division so we went at them twice each year. We knew them and they knew us. They played tough, it was a good rivalry. The Redskins had beaten us 9-5 earlier in the season while I was on the injured list and we wanted them.

I definitely wanted them. By shooting my mouth off about "turkeys" and "feathers" I had put a whole bunch of pressure on myself. John Riggins had said I was a "hot dog" and I didn't argue with him.

But they didn't give us any kind of a game. After all the talk they came out flat. We were ready, didn't matter what they came at us with we handled it. They tried to manhandle us but it didn't work, we just busted them back. The offense put up thirteen points in the first quarter and we shut the Redskins down cold. Drew Pearson caught a fifty-seven-yard touchdown pass from Staubach three minutes into the second quarter and we led 20–0 at the half.

Jean Fugett, now with Washington, was trying to brother-in-law me at the line of scrimmage. " 'Wood, how you doin'?" he said as he went into his crouch. "What's goin' on in Dallas?" Here we were lining up to tear each other's lips off and he wants to talk. Forget that. I wasn't getting lulled to sleep by no chump trick.

I was out there on all the special teams and they were double-teaming me, putting two guys on me all the way down the field. Plus, each time I'd come to the line I'd hear some Redskin yelling, "Wolfman Right!" or "Wolfman Left!" Finally I asked one of them, "Who the fuck is Wolfman?" He said, "You are, Henderson." Then he tried to cut me at the knees. Didn't work.

All day long they set up their returns to the side away from me. They thought they were fucking with me but I took it as a sign of respect.

Doomsday II, our defense (our original Doomsday Defense had aged out of football by this time), beat them all to hell. The Redskins punted nine times that day; they weren't going anywhere. We were up 37–3 before they finally got a fourth-quarter touchdown, but that was it.

37–10. Feathers all over the field.

In the locker room I showed up for the postgame interviews with a piece of tape over my mouth. Pulled it off in a hurry. "You guys knew it wouldn't be on long, didn't you?" I laughed.

I liked all this attention. After a while it came my way without my chasing it. Like the confrontation I had set up for me with Russ Francis.

Russ Francis was a big tight end who at the time was playing for the New England Patriots. We were going to play them the Sunday after the Redskins game and he was going to be my responsibility. Well, all the so-called experts were just about ready to make him All-World, the best tight end ever to step on the football field, unstoppable, overpowering, completely out of this world. I don't know if the Cowboy management put him up to it or not but early in the week one of the Dallas sports columnists, Skip Bayless, wrote in his column something like "If you don't think that Russ Francis is a blockbuster, the world's greatest tight end, watch him whip 'Hollywood' Henderson this Sunday at Texas Stadium."

That's all I had to hear. I guess I had set myself up for this kind of stuff by now, telling people how good I was, hunting down cameras and writers—If I saw a writer come into the locker room I would run and grab him, "Look, I've got this quote for you"—but here it was now in my face. I was seriously challenged.

The guys all read the papers, they know what everybody else is talking about and they talk about it too. Everybody was giving me the eye, teasing me about how I was in deep trouble now. Even Drew Pearson said, "Boy, you're in for it. He's a big motherfucker. That dude is six six, 250 pounds. He and that other one, Hasselbeck, that sucker is six eight. Henderson, what are you going to do?"

I said, "Drew, I'm gonna fucking whip his ass."

"All right!" Drew liked to hear that kind of talk. Showed you meant business. Didn't want to show fear on the field—ever. "All right then!"

I was scared shitless. I had met Russ Francis at the Coaches All-American Game in Lubbock, Texas, four years before and I knew just exactly how big that motherfucker was. He was huge and he was as good-looking as Elvis Presley. Grew up in Hawaii, tough, strong. Shit.

But I knew that I could whip him. I didn't know how but I just knew that I could reach down to my cow-pasture football days in the clay dirt of Langston University and find some way, somehow, to beat him.

I didn't do any cocaine from Wednesday on. Gave it up for the week. It wasn't an easy thing to do but I wanted to be in top physical and mental shape for this. I worked and worked and finally came up with a way to stop him.

I didn't give him a chance to get started, didn't want Steve Grogan, the Patriots' quarterback, to toss him a few and let him feel like it was his day. It wasn't. It was mine. The first play of the game I stuck my helmet in Francis' chin. He raised up from his three-point stance and I sprung from a squatting position and fired on him. I didn't care what the play was or what else was going on on the field; this first three seconds was going to determine who was going to control my side of the field that afternoon and I made damn sure he knew it was going to be me.

I rocked him. It was an extended explosion, not just one pop but me driving through the man's whole damn system. I knocked Russ Francis into his own backfield on his can. He was stunned. I told him he could expect more of the same and then I kept giving it to him.

By the second quarter Francis was trying to brother-in-law me at the line of scrimmage, inviting me to Hawaii. "You ever been over there? I got a house over there. I got a condominium." Right. For all the good he did that day he could've been Francis the Talking Mule.

We beat the Patriots, 17–10. In Monday's paper the headline to Skip Bayless's column was "An Apology to Hollywood." He wrote: "Dear Hollywood: I am deeply sorry I even suggested that Russ Francis, New England's blockbuster tight end, could block you. You embarrassed him and me. Forget Ali; you are the greatest."

But better than that, Coach Landry finally had something nice to say about me. At the first meeting that next Monday he got up in front of the whole team and reviewed the game. Of course he couldn't do it flatout, he had to keep me on my toes even then.

"I want to talk to the team today about Thomas Henderson," he began. I wasn't usually Coach Landry's first order of business and I listened as the chairs scraped the classroom floor. "I hate to praise Thomas Henderson because giving Thomas a compliment is like adding fuel to a fire. We all know Thomas." The team kind of rumbled a laugh but Landry went on.

"We all know Thomas does his thing"—I loved it when Landry picked up on some street expression; usually about five years after everyone else—"and I have no problem with Thomas doing his thing as long as he keeps doing what he says he's going to do. I don't mind anybody bragging as long as they can back it up. Until it affects the team I have no problem with it.

"Last week you all know that Thomas had quite a bit of pressure put on him by the press . . ." he paused, "and himself . . . that he was going to get whipped by Russ Francis. Well, as you will see today in the films, Thomas whipped him. Thomas played tough as nails. He made a lot of big plays, he performed better than I've ever seen him perform. But that is what Thomas is all about: He performs under pressure.

"The next statement I'm about to make I very seldom make," he said. "Thomas Henderson is a pro."

I had been there four years and I had never heard him call anybody a pro. I was so proud I could've died right there and been happy. I didn't go up and thank him afterward, I wouldn't have known what to say and I was afraid that he'd say something that would take it back. I just tucked that speech away and kept it with me from then on.

That week I was standing on the sidelines during practice when Gil Brandt, the Cowboys' vice-president and Tex Schramm, the president and general manager, approached. I was dirty, sweating, in full gear, waiting to get sweatier and dirtier. Tex Schramm, the president of the entire organization, whispered me off to the side. He put his hand on my shoulder pads. "Thomas," he said. I could barely hear him. "You were voted to the Pro Bowl today."

Making the Pro Bowl is pretty cool. The top players at each position are chosen by the players and coaches themselves; it's the judgment of your peers that you are the best. I'd been injured for a third of the year and still I'd made it.

I moved to jump but he had my pads. "Don't," he said. "Don't make a big fuss about it. Take it graciously. Don't rub it in."

The man did not want me to enjoy this. I was the rogue Cowboy who had bucked the system and won, and he wanted everything kept under wraps. Any other player and they'd have been proud. "Be discreet about it," he confided.

I turned from him and looked out over the field.

"I MADE THE PRO BOWL!!"

Top of my lungs. I grinned back at him over my shoulder. His face was flush red. He rolled his eyes and shook his head like, "Oh, Lord, what have we created?"

We won our last two games, on the road against the Eagles and Jets, to finish at 12–4 and win our division. The Atlanta Falcons were a wild-card team and we were supposed to run right over them in the first round of the playoffs but they gave us a tough game. We scored first on a field goal by Rafael Septien but they came right back and went up on a 14-yard touchdown run. Scott Laidlaw bulled it in for us from the 13 and then we traded field goals. But Steve Bartkowski burned us from the 17 and we were down 20–13 at the half. Worse than that, Falcons' linebacker Robert Pennywell sacked Roger Staubach, knocked him unconscious and gave him a concussion. Roger was through for the day and things didn't look too good, but Danny White came in and we sucked it up. We tied the score in the third period and Laidlaw rammed it across in the fourth and we beat them 27–20.

We were going to Los Angeles to face the Rams in the NFC Championship Game. I had missed our regular season game against them with my bad ankle, had to stand on the sidelines in my beaver coat and watch them kick our ass. I hadn't liked that one bit.

Since I had taken the lead in mouthing off to the papers, the press tried to get me to comment on this matchup. I knew it was going to get a lot of play so I tried to plan what I was going to say when the media massed around me the first day of practice that week. I remembered how horseshit I'd thought Coach Malavasi was and when they hit the locker room in Dallas that Monday I had it.

"You know what?" I told the reporters. "The whole Ram organization hasn't got any class. The Rams don't have enough class to go to the Super Bowl."

That was the line that did it. The shit hit the fan. Writers came from all over the world. What did I mean? "Hell," I said, "they ain't been to the Super Bowl, what makes you think they have enough class to go now?"

Each time someone asked me about it I added a line. "Why haven't they been to the Super Bowl? They're not a class outfit."

"They're not a class team."

"Well, if they do have class it's only third or fourth."

"They're gonna choke."

"If they don't choke, I will choke them."

I kept up the chatter. TV crews showed up, hate mail started to pour in. "You ain't 'Hollywood,' " one genius wrote, "you're just El Segundo."

When we got to Los Angeles I started receiving death threats at the hotel. "Nigger, we're going to kill you," and all this. Football fans do take their game seriously. I didn't think anybody was going to kill me because I called the Rams low-rent but this was California so I couldn't be absolutely sure.

I limoed to the Coliseum. Called my driver Benny, who I'd met some years back with Anita Pointer. "Benny, pick me up. I'm not riding in that damn bus to watch Tom Landry, and I'm not taking a damn cab. Come get me."

"You want me to wait?" he asked.

"Yeah. Wait on me. It's a big night."

I packed my nose full of cocaine before I left the hotel. My nose was hurting and I didn't want my sinuses to be bothering me the whole game long. I didn't want to be blowing my nose so I anesthetized it a little bit and then stuffed the rest of the coke way down in my bag. If I had a notion to take some I'd have to dig through a lot of stuff to find it.

The guard at the Coliseum ramp wasn't going to let us in. That was completely unacceptable. The whole point was for everyone to see me climb out of this brand new stretch in my fur coat. "Look fella," I told him, "I'm 'Hollywood' Henderson. There've been death threats made against my life.

I've got an armed driver here and I've got to get down close to the gate 'cause I don't want to get shot before the game.''

He bought it and I rolled up in my limo to the locker room.

Part of my pregame ritual was to take a couple of uppers, a Percodan and a Codeine 4. Taking these pills was a routine, like taping my ankles. And I wasn't alone. I would say that around 40 percent of the team would come to me to get a pill or two, or had a supply of their own.

I got into these pills through the Dallas Cowboys.

You've got to understand something about how the game of football is played. It is played in pain. Football players are in constant pain. Your back, your hip, your shoulders, your head and neck. Especially for a linebacker it's your head, neck and shoulders because you're constantly taking on guards, taking on tackles, taking on running backs, hitting people with your head. A linebacker is expected to be a vicious dog, and we can be, but to do it all the time you need something to anesthetize the pain.

You're expected to live with the nagging injuries, the pinched nerves and headaches and back spasms. For anyone who works behind a desk all day these things would send you home in a hurry. For football players they're part of the game plan.

I started learning, when I woke up each morning, to check myself. If, say, my shoulder was inflamed I would go into the trainer's room and he would put an ice pack on it. The doctors would look at my shoulder and say, ''Well, we just have to keep playing.'' They'd tell me, ''Well you know, it won't heal, you're playing every week so it hasn't changed much, has it, Thomas?''

''No, it hasn't changed. I think I have a separation there.'' You get to be an expert on your injuries once you get them.

''Yes,'' they'd say, ''you do have a separation. But you have calcium deposits and over the years you've always been a linebacker.'' They would explain to me the medical reason why I was hurting and then tell me it was something I had to live with. If it just hurt too damn much they would give me an injection of cortisone, which would take the pain away for the day.

When my shoulders were banged up I'd get injections of cortisone and Xylocaine, as well as two codeines, a couple of hours before kickoff. Otherwise I couldn't have played the whole game.

Afterward, when we were on the road, two hours after the final gun sounded, win or lose we'd get on the flight home to Dallas. I'd be wearing a nice three-piece suit but I'd be sitting there on the airplane with my shirt off and a bag of ice wrapped onto my shoulders.

The trainer would walk up and down the aisles and check the wounded, like leaving Vietnam. He would be carrying seven or eight bags of ice that he had prepared for the knees, thighs, hands, wrists, necks—wherever you were hurting. In his other hand he had his arrangement of pills.

He'd have antibiotics for the guys who had gotten cut up and bruised. For the aches and pains he'd have Codeine 3 and Tylenol 3 and Codeine 4. The strength of the pill depended on the nature of your injury. I'd be over there wincing in agony, making faces. I'd look so ugly when he got to me he'd give me two Codeine 4's without question. I'd wash them down with ten or twelve beers and when I got off the plane in Dallas I wouldn't be able to slip my feet into my nice Italian shoes.

It was a common practice. Anybody who was playing regularly was going to be in pain, so there wasn't hardly anybody who couldn't qualify to get a bunch of pills if they wanted them.

The combination of the pills, the cocaine and all my talking really set me up. I get psyched when I know the other team is concentrating on stopping me, and this Rams game was a pleasure.

We came out smoking but the game was tight. I knew they were after me and that was fine. In fact, it backfired on them. The Rams were driving and then got stalled and had to try a field goal. I was on the field goal defense team and I was blocking field goals that year. Got a couple. I was always pretty quick jumping through the gap and getting in front of the kicker, forcing him to look up at me just a little, to lose some concentration. This time they sent a guy to get me.

The Rams had designed a special play where the up back, the man standing between the linemen and the holder, crossed from his side all the way over to mine to try and cut me from behind. It's a cheap shot. A crack-back block can ruin a man's legs, put him out for all times. On their first field goal attempt they ran this guy all the way across the field, in front of Frank Corral, the Rams' kicker, to trap me. I avoided him and he rolled out of the play. Not only did the blocker miss me, he distracted the holder and made Corral miss. I laughed at all of them. I ran all the way to Malavasi's sideline and yelled, "Hey, fatass, you know that's a bad play. You know you're not supposed to do that. I didn't have to rush it, your own guy fucking got in his way!"

The score was nothing-nothing at the half. We were shutting them down. In the second half Charlie Waters made two nice interceptions, Tony Dorsett scored from the five, Scott Laidlaw scored and we were leading 21-0. The Rams were going nowhere.

In the fourth quarter the cameras panned onto me on the sideline with the microphone on. I told the several million viewers, "It's 21-0, the Rams are choking, and I ain't through yet."

I got back out there, under two minutes left in the game. I was covering Jim Jodat, who they called a "fast white boy." He had a pointy nose so I should have figured it. When I was growing up, if a white kid had small ankles and a pointy nose he was fast. Jim Jodat and Golden Richards both fit that.

Jodat was a pretty swift player. He ran an eight- or nine-yard out pattern to my left. I had to protect my inside because if a guy beats you to the inside it's Can You Catch Him? Jodat ran a wonderful route, a route that beat me. But the Rams' quarterback, Vince Ferragamo, held the ball too long. When Jodat made his break to the outside I was still very much to the inside. He had two yards on me. If Ferragamo had thrown the ball on a timing pattern there would've been no way for me to cover it. But he looked to another receiver on the other side of the field and by the time he came to Jodat I had made up the ground.

I could not believe he threw the ball. I was on a dead run into Jodat's route.

I was never known to have great hands. It was very difficult for me to go from a defensive psyche to an offensive psyche. I felt my job was done, and well done, if I knocked the ball down. My coach used to get furious about that. "Why didn't you try to catch it?" "I play defense, knock the son of a bitch down. The offensive guys catch it, I knock the ball down and knock them down."

This ball stuck to my hands. Not a juggle, just *thock,* right in there. I shifted it to my left hand and headed straight down the sideline. For about twenty yards Jodat was in hot pursuit, I could feel him breathing on me. I cut to the inside and saw this big fat lineman. I laughed at him, it was like playing with some big doofus, juked and was gone.

It was a sixty-eight-yard interception return for a touchdown. I'd been in the end zone before and my thing in the end zone was always to slam dunk the ball over the goal post. But my legs were dead. My cocaine use was starting to age me. So in order for me not to be embarrassed—I didn't want to try the slam dunk and get pinned on the crossbar—the grass was soft and I just did a finger roll. The newspapers called it adding "insult to injury."

Right there ABC-TV invited me to be in the SuperStars competition. I wouldn't have to crash the team's contest this year, I was in as an individual. They figured, "Well, the sucker did what he said he was going to do, let's invite him."

I was a phenomenon. It was incredible. I'd made All-American for two years and it hadn't made news. All of a sudden my Mouth of the South routine had made me a national figure. People all over knew who I was. This was hard to believe but I was going for it.

8

Super High Bowl

We had a week in Dallas before we took off for Florida and Super Bowl XIII. We were the defending Super Bowl champions, going to play the Pittsburgh Steelers in the Orange Bowl in Miami. Football was making a real bid to pass baseball and become the true American national pastime and here were the two best teams, peaking.

It's no secret that the Super Bowl is a big hype. In my opinion it is the most overrated game in sports. Lots of teams can win a big game on any given Sunday. The damn thing only lasts sixty minutes. Let them try to do it back-to-back. If the Super Bowl really wanted to determine which team was positively the best they'd get the champions of the NFC and the AFC and let them face off two out of three. Let them play Friday, the following Wednesday and the following Sunday. Three games in a ten-day period. Teams have played a regular game and then one on Thursday, they can do it. Let them get really prepared, then let them have to make the mental and physical adjustments, stay healthy, and fight it out. Make it a series like in baseball or basketball, make the teams really face each other.

That would be my Super Bowl format. But this was theirs and I figured out how to play it.

Terry Bradshaw was the Steelers' quarterback. He was not noted for his intelligence. He had taken a lot of shit for being dumb. I didn't know how dumb he was, I just knew that he and I would be sharing the cover of *Newsweek*. Not him and Staubach or him and Dorsett—Bradshaw and Hollywood. I had caused so much talk with the Turkey Day Massacre and the No-Class Rams stories that now I was the story. They polled the writers covering Super Bowl XIII, asking who, in the entire NFL, would be their first choice to interview. The winner: Me.

I started things off by telling the newspapers that Bradshaw was so dumb he couldn't spell "cat" if you spotted him the "c" and the "a." I told them that I didn't like Steelers linebacker Jack Lambert, " 'cause he don't have no teeth." As for Randy Grossman, who would be starting at tight end because their regular, Bennie Cunningham, had knee problems, "How much respect can you have for a backup tight end? I mean, he's the guy that comes in when everybody else is dead. He's the last hope." They tried to make me say that the Steelers had no class but I wouldn't because they did. They had won two Super Bowls already and they were a good team. I just said ours was better. They were the Steel Curtain. I said I'd bring my acetylene torch to the Orange Bowl and cut them up.

Nobody before me had been such good Super Bowl copy. They'd had to squeeze the things they got out of Joe Namath at Super Bowl III. I put on a show for them and I did it naturally. And even I was shocked by the coverage I got. The normal pregame hype is started by the league and continued by whatever the working press can get out of the players. The teams are set up in separate banquet rooms, each player at his own table, and the reporters are free each day to wander from man to man picking up tidbits, scoring anecdotes to tuck in their columns. They'll encourage a defensive back to snipe at the receiver he's going to be covering and then shuffle over to the receiver in the next room and try and get him to rag on the defensive back. It's all part of the game.

If there were 500 writers in the room, 442 were crowded around my table. They had to set me up my own press conference. Even some of my teammates came in to watch. Drew Pearson, standing on his tiptoes to see over the standing room, called me an overnight sensation. I wasn't about to tell them what I was doing overnight.

At the coaches' press conference the first question they asked the Steelers' Chuck Noll was about me. The first *seven* questions they asked Coach Landry were about me.

And I wasn't making things up. Football players are an arrogant bunch of guys, you've got to be to keep getting belted around and come back for more; you've got to give better than you get or else you don't last long in this league. Some athletes have a lot of couth, they won't go out on a limb and call some team a sorry bunch, some player a fool, some coach incompetent. They think it, they share it in the locker room, but they're not big enough to say it where it can do some damage. If some team wasn't worth a condolence call I had the nuts to come out in public and say, "Hey, they ain't worth a quarter."

After practice one evening that week Roger Staubach told me across the lockers, "You know what, Henderson, you've taken all the pressure off of us. All we have to do is play, **you** have absorbed all the pressure. You have opened your big mouth, Henderson, I love it."

But not all my teammates loved it. I was a part of the team but apart from the team. Preston Pearson said I wasn't a team player. There's a difference between being a team player and being a company man. I said what I thought and I gave everything I had on the field for the Cowboys. But I was no longer interested in practice, I was no longer interested in Bob Breunig and his moral leadership, I was no longer interested in listening to Charlie Waters or anybody. I just wanted to play the game and go do my thing.

This was my third Super Bowl in four years and somehow—maybe it was because I was the center of attention and I had nothing to look up to—it was really no big deal. I was looking for the really good Super Bowl parties.

My friend Joel McQuade lived in Fort Lauderdale and he came and picked me up and drove me to this special cocktail party at the Yacht Club. It was early in the week and all the celebrities I had seen were my teammates.

This party was for high-rollers. O. J. Simpson and I were the only blacks who weren't serving hors d'oeuvres. O. J. introduced me to his Hollywood agent, Jack Gilardi, who told me he had been hearing a lot about me, gave me the once-over, probably seeing what I was worth. As coked up as I was I was still looking good. I told him, "I want to be a star, man. I want to be an actor. I've always been an actor. They think I'm a football player but I'm still an actor." We exchanged phone numbers.

Andy Williams, Mr. Moon River, sang a song. Foster Brooks did his drunk impression. I was sitting with O. J., my friend Joel, Telly Savalas and John Y. Brown, who owned Kentucky Fried Chicken. I don't believe John Y. Brown was governor of Kentucky yet. The man was just rich. Everybody there who wasn't a celebrity, just lounging around with a drink in their hand, was rich or looked rich. Everybody was rich except me. I had money but these people paid sales tax with the money I made.

We were sitting there watching Phyllis George, John Y. Brown's date, play tennis in her shorty outfit with the bloomers showing. You could see the proud look in Brown's eye. I had a feeling he was politically inclined and it was nice to have Miss America on his ticket. But, you know, I'm sure she was fine the night she won Miss America but on this particular day, in the sunlight, live and in color, with my twenty-twenty vision I could see the woman had cellulite on her legs. All the men were talking about how pretty she was and I said, "Yeah, yeah, man, she sure is pretty." I turned to O. J. and whispered, "See that cottage cheese, man?"

* * *

I started the next day the way I started all days, by dealing with my nose. I had brought a little piece of brown Mexican cocaine with me that I'd gotten from Macaroni. It wasn't great stuff but it served its purpose. Every morning now I was going through my ritual. I would run the shower as hot as I could and work up a roomful of steam. Then I would look for something, anything, that I could slide inside my nose to tickle it and try and make me sneeze. I would work at it until my nose bled, the hot water loosening the scabs and easing the pain. I'd sneeze as long as it took to clear it all out. Then I'd stick some more coke up there to anesthetize the sore, then snort some to get me going, then head out into the day.

Another friend of mine, Cliff, picked me up at the hotel that afternoon in his shiny black Maserati. I waded through autograph hounds and the pageantry that never seemed to stop around that lobby and got in. Cliff wheeled me around the town, down streets I didn't know existed, until we got to this real exclusive area on the inland waterway, a little gated villa, and got out in front of this magnificent home. He had a hundred-mile-an-hour speedboat moored out back. Cliff was doing all right.

"You're rolling, man."

We went inside and he said, "You want a toot? I got some of the best shit in the world."

"Sure."

Cliff dumped out about nine grams across the mirror. Just took it and dumped it out of a bag.

"I don't want to die, I just want a toot," I told him. But, tell the truth, that's the way I liked it. I hated coming and putting microscopic lines out in front of me. Let me get down with it.

I just chopped it with an old matchbook cover and took a couple of good whiffs. This shit was excellent! That old brown crap I had back in my room was going to be given away because I had this new supply.

Cliff and I hadn't seen each other for a while and we just sat back and talked. Cliff would send me cocaine through the mails, half ounce, quarter ounce. Sometimes I got crazed and told him to send me an ounce, and the sucker never would charge me for it. He wanted tickets to games, or to meet women when he came to town. I covered his bases for him, he didn't need to make any money off me.

Cliff knew me and he was amazed that I could say all the things I'd been saying and still come out smelling like a rose. "I've been watching your ass on TV," he said. "You're a crazy son of a bitch, man." I was so crazy that I had to step away from these nine grams and go back to the Cowboys' evening meeting that Landry had called.

"Before you go," he said, "let me show you something."

He took me through the living room, back off his master bedroom and opened up a closet door. My heart almost stopped. There, like body bags, were kilo packages of cocaine stacked in two separate rows from the floor to the ceiling.

I was sure that everybody in the United States had a camera on me at that very moment. I have never been so scared in my whole life. They find me in that room and they put me in jail for *two* lifetimes. I thought the DEA, the federal government, the whole Miami crime force was going to bust in and shoot me dead.

I sprinted out of his bedroom, through the kitchen, out the back door. I started to dive into the water but I turned and ran into the street. I ran for two blocks before I had to stop. The coke was always fucking up my respiration. I started to walk. Panting, frightened, I was sure I was busted and everybody was going to know about it.

Cliff pulled up beside me in his Maserati and the window rolled down. "What the hell is wrong with you?"

"Are you a fucking cop?" I didn't stop walking. "What's going on with you? Keys to the ceiling!" I was completely fucking shook.

"Get in."

"You got any dope in your car?"

I couldn't control my laughter. I went into this wild blast as we were driving down the road. "You son of a bitch! You scared me so much! And you know what the bottom line is?"

"What?"

"Will you bring me an ounce over later?"

"Sure."

"You can pick up your tickets then. Drop me off on the corner."

I walked to the beach. I had to be at the team meeting in twenty minutes but I didn't care, I had to settle down. I took my time, walked back across the bridge, got my playbook and strolled into the meeting after Ditka had begun calling the roll. With my escalating schedule of fines that two minutes cost me about two thousand dollars but what the hell, I was in the Super Bowl, take it off the top of the check, asshole.

The stuff Cliff delivered was all rocks. Boulders. The best. "I scooped this off the top for you," he said. When I busted them open it was like glass on the inside, had kind of a yellow-beige tint to it. I immediately went to work.

Cliff had taught me this technique of making liquid cocaine. I took a squeeze bottle, like a Vicks Inhaler or Afrin spray, emptied it, washed it out. Then I dissolved two grams of coke in enough water to make it kind of pasty, like the texture of cream, not too thin. I squeezed the bottle all the way empty and then sucked the cocaine liquid right up into it.

Liquid coke. I didn't have to pick at my scab anymore, I could spray it, soothe it, and get high at the same time. This seemed to me like a godsend.

I gave the two grams I had left of Mexican coke to a teammate. Served two purposes. Made a friend and kept people off my back; when anyone asked for a toot I could say, "Go see whatsisname, I think he has some."

Super Bowl week went on too long. I started actually feeling guilty about the attention I was getting. I loved it but I knew there was something not right if this biggest hype in sports had somehow come to be centered on me. It really was just a game. It wasn't a cock fight, we weren't going to have razors on our feet. If everybody wore swords it would be something different. A game to the death might live up to the expectations. I didn't see how this could. I was glad when game day finally came by.

There's no rule that you have to ride the team bus. This wasn't Langston. Any stadium, any time, anywhere, it's the player's option. I didn't want to. Too Tall asked me if I wanted to ride with him but I said, "No, I'm gonna go by myself."

I had made sure I didn't do too much coke the night before. I'd taken a couple of Quaaludes and gotten a good night's sleep and an early wakeup. I wanted to play well out there.

It was a nice, quiet cab ride to the Orange Bowl that morning. The day was warm, it was too early for a lot of hoopla in the streets. I just kind of breathed and watched Miami go by out the window. I took out my Inhaler, shook it up real good and squirted two humongous shots into my head. I managed to keep from blowing my nose until I got there.

I got to the stadium three hours early. The team was required to be there two hours before kickoff but I wanted to be alone. I went into the john and went through my ritual. I showered till my nose stopped bleeding and then, still blowing it, walked dripping over to my locker, took out my Inhaler, went back to the toilet stalls and serviced both sides.

The place was nice and quiet. I kind of had it to myself for a long time there. D. D. Lewis and John Fitzgerald were there but they weren't saying much. I got my ankles taped and then the players started filtering in. Twos and fours, then tens. In no time at all, it seemed like, the room was filled with the team. But it was funny, it felt like the locker room as usual. For all the hype that everybody on the outside was putting on it, inside there was nothing special about the day. It was almost like a preseason game, a midseason game. It's just not what people think it is in there. I kind of wished it was. The only pressure, it seemed, was coming from outside forces.

And the outside forces were out in force. The press was climbing all over us one last time. The locker room is the hippest spot for hangers-on and people had pulled strings to get them in there. A couple of hours before game time, when all you can do is stretch, worry and think, here are a thousand pairs of eyes and ears and pads and pencils all around you and getting in your face.

There's a lot of pregame superstition in football, lots of guys doing the same thing every time for fear that they will get hurt or not play well. I had my own way of getting ready. I had to get up and check everything, all the parts of me, my vitals. Like a mechanic before the Indy 500 checking the engine, the carburetor, the brakes. I checked my knuckles to see which ones were sore from the last time I played, I would either tape that joint or leave it alone. Usually if I left it alone I hurt it during the game. I had my own little manicure program going. I clipped my toenails and fingernails to make sure I didn't rip one of them off. Being a linebacker and using your hands all the time every time, you find out quick that there is nothing worse than when a finger is hurting. If you ever rip a fingernail off playing football you'll know that you would rather break your leg first.

I had to take my shower at the same time each week, get my ankles taped the same time, take my pills at the same time and in the same order.

Everybody had their thing. Drew Pearson vomited. He had a bleeding ulcer or something wrong with him. The guy would catch a touchdown pass, come back to the sideline and you'd congratulate him and he'd puke on you. I played with him for five years and I never played in a game where he didn't puke. I saw him talking to Landry one time during a game and the coach jumped back. Landry didn't move that fast. Here was this corn and pancakes coming through Drew's face mask.

At kickoff time I felt great. All the pressure was gone. My legs were bouncy, I was strong, quick, fast. My Percodan had kicked in, and my codeine. My nose was okay, the passages were open, I could do what I had to do. I think I could understand how Ali felt when he fought Foreman, or how Michael Spinks felt when he fought Holmes. I knew this was an important performance for me. I remembered what had happened to Fred Williamson in Super Bowl II when he was with the Kansas City Chiefs. The Green Bay Packers came around and made a point of knocking him out. He had been running around all week calling himself "The Hammer." They defeated him in the Super Bowl, they defeated his character, they defeated his football ability, everything in front of everybody. I wasn't going to let that happen to me.

Standing in the tunnel, about to run out on the field, the feeling hit. I had played in Super Bowl X and Super Bowl XII and still the strange uneasiness of the Big Game came over me. Even if on the inside you know how this show operates and you see all the strings being pulled, when you hear the roar of the full stadium and you know that millions of people around the world are glued to the tube watching you, it moves you. There is energy in the air, excitement. And the butterflies, the anxiety, the fear, the whole spectacular game plan hits you at the same time. It was like a cold breeze came up in the Orange Bowl and rolled around my body. I broke out in a cold sweat. Throughout the whole game, most of what I was thinking was, "Thomas, no mistakes. No mistakes."

Too Tall, Charlie Waters and I made the first tackle of the game on a toss play to Franco Harris and from that point on the fear went away and I was in Bradshaw's face all day. The game was completely intense, everybody hitting, the best Super Bowl in history.

Early in the first quarter I was running down the field to cover a punt and the Steelers were letting me run free. I couldn't figure it out but I barreled ahead. After about forty-five yards I had a perfect bead on the return man. He was going to take off to my left and I was headed for him fully prepared to administer some punishment. Out of the corner of my eye I caught a glint of what seemed to be an oncoming vehicle. It was Dirt Winston, a Steeler linebacker and special teams man. He would have killed me.

If I had not seen him and covered up just a little, Winston would have planted his helmet in my ear. I know about that kind of hit. I would have been dead. I raised and took it on the shoulder and tumbled seven or eight yards in a cartwheel. He really got me. When I got to my feet I headed for the wrong sideline.

They had specifically put that play in to hurt me. And they did. But I knew that if I played hard nobody could get me, I'd get them.

Early in the second quarter with the Steelers on about their own forty yard line Landry called a read to blitz; if the back stayed in the backfield to block I was to go on an all-out blitz.

The back stayed in.

Bradshaw was rolling right and I went around the blocker and chased him down. Terry tried to get away but in a couple of steps I was on him, grabbed him. No way he could outrun me. He was trying to cover up, to cradle the ball and go down, but I pinned both his elbows in the middle of his back and shook him, trying to make something happen. Mike Hegman, who was blitzing from the other side, grabbed the ball from Bradshaw—stole it like a kid on the street—and ran thirty-seven yards for the touchdown. Put us ahead for the first time in the game, 14–7.

As I'd predicted, Randy Grossman was the worst tight end I ever played over in my whole life. He had what I would call "route" skills; he could run a decent pass route and had good hands, but as far as blocking me, the man did not have a clue. Franco Harris was going nowhere all day because they weren't opening any holes for him.

In midseason we had picked up an old-time tight end from the St. Louis Cardinals, Jackie Smith. Jay Saldi, one of my running mates and the backup to Billy Joe DuPree, had hurt his knee and was out for the year. As far as I was concerned, Smith, thirty-four years old, was the elderly statesman, but the man was good. I could not believe it when he came on the field for the first time. Trim, six four and a half, 235, red freckles all up and down his arms. He had played against my coach, Jerry Tubbs, and Jerry went to telling me about the time Smith had gone after Jerry but had knocked all of Lee Roy Jordan's teeth out instead.

Smith hadn't been to the Super Bowl in his sixteen years in the NFL but the first time I went up against him in practice I felt like I had put on my uniform and was blindfolded and somebody had put a forklift in front of me. The man had iron hands. I felt like I had gone back two decades of football, like this was a real football player here, not one of these Russ Francis types who did a better job in a bikini than a uniform. The man was hard. He played his half season well for us, caught passes, blocked well on the line. He had done a good job.

Late in the third quarter, with us down 21–14 but the ball on the Pittsburgh ten yard line, Jackie Smith got wide open in the end zone. Wide open. Nobody around him. He was the only one in the movie theater. Staubach saw him—he was impossible to miss!—and feathered a pass at his numbers. Because Smith was so wide open Roger took a little something off the throw, just to make sure it was easy to cradle.

Smith dropped it. It hit right off his chest and fell to the ground. So did he.

The touchdown would have tied the game and turned the momentum all the way around. We settled for a field goal but we were still four points down and had to play catch-up.

I despised Jackie Smith. I went to the sideline after the field goal and hated him. Then I looked at his son, a fourteen-year-old little Smith who looked just like him, red hair and freckles and the whole program, and said to myself, "He must be feeling terrible." I couldn't hate Jackie Smith. I just wished like hell he'd held on to the ball.

I was playing my heart out. There was nothing I could think of to do that I wasn't doing. I pounded Bradshaw, I ran with Franco, I covered ground.

By the third quarter I needed something. NFL uniforms have two little pockets where you can hide stuff, one right behind your knee pads and the other up around your waist. I had tucked my Inhaler in the higher one; I didn't need a little bottle digging into my knees when I hit the ground and I sure as hell didn't want anyone fishing in there if I got an injury.

Everybody knew I had sinus problems, I was carrying around a roll of toilet paper at team meetings and sniffling like I was living in the snow, so it wasn't going to cause any talk if I pulled out my Inhaler and gave myself some drops. I walked to the side while we were on offense and took a couple of deep belts of my liquid cocaine. My nose was getting raw from all the hits on the field and the Miami humidity was making even simple things like breathing pretty hard, so I just wanted to anesthetize it once more, open things up. I took another couple of jolts. I wasn't doing it to get high, I was on full-alert as it was, I just needed to keep the pain off of me. My teammates would have known what I was doing if they'd been watching but they had the Super Bowl to think about. The coaches were out in the cold.

I was in Bradshaw's face again when Harris came over and said something smart to me. I told him, ''Fuck you in your ass, and your mama too.'' That can get on a guy's nerves and Franco went back to the huddle mad as hell.

On the next play we were in a 4–0 defense, the nickel defense where I was the only linebacker on the field along with six defensive backs. It's designed to stop the pass. This was the defense I had been playing all year, where I had to cover the back out of the backfield man to man. I'd been up against Payton and Metcalf and Foreman all year, now it was Harris. I was supposed to mirror him across the line of scrimmage. Third down.

Charlie Waters had priors. Harold Jackson of the Rams had beaten him for four touchdown bombs one Sunday and I think Charlie had a shell-shock problem going in the nickel. He would often ask me to help him by bumping his man before I got to my own. Sometimes I told him to shove it—''You can cover the son of a bitch''—but Charlie knew his stuff, he was the defensive genius out there, and when he ordered me to do it I usually did. Coach Landry didn't know we had this system worked out between us.

Charlie's man on this play was the tight end, Randy Grossman. Charlie told me to hit Grossman, slow him down, and then go find Franco and do my job. I didn't want to, I thought about telling Charlie to fuck off, but I said okay. I could handle it, but in the meantime Charlie was supposed to cover my ass if the Steelers ran a draw play.

Franco Harris had stormed back to the huddle. I like it when a guy gets mad; sometimes he gets reckless. I lined up over the middle of the field to cover him, then moved over so I could get in the pop on Grossman for Charlie. Well, Terry Bradshaw wasn't as dumb as people said. He saw me move, audibled off and called a draw. With me on the outside trying to get in my chuck on Grossman, Franco ran right through us for a twenty-two-yard touchdown.

The Steelers loved it because I had just smarted off to Harris and here he was scoring on me. No one knew that I was doing Charlie Waters' job and that Charlie hadn't covered for me. From the Cowboys sidelines it didn't look like my fault or Charlie's—he had gotten screened by one of the officials and hadn't been able to make the play—but I felt lousy about it, a touchdown had been scored and I hadn't prevented it.

We were getting some extremely bogus calls from the officials. Benny Barnes got whistled for tripping Lynn Swann on a play where Swann actually interfered with him, setting the Steelers up on our twenty-three. They scored two plays later.

With under seven minutes left in the game and down by two touchdowns, a field goal and a point, 35–17, we started to make a charge. Staubach scrambled for eighteen yards, Dorsett ran for twenty-nine, and Billy Joe DuPree caught a seven-yard pass for one score: 35–24. Dennis Thurman recovered Rafael Septien's on-side kick, Drew Pearson got twenty-two on a pass from Roger, and Butch Johnson caught a touchdown pass from the four to pull us to 35–31 with twenty-two seconds left.

I was out there on the on-side kick team, dying for a shot at the ball. I knew if we got a hold of it now we were going to win. No way we weren't scoring on these suckers.

The kick hopped right up for Rocky Bleier. He held on and the game was over.

I sat in front of my locker and cried and cried and cried. I couldn't stop. I felt like I'd given all I had. I'd played hard, done everything I was supposed to do, hadn't made any mistakes, and we had lost. I kept going over in my mind the incidents that cost us the game, the bad calls, Harris' run, the drop, a fumbled kick, and I just kept crying. I wanted that championship ring, the one that said you were the best in the world. We could have played them the next week, or twice more, and we probably would have beaten them. We had a better team than the Pittsburgh Steelers that year but they beat us.

I don't care what anybody says, after an important game every football player goes through the same thing. You don't think about the loss, you think about all the turnovers, fumbles, mistaken routes and blown coverages that were not in the game plan, and ten times out of ten a guy will go, "Well, I didn't make any mistakes." You wouldn't say it purposely, and you definitely wouldn't say it to a reporter, but everybody thinks it: "I played great today." Or, "I sucked."

I played great in the Super Bowl. I had run my mouth all week, been the center of the major spectacle of sports, and when we lost everybody had an open shot at Hollywood. But nobody could take it; I had played too well, tried too hard. I wasn't the buffoon that people had hoped I'd be, I was a hard-nosed football player on a team that had lost.

I felt in some ways that I'd won. I'd won my battle for respect as a player, I had won my position. I was aggressive, tenacious, daring. I could have blurted out, "Hey, go watch the films. If everybody had played like me we would have won." I was thinking it but I didn't say it out loud. It's arrogant, but you've got to be arrogant to be a good football player. I praised the Steelers, said they were the better team that day, that they'd beaten the best team in football and now they were the best. And I cried.

In the back seat of the limousine that was taking me to the first round of post–Super Bowl parties I got into my cocaine. I took some tremendous whiffs. Then I got drunk. I think I drank a whole bottle of Dom Perignon but everything else is a blur. It was my first blackout. More truly a whiteout. The combination of cocaine, alcohol, pain killers, speed and the emotional devastation of playing my heart out and losing all combined to put me under. My eyes didn't close, my actions didn't stop, but my ability to recall what I actually said or did that night—and several nights to follow—just disappeared. When I came to I was back in Dallas. I didn't know I'd had a blackout, I just figured I'd had a good time.

The Pro Bowl was the next Sunday. It was being played in Los Angeles. Might as well go and be Hollywood where it counts. I met with Jack Gilardi at International Creative Management and he took me on as a client. I was up there with O.J.! Ahmad Rashad was on the Pro Bowl squad and he and I hit it off. Ahmad's a classy man and we sat around and talked for a while.

The Pro Bowl is an honor—the players and coaches from each conference choose who makes it, so it's not just a popularity contest, it's an affirmation—but it's also a lot of public relations for the league. There are parties and dinners and a whole show. With it being held in Los Angeles, where I had just called the Rams chokers and had run back my touchdown, I was not loved. When I was introduced the fans really got on me. I got a round of boos, a standing round of boos, a standing boovation.

Dick Butkus had just been elected to the Pro Football Hall of Fame and they were interviewing him on a pregame show with all of us there on the sidelines. When they'd asked me about Butkus I'd told them exactly what I thought: Butkus was a lineman standing up. He was a hell of a hitter and a great player, but he didn't have the moves, he couldn't cover a back or get back quickly into a zone. I gave him credit: He was a mean son of a bitch and if you were looking for someone who would run over you and control the middle of the field and beat up on everyone around him, Butkus was your man. He was a dominator, a monster in the middle at a time in football when you needed a monster in the middle. The best of his time.

They asked Butkus what he thought of today's linebackers. He said, "I think the best linebackers in football now are Thomas Henderson, Bill Bergey and Brad Van Pelt."

My ears were burning. Swear to God I almost fainted. It was the best compliment I'd ever had in my life. Nobody, not Landry or anybody else, had ever said anything like that to me, that I was one of the greatest linebackers in all of football. And coming from Butkus! I knew then that I had arrived.

The day of the Pro Bowl game I stepped out of my limousine in my full-length beaver coat and there in front of me, wearing a Rams' cheerleader's uniform under a red fox coat that must have cost ten grand, was one of the most beautiful women I'd ever seen. I winked at her and then chased her down to the Rams' trailer. She ran in the door, then peeked back out and all the cheerleaders were buzzing. "My name's Hollywood," I said. "Who's that little girl just went in there?"

"Oh, you mean Patty?"

"Yeah, Patty. You tell Patty to meet me after the game."

"What do you mean?"

"Tell her to meet me after the game, she's going with me." I was joking and they were laughing with me.

I had some fun at the Pro Bowl. There's none of that do-or-die feeling of the regular season or the Super Bowl, it's just the guys doing what they do best. Roger Staubach was on the sidelines rooting for me as I ran down the field on the specialty teams and I was pulling for him on offense. Roger is a warrior, he doesn't like to lose. We won.

In the tunnel after the game I saw the girl in the red fox coat standing in a corner. "Hey," I called to her, "you coming with me or not?" It's amazing what complete arrogance can do. She ran right over and jumped in my limousine. She still had her cheerleader uniform on. I wouldn't let her take it off all night. She slept in it, **or** at least parts of it.

Next stop, the SuperStars competition. That year it was held in Freeport, the Bahamas. I packed for the festivities and carried it on with me: a half ounce of cocaine, an ounce of incredible Thai sticks and about thirty Quaaludes, each different high in its own plastic baggie. I was a Cowboy on the field and off. Got off the plane dressed in my cowboy hat, cowboy boots, jeans and a big old cowboy belt buckle, waving to the fans. I was getting recognized all over by now, people shouting "Hollywood!" and asking for autographs. It was amazing how the magic of that name started to really make me go into instant character, instant antics when anyone called it.

I'd been on the airplane taking a toot here and there so when I got to customs I was loose. When they asked for my shoulder bag I gave it to them without hesitation. Then I realized what I'd done. "Oh, my God," I said to myself. "I'm busted. This is it, I'm going to jail, my life is over." I was traveling with my friend and former teammate, Percy Howard. Percy liked me a lot but he put about thirty feet between us.

This jet-black gentleman, obviously 150 percent Bahamian, was the customs agent and he was pawing through the bag like a pro. He opened the sides and slid his fingers down where I would have been hiding stuff if I'd been hiding it. The baggies were sitting out in the middle of my satchel like letters from home. He looked at them. I saw him run his fingers over the packages. I looked him in the eyes.

"Hollywood," he said in his British Bahamian lilt, "have a good time. I see you have brought everything you might need."

I'm a star! They don't bust stars! I was invulnerable.

Back in Dallas I was starting to scare my friends. James Suite I think I always scared, Jeff Cohen was more and more worried about me, and I began to give Philip a hard time. I was on the cocaine train and it had left the station. I was running to Philip's house three and four times a day to buy grams. I'd call him at four in the morning and if he told me he was tired or asleep or didn't have any or was busy I'd say, "Look, motherfucker, you can either sell me a gram or you can sell the police the whole bag 'cause I'm going to call the fucking cops if you don't sell me some cocaine." When I said it once it became a habit. And people believed me, they knew my desperation, they knew I was tweaked, they knew I was sprung, they knew I was in trouble and that it was just a matter of time before something happened.

I didn't have any friends. I knew that Too Tall had friends.

He had an old guy named Sid and his wife, and a guy named Kermit Cane who worked for Exxon, and Dr. Drummond and Dr. Washington were his friends. He often went to their houses for dinner, they went on dinner dates together to restaurants and such. All my friendships were drug-related. All my friendships were What You Could Do for Me. I had no sit-down, let's-talk-and-watch-a-football-game friends. It was my family, my coke connections and my women. I was not capable of being a friend because my motives were not clear. I wanted to party and if a girl wanted to be my friend we had to screw first.

I'm not real proud of this but it's the truth. In my five years in Dallas I must have had affairs with over a thousand women, from one-night stands to three-day romances to four or five women a night at the orgies. That's just the way it was being a football player in Dallas, Texas. The only man I know to have had more women than me was Too Tall Jones, he was the king of that program.

My spiritual base was zero. I felt godlike, I felt rich, I felt untouchable. My experience at the Bahamas airport had put me on a new plateau: You don't mess with guys like me, I'm too famous. I was on top of the world, I'd been in three Super Bowls, I was the best in my profession, I had climbed the mountain—but I was all alone. I hadn't dug any footholds, hadn't built any platforms on the way up.

All my friends were white. I just never wanted to go back to where I had come from. I preferred the intelligence of white culture. I knew all about hip, slick and cool, the rhythms and struggles of my people. I knew about black pride but I felt that anyone who claimed that he'd been blocked by racism was just a poor soul himself. Immigrants had come to this country from everywhere and done very well; I was born here; there was no excuse. I just had to get out of my community because I thought it was killing me.

I didn't have any friends and I started to act like I was bigtime. People felt that I was unreachable and no one tried to reach me. I was busy. When I was awake, doing cocaine all night, most people with any normality to them were sleeping with their families.

I'd call some doctor I knew and say, "Hey, Doc, let's go and have lunch." A friendly thing to do. But I had a motive, I wanted to get sixty Quaaludes out of him. And I would get them. There was a time when I could talk a hungry cat off a fish truck.

I used friendships and nobody ever called me on it. I smiled through gritted teeth, looking at people as they were watching me work them. And they would let me work them. I always felt good about the conquest, and the fact that I could do it again and again. But there was still something very empty about it. I'd leave them high and dry and the next time they saw me it wasn't to say, "Hey, let's go have a drink at happy hour," or, "What are you doing tonight?" or "Let's go shoot some pool." It was during office hours, during pharmaceutical hours. The bottom line was that with no spiritual base, with no serious values, I was lost. I was out of control.

9

Tom Landry and the "Terrible Towel"

Wyetta wanted to have our baby on my birthday. She only missed by a couple of days. I turned twenty-six on March 1, 1979, and six days later I took Wyetta to Baylor Hospital.

At the height of my career, with a million people in Dallas and everybody knowing I had a baby coming, I didn't have anybody there to say, "Hey, man, I'm going to keep the vigil with you and see how you're doing. I'm going to take you to the hospital and hang out with you and get drunk with you, help you buy some cigars." I didn't have that. Success had built a wall around me that I didn't want; all that people had to do was come into it, but nobody dared.

Too Tall wouldn't come with me. A friend of mine from Oklahoma City, Roosevelt Turner, happened to be in town and called that night. I said, "Man, look, I'm about to have a kid tonight. Can you take me and my woman over to the hospital and stay with me?" He said sure.

I took several shots of moonshine and brought along enough cocaine to last me the night. At first nothing was happening. I said, "This is gonna be a long wait," and Roosevelt left. I started cruising the hospital, made just about every rest room on every floor, doing my Standard operating procedure. Finally I settled back in the labor room at about 9:00 that night.

It was a wonderful hospital but the room was a little pillbox with a concrete floor. There was a bed only, not a chair in sight. I hadn't taken any Lamaze training or anything like that so a nurse came in and said, "Let me show you a couple of things." She showed me how to rub Wyetta's back and get her to breathe properly when she went through her contractions. They shaved Wyetta and I started joking with her— "You're bald!"—to try and keep her in good spirits. I was doing my best.

The wait seemed endless. We were there seven or eight hours. I took a pillow off the bed and lay down on the floor. I was on the floor in the labor room with my kid on the way, I put the pillow under my chest and I was making lines of cocaine on the concrete. I made them long. A fifteen-inch line of cocaine. I had a credit card that I was chopping the stuff with and I was lying there messing with it. Then I rolled up a hundred-dollar bill and snorted halfway down the line with one side of my nose, then went to the other nostril and sniffed the rest of it up real good.

Wyetta was in labor a long time, hurting and really hollering. I rubbed her back and said everything was going to be okay, tried to tell her jokes. I had a face that used to make her laugh. We'd been at home watching a Jerry Lewis movie and he had this look like, "Please don't hit me!" where his lips went up and his nose flared. I could do that face—Wyetta said I looked like a monkey—and no matter where we were she'd bust out laughing. I swung around the bed and, with my skull frozen from cocaine, did my monkey face for her. A smile came across but she was in too much pain to laugh.

Finally it came time. The doctor told me, "Mr. Henderson, I would like you to come into the delivery room and watch the delivery." They took Wyetta away and prepped her while they put me in a hospital gown and gloves. About twenty minutes later the doctor came out and told me, "We have a problem."

"What's happening? What problem?"

"I'm afraid we're going to have to do a C section."

"Now wait a minute," I bellowed. "What do you mean you have to cut her? You are not going to go butchering up my woman."

"Then you are going to lose both of them, Mr. Henderson."

I had to make a decision in a hurry. I stood there for a moment and then said, "Let me tell you one damn thing. If anything goes wrong, don't you bring your ass out of that room; you better cut your own throat in there."

They wouldn't let me in the operating room. "You are too high-strung right now," is what they told me. "You're not ready for the blood of surgery." I said, "Man, I've done saw people dead in the street, don't tell me about blood." He looked at me as if to say, "I know you're loaded, son," and would not let me in.

Wyetta gave birth to a beautiful seven-pound, six-ounce baby girl. I held her in my hands moments after she was born. They had barely washed her and I was standing at the door when they walked out and gave her to me. I held the life of my child in my hands. This human person that was part of me. It was the most beautiful moment in my life. I said to myself, "I don't need any friends, I have a baby girl. She'll be my friend no matter what." I broke down and cried. The nurse had to take the baby away from me.

I realized at that moment that I didn't have any friends. One had to be born that would understand me. She was the only person who was ever going to really love me, the only person who was going to be my true friend.

I named my daughter Thomesa Holly Henderson. Wyetta didn't argue at all, she was very happy with that.

Roosevelt was back and taking pictures of me and the kid. I couldn't get enough of looking at her. I called my mother and my grandmother, my sisters and brothers to let them know that I had a healthy young baby girl. March 8, 1979, was the proudest day of my life.

Drew Pearson, who had started out as a free agent and worked his way up to a $175,000-a-year salary, lived in a very attractive house he had bought from a developer. I liked Drew and respected him. He was a feisty character with chicken legs but he had a big heart, he would catch the pass over the middle where a lot of other guys would worry about getting popped. I was welcomed at his home and I was over there quite a lot. He didn't do cocaine, which shocked me.

I liked his house so much that I wanted one too. Drew's developer sold me one in Roger Staubach's neighborhood. I finally had my beautiful home.

Jack Gilardi called in June to tell me that 7-Up wanted me to do a commercial. In New York. The baby was three months old so I took her and Wyetta with me. I also took a half ounce of cocaine; it would be a week's work.

It was me and Frank Gifford and Earl Campbell and Pat Hayden doing some in-house promotional films before the actual filming of the spot itself. I found out quickly that the cameras were a snap. The cue cards were easy, the lights didn't bother me, when they said "Action" I got into gear.

I also found the parties in New York. Drank whole bottles of Dom Perignon, was invited to do some Quaaludes in the notorious basement of Studio 54 but went and did my own cocaine instead. I was expecting a little private room down there, at least a carpet and a couple of couches, a mirror, some razor blades. The place was a dump, barrels lying around, just a private place to do terrible things.

We limoed from a Studio 54 all-nighter to Veterans Stadium in Philadelphia for a 9:30 A.M. shoot. On the way down I lay down on the floor, been drinking all night, wasted, my nose hurting, and kept sticking my finger in my coke bag and then ramming it back up my nose.

At the stadium I stepped out and everyone was shouting "Hollywood! *Da da da da da* Hollywood!" They had to carry me from the car to the showers to straighten me up. Then I had to go through my bloody shower ritual. It took forty takes to get the shots right. I felt like Elvis.

The commercial was a big success. I couldn't go anywhere without seeing myself on the tube or plastered all over a print ad or a billboard. I was Hollywood and Hollywood was a state of mind.

I pulled into the Thousand Oaks Cowboy training camp that July in a stretch limousine. I had picked up some more coke and a couple of bottles of Dom Perignon for the ride down and I fully intended to do them. I told Benny, my driver, to jump the curb and pull the car right out onto the running track that circled the field. Over the years we'd had all kinds of Rolls-Royces come out to camp and nobody bothered them so I knew no one was going to check our ID. I just sat there behind the smoked glass for an hour and a half and did my cocaine.

Finally I instructed Benny to open the limo door and in my sunglasses, my cowboy hat, my short-sleeve shirt, shorts and cowboy boots that ran halfway up my legs, I stepped on out.

Dennis Thurman, a second-year cornerback out of USC, just about fell on the ground. "I told you it was him!" he was cackling. TV camera crews were rushing toward me, the guys with the batteries chasing behind. I walked right up to Landry and stuck out my hand. I must have reeked of alcohol and probably had stuff hanging out my nose.

"Hey, Coach!"

Landry looked at me. "Thomas, Thomas, Thomas," he sighed. It seemed like he was carrying a 150-pound dumbbell, because it was a struggle for him to get his hand up to shake mine.

"I'm just kind of cruising around here," I told him, "being Hollywood, doing my thing. You know how I am." He didn't speak. "When I get to camp I need to speak to you," I told him.

"Yes, we need to have a meeting, Thomas. We definitely need to have a meeting."

The veterans had to be in camp by noon, or seven o'clock, I can't remember. I knew the rules and I knew how to work the rules, I knew the rules that worked. Five minutes before deadline I strolled in. Landry greeted me. "Glad to have you with us, Thomas. You're five minutes early."

The next morning we had our meeting. I hadn't slept in three nights so I got a good night's sleep, got up, took a shower, went to breakfast and then walked over to his office.

We talked for an hour and a half. I started off by telling him that I was underpaid, that I was only going to make $90,000 that year and that I was the hardest-working man on the team. "I play kickoff," I told him, "I play kickoff return. Punt. Punt return. I'm on the regular defense, I'm on the special defense, the nickel defense. I cover backs man to man out of the backfield, I rush field goal kickers and play field goal defense. I work hard, Coach, and I want to be paid for it."

I told him I wanted $250,000 a year salary.

"Roger doesn't make that much," Landry said. "You have to talk to Tex and Gil on that, Thomas, because I don't deal in the negotiations of contracts. But in my opinion you're making too much already.

"Let me tell you what's going on here," he continued. "For the past couple of years, Thomas, you have gotten away with a lot of things. You've played some excellent football for me. You're a good linebacker, one of the best I've ever had. But last year you came to camp with hepatitis, then you hurt your ankle, you were out, you didn't get to practice much last year. You played well, you made the Pro Bowl, but I can't have you missing practices anymore. Not for colds, not for headaches, not for any reason.

"I'll make a deal with you. Here's the deal: If you miss any practices during the season, you do not start that week."

"Does that rule go for the whole team?" I asked him.

"No. Just for you."

"Why are you making up a certain set of rules for me?"

"For the last couple years, I'm telling you, Thomas, you've caused a lot of trouble with the staff here. You've talked bad to Don Cochren and Ken Locker, our trainers, you've used foul language, you've threatened them, you've belittled them." It was true, but only because they didn't believe me when I told them I was hurting. "You take off when they tell you not to. You've missed a lot and I'm not going to have you miss any more."

I said, "Okay, fine. It's your team, you're running it, but I don't think it's right to give me a certain set of rules and have everybody else live under something different. But I'll tell you what I'll do, Coach, I'll do the best I can."

I left that meeting and ran right into Gil Brandt's office and said, "Look, man, I want my contract renegotiated or I want to be traded." I walked out of his office and walked down to Tex Schramm's. "Tex, I want a new contract or I want to be traded." Walked out and went back to my dorm.

Too Tall Jones had retired to pursue a boxing career. He had told me he was going to do it but I didn't believe him, figured it was just a negotiating ploy, he'd show up in camp. When he didn't I knew that Charlie Waters and I were going to have to tighten our jocks because he wouldn't be there in front of us to intimidate opponents and slow them down. I also knew that I had no one to talk to.

I started out training camp with a boom. I was hitting hard, embarrassing rookies if they didn't come in with some strength. Some players were always talking football, discussing plays and structure. My football started when I put on my shoulder pads, other than that I didn't want to talk about it.

Ron Springs, a big rookie running back from Ohio State, embarrassed me in the chow hall. The rookies traditionally had to sing for their chow; I'd had to do it and so had all the other members of the Cowboy team. When I told Springs, "Sing," he said, "I ain't singin' nothin'."

The whole damn cafeteria laughed at me.

At the team meeting that night I told the team, "You know, y'all all laughed at me when Ron Springs disrespected me."

The guys started laughing again.

"It was funny. He didn't have to sing," I told them, "but

he disrespected all our traditions, he disrespected everything. He's a rookie, he not only disrespected me he disrespected all you assholes." I sat down.

For the next week in training camp Ron Springs had hell. Every time we had a drill with the backs, I drilled him. Whenever we had scrimmage with the backs and there was no contact, I hit him. Whenever there was a blocking drill I ran over him. Harvey Martin started to hit him. Larry Cole hit him. Bob Breunig hit him. Cliff Harris hit him. Everybody started taking their shots.

Springs came into the chow hall a week later and started singing. The whole team started to laugh. He walked over to my table and said, "Henderson, will you call them off?"

Ron Springs made the team.

I woke up in my training camp bed about three in the morning and my left arm was dead, my chest was burning, my heart was beating hard. I couldn't belch, I couldn't move, I felt like I was about to strangle. I had done some coke that night but I'd taken some Quaaludes to let me go to sleep.

I stumbled out of bed grabbing my chest and struggled across the parking lot to the trainer's dorm room, banged on the door.

"I'm dying . . ."

They woke the doctor up and he checked me. "Your heart is okay right now. We'll check you out in the morning."

We were going to Seattle to play a preseason game against the Seahawks the next day and my chest felt like it was about to explode. The doctor checked me again and the trainer said, "You're going with us. The doctor said you are okay."

"I am *not* okay. I am *not* going to Seattle. I am going to the hospital with or without your help!"

Everybody was preparing to get on the bus but I stood in front of the dorm holding my chest. When Landry came out I said, "I need to talk to you!" He stopped and looked at me.

"My chest is hurting. I think I had a fucking heart attack. I've got to go to a hospital!"

Landry turned around and walked back into the building and said a few words to Dan Werner, the administrative assistant. When he walked past me on his way back out the coach said, "You'll get taken care of, Thomas. They're going to take you to Dallas."

The Cowboys were leaving nothing to chance. When I got in from California two representatives met me at the Dallas airport and drove me straight to the hospital. I was feeling a little better by then. The doctors put me in a private room and were going to examine me the next morning. That night I slipped out and went to see a girl I knew, did some coke, slipped back in before dawn.

The pain blew up again and I pushed the panic button. Nurse rushed in. "I'm having a heart attack!" They went nuts with the needles and tubes until they got me stable. Then they examined me.

"Mr. Henderson," they told me, "you have a hiatal hernia." They explained that the flap over my esophagus wasn't opening properly and pressures and gases build until, yes, it feels like you're having a heart attack.

I didn't tell them but I think I had frozen my esophagus flap with all the cocaine.

They were concerned for me when I got back to Thousand Oaks two days later. The surgery for a hiatal hernia involves cutting you from the middle of your throat all the way round to the middle of your back. I hoped I wouldn't have to have it. Tough to be a linebacker with that kind of a zipper.

When the doctors reported back to him Landry finally believed I wasn't fooling around. They stacked bricks under the head of my bed so I would be sleeping on a vertical angle; I was slipping out the bottom of the sheets but I was getting better. Slacking off on the cocaine also helped my condition. I went back to practice.

Every year in preseason the Cowboys play the Houston Oilers for the bragging rights to Texas. The Oilers' main man, in his second year, was Earl Campbell. He had run over a lot of people when he was playing at the University of Texas in the Southwest Conference and now he was running over them in the pros. The man was a hog. He was huge in the hips and thighs, brutally strong, not a lot of finesse, just pure power and the will to use it.

Landry had put me in on the goal line defense at the middle linebacker position because of my tenacity, the way I liked to hit. Some linebackers hit with their shoulders, which is a safe and conventional way to tackle. I tended to want to put my hat on people, to put my size-eight helmet into them and knock them down.

The Oilers were driving. They got down to the four yard line and it was goal line defense time. They lined up, barked their signals and snapped the ball. Earl Campbell took a pitch to the outside and headed toward the end zone. The outside linebacker was cut down by a blocker and there was nobody out there except me and Earl.

I had to make a decision. It's only a fraction of a second you have to make up your mind, but you do make clear-cut decisions on the playing field. It's never going too fast to think. I thought, "Well, I can trip. If I wanted to avoid all this I could fall down and say my feet got tangled going for him. Or I can try and tackle him, just get my arms around him and hope for the best. Or I can knock the fuck out of him. Okay, I'll knock the fuck out of him. I'm not going to let him embarrass me, it's too wide open to do anything but go after his ass."

I hit Earl Campbell right in the face with my helmet. Most guys it would have stopped cold, driven them into the ground. Not Earl. Campbell didn't run over me and I didn't knock him back. He was headed north, I was headed south, and we both ended up going west till we went out of bounds. He didn't get his touchdown. At least not on that play. That whole year I think it was only me and Jack Tatum of the Raiders who stopped Earl Campbell one on one in the open field and I was proud of it.

When the season started I was ready to go. I was still angry about my contract. But I knew that after this year they were going to have to pay me and they were going to have to pay me big. I didn't have an agent. I didn't need a 10-percenter like Abner Haynes, and I figured I was in charge and could handle it. I didn't have any of the information that an agent would have, like comparative salaries or industry standards, all I had was the knowledge that I was working harder than I was given credit for and getting paid less than I deserved.

Brandt told me I was making more than most linebackers. He threatened me, dared me, to take Jack Lambert's contract. Made me feel like if I took it I was going to lose money. Lambert was a star linebacker with the Pittsburgh Steelers and Brandt kept saying, "Do you want Jack Lambert's contract? You really want that contract? I'll draw it up. You really want that contract?" I didn't have any idea what Jack Lambert made and since Brandt seemed very anxious to give it to me I said, "No, I don't think so." Turns out Lambert was making a lot more than I was and I should have taken it. He faked me out. Gil Brandt is a damn good general manager . . . if you call screwing people a good job.

Wyetta slapped me with a paternity suit. She told me, "Somebody came and told me my child is illegitimate." I said, "I don't know who the hell told you that. Illegitimate? I don't understand that law. Because I'm not married to you? I support Thomesa, gave her my name, made her the beneficiary on my NFL insurance policy. Of course she's legitimate."

I thought the suit was funny. When the reporters asked me about it I told them I'd never denied that it was my child, I'd given her my name. Wyetta hired a lawyer and I spoke with him. I was prepared to support the child, I loved the child, what did Wyetta want? Her attorney told me they wanted half of everything I had and half of everything I was going to get for the next five or six years. That included my new home, whatever money I was going to get on my next contract, commercial work, all of it. I told him he was out of his mind. I said, "Seriously. Let's talk serious here." He said, "I am serious, Mr. Henderson."

We had a hearing in midseason and it appeared to me that

they had the judge wrapped up. He appointed an attorney as my daughter's guardian. They took away my daughter.

My attorney was Charles Caperton. He had represented Waylon Jennings and had been the attorney in Rayfield Wright's divorce. Charlie was my friend but he told me his fees would run around twenty-five thousand dollars. After meeting with him, and his explaining the court proceedings and custody and the odds against the court siding with the father in a case like this, I said, "You know what? I'll just marry her. Whenever I get ready I'll marry her."

I went to Wyetta and told her I wanted her to drop the suit, that I was willing to marry her, though we didn't set a date. Before she dropped it, though, we had to appear in court. She got up on the stand to say that she was abandoning the case. Her attorney, who stood to lose a whole lot in legal fees, publicity and referrals, asked her on the stand, Are you sure Mr. Henderson didn't threaten you or do you bodily harm? She said I hadn't, that she was dropping the case. It looked like I was getting married.

I wasn't in Coach Landry's real good graces when we opened up the 1979 season. Still, I was a starter. Third year in a row. And once you win a starting position with Landry and the Dallas Cowboys you remain there. They are constantly reevaluating players, but once the decision gets made at the end of training camp you really have to fuck up to lose your spot. I was a Pro Bowler now and I meant to keep on being one.

We opened against the St. Louis Cardinals and I had to go up against Terry Metcalf again. That was never fun. A friend of mine, J. V. Cain, was the Cardinals' tight end. If J.V. got the best of me I'd hear about it for the rest of my life so we had to tussle and struggle out there.

I took to talking to myself between plays that year. I was running my own audibles, just a little on-field commentating. I was always the guy who was late for the huddle. I'd look up from a play and these guys were already huddling up. "Hey, man, the play was over here. How'd you get back there so fast?" Every game, Charlie Waters or Bob Breunig and I would get into an argument. They'd be going, "Thomas, get in the huddle," and I'd call over, "Oh, fuck the huddle. I know what you're going to call. What are you doing this for, TV?"

I'd be out there on the weak side going, "Oh, this is a tough goddamn life. I knew that sucker was coming around here. Yeah. He's going to try and run it over here again." I was dissecting their game plan out loud.

That first game against the Cardinals I came to the line of scrimmage on a punt rush and looked into the face of the guy across from me. He was a new guy on their special teams unit, someone I hadn't seen before. I looked into his face and I looked into his eyes and, man, he was ugly. One of these guys, you look at him and he'd say, "Okay, I know I'm ugly." I was surprised. Even on the football field you don't normally get guys that look like gargoyles. I looked at him and said real loud, almost a moan, "Oooooh oooooh! Boy, you are an ugly motherfucker! I bet if I followed you home somebody ugly would open the door!"

The whole field busted up laughing. Chuckling and jiggling along the line of scrimmage. His teammates too.

Along with their great receivers and ace quarterback the Cardinals had an excellent offensive line. In my opinion it was the best in all of football: Dan Dierdorf, Tom Banks, Bob Young and Conrad Dobler. Dobler was the meanest motherfucker out there. He'd stomp on your crotch and spit at you. I can't imagine anybody meaner except Ray Nitschke when he was drunk.

Ed Jones had a lot of respect for the Cardinals' line. After one game in St. Louis he and I were coming out of the locker room and turning into the corridor to go to the bus when I said, "Hey, Too Tall, there's Dan Dierdorf." Too Tall looked at me. "No," he said, "that's Mr. Dierdorf."

We beat the Cardinals in St. Louis 22–21, to open the season, then beat the 49ers and the Bears. I was handing out some serious hits. Against Cleveland I really laid one on their quarterback, Brian Sipe. Quarterbacks have to be able to take a lot of pounding, it comes with the territory. If they're not going to stand in there and take what's coming at them they're not going to hit their receivers and they're not going to stick around long. Some guys pride themselves on standing up under it. I really smacked Sipe and he pulled himself up off the turf and gave me one of those, "Can't you do any better?" quips. That's the quarterback's only answer. That and a touchdown pass. A friend of mine visited with Sipe after the game and Sipe told him, "That guy Henderson almost killed me."

One time we were playing the New Orleans Saints and I blitzed Archie Manning. I motored right through, really popped him. Archie dragged himself to a standing position, looking at me cross-eyed, delirious—he'd suffered a concussion right then and there—and said, "Is that the best you've got?"

I had the opportunity to hit Joe Namath once in my career. Couldn't do it. The man was my idol. He was playing for the Rams and was wearing two huge braces, one on each knee. He looked like one of Jerry's kids. I backed off.

We played Cincinnati and Archie Griffin, the two-time Heisman Trophy winner, caught a swing pass against me for four yards on the nickel defense. I was mad at myself because I read the play the whole way but still didn't get there to stop him for no gain. Later, in the second half, they ran the same play. This time I was ready for it. As he caught the ball and turned to run I hit Archie Griffin so hard I knocked the Heisman Trophy off his dresser at home.

We won seven of our first eight games and were on our way to another playoff season. There was no question in my mind that the Cowboys would be in the NFC Championship Game against whoever met us there and we would be going back to the Super Bowl.

It was cold in Dallas the day we beat the Cardinals for the second time that season, 22–13, and I had caught a little bug. I had been a good boy all year, had gone to work every day, and Don Cochren told me to get healthy and take a day off.

The day before our next game, a rematch of the Super Bowl against the Pittsburgh Steelers, I was sitting in the dining room of our hotel in Pittsburgh having a good time talking to Guy Brown about defenses. Mike Hegman was injured and so if anything happened to me that day Brown was the guy who would play. I was sitting there with D. D. Lewis and Hegman and Bob Breunig, telling Brown about specific defenses and certain situations that might come up—"This is what you do," and "Listen to Charlie"—and Landry casually walked over to our table and sat down between me and Guy. He looked me straight in the eye.

"You know what our deal is."

I didn't know what the hell he was talking about.

"Guy is going to start tomorrow."

Landry looked around at all of us, got up and went back to the coaches' table.

I started to boiling, fuming. My stomach was jumping like I was going to be sick. I looked at Bob and said slowly, "Breunig, he can't do it to me no more. No fucking more. Not tonight, not tomorrow, not ever again. I'm not scared of that bald-headed son of a bitch, fucking God on earth."

I walked over to Tom Landry's table, came up behind him and tapped him on the shoulder like a cowboy in a saloon. He looked around at me. The coaching staff sitting around with him all stopped and looked at me. I said "Coach, if I don't start tomorrow I ain't playing. Now you deal with that." I walked out of the dining hall.

About a half hour later Bob Breunig knocked on my door. "Thomas, I just had a talk with Coach. He said if you ever do that again he's going to get rid of you."

"Bob, he can do whatever the fuck he wants."

"Settle down, man. You and Landry have been going at it for a while now, but for you to front him off in front of the coaching staff . . ."

"He fronted me off in front of you guys, what's the difference? This is his team, sure, but goddamn, he comes over and disrespects me and is going to start a fucking rookie in this game just to fucking punish me for missing practice on a deal he made with me that doesn't apply to the whole team? And I had the doctor's permission! It's not right, Bob.''

"I know it's not right, but Thomas, don't front him off in front of the coaches.''

I wasn't budging. This was the Steelers. A rematch of last year's Super Bowl. This man was trying to break me and I wouldn't be broken.

I reported to Three Rivers Stadium, went to the locker room, took off all my clothes and put on a jock, a pair of socks and a T-shirt. I didn't get my ankles taped, nothing. I sat in front of my locker, I was not going to go on that field.

Ninety minutes before kickoff Landry walked over to my locker and stood in front of me. "Thomas," he said, "you win this time. You can go ahead and start today. I talked to Don Cochren and he said you did have a fever and that's why you missed a day's practice this week." What did I need, a note from my mother?

We lost that game 14–3. Nobody on either side did anything spectacular, myself included.

All the following week I felt like something was boiling and bubbling in Landry and everybody else. The coaching staff quit talking to me because I was foul-mouthed. Mike Ditka, though, who would probably argue with Satan, said to me, "Buffalo sure is cold in the winter." He was telling me that I was getting traded.

We beat the Giants, then Philadelphia beat us on Monday night. The next game was in Washington. I was sick again, full of flu phlegm and cocaine, I didn't know which was making my nose run and my eyes water more. I had the full bug this time, I was weak.

The Redskins were up for us. I had called them turkeys the year before and it was the first time I had seen them since. It was not a good game. I was overpowered, I got used by the tight end. I couldn't make any moves, he was all over me. I don't think I made a single tackle the entire game.

Preston Pearson had designed this "Terrible Towel" with Cowboy stars and stripes on it that he was trying to get placed in all the 7–11's and sports stores around the country. We had sat next to each other on the airplane going to Washington and he had given me one. He knew how I was with cameras on the sidelines; the crews always came to me and the red light would go on. He said, "Listen, if you get some air time. . . ." I said sure.

During the second half I picked the towel up and waved it in front of the lens and said, "Cowboys Number One!" No big deal.

Up in the press box my coach, Jerry Tubbs, saw it. We were losing and we finally lost the game 34–20 and he objected.

In the locker room afterwards I didn't feel I'd done anything wrong. I was thinking about how I had gotten pushed around out there and how I didn't like to get my ass kicked and I didn't like to lose. I had forgotten all about waving at the camera; I'd done that all the time. I hadn't done anything intentionally malicious, hell, I wasn't getting anything out of that towel, it was Preston's.

Coach Tubbs approached me and I had never seen him this mad. "What are you doing on the sidelines mugging for the camera when we're losing the game?" Real fast and agitated. "You know what, Thomas, if I was the coach I'd cut you today. I swear to God I would. I can't believe you and how inconsiderate you are of this team!" He rushed on and on.

I stopped him.

"Get out of my motherfucking face, punk." The speed and coke and pain-killers were swirling around in me. "Get your ass back over where all them other punks are. Fuck you! I can do whatever the fuck I want. When the camera comes on I can do what the fuck I want. You can't tell me what to do, I'm a grown fucking man!"

The whole locker room turned to look at our gunplay.

"Get the fuck away from me!" I made a move like I was going to bust him over the head with the helmet that was in my hand.

He walked away.

Jerry was a good man. I knew right then it was over but I didn't quit there. I got in the shower and called everybody out. "Fuck all of you punks!" I shouted. It echoed around the tiles. "All of you hen-pecked, kiss-ass motherfuckers around this fucking franchise! Ain't none of you got no fucking balls. Those fuckers say 'Jump,' your ass comes a mile high. They say, 'Go to church,' you all pile in there. All of you doing drugs before the goddamn games. All you married assholes out trying to fuck cheerleaders and every little bitch you can catch on the road and you look at me and judge me, you punks. I see all you fuckers!"

I started taking everybody's inventory. "I see those bitches leaving your rooms. I see the bitches meeting you every week at these places. Your wives don't know but I know! Even some of you fucking coaches. But I'm the bad boy. I'm bad. Just 'cause I ain't cool like you all. I ain't married, I can fuck whoever I want!" I just was ranting on. I'd just had enough. And I wasn't lying.

The press, who were swarming all over the locker room, never quoted a word of it, they're wrapped up so tight.

On the flight home I got wasted. I took a Quaalude after the game and snorted a noseful of coke in the lavatory, had the stewardess give me a couple of those little bottles of gin, and I started talking loud.

"Trade me, I don't give a fuck about this." I walked through the first-class section and looked at Coach Landry like he had shit on him. I went up to the cockpit with Wally the pilot. He had heard the noise and looked around at me. "Thomas, you okay?"

"Yeah, I'm okay, Wally. I can't stand these motherfuckers around here, trying to force their damn beliefs, trying to control me, they won't let me do my thing. People coming up in my face and getting on me."

"Settle down, man, settle down."

I walked back and gave Jim Myers a look that said, "Don't you say nothing, I'll bust you in your nose. I've got nothing to lose here." Walked through the press section and said to the whole cabin, "I want to get traded from this franchise, all these sorry-ass motherfuckers. Nobody on this plane's got nuts."

Nobody said a word.

I got off the plane and headed straight to Jeff Cohen's house. Bought a couple of grams and stayed up half the night talking, then went home, took a couple of 'ludes and fell asleep on my couch.

About 7:30 in the morning the phone rang. It was Marge Kelly, Landry's secretary. "Thomas," she said, "Coach Landry wants to see you this morning."

I yawned. "Can I see him after practice?"

"No," she answered, "I think you better see him before practice."

I took a shower and went through my ritual of steam and blowing my nose and packing it with cocaine. I looked in the mirror, put some Visine in my eyes to clear them up, laid out a line of coke about a half a gram long and snorted it all. Got dressed, got in my Mercedes and headed on over.

I figured he'd tell me I had fucked up bad yesterday, been a bad boy, and put some new restrictions on me. I was ready for him.

The whole Cowboys office was empty, all the doors were closed. There could have been sagebrush kicking down the corridors, like it was cleared for a gunfight. I walked straight into Landry's office. The coach took his glasses off, got up, walked over and closed the door. Uh-oh.

I stared him straight in the eye and snorted a whole honk like I was trying to clear my nose. My eyes were glassy as I slouched in the chair in front of his desk.

"Thomas," he began, "we had a deal this year. You did pretty good, up to a point. I don't know what's wrong with you. You have shown great disrespect to the staff, you've been a disruptive influence on my team, and your behavior in Washington last night is unforgivable. Coach Tubbs never uses foul language and I do not understand what Jerry said to you that would have caused such an outburst. What you did on the airplane . . . players never approach me like that."

He looked at me for some kind of response but I wasn't moving.

"I know you didn't have a daddy, that you didn't have any

279

discipline growing up, I understand all of that. But you are up one day and down the next, your attitude has gone from bad to worse.

"I have a couple of options here, Thomas. I could bench you, but that would not be in my best interest right now. You would be too disruptive if I benched you."

What else could he do?

"I'm not going to try and trade you. I . . . this is the damn toughest thing . . ." He broke.

I watched Tom Landry as tears welled up in his eyes. I had never seen the man this way. He was feeling pain for what he was about to do to me. "You can play football for somebody else. I just can't handle you anymore. I'm putting you on waivers."

Canned. And wired. I snorted again. He didn't say another word.

That's it?

"Well, you do what you've got to do." I was sitting there as arrogant as a kilo around company. The most important thing in my life was not my job, playing professional football. It wasn't my relationship with Tom Landry or my relationship with my family, it was my relationship with cocaine. I felt quite comfortable sitting there with my career in the balance, watching this sorry motherfucker shed these tears for me. Hell, I was happy to get out. No more practices, no more bullshit meetings, no more training camp, no more doctors, no more needles, no more nothing. The cocaine in me was saying, "Fuck Landry, fuck football, fuck rules. Fuck all this crap! You're free!"

I guess he expected me to apologize or talk my way out of this deal, and I think if I'd made an attempt I might have won him over. But I didn't. I just sat there and started to steam.

"I ain't making enough money here anyway to go through any more of this bullshit!" Then I began to let it out, the words coming out in a rush and my voice, which I thought I had under control, beginning to rise.

"I've been underpaid, I've been overworked. I don't get no credit. Landry, you know you never told me I could play football. You never told me I was good but once. Once. You used to brag about other people . . ." I started getting emotional too.

"But I'll tell you what. You are going to miss me."

Landry wanted me out of there. "Thomas, I'm going to put you on waivers. Probably the 49ers will pick you up."

"No, no, no," I told him, arrogant and confident and rushing. "You ain't going to put me on shit. You can't fire me 'cause you know what I'm going to do? I quit. I'm retiring as of this moment. I quit! You can't do no more to me, Landry, you can't do nothing else to me! And you know what else? You ain't going to the Super Bowl this year, and no other year. You'll never go to the Super Bowl again without me, Landry. You're never going to win another Super Bowl!"

I stormed into Gil Brandt's office. "Set up a press conference, I'm retiring!"

I blared my car radio all the way to Cohen's house. Reached in the glove compartment and grabbed me a good joint and fired it up. I was numb.

"Jeff, they fired me," I told Cohen when he answered the door. "I need some coke."

"I bet you do. How much you need?"

"Give me a quarter ounce, seven grams." I paid him and drove home. I couldn't even put the bag in my pocket. It had to be in sight. I opened it and started driving with my legs, sticking my Mercedes trunk key into the baggie and then filling up my nostrils with the coke. After the first few hits I started feeling fine. Couldn't feel a thing. I was anesthetized and arrogant, relieved and lost.

Wyetta and Thomesa were awake when I got there. We weren't living together but they were there that morning. I poured a gram on my bedroom mirror and started chopping it. Then I walked into the kitchen.

"Well, Wyetta, I'm not a Cowboy anymore."

"What?!" Tears filled her eyes.

I started laughing at her. "What are you crying about? I'm the son of a bitch that should be crying." I turned to my daughter. "Hi, Thomesa, hi, honey. How's my little Holly?"

I picked her up and tossed her in the air. "You know, it doesn't matter. I've got Thomesa. This is my little friend right here. She is my only friend. Thomesa is the only friend I have in the world. Her mama files paternity suits on me and the Cowboys fire me." Then I started to cry.

The phone rang. The Cowboys had set up my press conference at the Marriott, right down the street from where I lived. They were making it very easy for me.

Jerry Tubbs called. "How do you feel, Thomas?" he asked quietly.

"Oh, I'm all right, Jerry. I want to tell you I'm sorry about cussing you out, man. I was upset."

"Thomas," he said, "if Coach Landry changes his mind do you think you could straighten out?"

I had my opportunities.

"No, Jerry, I don't want to play for Tom Landry no more. I can't take it. Thanks anyway. See you later. 'Bye."

Wyetta was still crying but the phone started jumping off the hook with reporters and people starting to get the word. I was still a star.

The press conference was a show. I might have been retiring but I sure was getting a lot of attention. I dressed up in a suit and tie, snorted up the rest of the gram and told the world that I was finished playing football.

That was a big mistake.

The way football rules work, if a player retires his rights remain with the team that last employed him. If he's put on waivers he can negotiate with whoever picks him. If nobody picks him up then he can negotiate with any team in the league. By retiring I gave myself to the Cowboys forever; they would have to be compensated before another team could sign me. I am convinced that that's why they set it all up. I had no agent, no attorney to advise me of my rights. Cocaine was my agent, cocaine was my attorney, cocaine made most of my major decisions. I was under foreign management.

I ran off to Las Vegas and partied with Sonny Vale, got back to Dallas and got down with one of my girls. Rita. I stayed stoned with her for two weeks solid, then I tried to get back into the NFL. I called Pete Rozelle and he told me that it was too late to catch on with another team this year; I had retired and it was a league rule that you couldn't be reinstated during the last thirty days of the season. My season was over.

Seven-Up withdrew my commercials, my income from the Cowboys abruptly stopped, my world was falling apart. Jay Saldi and Aaron Mitchell came around often but other than that I didn't see anybody. Too Tall never called.

The Oilers kicked the Cowboys' ass. Beat them 30–24 in Texas Stadium. Earl Campbell ran right where the hell I'd left from, dragged Mike Hegman and Bob Breunig for something like 190 yards that day. I guess the Oilers' coach, Bum Phillips, felt like, "Henderson's vacated the spot, they've got this new kid in there, let's attack it."

I watched on TV as the Rams beat the Cowboys 21–19 in the first round of the playoffs. Late in the fourth quarter the Cowboys were in a zone defense and Rams' wide receiver Billy Waddy caught a pass over the middle and ran it in. Mike Hegman jumped as high as he could to knock the ball away and just missed it. I could always out-jump Mike Hegman. As far as I was concerned Tom Landry lost that game when he fired me. We had been to two straight Super Bowls; *they* had gotten bounced. I sat there with a bag of coke in my lap and I loved it.

Within a couple of weeks my intake of cocaine and my habit doubled. It was what I had to do. I bought an ounce from Suite. I got into cocaine cigarettes, emptying the tobacco and filling the tips with coke. I'd sit around the house, matches everywhere, tobacco strewn all over everything, putting more and more and more cocaine into the butts until they wouldn't even light up. My weight dropped from around 220 to under 200 pounds. I had bags under my eyes.

Right after Christmas I got a call from John Wooten, who worked with Gil Brandt at the Cowboys' office. He had been an agent, represented Drew Pearson and Billy Joe DuPree, and then all of a sudden had gone organization. The guys called him 007, James Bond, because he was a double agent.

Wooten wanted me to meet him on Park Lane and Central Expressway, like a Mafia drop. I said, "What's happening?"

"Just meet me, Henderson."

We left our cars far apart and met in the parking lot. "You don't look too good," he said when we shook hands.

"I don't feel too good, John."

"I just want to tell you something," he said. "Some people are watching you closely. This James Suite you're hanging out with—I don't know the guy but I know his name—he's been dropping your name because he's in a little hot water himself. They're going to bust you if you don't quit it. Are you sick?"

"No, I'm not sick." I said it quickly.

"Well, I just want to tell you that they're going to bust you if you don't stay away from these people you're with. Thomas, you need to go get some help."

I said, "I don't need no help, John. I appreciate the information. I know Suite but I don't stay at the sucker's house long enough to get in no trouble."

I was no longer under the Cowboys' umbrella. They had covered for me and other players in their time but Wooten was letting me know that it was over. He was kind to do it. The Cowboys knew I was into cocaine. When Landry later said that he didn't know about my cocaine use, I think for the first time in his Christian life he lied.

I told John thank you and walked away. I was cool in his face but I got to my car and I was shaking, my breath was short and my pulse was racing. I was afraid because in my heart and my head I knew one thing: I could not stop. Didn't matter who was watching me—from now on, I said, I'd be even more wary—I would not quit. I could not quit. I wasn't able and I didn't want to. I was possessed.

In January I began to spend a lot of time with Rita and the girls. Rita freebased. She had showed me how to cook up the stuff and had given me several hits over the past couple of months but it had never really taken. Plus, she'd take my two grams and dilute them with water and boil it on the stove and when I got them back it just didn't look like I was getting my two grams' worth. I needed to keep putting the stuff up my nose just as maintenance. Without the toot I couldn't function, couldn't even breathe. But finally I took the hit that did it.

I knew why the Liberty Bell cracked.

I went and told Jeff Cohen, who snorted every day, and he tried it. His eyes dilated, he was panting, and he looked straight at me. "Fuck," he gasped, "I'll never hit that shit again. That's too good, Thomas, it's too good."

He was right on time. Freebase was too good. It did too much to you too quickly. The Euphoria. The Explosion. It was the mushroom cloud of the drug universe.

My nose was telling me, "Henderson, you've got to take care of me, baby, 'cause you're going to be whistling through me in a little bit." I was already snorting three or four hundred dollars a day, I couldn't afford to smoke two thousand dollars a day. I managed for the next several months to run from it. I just stayed away from Rita.

I called around trying to get back into football that winter. I called the Cardinals, I called the Rams, I called the New Orleans Saints. The Saints had the worst defense in professional football and they wouldn't have me. Their coach, Dick Nolan, was a good friend of Tom Landry from their days on the Giants and I think Landry got honest with him: You don't want him, he's trouble.

Finally Gil Brandt called me and said, "Henderson, Bill Walsh of the San Francisco 49ers is interested in you. We think we can get a deal with him. Would you be interested in going to the 49ers?"

"Like I've got a choice?" I said. "If you trade me to Japan I've got to go." They weren't about to give me my unconditional release. I said sure.

Coach Walsh invited me to his house. This was unprecedented. Coach Landry hadn't invited me to Kentucky Fried Chicken. Wyetta and I jumped on an airplane and flew out there. I had an ounce and a quarter of cocaine right on me.

"My wife went to pick up some ribs," Walsh told me

when I called to say I'd arrived. I was offended. He was trying to make me feel at home with what he thought he knew about my home, but I would have preferred caviar. Didn't matter. They were good ribs.

When I got there his wife was still out and Walsh had to take a shower so I took a walk around the neighborhood. I strolled several blocks down the street and stopped. I don't know how conspicuous I was, a black man in a white neighborhood, sticking a credit card down into a plastic bag, coming up and snorting two big nosefuls of powder.

We talked contract over dinner. "What do you expect, Thomas?" he asked.

"Somewhere in the neighborhood of $200,000, Bill."

"Thomas, I don't think I can go that far. I'll tell you what I'll do. We'll get a working contract that you will be happy with."

We ended up calling it a laughing contract, because we laughed all the way through dealing with it. We started out with a $125,000 base salary. Then he gave me $500 for every week I wasn't fined. He gave me $1,000 for every week that I played on specialty teams, $1,000 for every week we won, $1,000 for every week I started. I'd get $10,000 if we made the playoffs, $10,000 if I made the Pro Bowl, $10,000 if I made All-Pro. If I had a good year I could make right up near my $200,000. I was happy to agree.

Lou Rawls was staying at the same hotel as Wyetta and I in San Francisco. I saw his limousine pull up and I went and introduced myself. He invited me up to his suite and I proceeded to get loaded with whoever was there. I took this big bag of coke and dumped it on the table. "You want some of this, Lou?"

"No, man, and I don't think you need any more either, Hollywood."

"What's wrong?"

"What are you doing running around with that much coke?"

I wasn't about to tell him I had a plan to cut it and sell it in the clubs in Dallas. "Oh, man, it's a long story." I started bragging. "This is the way I do it, this is the way I function."

"Man, I don't know you that well, Hollywood, I just met you, but man, you are fucking with some bad shit. You need to leave that shit alone."

I filled up a cigarette, honked on my nose and invited him to my room. "I want you to meet my wife," I told him.

It was three in the morning and I shook Wyetta awake. "Wyetta, Wyetta, guess who's here."

She was pretty groggy. "Who?" she squinted.

"Lou Rawls!"

And in that deep deep voice of his he purred, "How you doin', baby?"

"Oh, it *is* him!" She pulled the covers over her head.

We sat around and talked. He said, "Man, I watched you play. You got too much talent, you are much too flagrant with this stuff. You run around getting high with people you don't know, you're running around in hotels and you don't know nobody in the whole city. You got to get yourself checked. You need to quit messing with this stuff."

I didn't want to talk about this. "Okay, Lou, man, thank you. Look, Lou, I'm gonna try and get some sleep. . . ." Rushed him off rather than sit for the lecture.

I finally asked Wyetta to marry me. She thought I was kidding. We were lying in bed and I said, "Will you marry me?"

"Don't play with me."

I pulled out a diamond ring.

Wyetta invited all my former girlfriends to the wedding. It was her moment of triumph. The closer the women had been to me the closer she put them to the front. She had staked her claim and now the papers were all drawn up.

My mom came in for the wedding. My sisters and brothers came in, my aunt and uncle from Austin. People kept coming out of the woodwork and I liked the activity. My house was full of people preparing for the day so I went and stayed at a local hotel for most of the week. I dropped over to Jeff Cohen's house and tooted up half the nights. We sat there, both of us wired on cocaine, and solved the world's problems. International affairs. We were world leaders those nights, fixed everything.

I told Wyetta, "Go and buy both your mother and mine dresses for the wedding." Wyetta went out and bought her mom a designer gown. She bought mine some chiffon bullshit looked like a ten-dollar number you'd find at a flea market.

My mother was furious. I was furious. How could she disrespect me and my family like that? I was loaded all that week and I was loaded that moment. I took her back into the bathroom and slapped her hard four or five times.

My mother started beating on the door when she heard the shouting. I let her in. "Quit hitting that girl!"

"This is none of your damn business. You get out of here."

"I mean it." My mother slapped me. Didn't take nothing off it.

I looked at her. "Don't you *ever* hit me again. Do you understand that?"

She slapped me again.

On nothing but reflexes I slapped my mother.

She slapped me again.

I felt shame. I had taken cocaine to anesthetize everything but this feeling was so powerful, so overwhelming, that it cut right through and left me for dead.

I ran out of the house and into the street, crying uncontrollably. I was shaking and wailing from the bottom of me. Hiccupping and bellowing. I asked God for forgiveness but I think he cursed me. I knew I'd done the worst thing in the world that a person could do and that I'd never be forgiven. People brag about never having raised their hand to their mom or dad and I had, on pure reflex and impure cocaine, slapped my mother.

I walked for about an hour and just cried. Me and my cocaine, what had we done? When I got back my eyes were swollen, my sinuses were all screwed up, my nose was running. My mother told me that she wanted to talk to me. She took me back in the bedroom.

"It's okay," she told me. "I had no right to hit you. You didn't hurt me. You didn't even slap me hard." She tried to take my pain away.

"Thomas," she said, "I don't want you to marry this girl." I stopped cold and looked at her. "This wedding does not have my blessing. This woman is going to ruin you. She's going to rip you off, she's going to spend your money, and you know what, Thomas? She is going to get a divorce and she's going to sue you. Just as soon as she's getting this wedding she's gonna get a divorce."

I was exhausted. "Mama, we've already made the arrangements and we're going to get married."

We had a giant wedding. May 5, 1980. I had just turned twenty-seven, had a daughter and now I had a wife.

I invited my whole team to come and a lot of my former teammates made it: Drew Pearson, Tony Hill, Benny Barnes, Rayfield Wright, Charlie Waters, Percy Howard, Robert Newhouse, Guy Brown, Butch Johnson. Too Tall gave my wife away. He also gave me a hell of a bachelor party. Tom Landry sent a silver tray, Roger Staubach a big glass vase.

A lot of people gave me another kind of gift: a gram of coke, two grams of coke, a quarter ounce of coke. I probably had an ounce and a half of cocaine after my wedding was over.

As she walked back down the aisle after we had said our vows and exchanged our rings, Wyetta announced to the assembled multitude, "I finally got him, I finally got him. How about that?"

My wife wouldn't sleep with me on our wedding night.

She would not make love to me. Wouldn't let me touch her. This had to be a first. I told her, "All these years you've been trying to get me, you'd come over all hours of the night, now when I marry you you don't want to sleep with me.

"Okay," I said, "I'll tell you what. I know somebody who will sleep with me." I got up and left.

I went to see one of my girlfriends. She wouldn't sleep with me either. "You just got married."

Skip that. I went to see old faithful, I went to see Rita. Sat there and got loaded and told her the whole damn story.

10

Base

Wyetta took all our furniture and furnishings and went ahead to San Francisco to set up a condominium I had rented when I was finally sure that I would be traded there, and I was alone in Dallas for a few weeks. I moved into a motel, the Double Tree Inn.

When an athlete becomes a star, whether it's on his high school or college or company team, he is given a safety net in his community. The umbrella. If he gets stopped for drunk driving the cops take him home, if he knocks out a neighbor's window everybody laughs it off and brags about being so close to the guy. But once you're no more use to that team, school, community, that net gets pulled. Some places faster than others, depending on the amount of good will you've built up while you were starring. I was out in the cold.

I was seeing a girl named Joy, or at least we were good friends for a long time. I had a key to her house and we were happy to see each other. I dropped over to her place.

Joy was shaking, paranoid, visibly upset. She was never that way. She would buy cocaine for me from different sources when I wasn't getting it from James Suite and, when I could finally calm her down enough to tell me, it turned out that two narcotics agents had followed her home from work the night before, gone into her house and threatened to bust her or plant something on her if she didn't cooperate with them. They wanted her to roll over on me, set me up so they could bust me.

I called everyone I could think of: the district attorney's office, the head of the DEA; I called homicide, family court, every agency in town and told them what was going on. They had threatened an innocent woman to set me up. What kind of police department were they running, I wanted to know; if those fuckers wanted to come at me don't come around the corner like some sneaking goddamn slime bag, come at me!

The district attorney's office finally squashed it but they denied in the press that it ever happened.

I went to a party the next day with some get-high buddies, got high, met this gorgeous young blonde named Prissy around noon and by evening she was coming home with me. I was sitting there with this fat bag of cocaine giving everybody lines but my paranoia was getting progressively worse— I was checking out the pool for vice cops and narcotics agents, I was suspecting my friends, started going through their house looking at the light sockets to see if there were microphones stashed or a video camera set up. But still I wanted this girl. I said, "Baby, I want you to go to the Double Tree Inn, check into a room under your name, then call me back here and I'll come on over."

She did all that. I was staying on the tenth floor and she got a single on the seventh. I walked into the Double Tree a half hour later and it was "Hi, Hollywood," everybody knew who I was. I took the elevator to the tenth floor. For all practical purposes I was in my room. I walked down the end of the hallway, took the fire stairs to the seventh floor, went in the girl's room and partied all night. I had about twenty grams of coke at the time plus some Placidils, some Quaaludes and a bunch of pot and we did them all and each other.

I woke up around two the next afternoon, took a shower

and went out to get something from my car. When I stepped out of the elevator into the lobby all the people at the front desk looked at me like, "You're here?" I said to the bell captain, "What's happenin'?"

He whispered like he was being indicted. "Twelve agents were here last night with shotguns, Hollywood. They went to your room. Where the hell have you been?"

Oh. So it wasn't paranoia; they *were* after me. The net was pulled. There were a lot of NFL players still under the umbrella, I just wasn't one of them.

I had the desk make up my bill while I ran up to my room to throw all my clothes in my suitcase and clear out. When I opened the door the place had been torn to pieces. Drawers open, the bed turned over and stripped, my belongings strewn all over. Ransacked. And right next to the dresser dangling from a stand-up lamp, was one of those paper-covered wire coat hangers. They'd written a note on it. "Mr. Henderson: We entered your room with a search warrant last night. We found a controlled substance in your room. Please call me," and gave me a phone number. Signed Sgt. so-and-so.

Sure I'll call you, Sarge.

I ripped off the note and jammed it in my pocket, threw my stuff together and checked out.

I called my attorney, Charles Caperton. If someone's going to get in trouble with cocaine in Texas, Charles Caperton is the man to call. He's got friends in the DEA, friends in the narcotics division, he's an old Dallas boy from Highland Park and SMU. He'd been telling me all along to stay away from James Suite and the people I'd been running with. He'd tell me the things I'd been doing, like coke in the men's room of Biff's, and if he knew so did the police. It wasn't no big secret in Dallas that I was on the coke.

"Charlie, they almost got me last night!"

"I know. I've been trying to call you, I didn't know where you were but I knew they had a search warrant." He was so well-connected that just through the legal process he was on top of my case.

I told him I was in a girl's room. "You lucky son of a

bitch,'' he said. "Okay, give me the sergeant's name and number."

The cops said they'd gotten some controlled substance out of the room, which might have been from where I'd dumped my coke out on the dresser and done a few lines. But if they scraped the dresser they only got a midget line and there are maids and porters and passkeys to that room, could have been anybody in there and left that. Charles said not to worry.

My dope was on the seventh floor. I called Prissy and had her scoop it all back up into the baggie I'd brought it in and come meet me with it. We rendezvoused and I headed out to the airport. I wasn't going home. Stood on line with half an ounce of cocaine, a hundred Quaaludes, Placidils and a stash of pot tucked into my socks inside my cowboy boots, bought a ticket under my own name and got on board. I was on my way to California.

My father had been in Los Angeles but he'd moved to Oakland when he heard that I had been traded to the 49ers; he wanted to be close to me. I limoed to his house, then checked up and down the block to see if I'd been followed.

My dad and I went out to a club called Daisy's to have a few drinks. I got recognized, introduced around. I'm not in town five hours and I've got a coke connection in California. Snorting it and rolling it into cigarettes I went through the rest of my fifteen grams in two days. Didn't sleep, just smoked and snorted and raved and ranted about how the Cowboys done me wrong.

I ran out of cocaine. Called the guy I'd met two days before about needing a little bit.

"How much is a little bit?"

"Oh, about a half ounce."

He said he'd give me a good deal, one thousand dollars for the good stuff, uncut. I'd been buying it in Dallas for fourteen hundred or more. I said I'd be right over.

My dad and I drove to his apartment. Fourteenth floor. It took him three minutes to unlock the door. We heard *clack, clackclackclack, bloomp, bloompbloomp, clackclack* as the deadbolts slid and the cylinders turned. "Oh, I got a few more here," and finally we were inside and he had to do the whole security check in reverse.

There were four pounds of cocaine sitting on the floor in various bags. "This is the good stuff," he said and picked up one package of about a pound. He was completely loaded. Sitting on the floor next to him were five plates of the stuff being cooked. Like on Ed Sullivan or at Barnum and Bailey, he had five plates going at once. "Don't smoke," he told us. "Don't light anything, this is ether." He was taking an eye-dropper and working his way from plate to plate preparing his dope. When he had it the way he wanted it he put the coke in his pipe, capped up the ether and threw a blanket over it and pushed it to the side.

I watched as he fired up this butane gas tank and heated the pipe until the white stuff melted. Then he smoked it. Sounded like some sort of deep-throated gurgling bird. Held his breath as long as he could, hyperventilated, then blew it out.

His eyes went from low beams to high beams like he was hitting a toggle switch.

I still had a little toot on me, I was in my little world, I was buzzing, my nose was tight.

"You want a hit of this?"

"Fuck yeah."

He took a razor blade and like an artist scooped and swirled and collected some of the cooked cocaine and dropped it carefully into the pipe. Filled it to the top. "I've smoked some," I told him, "but I've never seen it done like this, with ether."

"I like the taste of ether."

I was ready for my hit. The guy told me first blow all the air out of your lungs. I did that. Then he lit the thing up.

When I hit this pipe I sucked every damn bit of cocaine out of it. The heat turned into a white smoke and it went in my lungs.

My dad was sitting there checking me out.

When I let go of that pipe my dad saw it and I felt it: My

eyes exploded. Something went off in me that never went off before.

My father looked at me and I looked at him. I let the smoke out. I was breathless, my heart was racing, I was panicky but I'd never felt that kind of rushing power in my life. I didn't want to move because it would shake up the universe.

I lost my voice. My ability to talk was gone. All this time I'd thought I was out of control, that was nothing. This was it.

It was five minutes before I dared do anything but breathe. I enjoyed that hit. That hit scared me so much I didn't want to hit it again. I said, "Can I get what I came for, I need to get out of here."

The guy sold me the half ounce and it was good coke, fresh, smelled good. We walked out of the apartment. "If you need anything," he said as we were leaving, "just call me."

"Do you just sit there and smoke all the time?"

He went, "Yeah. Why not?"

In the elevator my dad looked over to me. "Thomas," he said, "I never want you to do that again. You should've seen your damn eyes. I thought you were going to have a heart attack. I don't ever want to see you do that again."

"Don't worry about that. The only reason you saw that was that it was a great hit, the shit's good."

I did the half ounce and was up for five days, no sleep. Then I decided to go to my wife and daughter in Redwood City.

Wyetta—Sherlock—saw the shape I was in and knew what I'd been up to. She'd gotten a couple of calls from Dallas, knew about the girl and the near bust, but she was happy that we were out of there and we were looking forward to starting something new here.

I slept for about twenty hours and when I came to I felt better. Wyetta went and bought half a dozen Afrins to keep the pain in my nose under control and I played with Thomesa, my little bundle of joy. I started playing Daddy. Bought a

296

bicycle with a kid's seat on the back and we rode around, my daughter and I. Before, it was always my annoying little kid waking me up before it was time. Now I wanted her to know that I loved her, I wanted to make sure she knew that I loved her more than anything.

We cruised down the streets in the warm sun, making gentle curves, me talking to Thomesa and her chattering her own language back. I loved having her close. There was an ice cream stand by the side of the road and we got off and I bought her a cone. I wasn't about to try and act like some proper person, I just let her go at it, and at eighteen months old she had ice cream everywhere. I didn't care; she was happy.

I didn't know a soul in California, just my daughter and my wife, and for a while that was good enough for me. I took Thomesa everywhere; we went swimming and to the movies and on our rides. Wyetta and I were getting along. She was cooking, I was eating. My weight, which had dropped to about 205 while I was doing all my cocaine, went back up to 220 where it should have been. I had cocaine in the house but I didn't do it. For three weeks I had a perfect marriage. I was the happiest man in the world.

But even the power of love and family were no match for the power and obsession of cocaine. I felt trapped. I couldn't shake the paranoia. My life was subject to surveillance, to invasions by the police, to anything going wrong at any time. I knew that and finally I couldn't ignore it. I knew I couldn't quit doing coke. I needed coke for my nose, I needed coke because my body craved it and I had nothing to replace it with. All I knew was to do more.

It was time for 49er training camp. I had made a few trips over to the facilities and met some of the guys. Steve DeBerg was the number-one quarterback and Joe Montana was just a skinny kid from Notre Dame. Willie Harper was a wonderful linebacker but the team had been a loser for years. It was just building and Coach Walsh was the architect.

Bill Walsh was really into names. He took Renaldo Nehemiah, the world champion hurdler who had never played football. He got Russ Francis, he wanted O. J. Simpson, he got "Hollywood" Henderson. He went after the big-name guys because the franchise had to get back on the road.

I packed up my Percodan and Quaaludes and my quarter ounce of coke and headed over. I hadn't done any coke for about four weeks, which was some kind of record for me at the time. The way it worked was that if I was under the influence of it I had to have more; if I never took that first hit I was okay. Except for the nose. My nose was killing me. The Afrin was doing all right but it was only a stopgap measure, the issue had not been settled.

I wanted to look good for the 49ers. I had a lot of pride in my playing and my reputation, but right away I had a problem. Somebody else had my number. I had worked hard to establish 56 as my number around the league. When Willie Mays was traded to the Mets they made sure he got number 24; the guy who had it was asked to give it up and he did it graciously. It was a sign of respect.

Fred Quillan, a second-year center, had my number and the 49ers didn't ask him a thing. I offered Quillan two thousand dollars to let me have number 56 but he refused, told me he had worked for that number. Now, I wasn't Willie Mays but I was All-Pro and it wouldn't have taken much to please me. Already I didn't feel wanted, didn't feel accepted.

The defensive coordinator was a guy named Chuck Studley. I was sitting in the room with sixty or seventy defensive players when he walked in. About five feet nine inches tall with a little bit of a belly, he wears his pants high enough not to let it flop over so he has an illusion of a look, but you notice right away that he's not letting it all hang out. He came into the room and reached the podium. "Gentlemen," he said in some Mary Poppins kind of voice, "I want you to imagine this." Then he went on to describe this *idea* of defense. Some kind of football metaphysics.

I had just left Tom Landry, the great defensive mind of all times, and I get this Amway lecturer. He's trying to motivate me but I ain't buying.

You have to be a twisted kind of guy to be a defensive

coordinator. You've got to be a motivator and what you're motivating is aggression. It's not a nice job, it's sort of like being a mule team driver. "Come on you lazy, slop-eating dog. You piece of dung." Did you ever hear a guy whip a mule? Like Festus on *Gunsmoke*, you call him all sorts of names and sooner or later he moves for you. Mules don't respond to "giddyap!" You need a certain sick sense of humor and the ultimate killer attitude: "I don't know his parents. Hurt him!"

Chuck Studley had the good manly name but the wrong attitude.

But he wasn't all bad. He pointed to me a lot. "Henderson, did you ever use this in Dallas?"

"Yes, we used it but it was different." This particular play he was describing was a man defense.

"What did you call it?"

"Forty-eight."

Studley kept using me in the meeting, picking me out like I was the mind in the room because I had played for Landry. I felt good and it was true; I had absorbed the best defense in pro football.

The 49ers linebacker coach was Norb Hecker. He had a smile that stayed on his face all the time and one of those infectious laughs. He was a good guy but he wasn't Jerry Tubbs. I was comparing everything to Dallas and it wasn't matching up. This team hadn't been to any Super Bowls. I was still pouting. I really still wanted to be a Cowboy.

My first few days on the practice field I was impressing people. I showed the young linebackers like Keena Turner and Bobby Leopold and even Willie Harper, already an excellent player and a veteran, some of the techniques for taking on a tight end and the quick blocks from the tackles.

There was a big tackle from Grambling, a giant of a man, and Coach Walsh watched me work on him one day. The linebackers were working on this take block, where the tight end blocks down on the defensive end and the tackle comes around and blocks the linebacker while the back tries to run between them. If the linebacker steps straight across the line instead of making a move right or left, if he keeps his shoulders parallel to the line of scrimmage, he can knock the tackle's ass off and get right to the ballcarrier. Superman can't do anything with that. The linebacker is working from the center of his strength and he can just wail on anybody near him. If you make a lateral move or if you follow the tight end in, that's something else. But it's the linebacker's job to have the knowledge and the vision to take that first straight step; it's vision and keying. As long as you stay parallel you can hurt him.

The Grambling giant didn't get it. You could put Conrad Dobler or Dan Dierdorf or Tank Younger or a Brahma bull in front of me and if I knew it was a take block coming you couldn't block me. *Pow.* I busted him.

"Let's try it again," the big guy said.

Pow.

"Let's try it again."

Pow.

Coach Walsh was standing on the sideline in his favorite pose, one hand wrapped across his waist, the other up at his mouth. Jack Benny with a clipboard. I was giving away about a hundred pounds and this big dummy wanted to block "Hollywood."

"Let's try it again."

I coiled this time and when the play came at me I fired. Instead of giving him my shoulder I squatted and plunged with my helmet right into his throat. He didn't want to try it again after that. Coach Walsh was impressed.

I hadn't done any drugs in a month. To control the pain in my nose I had the trainer carry around a bottle of Afrin all day and when it got bad I would walk over to him and take a couple of deep pulls. This was regular Afrin, not my special mixture. The trainer said, "Be careful. You might get addicted to this stuff."

"Don't sweat it," I told him.

I hurt my foot the first week of practice and couldn't play for a few days. Then I had to have a tooth extracted. The dentist wouldn't give me any drugs to kill the pain so I did my own drugs, my own Percodan. With nothing to do all day while the guys were practicing I decided to give my nose some medicine. One hit of cocaine and I was sprung again, my body started its craving and I could not resist. I made some phone calls and got a half ounce to last me the rest of camp.

My nose went back to acting up. At night in the dormitory I'd be blowing and honking, two or three o'clock in the morning. Your nose makes some incredible sounds when you've been blowing it for several years and it's numb. I sounded like I was trying to start up a car or kickstart a cycle in the hallway. People would see me the next day and say, "What the fuck's wrong with your nose, Henderson?" So it got around. Pro football players aren't completely stupid.

Tight end Charles Young approached me. "Hey, man, it's out about you and the coke."

"No sweat," I told him, "my nose is fucked up. But as far as the coke is concerned I'm not on no coke. I just need surgery on my nose."

Several times I left camp and drove home. I would lie in bed with my wife and blow my nose all night long and in the morning tell her to call Walsh and tell him I was sick and couldn't make it that day.

By the middle of August 1980, I couldn't take it anymore. I made an appointment with the 49ers team physician. I assumed it was a confidential doctor-patient interview and examination. I said, "I'm sick, Doc. I've got a problem with cocaine. It's eating my nose up, it's keeping my wife up, I can't sleep. I need some professional help but I don't know where to go, I don't know what to do." I sat there and started to cry.

The doctor prescribed me some nose salve and said he'd look into it. In his report it says I had URI with sinusitis and bronchitis.

From the day I met with the doctor, Walsh stopped talking to me. We used to have these little conversations after our "laughing contract" got finished but now he wouldn't speak to me. Quit cold.

I had to wonder about the professional ethics of team physicians.

I had played well in preseason games against the Raiders, Chargers and Seahawks, but in the second half of our game against the Kansas City Chiefs I made a tackle on J. T. Smith and I was out. I hit him like I usually hit people—hard—but this time I didn't get up.

They pulled me off the field and into the locker room and left me there until it was time to go. When I went to the hospital to get my neck examined, the team doctor diagnosed it as "mild concussion, probable cervical sprain syndrome." The orthopedic doctor said, "Cervical spine sprain. Question fracture." They took front, back and side X-rays but not a CAT scan or tomogram, which would have showed them something I believe they did not want to find: I had broken my neck. Instead of putting me on the injured reserve list and placing me in treatment for cocaine abuse, the 49ers put me on the active roster for the 1980 season.

I couldn't play football at all but I was on the roster. I couldn't comb my hair, I couldn't lie down without pain. If I was lying down I couldn't get up, the slightest move would send a tremor of pain through my whole body. Tough to play linebacker that way.

Charles Young came and told me that Walsh had said to him, "I have reason to believe that Thomas is on cocaine and I'm making a decision about it right now."

Two weeks after I got hurt the 49ers were going to open their season against the Saints in New Orleans. I was on the team and was supposed to dress for the game but I couldn't play, I couldn't hardly brush my own teeth. I knew something was happening because people had stopped talking to me, so I stopped talking to them. I didn't go to the defensive team meeting, the film meetings, the whole squad meetings. I met with Sonny Vale, who flew in from Dallas with a quarter ounce of coke.

Sonny and I were sitting in my room talking and snorting. The salve was working but I thought that cocaine and salve together worked even better. At about 10:30 Saturday night there was a knock at the door. Here was Fred Quillan.

I hadn't said anything to Fred Quillan all camp except about my jersey number. He'd said no and left it at that. I didn't know Fred Quillan, I didn't know if he smoked cigarettes, if he ate fish, if he liked Willie Nelson. But on this day Fred Quillan came to my door and asked me if I had any cocaine.

"No," I told him, "I don't have any cocaine, Fred. No, I sure don't." I was looking at him like, "You don't know me." And I was thinking, "What the fuck is this? What's going on?"

"Don't you have just a little?" he kept on.

"No, Fred. Sorry." I closed the door. I turned to Sonny and just shook my head. To this day I am convinced that Walsh put him up to it. Quillan never spoke to me again. Not on the plane going home, not at practice, not ever. I don't suspect it was some introduction to a friendship he was trying to establish, I think he was a pure kiss-ass snitch.

The day of the Saints game I wanted to play. I didn't like being hurt or being on the sidelines. I'd come to play and I wanted to. I was even telling Walsh, "Look at me, I think I can move today." I was out there trying to warm up, looking like a robot, wearing a neck collar, turning my whole body every time I tried to turn my neck. Herman Munster. Never got in the game. We won 26–23.

I went to practice all the next week and still stayed up three or four days doing cocaine. The next Sunday Walsh put me on the field covering wide receivers. I pulled a hamstring muscle trying to make the coverage and didn't make a tackle the whole game. Didn't come close.

I fell asleep doing the stretches during practice the next week. I was down in the sitting hurdle position, one leg out front and the other tucked behind me, lying back on the grass, and I fell out. When I woke up the whole team was sniggering down on the other end of the field.

I went to do some drugs with one of the secretaries in the 49ers office. I didn't know that the house where we went was under surveillance by the drug authorities. The girl got busted, then fired. The girl told Bill Walsh everything she could about me to try and keep her job. She couldn't say we'd fucked, we were too busy doing cocaine. Wyetta called Walsh to make sure he was going to fire this woman for fooling around with her husband, and while she was at it she gave him my whole drug history.

That day John McVay, the 49ers' director of player personnel, was out there on the field. There were several other people on the sidelines who I hadn't seen around. Walsh walked up to me on the sideline and said, "Think you can play? I'm going to start you this week if you can play." Then he told Chuck Studley, "Okay. Henderson is going to start at linebacker this week." I went out on the field and walked through the three plays they ran at us.

I went home and got some sleep that night. Woke up refreshed for a change. My wife cooked me my favorite, pancakes and eggs and a pound of bacon. The phone rang.

"Hello, Thomas, this is John McVay."

"How're you doing."

"Thomas, we have placed you on waivers and the decision is final. R. C. Owens will be by with your check in a little while."

Walsh had set me up. He had signified that I could perform by letting me walk through a series of plays when he knew and the doctors and everyone knew that I was in no shape at all. It was the lowest thing a coach could do. I was sick, I had asked for help, but instead of trying to heal me the 49ers were letting me go. Walsh had been waiting for me to get physically well enough to let me go but I had taken too much time and he'd gotten impatient.

It wasn't my injuries. The fact was that Walsh didn't know how to handle a man with a drug problem so he decided simply to get rid of him. It turns out that he'd been trying to trade me to another team; he was ready to trade my drug problem for a draft choice, which was the real bottom-line NFL mentality.

It is part of the agreement between the NFL and the Players' Association that a team may not release a player while he is injured. If I had been placed on injured reserve they would have been obligated to pay me my whole salary, and I should have been put on injured reserve for two reasons: my neck and the fact that they were aware of my cocaine addiction. Instead, they figured out how to get rid of me.

I hung up the phone. "Well, Wyetta," I said slowly, "I got fired again."

The Houston Oilers needed a linebacker. I called their head coach, Bum Phillips. All us Texans know about each other. After a couple of hours negotiation between me and their business people I was signed. I was still making over six figures so I hadn't lost anything. My neck was still hurting but I was determined to try to play through it. Football was what I did, who I was. I wanted to play.

Bum Phillips was a player's coach, he wanted to keep his team happy and he went out of his way to do it. For example, on the flights to and from away games the players were the ones who sat in first class. Not management, not the coaches and their wives, the owner's wife, the president and his wife; it was the offensive linemen, the receivers, the starters. Earl Campbell, Ken Stabler, Robert Brazile, Kenny Burroughs, Bill Casper, Billy "White Shoes" Johnson—the guys who did the work for Bum. And it worked on the honor system; everybody knew who deserved first-class treatment. In Dallas it was just the reverse.

And there were some goings on. After the first game I got there, against Cincinnati, I went to use the lavatory one flight up in first class and stood there beating at the door for about fifteen minutes waiting for the Occupied sign to flash off. Finally the door opened and a flight attendant stepped out. I moved to get inside. "There's someone in there," she told me. Sixty seconds later, Earl Campbell came out. I don't know what they were doing but there was a wet spot on his trousers.

Earl Campbell, I found out, was the laziest football player I'd seen in my entire life. He was Mr. Houston but he was the first guy I ever saw spend time at practice stretched out horizontal in full gear with his head propped up against his palm. Whenever he wasn't on the field he would just lie down. Earl used to get up real slowly after he got hit and when people asked Bum about it the coach, quick as a fox, said, "Why does he get up so slow? Because he goes down slow." It was a great line but I knew soon after I saw him that Earl Campbell was never in condition to play professional football.

Earl was gifted and powerful, he could run right over you, but he was lazy. If he had played for a coach like Tom Landry or Don Shula they would have made him work hard and he would probably still be playing and gaining more yards than anyone in pro football history. Earl Campbell got up slow off the ground because he was so damn tired.

If first impressions are everlasting, when I walked into the Houston Oiler practice facility I felt like I'd joined a second-class organization. The lockers were wood and old chicken coop wire and they were dirty. There just didn't seem to be the care and attention to detail that the Cowboys had defined as professionalism.

The head Oiler was, of course, Kenny Stabler. He was on his last legs after a great career with the Oakland Raiders but he was another of Bum Phillips' kind of guys. He and I didn't party, we didn't have a lot to do with each other, but he was friendly. The first day I walked into the locker room he shook my hand. "Hey, hoss." With his silver beard and long scraggly hair he reminded me of Howard Hughes.

Robert Brazile was the Mary Lou Retton of linebackers. At six four, 235 he had all the tools. He could run, he had a little waist and looked good in his uniform. He was good and he was all the time telling me how good he was. But he was a showman. Robert would make his share of tackles but a lot of times he would run forty yards out of his way to be part of the play for the cameras. The tackle was already made and here comes Brazile flying from the side, doing a flip over the pile, somersaulting on the ground and then jumping three feet in the air. It was like he was looking for the judges—9.8, 9.9, 9.9—with more points for degree of difficulty.

My neck was still hurting but I wanted to play and show the coaches that I still had it. The third week I was with the Oilers we were 3–2 and playing the Kansas City Chiefs. A receiver had caught a pass on Brazile and I was helping run the guy down when my hamstring snapped. The same hamstring I had injured in San Francisco. My cocaine had messed with my conditioning and my body was starting to go.

I felt like I'd been shot by a high-powered rifle. I went right down. Bum Phillips put me on injured reserve.

It didn't take long for me to run down my cocaine connections. Several Oilers were freebasing—they got busted a couple of years later—and I got introduced to this guy named Travis.

Travis was a slim, very good-looking black man, wore loud clothes, sharp, pimp-looking kind of dude. He ran the party house and was a big football fan. I went over there to buy some coke. Coke to go.

"What're you going to do with it?"

"I'm going to snort it."

"Man, why don't you quit fucking wasting it?"

"Well . . ." He had a pipe going. "Give me a hit of that."

There comes a time in all addicts' lives when they take the hit that pushes them over the line. This was mine. I took the pipe and it took me. It changed my life.

First thing it did was go right through me. I went straight to the bathroom. When I got back out my ears were ringing, my breath was short, my heart was racing, my pulse was too much over too much. I was wired. And I wanted to hit it again. And I kept hitting it. Again. And again. And again.

I got to Travis' house at one in the afternoon and left at 9:50 the next morning. I had smoked $2,100 of his cocaine. The $2,100 didn't hurt me. What hurt me the most was leaving his coke. I could have sat there that day and smoked another three or four thousand dollars worth.

Travis was cooking it all up for me. He broke me in rather expensively. But I knew I had found it. Some people search for enlightenment, some search for the truth. My search was for the ultimate high and I had found it. It had a kind of hum to it, a harmony, like your whole body comes alive, or dies, I'm not sure which. You can take a hit and maintain that level for a long while, but when it fades you've got to get back there. The first hit that meant anything to me was right there, I'll never forget it as long as I live. But the overwhelming fact of freebase is that I tried to get that hit again for the next two years.

I wouldn't have left if I hadn't had to go to work. I was late to the 10:00 meeting.

I was on injured reserve with the Oilers so I wasn't part of the practice process. In Dallas you go to practice and stay the whole damn day and sometimes afterward. They check up on you. "He's getting his treatment, isn't he? Where is that sucker? Oh, there he is." You better be in getting your treatment or they'll fine you. They give you a harder time about injuries and getting well quick than they do about anything else. "Oh, you're late. We'll tell Landry on you." There was a two-hundred-dollar fine for being one minute late to a doctor's appointment.

In Houston it was kicked back. I got out of practice at 11:45 and ran right back over to Travis'.

Before I took the first hit we had to talk. I said, "Look, man, you charged the fuck out of me last night. I'm gonna have to start buying my dope elsewhere or you're going to have to give me more, 'cause you cut up a little rock and charge me one hundred dollars, it's not that much dope."

We cut a deal. I'd buy three and a half grams for five hundred dollars. It was expensive, but I was basically renting his pipe, his house, his torches. He started inviting girls over. . . .

For the next nine weeks in Houston, with freebase in my lungs and controlling my mind, I forgot everything except the pipe. My nose was still bothering me whenever I came down or woke up, but it seemed less important now.

I was lucky I didn't kill somebody. I was lucky I didn't kill myself. In the next nine weeks, the rest of the NFL season, I spent $110,000—my whole salary, minus taxes—on cocaine. The first time I went there I had twelve hundred dollars on me, so I left owing him nine hundred. The next day I didn't have any money but I told him I was getting paid. I told him what I made. I said, "This is yours." I actually showed this guy my NFL contract.

I was an animal. The obsession with freebasing took me by storm. While the Houston Oilers were playing Tampa Bay and the Bengals, the Broncos, Bears, Jets and Browns, I was madly stalking Houston full of freebase. I would barely make my physical therapy and ice-down sessions for my leg in the morning, then fall over by Travis' and base out. I would go home after freebasing and not seeing my wife for five days and I'd accuse her of cheating on me. I'd grab bags of garbage from the trash and pull them inside and throw them on the floor—"Who drank this? Who ate this? Who are you fucking? Who are you messing with?" Total paranoia. Finally I moved out on her, got a room at the Marriott. That was my home. That and Travis'.

I was completely gone. Whatever there was of Thomas Henderson had been destroyed and in its place was this madman.

I started owing Travis money: $2,000, then $2,600. Before I even lit up another bowl each noontime I'd be $3,100 down. He said he needed something to hold. I went and got him my fox jacket as collateral until I could get to my bank accounts in Dallas and San Francisco where I had stashed some extra funds. I knew I was spending a lot of money but I couldn't stop.

Freebase holds a lot of power over women too. The things women will do for a hit are unbelievable. The women Travis controlled. It's a slave-maker.

The paranoia was also incredible. I'd lock myself up in Travis' bedroom and just hit the pipe, don't bother me, don't come near me. Then I'd tell him I needed some more cooked. He was cooking it for me and ripping me off royally but there was nothing I could do about it. I wanted the cocaine, I needed the cocaine, I wanted to be where the cocaine was.

I learned how to cook it up myself, freed myself from

Travis' house but got even deeper into the drug itself. Now I could do it anywhere.

Late one night in my room at the Marriott I was standing by the window smoking the shit when I was sure that I saw policemen in the parking lot. They were after me. They were going to bust me. I packed up all my stuff—my cocaine, my pipe, my lighter—put on my full-length fur coat, don't ask me why, and walked out of the hotel. I needed to go somewhere safe.

The Marriott was about fifteen blocks from the Astrodome. I would be safe at the Astrodome, it was the one place where I would probably get a break.

Clutching my freebase tools, the bag of coke rocks in my hand, I walked the fifteen blocks. Houston that night was hot and humid and as I stomped toward the stadium I was wired for hire, smoked, tweaked. The paranoia set in about the third block and I was looking in all directions, storming forward but watching my peripherals to see that nobody rushed me and busted me and took my cocaine away.

I got there. Felt like I'd been walking through the desert. Forget about going inside, it was all cooped up. I walked to the very middle of the parking lot and just sat there. I could see all the streets from there, all of them except for one where, 150 yards away, some weeds hid the view.

There were cops walking through those weeds. I was sure of it. Cops on these streets kept passing. Every car that came by seemed like it doubled back. They were closing in.

I pulled the coat over my head and lit my pipe and pulled on it—got that long, low snuffle of a sound—and smoked my cocaine.

I peeked out from behind the collar. My mouth wouldn't move, per usual. Freebase robbed me of my voice. I put the pipe on the ground and looked around. There was a rustling in the bushes. My voice returned.

"I know you cops are there!" I screamed. "I know you're there. But let me tell you something. If you try to run out here and bust me I'm gonna break the pipe and throw the coke all over the parking lot! You'll never get me!"

I was sitting there under a fur coat, perspiring, in the middle of the Astrodome parking lot at three o'clock in the morning, shouting and freebasing cocaine.

I hunched over under my coat for forty-five minutes, peeking and screaming. I smoked until the pipe got so clogged it wouldn't draw; I was putting rock after rock on and the damn stuff finally just shut it down. Only then did I stand up.

"You see this?" I shouted to the phantom forces. "This is a pipe. I'm gonna break the pipe! I have no more coke!!" I reared back and flung the bowl as far as I could throw it. The glass broke like a bell going off somewhere else. It skittered along the concrete.

"I threw the coke away!" I yelled. The parking lot absorbed nothing, my voice sounded thin in the air. "I don't have any drugs on me! I'm going back home now!"

With the lining of my coat drenched with sweat I staggered back to the Marriott. I had more rocks in my hand.

My hamstring finally healed and I got back to playing football. I was back, but I also brought back my cocaine addiction. I was obsessed. This freebase has cracked my brain. I didn't know about bills, I didn't know about responsibility, I didn't know about my wife or how my big three-hundred-thousand-dollar house in Dallas was doing. I knew nothing. All I knew was I wanted to freebase cocaine. And that's all I did. I slept three nights out of the week. The rest of the time I was at the pipe.

I missed seven games with my hamstring and when I got back the Oilers were 8–5.

My first game back we beat the Steelers 6–0. I had never taken a pipe to the Astrodome, never taken it anywhere near work, but this time I took it into the locker room. I freebased in the commode stalls before the game and played spectacularly.

The following week we were going to play the Green Bay Packers. I had gotten into the groove of not practicing while I was injured. I never wanted to practice, I wanted to play. I was playing with the defense on special pass situations and when the coaches called for the scout team to play the Packers' defense I did what Robert Brazile and other leading defensive players did, I walked off the field. This wasn't my job. I was in good company, standing on the sideline with Vernon Perry, Kenny Burroughs, Earl Campbell.

Out of the blue this loud voice came across the field. It was Mike Stensrud, number 67, a nose tackle who ran about six foot five, 300 pounds. "Hey, Hollywood! Why don't you get your ass out here and give them a defensive look. Who the fuck do you think you are! You've got to work like everybody else around here. Get your ass out here and work, you fuckin' dog!"

I had been up for three days freebasing cocaine and I don't take no talk like that from some fat stranger. If you're a friend of mine, maybe. Not from no fucking third-year stranger.

I looked at Kenny Burroughs and he kind of looked down at the ground. I put my headgear on, buckled my chinstrap and walked straight for Stensrud. Forty yards to where he was.

"Say, man, I'm tired. I'm trying to rest my hamstring muscle," I said to him softly. "And let me tell you something else. You don't call me a dog. Don't you ever in your fucking life call me a fuckin' dog again."

Stensrud said: "You fuckin' dog."

I hit him with a left hook and he dropped like a sack of potatoes. Six five, 300 pounds. Dropped. I knocked him out.

When my vision refocused I couldn't see him. When I looked down he was sitting on his ass propped up like a baby and kind of swaying. In slow motion he handled his jaw from side to side. He wouldn't get up. He had no fight in him to get up and come after me.

Bum Phillips looked at me, defensive coordinator Eddie Biles looked at me. I looked over and Robert Brazile was on the ground laughing. Kenny Burroughs was on the ground. Vernon Perry, Earl Campbell—they were about to die laughing.

I was mad, tired, based out, walking away, but they got me to laughing too.

I carried a pocketknife all the time, something I cut my coke with. When I got to the sidelines Robert Brazile told me, "You better watch that boy. That's a big motherfucker, you better watch him."

I said out loud for everybody to hear, "I'm gonna cut that boy's heart out if he fucks with me!"

I went to take a shower and put the knife in my mouth, blade open across my teeth like a pathfinder. My eyes were twitching, I was crazy, based out. I would have cut the motherfucker if he had come after me.

The next morning I went to the coach's office and saw Bum about it. I said, "I'm sorry. The guy called me out, he called me a name. I'm sorry it happened."

"Oh, it's all right," he told me. Bum didn't care.

We went up to Green Bay and won. Coming back on the plane Stensrud was getting drunk. He was a very large fellow. Robert Brazile came down the aisle and told me, "Hey, man, you better watch Stensrud. He's getting drunk, you better watch him."

Stensrud didn't know that I had gone from a three-inch blade to about a four-and-a-half-inch blade on the knife program. I sat there in my chair with my dark shades on. I had quit drinking beer but I was carrying a little bitty base pipe so I went back into the lavatory and got myself tweaked.

My paranoia rose like a shot when Brazile told me this big dude might try and repay me for decking him. We were thirty-eight thousand feet in the air going back to Houston from Lambeau Field in Green Bay and I leaned back in my chair and looked down the aisle and here was this big motherfucker coming right for me.

I eased my knife out of my pocket, slipped the blade open and locked it in the stabbing position where it wouldn't close on me. I was sitting against the window and the blade was in my right hand against the wall. I was ready to stab this motherfucker right in the throat if he came at me. I was dead serious about not letting him hurt me.

Stensrud was drunk all right. His tie was slipped all the way to one side of his chest and he was kind of rolling and tumbling down the aisle. The closer he got to me the more nervous I got. Two steps away from me I was ready to jump up and go, "Look, motherfucker, don't come back here fucking with me!" But I didn't, I just stayed ready.

He walked right up to the seat on the aisle and started leaning toward me.

I came within a fraction of committing murder. He came at me looking drunk, looking mean, looking ready to knock my head off. He leaned toward me and I gripped the knife tight.

"Hey, Hollywood." He was right up in my face. "Look, man, I've been drinking a little bit. Everybody thinks that I'm going to try and retaliate on you. I just want to let you know, man, that's it all over. I was wrong to call you out like that. I want you to know it's okay, man."

My heart started again. "It's all right, man," was all I had to say.

I was so doped up, so completely fucked up on freebasing cocaine that I had almost committed murder. His neck had been wide open and I would have stabbed him in it. I wouldn't have cut him, I wasn't about to slice the big monster and have him come after me. He would have died on the spot. I was going to murder him. He was dead! Cocaine had almost made me a murderer!

But freebasing, smoking cocaine, was the most important thing in my life by then. There was nothing that came in second. It was all I thought about and all I did.

I had learned to recognize my paranoia level, even if I couldn't control it. I knew before I took the first hit, for example, that at some point during the night I would get overwhelmed by the absolute certainty that people were watching me. So therefore when the urge came to go peep into a light socket to see if there was a microphone or camera in it I could hold myself back for a while. I had actually torn lamps apart in hotel rooms, torn apart furniture in my own house thinking I was being bugged. That's freebase.

I was basing in my room at the Marriott with two of my

teammates when one of the guys went over to the window and looked out. I had looked out that window many times. It was a large parking lot butted up against a tree-lined area close to a man-made ravine, a concrete-bottom creek. The cocaine I had was excellent and I knew what was going on in his head.

He stayed at the window for maybe ten or fifteen minutes, peeping out through the Venetian blinds. If anybody was staring in with binoculars or a telescopic lens they wouldn't have been able to see him. It was one o'clock in the morning and he was studying the parking lot. When he turned back to the room his eyes were on high beam.

"There are thirteen cops out there," he whispered. "All over the damn parking lot. I've got to get the hell out of here!"

I had never seen anybody do the paranoia deal except me. I wasn't arguing with him, I just watched.

The other guy, not wanting to bite into it, raised up and went over to the corner of the room, exactly where the first guy had been sitting. I was 100 percent sure there was no one in the parking lot. The parking lot was just a parking lot. But in the midst of paranoia you can conjure up anything you want.

The second guy stayed a little longer, standing over by the window for about twenty minutes. When he turned back toward us with the high beams on he said, "I only see twelve."

I knew their time in the room was short because once you get that paranoia you can't sit still. The best thing you can do, it seems, is to get in the car and drive. You don't feel so trapped that way. You still trip—every car is suspect and your peripheral vision is filled with intruders—but you're moving. It's a dangerous thing, paranoia. It can almost drive you to suicide. You're completely convinced that you're being watched, looked in on, violated. It's like you're in prison. There's nowhere to hide.

They left. I went over to the window and looked out. After I got to the fourth cop I quit.

* * *

In a ten-week period in Houston, Texas, I was literally consumed by cocaine. I didn't even snort it anymore. I forgot about my nose, there were more important things to think about, like when I was going to get the next pipeful. Even football didn't matter. Bum Phillips had to move me through waivers in order to reactivate me off the injured reserve list but he did it with no worry; no other team was going to claim me. I was the bad boy of the NFL.

I came back late in the season and the team was in position to get into the playoffs. Nobody likes to back in and if we beat the Minnesota Vikings in the last game we guaranteed ourselves a spot.

Eddie Biles was the Oilers' defensive coordinator and he didn't like me. I often told him point-blank that I was a better linebacker than Robert Brazile, and Biles didn't want to hear it because it seemed like he felt he personally had built Brazile. But Bum Phillips wanted me on the field; he knew my ability to cover backs out of the backfield. He was responsible for my being an Oiler in the first place.

In the fourth quarter of the Vikings game Biles didn't want to but he threw me in. The Vikings were threatening with under two minutes to go. We were ahead 20–16, but they were about at our thirty. They could beat us if they scored a touchdown.

The Oilers called a straight zone coverage. (If you could count to three you could play for the Oilers, they were not a high-tech system. I never saw a playbook while I was there.) When the ball was snapped I dropped into my zone out in the flat.

When a linebacker drops into a zone he has to look at the back to see if he is doing a swing pattern, which is an arc, or a sideline. If the back heads for the sideline you've got to think, "Do I bite on the short sideline or are they really trying to do something behind me?" With my experience I got a good deep drop, laid there and hung. I keyed on the Vikings' quarterback, Tommy Kramer.

Ahmad Rashad ran a deep comeback to the outside. If he caught that ball he'd be on the ten yard line and we'd be in trouble. I laid in my zone and watched Kramer. When I saw that he was going to throw the ball behind me I took off at top speed for the sideline. I was running at a forty-five-degree angle and right in front of Rashad I leaped as high as I possibly could and caught the ball with my hands, just my hands. Came down inbounds with the interception before my momentum carried me out right in front of the Oiler bench.

I'd saved the game. I had stopped the Vikings' drive. We were going to win. We were in the playoffs!

I was lying there, the ball in my arms, just about to party, when Eddie Biles dove on top of me. "Don't make a fuss out of this," he whispered in my ear. He was holding me down. "Don't make a fuss out of this!" I was ready to run out on the field with the ball, hold it high, show it to the fans, the whole routine. But Biles didn't want me to celebrate because he hadn't wanted me in the game to make that play in the first place. I'd never seen a coach suppress a player like that before. He wouldn't let me up until the ball was gone and the time had passed. (What I didn't know but found out later was that Biles was undermining Bum Phillips and angling for his job.)

We went to Oakland the next week to play the Raiders. I spent most of that week basing and when I got to San Francisco I called some of my early-season contacts and had a party in my room.

We lost to the Raiders and I don't remember much about the game. I think I played well on the specialty teams but I can't be sure. I was going through blackout phases and don't remember much of anything. I just know that I was numb and full of Percodan.

I got back to my coke. Cooking it myself I'd take a two-and-a-half-inch glass vial with a pressure cap and I'd dump my dope in it. Street people put a quarter of a gram, a smidgen, inside and cook it up to try and turn it back into a rock. Not me. I'd drop two grams in the vial and put in a half gram of Arm & Hammer baking soda, then I'd put about an inch and a half of water in a pot on the stove, get the water to boiling, put the vial in the water and watch the magic happen.

As the heat melted the cocaine it would rise to the top then all of a sudden it would drop and start to harden. I would loosen the pressure cap, put it back on the fire and boil it some more. When the cocaine turned an almost yellowish tint I would take the vial in my hand and flick it with my wrist to mold the coke into a solid ball, a rock. It became an art, that flicking.

The whole thing became a ritual. As I put a pile on the stove the saliva would actually start to run in my mouth. I would sit there and drool like Dracula. I could taste it, my lungs strained for it.

I didn't do freebase like other people. Some people could just take a hit and put the coke back in the drawer. My deal was to do it all. That was how I did drugs, that was how I did alcohol, that was how I did everything. I did not do it sociably, I did it to get screwed up. And I stayed screwed up.

My wife had taken my daughter and left me during the season, kicked me out of my house. She went to court and had a peace bond put on me so that I couldn't even come close to my daughter or my house. After one particularly nasty confrontation I phoned her and a policeman answered. "Mr. Henderson," he told me, "we think you should get out of the area before we put you under arrest."

I was sure they were going to bust me. I didn't even go back to the Marriott. I left a couple of suits, a briefcase, a couple of pairs of shoes, all my papers, my driver's license, and went straight to the airport.

I went back to Dallas and moved in with a beautiful, sweet young woman I'll call Sally Ullman. I'd met her just before I'd married Wyetta and I'd known then that I was marrying the wrong woman but it had been too late. Sally truly cared for me; I quickly fell in love with her. I don't know if it was that I needed a shoulder to lean on or the fact that she was kind and soothing and lovely, but I cooled out when I got there. She was everything I needed but probably didn't deserve.

For one whole week I didn't freebase. I could get like that.

I didn't crave cocaine until I had the first hit, then I needed it to live.

But my abstinence didn't last long. I ran into an old friend of mine named Will who had the bag. Will was freebasing, he lived five minutes from Sally's place, and I took off. I went to the bank and withdrew my 7-Up commercial money. In three weeks I went through fifteen thousand dollars in cash and ended up owing him another five grand.

I wasn't sober but I'd woken up dry the day of Super Bowl XV, the Raiders against the Eagles at the New Orleans Superdome. I was at home with Sally and I started watching the game. By halftime my whole life was passing in front of me. I wanted to be out there playing but I had fucked up everything. My career was in jeopardy, my body was going, my money was going faster than my body.

I jumped up and left the house and went back over to Will's. "Give me a half ounce," I told him. "I'll pay you the money as soon as I get to the bank." I started basing there.

I came back home that night and started basing in the house. Sally had never seen me freebase. She looked at my eyes and started crying. "You ought to see yourself. Thomas, this is not you. I cannot believe the way you look when you're doing this thing." I could see in her eyes the questions: "Where, in this sickness, lives this man? Why, in this sickness, lives this man? How, in this sickness, lives this man?" She said, "Your eyes are so sad. Why are you doing this to yourself?"

I couldn't say a word. All I wanted to do was go back upstairs to the bathroom, lock the door and freebase some more. I'd been running and running and running and I couldn't stop. There was nowhere else to go. I was holed up in this young girl's house and I thought I was going to die.

I was sitting around that night, zombied in front of the tube, when the Super Bowl highlights came on. There, on the sidelines in one of the replays, was Charlie Jackson, head of NFL Security. He had come to all of the training camps I'd been at, giving his little lecture on the danger of drugs.

The last time I'd seen him had been on the practice field at Houston. He'd pulled me over and said that he had heard a lot of stuff about me in San Francisco, that he knew about the situation in Dallas and the police inquiries. NFL Security was well aware of my escapades. He hadn't said any more than that, just that he was watching.

The next morning I called the Hyatt Regency in New Orleans and asked to speak to him. I knew he'd be staying there. Jackson wasn't in. They gave me his room number and I said I'd call back later. I took off over to Will's place and came home with a big bag of coke. Then I called him again.

I was sitting in the living room. Sally was sitting across from me, crying, in tears. She couldn't believe I was slouched there smoking this cocaine, couldn't hold a conversation, my tongue was not working. The only thing that was working was that I could suck the cocaine. Bathing wasn't important, speaking wasn't important, nothing was important.

I sat there with a Bic lighter, gurgling, smoking from my freebase pipe. I got Charlie Jackson on the line.

"Mr. Jackson . . ." My voice was coming and going as I swallowed the smoke. Sounded like I was going under. "This is Th . . . Th . . . Thomas Henderson. . . ."

"How're you doing, Thomas?"

"Uh . . . Charlie . . . I'm fucked up. I'm freebasing. *Right now I am freebasing!* While I'm talking to you! I'm sick. I need some help. This cocaine is killing me!"

Sally sat up in her chair across from me. "Ho . . . Hold on a minute," I told him. I put another large rock on the pipe and lit it. When I put the pipe down it was still smoking.

"You still there, Charlie?"

"Yeah."

"What can I do, man? Can y'all help me? I'm sick. This coke is killing me. It's ruining my life. I don't know what the hell I'm gonna do. I'm spending all my money. I'm goin' crazy, man!"

"You hold on. Let me call you right back." He was frazzled. I think I stunned him. He was supposed to smoke out drug users. Having drug users come to him was a new experience. But I didn't know where else to turn. I had told a doctor in San Francisco and gotten turned out of there in a flash, nobody had helped me. Dallas knew, the organization knew, but nobody knew what to do. They were trading dope addicts, they were cutting alcoholics. They were getting rid of the problems, not trying to fix them or see that people got treatment.

While I waited for his call I smoked and smoked and smoked. Finally he called me back.

"I want you to go see this psychiatrist tomorrow morning first thing. Then we're going to try and get you into a drug facility."

I didn't argue with him.

"I'm going to call you back and give you the information."

I made an appointment for the next day. But I still had this whole bag of cocaine to smoke through. Sally talked me into letting it go. She made me a gin and tonic, Tanqueray and tonic. "Here, drink this and settle down, please. Come on." Refreshing drink but it got me drunk. I went upstairs and got two Quaaludes, broke them in half so I had four pieces, and ate all four while I drank this tall tumbler of Tanqueray and tonic. That took the edge off me and I managed to go to sleep that night.

I was driving my Mercedes with my legs again, holding the pipe in my hand, sucking on a few rocks on the way to the doctor's. Sally was sitting next to me, crying again. Nothing I could do about it, my body just needed this cocaine and I couldn't fight it.

The doctor's office was in a shabby little building in East Dallas. The doctor, a clinical psychologist, came out of his office with his spectacles lying down on his nose. Didn't look to me like a man in touch with the modern world. "Are you Mr. Henderson?" My mouth wasn't working again because I was under the influence and I sounded like a seal.

"Yeah. Yeah."

"Come right in, sir." The man had a timid voice, like a

schoolboy whose only friends were his books. He sat down behind his desk and took out a long legal pad.

"Mr. Henderson," he mewed, "how long have you been using cocaine?"

"Five years off and on," I stammered, "but it's gotten real tough here the last year or so. I've just started freebasing recently and I can't stop. I can't quit."

"Do you want to quit?"

"Hell, yeah, I want to quit but I just can't. The idea of freebasing seems more attractive than anything I know right now. It means more than love, it means more than my daughter, it means more than my career in football, it means more than anything." I put it straight to him. "The idea of smoking cocaine means everything to me right now."

The doctor was taking notes. Then he looked up. "Mr. Henderson, tell me a little bit about your childhood."

I exploded. "Man, fuck you! What am I going to tell you about my childhood when I've got coke out in my car? I'm going to go smoke some more goddamn coke right now. I ain't going to sit here and get fucking analyzed by you, what is this shit about my childhood? What about some drugs? I need to get off this shit! I don't need you sitting there psychoanalyzing me. Fuck you. Fuck you! I'm gone!"

I got back in the car and grabbed the pipe. I was parked right in front and I could see the guy looking out his window, looking at me. I took my freebase pipe and took my lighter and gurgled as I sucked the hot coke in and saluted him with it, waved the thing at him and drove away.

I went back to Sally's house. Within two hours the NFL called. "Thomas, we heard about your interview. You're in bad shape, aren't you?"

"I'm freebasing right now, motherfucker. Just like I was yesterday. I haven't stopped yet."

They put me into treatment. I told them I didn't have any money, "If I did I'd buy some more base"—dopers will lie to you—so they bought me a plane ticket and sent me on my way to Camelback Hospital in Scottsdale, Arizona.

Before I left I went by Will's and got me three and a half

grams, figured that ought to last me for the trip. Cooked it up. Sally said, "I can't believe you. I have no more tears. You are crazy. You need to go stay in that hospital. Forever. I love you, Thomas, but goddamn, you are crazy. You're losing your mind."

I was cold. "Leave me alone."

I freebased on the airplane to Scottsdale. Went to the lavatory and smoked, sat back down. Five minutes later I went back and did it again. Smoked all the way there.

I grabbed a cab at the airport and told the cab driver to take me to Camelback. As soon as we were on the highway I pulled my freebase pipe out of my bag and fired it up.

"What is that?" he asked in the rearview mirror.

"This is my asthma medicine."

"Oh, sure, that's asthma medicine. What the fuck are you doing back there?"

"Well, I'm sick, man. I'm going to the drug rehabilitation center and I'm smoking the last of my cocaine."

"What? You're smoking cocaine? You damn sure need to be in a hospital, doing that shit!"

I freebased all the way to Scottsdale, Arizona. Gave the taxi driver a twenty-dollar tip. He said, "You don't come out of there until you're well, Bud."

I had flown all across the desert to be at this place and at least I had come in by myself. I could say that much for myself. I sat on the steps of this brand-new hospital and decided to smoke my last rock. I lit up the half gram I had left. Because it was there. I took five or six good hits, looking behind me, looking to both sides to see if anybody was coming. Finally I stood up. This was it. I turned and threw the freebase pipe against the concrete hospital wall, listened to it shatter and walked inside.

I was tweaked, sprung, my high beams were on. "I'm Thomas Henderson," I told the receptionist.

"Oh, Mr. Henderson. We've been expecting you. Please have a seat."

I was moving too fast to be sitting down. "No, I'll be outside," I told her. The room had got to me.

I was pacing the steps. Tweaking. Full of it. Every hair of my body from my toes to the top of my head was possessed by cocaine. I was looking at the wall to see if maybe I could find some of the stuff I'd thrown away and put it in the end of a cigarette when two men came walking through the door. One was Mr. Civac, a psychologist, and the other was a black man who was running the program. They came and sat on either side of me.

"We're happy to meet you, Mr. Henderson."

"Hey. I want to let you know that I'm wired up, I got loaded all the way over here, and do you have something to bring me down."

"We'll get you something, Mr. Henderson. Why don't you come on in."

I was rushing. "Do I have to sign anything? Do I have to fill out anything? I don't want to fill out shit, I just want to come down. I want to just come down. I want to lay down. I've been up for a few days, I just want to lay down. You go into these hospitals bleeding and shit and they want you to sit there and fill out forms, ask you who your insurance is. I don't know, man. I just want to lay down. Can I just lay down? That's all I want to do."

The doctors were very calm. "We'll have you fill out the papers when you feel better. Why don't you just come on in."

I walked through the doors with Dr. Civac on one side and the director on the other.

I was the first NFL player to go public with his cocaine addiction. I wasn't the first man to have this kind of problem and play in the league but I was the first to say publicly that something was wrong and that I needed help in dealing with it. I had been looking for some way to escape my addiction for almost a year but I hadn't known where to go. I don't think the NFL knew how to handle it either, the whole thing was too new. I definitely did not want to be the trailblazer for the league's drug rehabilitation program—I didn't want to have the problem to begin with—but I was, only because I thought I was going to die and I didn't know where else to turn.

In my hospital room the nurse gave me a large dose of Valium, which she said would probably help me rest well for a day or two. Then she picked my bag up off the floor and started to go through it.

"What are you doing?" I barked.

"I have to search your bag."

"No you're not searching none of my goddamn things. I left the drugs outside. You have no right to search my bag."

"I'll send the doctors over," she said.

The doctors never came, they left me alone. I didn't want them to find the half ounce of pot I had brought along for comfort. Skunk weed was not my problem, I thought; drinking was not my problem; my problem was cocaine and cocaine only. The Valium came on and I passed out.

I had nightmares. I was dying and waking up in a strange place, felt like I was in prison.

I slept for two days solid. When I woke up I wouldn't come out of my room.

Three days after I got there I ventured out into the hallway. Dr. Civac was my assigned psychologist and we began talking. I opened up to him. I told him how I used; I never could tell him why.

I went to my first therapy group and there was a nurse at the blackboard telling this small roomful of cocaine abusers about the chemical properties of the drug, what opiates are, what they are derived from, what they create in your body. I was sitting there thinking, "Yeah, okay, this is interesting stuff. But I'm coughing up black phlegm, what can you do for me?" I raised my hand. "Excuse me, ma'am, may I ask you a question?"

"Yes."

"Have you ever gotten loaded?"

"No," she said, "but my son has smoked marijuana."

Not good enough. "I don't want to listen to you. I need to talk to somebody who's gotten high, who's felt what I've felt, who knows how I've felt.'' I got real agitated and walked out.

Dr. Civac came to see me in my room. "I'm killing myself with this shit. I need to talk to somebody who's done it and can tell me how to stay off it.''

"Thomas, that's the educational process," he told me. "If you'd stayed a little longer she would have told you what it does to your body and how you can get addicted to it and how to release yourself from your addiction.''

I returned to the meetings but I was bored. I told the nurse that marijuana wasn't my problem, beer wasn't my problem. She told me, "Any mind-altering chemical is your problem once you become addicted to one of them. Once you become addicted, any mind-altering chemical will ultimately take you back to your drug of choice.''

"No," I argued, "that ain't true. That ain't true." As a matter of fact, I wanted to tell her but didn't, I smoked a joint just this morning. In the midst of treatment at Camelback Hospital I was smoking pot.

The group played out psychodramas, put individual members under hypnosis and drew them through some trying times. They wouldn't do that with me because, as big and strong as I was, they were afraid that if a lot of my true feelings came out about Tom Landry and the Dallas Cowboys I would become too violent for them to handle.

After I'd been at the hospital two weeks and hadn't had a touch or taste of cocaine they began to give me passes. I could go out into Scottsdale for the day. The Oakland A's baseball spring training camp was about six blocks from Camelback and I rented a car and drove over.

By this time the NFL had released to the press that I was in drug rehabilitation, so that was a topic of conversation. It became a daily thing for me, get a two-hour pass and go hang out at the ballpark.

I met Mike Norris, a talented A's pitcher, and told him what I was doing. "Good, man. I'm proud of you, Hollywood." A couple of times I went back to his apartment. He was snorting cocaine, I'd be smoking marijuana telling him,

"Leave that coke alone. I'm telling you, that stuff is terrible. You ain't basing yet?"

"No, I'm just snorting it."

There I was in drug rehab, drinking beer and smoking pot and giving advice.

The Camelback program lasted twenty-eight days but I was sure that I was going to stay a lot longer. I was getting comfortable with the idea of hanging around this place because I wasn't doing any cocaine.

Dr. Civac found me one morning in my room. "Thomas, we have a problem at the front door. We have a man who wants to serve you with some papers. We can stop him from serving you but ultimately you are going to have to face this. He'll just wait in the parking lot until you leave on a pass. Why don't you go get them."

"What are they?"

"I have no idea," he said. "They're sealed."

I went to the front door of the hospital and this guy hands me an envelope. "Are you Thomas Henderson?"

"Yes."

"Here, take this." He put it in my hand and walked away.

My wife had filed for divorce.

My marriage had been over for two years before it even began—we had stopped loving each other a long time before we signed the documents that put us together—but still I stood there holding my divorce papers and started to cry. I sat down in the lobby and flipped through them, tears falling on the pages.

All the time I'd been in the treatment center my wife hadn't called. I couldn't call her; Wyetta had changed the number. I called my mother-in-law to find it out. I was still paying the bill but she told me she wouldn't give me my own home phone.

I got a pass that night. They didn't want to give me one but I talked them into it. Went out, found a bar, got drunk, met a girl and went home with her. I had an eight-hour pass but I stayed out till six in the morning and when I got back to the treatment unit I was singing. The nurse told me she was going to give me a urine test. "Hey, don't worry, I didn't do any coke," I gargled. "But you might find some skunk weed and some beer in there!"

They put me in psychiatric lock-up. It was either that or throw me out.

"We are trying to get through your head that it's good that you have not done any cocaine but you're defeating the process if you continue to drink beer and smoke marijuana."

"Those are not my problems, sir," I argued. "My problem is cocaine. Don't you understand? My problem is cocaine, and I haven't done any cocaine." But I had made a few phone calls to try and get some. I was ready to have a little bit to see if it was any different.

They locked me up. Took all my clothes, all my cigarettes, all my matches. I could walk the halls in hospital-issue pajamas and robe but they locked me in my room at ten o'clock at night. I argued with them that beer and pot were not my problem but they kept me locked up. Sally came and visited me—with my wife filing for divorce I told the doctor I needed my girlfriend for support—and when she saw me on the ward with all these senile and seriously damaged patients she broke down and cried.

When they finally let me go back to the regular ward the doctors told me, "One more prank like that and we're letting you go."

I was well into thirty-five days at the center and I told them I wanted to stay through a whole nother program. "I don't think I got it the first time around."

I stayed at Camelback for two full sessions, about sixty days. When I checked out I just felt it was time to move on. I hadn't done cocaine in almost nine weeks and I was satisfied that I was no longer a user.

Spending so much time around a hospital I figured I'd get my nose fixed. I went to see a specialist and he said, "My God, what have you been doing, poking your nose with an ice pick? I've never seen anything like this." He gave me some millimeters and centimeters and told me he was going to cut out what the cocaine had destroyed.

I asked Bob Breunig to wheel me into surgery. Bob had gone to Arizona State and his parents lived in Phoenix. He has a real good heart. He had been concerned about me going into treatment and invited me over to his parents' house for dinner. It was wonderful to see him. I cared for him much more as a guy than I had as a teammate, and I believe he felt the same. I drank about two six-packs over dinner and talked about my operation.

"Bob, I'm scared about going under the knife."

"What are you going under the knife for?"

"My nose is all screwed up from doing all that cocaine."

"You know, I never knew you were snorting coke. I knew you blew your nose a lot, and came in all excited sometimes and then came in all grouchy. Are you going to stay off the stuff?"

"I have to, Bob, I have to." I sat back in my chair. "Can I have another beer?"

The surgery was successful but it left a permanent hole in my nose. It was real painful and the doctor gave me a prescription for Percodan—"refill as needed"—to alleviate the suffering. For ten days straight I took four Percodan every four hours and spent a considerable amount of time running to the pharmacy.

The pain, the Percodan, the beer and the marijuana sprung me again. I wanted some coke. I called Houston and had one of my connections fly to Phoenix and bring me a quarter ounce. I paid for his flight, his room, his time. I took the seven grams of coke and I freebased.

I went back to Dallas and kept at it. Everybody around the country thought I was well. After all, I was three weeks out of a double session at the rehab center. But I was also in the middle of a divorce, went to see lawyers, spent time in court, finally settled with Wyetta, and started back to freebasing again. I was back to my old self. I found myself at a dealer's apartment one night at four in the morning and he wasn't going to give me no credit. I gave him my full-length beaver coat, worth five thousand dollars, and I gave it to him for a quarter ounce of coke.

Still and all I wanted to play football and in April I began shopping the league for some team that might accept me. I called St. Louis, Philadelphia, they didn't call me back. I called Gil Brandt at the Cowboys. No.

I called Don Shula. Just called him. "Coach, are you interested in a good linebacker? I've been in treatment, I'm better, I want to play ball."

Shula checked me out. He called Camelback and confirmed that I had spent sixty days there successfully sober. He called me back.

"Listen, Henderson, I'm coming through Dallas. Why don't you come out to the airport and meet me. I'd like to see you, talk to you."

I got to the airport nervous. I was loaded, sweaty. I'd been freebasing all night. I left a half-lit pipe on the floorboard of my Mercedes in the parking lot, went to the rest room and threw water on my face, tried to clean up, put on some shades and went to meet Don Shula.

"You've gained some weight," he said when he saw me. I had put on ten pounds and looked healthy. He couldn't see my eyes. We talked for a half hour and he said he'd give me a tryout in May. I was in. If Shula liked me I was going to play.

Meanwhile I was going to base. I still had some money but the payments on my three-hundred-thousand-dollar house were putting a severe dent into my ability to buy cocaine. I went to Roger Staubach, who I trusted in things like finance and money, and told him I wanted to put my house up for sale. He got an agent and put it on the market. My dream house or a continuing supply of cocaine; I couldn't afford both. I chose the dope.

I was staying with Sally. I was this vagabond ex-superstar dope addict but she was still putting up with me.

I went to the tryout in Miami looking healthy but with my mind fogged. Still, I was serious enough about this gig that I went to Florida without cocaine.

When I landed I went straight to the Dolphins' training camp at Biscayne College. Shula and I had a talk. He talked.

"Thomas, do you plan to be in after-care? Are you going to go to meetings and stay sober? You've got to go to those meetings, you know that, don't you?"

I was surprised that he knew so much about the rehabilitation process. I didn't ask him how he knew.

"I'll do whatever you want me to do, Coach."

"You look heavy."

"Yeah, I'm about twenty, twenty-five pounds bigger than I've ever been."

"What do you weigh?"

"I don't know. Let's go over to the scale and weigh me." I was 242.

"You are big."

He set me up to run a forty-yard dash. That's linebacker territory. If you can't run the forty you can't run; you've got to get there in a hurry when you're a linebacker.

I went out to the field and warmed up. It was a humid day in May, Miami, 1981, and I warmed up seriously. I wanted to run good. I spread out on the ground warming up my hamstrings and my groin muscles, my calves and thighs. I knew I could run, I'd always been able to run, I just had to work a little harder than normal to impress him.

But this 242 worried me. And the fact that I was running on grass. The field hadn't been mowed, I was going to run in about four inches of uncut grass. I wasn't on Tartan Turf, I wasn't on asphalt. I had to trudge the grass and run too. I couldn't afford to run a 4.9, no, I couldn't run a five-flat.

Shula didn't trust the stop watch to an assistant coach, he was going to clock me himself. I knew that this run would decide everything, this run would make me or break me, this run would determine whether I would ever play football again. Nobody else was calling.

When I pulled my hand up off the ground and took off toward Shula I was running for my life.

I charged past the coach like a horse. Didn't stop at the

finish line, I ran eighty-five yards, galloping, cantering at the end. I doubled back as he looked at his watch.

"Damn, that's a 4.6! That's fast enough." He looked at his watch, then at me. "Run another one for me."

Normally I'm not real good at running sprints again but I didn't have a choice.

"Are you sure he's behind the line?" Shula called to his assistant.

"Yup, sure is."

"Are you sure you marked off forty yards?"

"We've been timing them here for years, Coach."

"Okay. Whenever you're ready, Henderson."

I ran a 4.6 again, in tall grass at 242, and made the Miami Dolphins.

I called Coach Landry late that week and asked if I could use the Cowboy facilities to do some training. "You never trained when you played for us," he cracked but he let me in.

The Cowboys are very conservative people, a very conservative organization, but once you've played for the Dallas Cowboys—good, bad or indifferent—you will always be a Dallas Cowboy. Me, Duane Thomas, Bob Hayes, Lance Rentzel, Pete Gent, whoever—gone astray or right on the straight and narrow—no matter what we do we're all still part of the family. It's kind of a paradox; while you're there they don't treat you very well but once you're gone you can always come back.

I ran into Randy White on the practice field. Randy was never a bad guy, in fact he was a real nice guy, but from the first day I had resented him. I was supposed to have been the Cowboys' number-one draft choice in 1976 but they had gone and traded way up in the draft to get him and I always felt that he had invaded my glory. Maybe if I'd been a second- or third-round draft choice there wouldn't have been a conflict, but there was.

Dr. Bob Ward was the conditioning coach and he always had some martial arts equipment out there because he was some kind of a belt in karate. That day he had these pillows with handles on the back of them and ropes that tied them to your waist. Grown men could have pillow fights with these things. It was a quickness drill, who could get in the first licks, who could counterpunch. You could deliver a real good shot with these things and fall just short of killing someone.

I had always woofed at Randy White over the years. "Fuck you, you big white son of a bitch, I'll whip you!" I used to yell at him. "Just 'cause you're big and got a roadrunner on your leg doesn't mean you can whip me. I'll whip your ass!" I knew I probably could outbox him, but Randy White is a monster and I also knew that if he ever got his hands on me Randy White could kill me.

"You want to try this, Randy?" I called to him.

After all this time he was ready. He picked up two of these things and I picked up two and we squared off. It was the first time Randy White and I ever went at each other.

Charlie Waters, Bob Bruenig, the trainer and some of the coaches were standing around watching. It's mid-May and there's a full but informal Cowboy workout going on.

I was getting the best of him. I'm a whole lot quicker than Randy and, *pow*, I hit him in the ear. *Pow.* Hit him in the head. *Pow.* Hit him in the chin, and I was getting away with murder. I was getting back with my head so quick that he couldn't get his counterpunches in and he wasn't quick enough to land the first one. For three minutes, about the equivalent of one round in the boxing ring, I just embarrassed him. He was clumsy, he was looking for me and I wasn't there. These pillows didn't hurt or anything but it was humiliating for him to keep getting hit.

I hit him with a left, hit him with a right, and he couldn't do anything. I beat him. It was over. When I walked away I turned and said, "See there, I told you I could whup your big ol' slow ass."

I was sitting in the locker room in front of my old locker. Somebody else's clothes in there but it was my old locker. Randy White came by and I said, half under my breath, "You are a sorry motherfucker."

He didn't take to it kindly. "Henderson," he bellowed, "just shut up! I don't want to hear your shit in here!"

I said, "Randy White, fuck you!"

I got up and I don't know what got into me but I slapped the shit out of him. Slapped him across his big dumb face. I had to have been way out of control to do a stupid thing like that.

Randy White grabbed me like I was a sack of cotton. He picked me up by the arm and the waist and threw me about ten feet into an open locker. I came out of there hurting all over and ran to grab him. It was like grabbing a deep freezer.

He treated me like a child. He threw me to the floor and held me there. He was so strong he pinned me to the floor against my will. Nobody had ever done that before. If he had wanted to beat the hell out of me he could have. But I knew that about him, I knew he wouldn't even ball his fist at me.

"Henderson," he said from on top of me, "you going to stop? You going to stop?"

Jerry Tubbs appeared, and Buck Buchanan and Don Cochren and Dr. Bob Ward, and Randy White continued to hold me to the carpet.

"Motherfucker, let me up! *Let me up!*"

Rayfield Wright came over and said, "Come on, Hollywood, settle down."

"Get this motherfucker off me!"

Randy White backed up off me and I jumped up. "You want to fight, man? Come on, motherfucker! Come on!" I was ready now. I wanted to go. I would not have backed down. I knew I couldn't handle him but I would not have backed down. We left it at that.

Before I left for the Dolphins' training camp I went around borrowing money. Tex Schramm, Roger Staubach, Drew Pearson all loaned me some bucks. I had no pride and no control. I also didn't have any money and I didn't want to run out of coke. I was trying to be straight when I started with the Dolphins—I knew this was my last chance—but just in case. . . .

In Florida I had to show up with the rookies. I did it and didn't complain. Don Shula took me aside early. "I know you went through treatment," he told me. "I hope you're clean. Every Wednesday night I want you to go to this meeting. You may not have a car and you may not know where it is, so my wife will take you or I will take you. But you will go to that meeting every Wednesday night."

The first Wednesday night we went down to South Miami Hospital, which is a major drug treatment center. Me and Shula! He cared about me, he wanted me to stay clean, to stay off the coke. And I was going to try and do the best I could.

I was up to about 247 by the time training camp started. I decided to become a vegetarian, no meat in camp. Salads, soups, more salad, fruits and salads. And it worked. In three weeks of training camp I lost thirty-two pounds. It was humid and I was drinking Old English 800 Malt Liquor at night and it was knocking me out.

My defensive coach was Bill Arnsbarger. He had a great defensive mind and I loved working with the man. I started working harder than I'd ever worked before, getting my techniques down, my tackling, hitting. I was going through the conditioning period and doing what I was told. I still couldn't run any distances. The team had a twelve-minute run, kind of like Landry's Hill in Dallas, and I came in second to last. The only man to come in behind me was quarterback David Woodley and Shula gave him a hard time about it: "Woodley, the dope addict beat you!"

The veterans were in camp but not dressing out and Shula told me he wanted me to play on the rookie scrimmage. Another test of my sincerity. I said okay. All the veterans stood around the field—Bob Baumhower, A. J. Duhe, Larry Gordon, Don Strock, the Killer Bees—and watched. Bum Phillips had just taken over the head coaching job with the New Orleans Saints and he brought his rookies over for the scrimmage.

They ran a slant play my way, I stopped it for a three-yard loss. They ran another slant, I stopped it for a four-yard loss.

They ran a draw play my way, I stopped it for a two-yard loss. Then they dropped back to pass and I blitzed and sacked the quarterback. Bum said, "Hold it, hold it, hold it. Let's run the other way so we can get something done."

Shula was proud of me and I was glad to see that I hadn't lost anything, I could still play this game.

One of the rookies kept missing practices, getting hurt, getting carried off the field. One day at lunchtime I saw him peeking out his door, looking up and down the corridor. I knew that look. Looked like Thomas in a hooker hotel in a run-down part of Dallas. I waited. I knew how long it took to cook base up, how long it took to get that first hit. I waited just long enough and then went up and knocked on his door real hard.

"Hey, man, open up!" Not a casual knock. "This is Hollywood. Open up!"

He came to the door and I saw that sad delirium in his eyes, like he was being followed by a pack of wild dogs and he was getting tired. I walked inside and closed the door behind me. There was the familiar odor.

"You're basing, ain't you, man?"

He didn't say anything.

"Give me a hit."

I started to seek him out and about the second week of preseason I started to freebase again.

I was still going to my Wednesday meeting. I wasn't out of control but I wasn't in control, either. One evening as we were cruising down the freeway heading down into Miami Shula said, "You know, Henderson, the reason that I'm involved in this thing and I am trying to get more education about drug abuse myself is that it hit pretty close to home with me, somebody close to me. I understand what you're going through and I'm trying to learn more about it." No coach had ever gotten this involved with me and I appreciated it more than I could say. Still, I was controlled by the substance, I didn't control it.

As the season approached I was in the best shape of my life. Even though I was freebasing, the conditioning and se-

rious attention to workouts had paid off. I felt great. I felt
wanted. The linebacker who had been wearing number 56
had been traded away so I even got my old number back.
Miami was happy with me, the organization was happy with
me, I was happy with me. I wasn't going out and freebasing
for five days straight; I figured anything less than that was
a good week for me. I was right on the edge but no one
knew it.

Shula wasn't starting me in the preseason games but I was
seeing some good action. He was monitoring my progress. I
felt he was watching and approving.

The final preseason game was on a Friday night in Miami
against the Kansas City Chiefs. Ever since my injury in San
Francisco I had worn a neck roll, one of those protective pads
that looks like a couch bolster wrapped around a player's
shoulders. I also wore flack shoulder pads which filled up
with air and protected you from some of the violent pounding
that went on. But that night it was humid, as Miami will get
in August, and I decided to take it off. My neck felt hot and
loose from the warmups, plus I felt really confined in that
collar. Without it I had more flexibility, visibility, my movement wasn't diminished, I could play better.

I was playing outside linebacker and in the second quarter
the Chiefs ran a normal slant play in my direction. It was a
fullback lead but I avoided the blocker and stuck my head
right into the running back, Joe Delaney. My neck snapped.

It was like being hit on the crown of your skull with a
sledgehammer. The pressure, the compression, I felt like I
was going to accordion right up. I blacked out.

I came out of it as any football player would: I tried to
play through it. I did not like the idea of being carried off
the field, even hurt. I struggled to stand up. My neck was
shaking, my body was shaking, my hands were shaking, I
got up like a man with Parkinson's disease and tried to shake
it off. All my life I've been able to shake it off—that's part of
being a player—but this wouldn't go away. My legs and back
tingled inside where I couldn't scratch them.

I did not want to leave the game; I thought it would wear

off. I'd felt the same way when I got hit in San Francisco. Identical excruciating pain. I'd lived. I was on my feet so my legs were still working, I was not dead, I was able to carry on. There's a whole pro ballplayers' ethos: Go. I could go. I'd seen football players hurt a finger and lie on the ground. What the fuck is wrong with your legs, boss? Get up and walk off the field and get the finger taken care of, but you don't fall down and hold your finger. If I was standing, my legs must be okay. Let's play ball.

I started to feel numb. I felt like I'd taken a giant Percodan; from my neck down, my whole body was feeling weird. It hadn't been any great hit, no sensational tackle, nothing that was going to show up in the highlight films. What's all this? I struggled back to the huddle.

I don't remember what defense was called. I was in a blackout as we huddled, a daze when we broke.

When I came out and lined up over the tight end the pain hit me. Ten times worse than when I'd made the hit. I felt like a thresher was running over me. Now.

They snapped the ball and I ran away. I didn't want anybody to touch me. The tight end was trying to block me and I ran twenty yards in the other direction. I was racing from him like he had a knife. When the play ended I just fell on the ground.

My neck was broken. If the tight end had taken me on it would have snapped my spine.

They came out and got me, took me into the locker room. A team physician examined me on a table and told me to stay where I was. They took my shoulder pads off and went back out to the field. I was lying in the locker room of the Orange Bowl with a broken neck and everyone left me to go back out for the second half of the game.

I tried to get up and take my pants and jock off and all I could do was stumble. My feet were dying on me. The numbness had spread to my legs and my arms, and the pain was incredible. I almost passed out. If I had, no one would have known about it.

At the end of the game the doctor came back and felt

around my head. He put a little whiplash collar on me and told me to go home. No hospital, no X-rays, nothing. Go home.

There was nothing doing back at the dormitory where we were all staying. I was hurting but I went with a couple of teammates to a party over in Key Biscayne. By the time I got there I was beginning to feel like I had club feet and I was starting to really stiffen up, to do the Frankenstein. I drank two bottles of champagne, took some Percodans, and asked one of the guys to drive me home.

I couldn't sit up in the back of the car. I couldn't lie down. I hunched there like a crab while they drove me back to the dormitory, then I crawled into bed.

The game was on a Friday night. Saturday everybody was off. Sunday everybody was off. I was in my little Biscayne College training camp room by myself, nobody around.

I woke up at four in the morning feeling like someone was turning a knife in my neck and slamming my head with a rock at the same time. I couldn't move. I tried to get out of bed but I couldn't. I couldn't raise my head off the pillow. My arms and legs didn't work. I started screaming. No one was there to hear me.

I screamed from four o'clock in the morning until almost 8:30. "Help me! Somebody help me! Is anybody around?! Please! Help!" Finally a maid who was cleaning down the hall heard me and opened the door.

"Please get a doctor!" I cried to her.

She ran and got the trainers. Junior Wade came and said, "Let me get you over to the training room. Let me get you up." He pulled my hand with one hand and put his other behind my head. It felt like my skin was tearing away from my bones. He got me sitting on the side of the bed but I couldn't stand on my own. He had to pull me up. The pain was unreal.

I had to walk down two flights of stairs and across a parking lot and I was in tears. What was normally a ninety-second walk took me ten minutes walking like a zombie. The trainer took one look at me and said, "We've got to get this guy to the hospital." They didn't call an ambulance, they took me in a van. The bumps shot through me like shrapnel.

They sat me in the waiting room and wanted me to sign some forms before they'd let me in. I started shouting, "Will somebody get me a fucking bed! My head! I can't sit up anymore!" Finally they put me on a gurney, wheeled me down the hall and put me in traction.

A team doctor showed up that afternoon and helped them take X-rays. He showed up Sunday to take a look at them. "I think you just have a pinched nerve," he told me.

"No, Doc, I think I broke my fucking neck."

On Monday they took me in for a CAT scan and tomogram. The team doctor stood over me and looked at the results. "Henderson," he said, "you broke your neck. You will never play football again."

The first thing I thought was, "You know, I broke my neck before—in San Francisco."

The team doctor decided to put me in a Minerva collar. I was hurting from my hairline up to my crown, under my skull, because I had broken the C1 cervical vertebra and cracked number two, and five and six were spurred. He started with the plaster, wound it around until after a while I had this huge bowl around my head. I was carrying thirty pounds of plaster wrapped around my skull, looking like John the Baptist with his head on a plaster platter.

I still needed the cocaine, though. I couldn't get by without it. From my room I called this girl who brought a quarter ounce, some baking soda, a test tube and pipe and I started freebasing. In the hospital. For three days. Unless you know the faint scent freebase is odorless, and the nurses didn't catch on. I'd tuck the pipe between my legs when they came in. I was one sick fellow.

A few days later the team doctor told me I was going to be placed on injured reserve, that I wasn't going to play anymore. He didn't give me any therapy, he didn't prescribe any off-season training, he didn't prescribe any medication for the pain. All he did was tell me to come back in December for my end-of-the-year physical so they could release me. A football physician's care depends entirely on the patience of the team, not the pain of the patients.

With this huge plaster bowl around my head I went back to the Dolphins' training camp. In front of the whole squad Coach Shula said, "I give Henderson all the credit in the world. He worked hard, he was going to be a contributor to this team, a good player for us." He took me aside and told me, "Thomas, damn, this was unfortunate. I had big plans for you this year. But you need to take care of yourself."

I was going to be paid my full year's salary, $125,000. I had nothing to do. I flew back to Dallas and moved in with Sally. Ken was the name of my new coke connection and he had the purest cocaine I'd ever smoked. His stuff would get so hard when you cooked it that you could throw it against the wall and it would roll back to you like a marble. I began to fullblown freebase all over again.

I went to see one of the best orthopedic specialists in the Southwest, Dr. David Selby, and he told me that what the Dolphins' doctor had put me in was prehistoric. He told me that proper orthopedic treatment would have put me in a halo, that this Minerva collar was unnecessary. He sawed the thirty pounds of plaster off and put me in a fiberglass collar instead. Finally I could lie down. It didn't take away the pain and stiffness but it did allow me to shower.

I later filed grievances and appeals with the NFL and the Players Association about my mistreatment at the hands of the 49er doctors and the fact that the Dolphins didn't pick up my option. I was in the league a year short of the new collective bargaining agreement, so I got cut out of severance pay.

I couldn't play football, I was living in pain, my past was catching up to me and I had no future. All I had was my salary and my cocaine. I was taking home about six thousand dollars each week of the season, sixteen weeks, and it all went for dope. Ken got each and every one of my checks. I spent my entire salary, every red cent, freebasing.

All I could see was the pipe. It blocked out everything.

Friends, family, food. Nothing else mattered. I'd wake up sweaty, nauseous, with my nose bleeding, my bones rattling, nerves screaming, wanting to die. Some days I didn't get up at all. I had nobody, no mother, no daughter, no wife. All I had was the dope man and the pipe. I don't remember much out of that sixteen weeks. It's all a blackout, a whiteout, a cokeout. I don't know what the hell happened in the real world. In mine it was me and the pipe. I was living in hell.

By December 1981 I was broke. Roger Staubach had sold my dream house and I had smoked up the several thousand dollars from that. I had pawned my Super Bowl rings to a friend for seventy-five hundred dollars and had smoked that up too. The Dolphins had made the playoffs and had one more check for me, and I was supposed to show up for a final physical, so I hopped on a plane for Miami.

The Dolphins' doctor gave me the once-over, wrote a report, dismissed me and said that was it. I picked up my check for fifty-six hundred dollars.

I hooked up with a club owner named James for a couple of days and partied with him and some girls. Freak parties. Sex parties. It always amazed me what women would do for freebase. I was at some wild parties when the pipe was hot. When I had the coke I could have all the women I wanted; when they hit it they always wanted more. They'd leave my door and then come back knocking. "Can I have another hit, please, before I go?" Then they would leave and come back. "Can I have another hit?" Any sex act you could think of, women would do just to get a hit of the rock.

There's one big problem with that, though: When you're freebasing steady, when you're hitting the pipe like it's batting practice, you can't get it up. There's no big sexual activity going on after a while because it would take a fork lift, a crane, to get it up.

By the time I was done with that party I had twenty-five hundred dollars and an ounce of coke left.

My divorce had become final and I had promised my daughter that I was going to be with her for Christmas. She and her mother were in Nashville. Thomesa was almost three years old and she knew who her daddy was. On Christmas Eve I called.

"Hi, Thomesa, this is Daddy. Daddy will be home for Christmas. You'll see Daddy. I love you, Thomesa."

I got up, took a shower, got out, put a rock on the pipe and fired it up. I hit the pipe and missed my flight. Hit the pipe and missed Christmas. Hit the pipe and missed my daughter. Hitting and missing, hitting and missing.

I came to on December twenty-seventh.

When I got back to Dallas I was broke. Sally had moved out. All I had was a Mercedes-Benz and my clothes. I scurried around and found five hundred dollars here, a thousand dollars there, tucked into bank accounts I'd forgotten I had, but I had no money coming in and my habit was draining me. I was barely making it from day to day. I would cruise around Dallas and stay with whatever girls I met or called. I was wearing out my welcome everywhere.

By pure luck I got a letter in the mail from the singer B.J. Thomas inviting me to a New Year's party at his house. It turned out that he had wanted to meet me and talk to me for a long time. At the party I found out that we had some similar problems. B.J. had had the same doctor in Nashville as Elvis Presley and had had a hard time with pills. His wife, Gloria, he told me, had saved his life. He seemed like a man who knew what I was going through.

A couple of weeks after meeting him I called B.J. up and started to cry. "Look, man, I don't have no money, I have nowhere to live." In January 1982, after all the high times—the game, the fame, the cocaine—I didn't have anything. My child, my wife, my career, my friends, my Super Bowl rings, all gone. I didn't have money to put gas in my car. I wanted to die.

The big money was gone. I could go to Drew Pearson and get a hundred dollars, to Tony Dorsett and get a hundred dollars to tide me over. My best friend Too Tall wouldn't give me a quarter; he knew I was on cocaine and he wasn't going to support that habit. And he was right, every time I got two hundred dollars in my pocket I'd go buy two grams. When I ran out of money I wouldn't do any but if I had five hundred I would go and spend that on a quarter ounce, and beg for a quarter at that price. All I had was my name and I began borrowing on that. To the public I was still "Hollywood" Henderson, they didn't know the depths of what was going on.

B.J. told me to come stay with him for a few days. When he and his wife bought a new condominium as an investment I ended up staying in the new place for nine months. The condo was in Arlington, Texas, which was great for me. I had to get out of Dallas. If I'd stayed in Dallas I would have been in the gutter. I didn't want to be in the gutter and I didn't want people to see me in the gutter.

For almost a year B.J. Thomas supported me. He paid the rent, bought the groceries, even gave me pocket money, basically kept me alive. It wasn't a longtime friendship but it was a friendship of understanding. I felt guilty for accepting his charity, and I promised to repay him with money I was going to get as workman's compensation from the NFL, but I wasn't capable of doing anything substantial about paying him back.

Still, despite his good intentions, B.J. Thomas was my enabler. He enabled me to continue my disease, to use cocaine. I had no responsibilities to anyone, let alone myself, and B.J.'s gesture of good will enabled me to take whatever money I conned people out of, begged for, promised to pay back, and use it to buy cocaine.

I got a job in an executive recruitment firm, shaking hands and impressing people while I tried to convince them to change jobs. I was an entirely different Headhunter of the Week. I was good at it, but the job had its hazards. I started going to lunch with the coat-and-tie-wearing people and I started getting into drinking.

I had decided at a very young age that I wasn't going to be a drunk. Seth and Whiskey, plus my mama and daddy, were people I didn't want to grow up to be. I never liked the taste of beer so I never drank a lot of that with the rest of the guys, and I didn't like scotch or whiskey or bourbon. But this Tom Collins wasn't half bad and this Tanqueray and tonic tasted great. Plus, I was a gulper. I'm like that with everything. I drank this stuff like it was lemonade and I wouldn't know I was going to get drunk until way after it had happened. I never caught on.

I'd have five Tanqueray and tonics at lunchtime, go back to the office at about two o'clock, then come back again at Happy Hour. They served doubles at Happy Hour and I'd down twenty to twenty-five more. By eight o'clock it'd be time to go but I'd tell myself the traffic was too heavy, that I'd wait it out. Of course, by two in the morning the traffic had died down a little.

I was very proud of the fact that I could walk out of the bars without stumbling. I could walk to my car and drive home without appearing to be drunk. But the blackouts began to fall together. Between 1982 and 1983 it got to where I didn't remember from one day to the next what I had done or what bar I'd been at. I began drinking a can of beer for breakfast when I got up in the morning to get me started. Then I moved on to a quart of gin a day. I became a full-blown alcoholic. I had a double addiction now.

I could grab a bottle of booze a lot quicker than I could get an ounce of cocaine, and it was a whole lot cheaper. It was a matter of economics. When I made some money I went and spent it on coke, but that money went fast and when I blew it I went back to my gin.

One time when I had put a couple of thousand together I bought an ounce from Suite and went back to the condo to cook it up. It was good to have this stuff again, I was glad to get back to it. I put the rock in the pipe and lit it up. Like I usually did, I took a deep breath, blew all the air out of my lungs and then inhaled as hard as I could and took a giant hit. All the freebase flew up into me.

When I woke up I was on the floor. I had bitten my tongue, there was blood in the corner of my mouth and a knot on my head from where I'd fallen. I'd had a seizure.

The first thing I thought was, "Wow. Now how did I do that?!"

I was so out of control that I was out there trying to have a seizure again. Heart attack? Stroke? Forget it! I wanted another hit just like that one! I put my feet in the same spot they'd been when I'd fallen, I blew out and inhaled once more. No luck. Not that night. I just kept missing. But from then on I knew what I was after. The ultimate hit was right up there with cardiac arrest.

Finally, B.J. and his wife asked me to leave. They kicked me out of the nest. I had borrowed from my employer, used my car as collateral, and gotten my own place. But when I looked at my job I found I was making a living, not living a life. I quit. I stopped paying rent in February and on my thirtieth birthday, March 1, 1983, I was broke again. I didn't even have my Mercedes-Benz. I had nothing.

I decided to do a geographic, go to California. I didn't know where in California, I didn't know anybody in California, but I was "Hollywood," why not. There was nothing for me in Texas. I owed everybody money.

Before I left I took one more turn around my friends and acquaintances, borrowing dollars. I could still talk. I retrieved my Super Bowl rings and even conned up a bankroll of about five thousand dollars. One day I was so tweaked, broke and needing more dope that I called the Cowboys and threatened to tell about everybody I knew on the team and in the office who was doing cocaine. They said they had nothing to hide. I knew that wasn't true but I didn't call their bluff.

I drove to the Coast. Didn't turn over the car to my ex-employer; in my own sick mind I felt that he had swindled me out of it. Imagine, making me give up my last sign of celebrity just because I owed him over ten thousand dollars. I filled my Mercedes up with clothes, boots, shoes, trophies, plaques, awards, footballs, and took off.

I averaged one hundred miles per hour all across the state of Texas, nobody stopped me. I almost drove off the road near Flagstaff, Arizona, pushing that car to its limits. I think I really wanted to die.

I stopped in Las Vegas and won eleven hundred dollars at the crap tables, freebased in my room.

In Los Angeles I dropped in on an attorney, Arnie Gold, who I had seen about suing the NFL, the Dolphins, 49ers, Cowboys and anybody else involved in my football career because of my injuries. I stayed with a friend named Howard for about a week, borrowed fifteen hundred dollars and left.

I scammed and worked odd jobs for several months in L.A. I didn't freebase because I needed whatever money I had to pay the rent on a small apartment in Long Beach and to eat. I wasn't sober, though, I was just dry. Then the dollar flow started up again.

Several years before, me and Too Tall and Drew Pearson and Jay Saldi had been in a movie called *Squeeze Play,* a low-budget film that starred the daughter of the producer. It was a ridiculous movie, a true pile of crap, might have played in a half dozen drive-ins around the South. But now, somehow, someone wanted to release it again. And pay me ten thousand dollars to go around the country promoting it! They were going to give me the cash in two five-thousand-dollar payments.

I called my connection. "Flo, we are rolling."

I smoked the first installment in a blur. Then I went on the road and did the promos. I didn't freebase on the road. All I did was hype this dumb movie and look forward to the next five thousand dollars.

When I got it I put it in the pipe.

I lost my Mercedes to freebase. I was smoking while driving and I hit a serious dip in the road, didn't see it until after I'd hit it. Busted the oil pan. If I'd gotten out and had it fixed everything would've been all right, but I was tweaked and couldn't be bothered. I looked out the rear view mirror a little later and there was black smoke billowing behind me. I was hoping that it would just go away but it didn't. The motor froze.

I pulled my beautiful Mercedes-Benz over in a driveway and left it there. When it gathered enough tickets it would get pulled to the pound. When they came for its owner they'd be looking for an executive consulting firm in Dallas. I was too tweaked to do anything but walk away.

Then came the worst day of my life. November 2, 1983.

I had bought a quarter ounce of coke and was preparing to cook it and smoke it. I needed some 151 rum, which is used to burn the stuff, plus some cigarettes and beer, so I walked to a store down the block from my apartment to get it.

There's a ruling known informally as the Son of Sam law, which states that a convicted felon may not make money off telling the story of his crime. I'm the last guy who wants to run afoul of that law, so I will describe what happened next only in outline.

As I came out of the store and was going home, two girls who were at the corner bus stop asked me for a cigarette. They noticed my Super Bowl rings, noticed that I was high, asked if they could get high with me. I invited them home. I cooked the cocaine and we all freebased from about 4:30 in the afternoon until about 10:00 at night. We did some fondling. One of the girls and I had sex. We all talked and freebased some more. It was a long evening. At one point one of the girls tried to rip off some of my money and I had to threaten her to get it back. (I had an unloaded gun among my stuff.) I put the gun away. We had more sex. We freebased some more. They left.

The next thing I knew the cops were at my door. The girls were underage.

My arrest hit the papers in the morning. My mother called from Austin. "Thomas, what's going on?"

"Don't worry, Mama, it ain't nothing. It's gonna be over soon." I had done much more outrageous things than this. This was lightweight as far as I was concerned. I jerked the phone wire out of the wall and started freebasing. I based and I based and I based.

I seriously wanted to die. My life was in ruins, my football career over, my money gone. And I needed the cocaine more than ever just to keep going. I wanted to stick a gun in my mouth and blow my brains out, but the police had my gun.

I sat in my apartment with less than two thousand dollars

to my name. There was no use to me paying rent, getting food, anything. Just base and hope I died. I based up that two grand in a day's time, and I was being conservative; instead of taking a hit every five minutes I tried to hold off for fifteen or twenty.

Arnie Gold, the attorney representing me, had called a drug rehabilitation center. He assumed that I had health insurance that could cover it since I was only out of the NFL less than a year. He was wrong. When he called and asked me if I wanted to go into treatment I said I was ready for anything. He told me I needed it. "You know, man, I care about you," he said. "Screw this case. You just try and get yourself straightened out."

Arnie came and picked me up in his little red Mercedes. He walked into my apartment and it was barren: no living room furniture, just what was left of my clothes and mementoes heaped in one corner. I squinted up at him from a box spring and mattress lying on the floor. Four days after I was accused of committing this crime I checked into the Comprehensive Care Unit in Orange, California. I was spaced out of my mind.

The Care Unit is run by Dr. Joseph Pursch. He had treated Betty Ford, Billy Carter, the astronaut Buzz Aldrin, Vida Blue, and he was going to treat me. I had no money, no insurance, nothing. I got an immediate good feeling for the place; they didn't make me sign anything when I went in. They gave me a whole bunch of Valium—about eighty milligrams, enough to make me feel comfortable—and put me in the detox section, midafternoon, November 6.

The detoxification section was a little room with a television and a bunch of food. Orange juice, milk, cookies, grapes. I sat there and ate everything in sight. I was still tweaking, having been basing for several days. The Valium hadn't shut me down.

The television was supposed to be turned off at 11:00 at night but I told the nursing staff, "I'm not going to turn this fucking TV set off, and if you don't like it I'm going to leave this whole hospital." They don't like for patients to leave the facilities while they're under the influence of detox drugs so they told me if I kept the TV down I could stay with it.

I stayed in there all night. At about 6:00 the next morning they came and gave me another forty milligrams of Valium. Still didn't do it. At about seven A.M. I was lying there watching cartoons when I looked over to my left and saw these pink elephant slippers padding into the room. I looked up and saw this woman in her robe and pink elephant slippers—tusks and all—and I thought that I had lost my fucking mind, this was the loony bin. Finally I fell asleep.

I woke up two days after I'd gotten there and I was shaky, embarrassed. Then I was told that I had to have a meeting with Dr. Pursch, the medical director, and Dr. Stone. "Thomas," Dr. Pursch asked after we shook hands, "do you want to get sober?"

"Well, yeah, Doc. I've been in treatment before but it didn't work last time. They didn't heal me, they didn't cure me." Both of them laughed.

"Thomas, don't you know that you'll never get well from this disease?"

"What disease?" I interrupted.

"Alcoholism," Dr. Pursch said.

"My problem is not alcohol," I informed him, "my problem is cocaine."

"Did you use cocaine or alcohol first?" Dr. Stone asked.

"Alcohol."

"Well, you're an alcoholic."

"No, no, no, I'm not an alcoholic, I'm a cocaine abuser."

"Thomas, let me tell you something. Until you concede that you are an alcoholic too you can't ever recover."

"Okay, Doc," I answered, "I'm an alcoholic. I want to recover. I'm an alcoholic, is that all right? Is that what you want to hear? I'm an alcoholic."

"Thomas," Dr. Pursch said calmly. "we're going to start you in therapy. We know you don't have any money or insurance but we're going to take a shot on you. We're going to help you. That is, if you want help. We are not going to put up with any nonsense like you leaving this place or using drugs within this institution.''

They put me in a group and assigned a man named Phil Allen to be my individual therapist. The group was a hell of a mix. There were about eight people in it—an airline pilot, a millionaire, a farmer from Kansas, a housewife who hid vodka bottles all over the house—and they talked about how they were sick and how they drank and how they used. I started listening, then I started telling them about how I drank and used and functioned.

Phil Allen asked me, ''Thomas, was your life unmanageable as a result of alcohol and cocaine?'' I said yes. ''Then you're an alcoholic.''

That burned. I didn't want to be an alcoholic, I was a drug addict, a cocaine addict and only a cocaine addict; it made me unique.

Along with these in-patient therapy session groups the hospital required that patients participate in other, larger group meetings, which had developed twelve steps to sobriety. About five days after I had arrived at the Care Unit a man showed up named Chuck D. Chuck D. told me he loved me and that he wanted to take me to a meeting or two. He took me to this dungeon of a church in Anaheim and I sat there and listened to all these people talk about their being drunks, that they had been sober for four or five years but they were still having problems.

They introduced themselves as alcoholics. ''Hi. My name is William and I'm an alcoholic.'' I was dry by then, five days away from freebase, and I could see something in this hospital, in this treatment, that had been missing at Camelback. People were admitting their disease. And my therapist, a sixties kind of guy who had been through that era, was himself a former drug addict.

I spent a lot of time at those meetings, and as I started listening I started getting better. I started meeting people who were as sick as I was, some even sicker. Other drug addicts were sitting there telling what they'd done to get some dope: guys who had robbed and flim-flammed for it, women who had prostituted themselves, given ten blow jobs just to be around the pipe. The treatment was starting to catch on with me. I was there a month and I still hadn't used, hadn't wanted to use, hadn't thought about using.

By mid-December I had been sober for almost forty days. Dr. Pursch called me in. "Thomas, we can't keep you here any longer. But because I want to monitor you and keep you close to the program and close to the therapy I'm going to send you to a hospital near here, which is just opening. It's called Starting Point and the director's name is Don Beld."

I didn't want to leave the Care Unit, my emotional nail marks are probably still all over the walls of the halls, but I had to go. I had been there forty-two days and met some wonderful people, people trying to get well. Chuck D. became my sponsor. He had been an alcoholic but he had been clean and sober for ten years so he had the experience and the success I needed to draw from.

I checked into Starting Point in Costa Mesa, California, and continued going to the meetings, kept hanging around people who knew what my life had been like. I didn't feel dry, I felt sober. For the first time in a long time I was feeling okay about Thomas Henderson.

I stayed at Starting Point for sixty days. I wrote some syndicated articles about being sick and tired of being sick and tired. I was beginning to be convinced that I had found a way of life that would enable me to stay sober. Someone had looked me straight in the eye and said, "Thomas, you don't have to live like that anymore," and I had finally paid attention.

I started addressing the meetings, introducing myself: "My name is Thomas. I'm an alcoholic." It was not something that I was proud of, it was just something that I was.

When I reached the point where I could admit that I was an alcoholic my life began to change. I recognized that if I drank even one beer there was no question but that I would end up on Sunset Boulevard in a cheap hotel with some hookers and some freebase. I could come up with the money, I could con somebody out of enough to get me loaded; I had to stay away from the desire.

I wasn't conning anybody, I wasn't borrowing any money, I wasn't talking anybody out of anything. People were being nice to me. They had given me thirty-five thousand dollars of free treatment at the Care Unit and it had to be two hundred dollars a day at the Starting Point, which I wasn't being charged for.

I was going to meetings and people were loving me, hugging me. I stopped calling myself "Hollywood." I was Thomas. Nobody was asking me for my autograph. I wasn't a star, I was a fellow alcoholic. And I was hugging these people back for all their problems as well.

I started getting sober from fear, straight fear. I had felt like I was going to die and I didn't want to die. But if fear helped me get sober, love helped me maintain my sobriety. I couldn't believe these people, the love they had for me. Unconditional love. I had never met people like this, people who could stand up no matter how tall or how small, male or female, heterosexual, homosexual, bisexual, didn't matter who they were and say, "I'm an alcoholic, I'm a drug addict, and I don't want to live like that anymore."

People were accepting me. They didn't look at me as this outcast sex offender, they would look at me and say, "You know, I did some bad stuff myself." All drug addicts and alcoholics have frightened skeletons drying out in their closets. I just happened to be a celebrity and couldn't keep my secrets. When they heard me share the hard moments of my life they loved me anyway. It didn't matter who I was or what had happened. I was overwhelmed.

I spent December, January and February, 1984, at Starting Point and met a whole new group of people. I met Larney and Thomas V. I had already met P.J., another Dallas boy every bit as sick as I was. He was my roommate and we understood each other, each of us knew what the other was going through because we'd been there. Going through therapy with him was very important. He has become the best friend I have in the whole world.

I found out that this group was made up of people all over the world trying to stay sober, one drunk talking to another, one addict talking to another. I was going to three meetings a day, sometimes four. My sponsor, Chuck D., insisted that I go to as many as I could. I wasn't working so I better go out there and work on staying sober.

There were Saturday sessions. One was mandatory. I went to four. We all sat around what looked like a shiny and official boardroom table. The doctor had given us all pillows and told us we could sit or lie down anywhere we wanted. One by one the group members went their ways until I was the only one left at the table. I couldn't see them. Was I supposed to be on the floor? I lay down on my back and put the pillow under my head.

The doctor took us on a journey. I don't know if we were hypnotized or not. I didn't think so at the time. He put us in the middle of the ocean, on our backs, swimming effortlessly. I was there, in the water, I could feel it. Then he had us dive. I stopped stroking and turned over and dove to the bottom.

There was a treasure chest sitting on the ocean floor. The doctor brought it into focus. He asked me, he asked all of us, to open it up. What did we see?

Each of us saw different things. What I saw was hope. That's what I wanted to see and that's what was there. The doctor brought us back to the surface.

Then we were in a hospital, far far away. Thomas was lying in a hospital bed, far far away, and I was dying. The doctors couldn't do anything else for me. The nurses didn't answer the bell when I rang for them, the pain medication wasn't working anymore, my mother and my family weren't coming to see me. I was dying.

As I lay on the floor of the treatment room, tears fell down my face. It was so clear to me, and so real, that if I didn't change my life I was going to die.

That day, that session, was my foundation. Everybody has his or her moment of clarity; mine was right there. I couldn't use any mind-altering chemicals anymore, I realized, or I would be a dead man. Not everyone at that session got something out of it, but I found that when you're willing, when you're ready, and when you make that decision to change, all the possibilities are open to you.

I met a girl in treatment. A very beautiful girl named Diane. She was an out-patient but she would often come to visit. We went to movies together and talked, we went to special places and made love. It was a whole new kind of lovemaking for me that actually involved love.

The time came for me to leave Starting Point and try and find my own place. Dr. Pursch and all my therapists and fellow addicts and drunks, and me, had brought me to sobriety. It was up to me to stay there. "Anything is possible in sobriety," Dr. Pursch told me. "Nothing is possible if you use."

But always in the back of my mind I knew I had to deal with the law. My preliminary hearing came up and I had to go to court. I was accused of doing all kinds of horrible things that I hadn't done, as well as the things I did. The prosecution was going to pull people in from all around the country and document my sins. The press, which I had courted and chased in my Cowboy days, was now in a feeding frenzy. Despite all the progress I had made, I wanted to die.

I contacted one of the girls who had brought the charges and asked whether she and her friend would take ten thousand dollars to drop the case. If a lawyer had done it it would have been negotiating a settlement. I got busted for bribery.

A series of negotiations resulted in a plea bargain: no contest to sexual battery and bribery. Sentence: four years, eight months in prison.

Dr. Pursch told me, "You thought you could buy your way out of another one, didn't you? But you didn't use, and that's what's important. You are not going to be a perfect human being in sobriety, life won't always be a bowl of cherries, but as long as you don't drink and as long as you don't do cocaine, you will be okay, Thomas. You'll make it."

11

One Day at a Time

I wasn't so sure. I was sober but so what? I was about to become a convict, I'd be a convict or an ex-con the rest of my life. There would be shame in my family, shame on me in all the papers, on all the networks, shame in front of everyone I knew. Why be sober when there's no life to live?

My Aunt Gwen telephoned me in prison shortly after I arrived. She told me my brother Allen had killed himself a few days before I went in. He had been one of Billy's sons, a corrections officer at Attica Prison in New York—and a freebaser. I had freebased with him in New York. Now he had committed suicide.

I started crying. A powerful cry, hard, moaning and wailing from deep down inside of me. But I wasn't crying for Allen, I was crying for me. I was crying for being a coward. That was what I should've done, I roared, I should be dead, I should have killed myself! Screw sobriety, screw living, screw everything! I had nothing, why didn't I just kill myself? Allen, you were brave; I was the coward. I didn't like feeling like a coward. Why hadn't I killed myself? Why hadn't I done it when I was on the outside when I'd had a chance? How can I do it now? I cried for several hours straight. For several days there in maximum security prison in Chino, California, I was in a suicidal tantrum.

Somehow I came out of it. I had my sobriety. It was all that I had and I clung to it.

The way prison sentences work is that for every day of good time you do you get one day off your sentence. Cause them problems and you serve it all. If I stayed between the lines I could get out in twenty-eight months and that's what I aimed at.

You'd think that in prison, of all places, you would be free of the temptation of drugs, that a maximum security sentence would mean enforced sobriety. You would be wrong. I was not safe from cocaine, marijuana or heroin in prison, they were plentiful. The police bring it in and so do visitors. The inmates receive it in the visiting room in prophylactics or balloons and stick it up their butts. It's called "kiestering," as in "Charlie kiestered in a quarter." Talk about fertilized dope.

The idea of me using drugs was preposterous. I was seven months and three days sober when I entered prison, I was living one day at a time and I knew that if I slipped now it was forever, I didn't have another one in me. I prayed to some power greater than myself to help me stay sober in prison.

I started getting mail. Hundreds of letters started coming in. Not from football fans, not from Dallas Cowboy fans. Letters from drunks. Alcoholics and drug addicts from my meetings were writing and telling me that they loved me. "It's okay," they were writing, "we'll be waiting for you." "You'll be clean almost three years when you get out." "Just keep doing what you were doing while you were out here. We know it was tough for you." And "Through your strength and through your staying sober and through your showing up at these meetings and saying, 'My name is Thomas and I'm an alcoholic,' you helped me stay sober."

I just lit up. I had brought some of my meetings' literature into prison but what I had also brought in, without hardly knowing it, was the friendship, love and understanding of all these people.

Prison was no picnic. I was out from under the NFL's umbrella and wasn't about to get any celebrity treatment. I didn't get sent to any country club setup like your basic convicted congressman or inside trader. They sent me to max. Susanville Correctional Facility all the way up north by the Oregon border.

I got off the bus on July 17, 1984, and a big black guy met me in the yard. Everybody knew I was coming. Convicts basically run the prisons from the inside and they've got a communications system that works like the drums. I was expected. In prison I was going to be Hollywood.

This guy was six foot five, about four hundred pounds. A big sucker. He was going to give me my orientation lecture. There were about thirty guys on the bus in but he got a hold of me and walked me around the prison yard. I knew about tough guys in the street but inside there were a whole new set of rules.

"Look, man, this is what's happening here," he told me. "Everybody knows what your beef is so you're gonna have to be extra careful. The one thing they don't like around here is a sex offender."

A six-foot white guy who must have weighed 230 walked by, covered with tattoos from head to foot. I turned to look at him after he'd passed and spread across his back, tattooed from shoulder to shoulder like a name on a football jersey, was "100% Pure Honkie." This must be prison. "Well," I said, "I have arrived."

"Henderson," the black guy said, "this is the way it breaks down. We've got the BGFs, the Black Gorilla Family; we have the Crips, we have the Bloods, we have the Pyroos, we have the guys from Palo Alto; we've got guys from the north, 415, which is the Oakland–San Francisco area; we have the North and South Mexicans and we've got the Mexican Mafia; we've got the Aryan Brothers and we've got the Nazis. Each one of these groups has a yard rep here in Susanville and we try and stay out of each other's way. Ninety-nine percent of the guys who come into prison, if they were not a gang member on the streets, try to hook up with a gang when they get here. You being 'Hollywood' I don't think you're going to have any problems with that but I don't know for sure.''

I said, "Fuck that." I was cocky in the beginning. I wanted to be a free agent. I wasn't joining up with anyone. Groups. Protection. In prison they call them "cars"; "You gettin' in the car, man?" I figured me for a one-seater.

I got settled in at Susanville. They had me working in the gymnasium, training inmates, putting them through calisthenics. The corrections officer/coach said I'd be getting paid thirty-eight dollars a month. I said, "That much?"

By mid-August I thought I knew how to play prison: Do your job and cover your ass. I was lying on a hardwood bench in the television room of my dorm about eleven o'clock one morning watching *The Young and the Restless*. Across from me this little Mexican kid had pulled the mattress off his bed, put it on the floor, propped a pillow behind his head and was watching it with me. I liked this kid. He was about nineteen years old, funny, talked about how he came out of Mexico but wasn't ever going home. Not if he could help it.

"What about parole, man?" I asked him.

"I'm an illegal alien, Homes." Everybody calls everybody "Homes" in prison, especially the Mexicans. "We don't have parole, Homes, they take us back to Mexico. And when we get back to Mexico, Homes, we come right back across. I already got my ID made up, Homes, got my little green card. . . ."

I liked him. I liked seeing him beating the United States Immigration. "Okay, man," I laughed, "go for it."

The dorm was a big Quonset hut with one entrance on each end. I looked up and saw about six Mexicans come through the back door. Another six appeared at the front door and they all had shanks, pieces of sharpened metal wound round with tape for a handle. They came in there and jumped on this kid and started sticking him unbelievably.

My years of living on the street came right back to me and I jumped back into a corner and watched this madness. They were sticking him in his feet, his back, his arms. He was doing his best and keeping them off of his vital organs but they were kicking him in his face and getting at him. He lay on his back clawing like a cat, kicking, kicking, kicking. But every time he would kick at someone they would stick him with a knife.

I couldn't take it. I started screaming at the top of my lungs. "You coward motherfuckers, get off that kid! Get off of him, you fucking cowards! Get off of him!"

They looked at me with rage in their eyes and left the dorm. Didn't run like they were scared, just hurried like they didn't want to leave their business unfinished. The police were in there in a minute.

I stepped outside the dorm and saw the guy who had eyed me throw down his blade. I saw which dorm he ran to. I wanted to tell the cops, "Hey, there that fucker is, right there," but I didn't. That one piece of street smarts probably saved my life.

The kid had gotten stuck fourteen times but nowhere vital. Just a bunch of punctures. His nose was swollen badly from getting kicked but he would live.

The whole place went on lock-down. We were all confined to quarters.

It turned out that the North Mexicans had attacked the South Mexicans. One of the shot callers had called it on this youngster and I had just happened to be there.

My name came up immediately. First it came up with the North Mexicans: "This fuckin' nigger's interfering with our business. He don't fuckin' know that it's been goin' on for a hundred years. We hit them, they hit us back, we hit them. They hit one of our boys down south yesterday. We've gotta hit one of them up here today." The kid had probably smart-mouthed one of them but he had been picked because he had a brother or a cousin who was big up in his own organization and the North Mexicans just wanted to hit him.

I saved the kid's life. They had planned to kill him. It was a contract hit, they never would've found out who did it. That's what scared me. I had got in the way and now it was me. My instincts were telling me, "Henderson, you got to grab one of these Mexicans, I don't care where he's from, and beat the hell out of him." It was called a "PC move," because if I beat someone they were going to ship my ass in Protective Custody to some other joint. But we were on lockdown status so I didn't have a chance yet.

At about 2:30 in the afternoon we were put on control release status for lunch. The prison administration knew who really ran this place and they didn't want a full-scale riot on their hands. They called all the yard reps out—the head of the North, the head of the South, the head of the Crips, the head of the Bloods, the head of the BGF, the head of the Mafia, the head of the Aryan Brothers, the head of the Nazis—and gathered them out in the middle of the yard. Everybody in the prison was watching. The reps said, "We want Henderson out there too."

Two corrections officers came and got me, escorted me to the middle of the field and left me with all these leaders, these shot callers. The BGF man, his name was Paul, said "Look here, y'all, we're gonna talk to him and then we'll let him talk to you all." All the black leaders took me and sat me behind the baseball diamond on a bench.

Paul said, "Henderson, look here, man, we know you ain't never done no time. We know you're not used to this prison life, prison rules, the way things work around here. I want you to know, man, the North Mexicans want to kill you. You interfered with a hit and they want to kill you, man." If I hadn't been "Hollywood" and I had just kicked back, Paul told me, in another two or three weeks, a month, two months, they would have caught me sleeping in my rack and I'd be a dead man.

He started telling me the rules. "Henderson, from now on, man, if you see a fight, if you see a hit, if you see a man get his head cut right off in front of you, you just turn your fucking back and walk away from it, it's none of your fucking business. These Chicanos have been killing each other forever and they will continue to do it.

"Let me tell you something, man," he said. "On the street

a Chicano could have killed a man's mama but when he comes in here it's down to South or North. If they're both from the same side of town, they're brothers. They'll tell him, 'We know he killed your mama but there ain't no retaliation on that end in here. We're down together in here. That shit's dead.' If anything happens to this guy who killed his mama, they're gonna kill him."

They told me the laws of the land and I guarantee you I wanted to leave the goddamn land.

I went over to talk to the North Mexicans, the ones who were offended. They had the captain and two lieutenants out there. They actually had rank and file in the joint, that's how organized they are. I told them, "Look, I didn't know what was happening. I had never seen nothing like that. I reacted. I'm sorry, man, I didn't mean to butt in. I didn't know anything about this stuff. I've been told the rules and you can all stuff hot tamales up each other's ass, I ain't gonna fuck with it."

Then I had to go talk to the South Mexicans. Their story was a little different. They told me, "Thank you, man, you saved the kid's life. We knew the hit was coming down, we just didn't know who it was on. Be down, Hollywood. Look here, man, we're gonna put a vigil on your dorm for a couple of weeks anyway. The South Mexicans down with you, man, 'cause you saved the little youngster, man. We appreciate that."

When I got back to the dorm one of these rough-dried-ass black guys who was going to be playing by these rules for the next forty years took me aside and told me the worst horror stories I ever wanted to hear about what could happen to me. "Forget this amnesty bullshit. In the morning, man, when the dorm is rackin' at 6:15, you got to be up, you got to be out of bed. No more naps in the middle of the daytime, Henderson. I don't give a damn how big you is, them motherfuckers will come in and rat-pack your ass. Some of those boys will be wanting to make a name for themself, come in here and killed 'Hollywood.'"

I was terrified. I never backed down from a fight in my

life but I wasn't taking on a dozen Chicanos and living to tell the story. I had to get out of there. For the next month I couldn't even stand in the chow line without my back to the wall. I learned quick that there is no rehabilitation designed into the prison system, no reform; prisons are warehouses. It took me two months to convince the prison psychiatrist that if I stayed at Susanville I was going to commit mayhem. Finally I got transferred out of there.

But it wasn't all horror stories inside. On November 8, 1984, I stood up at a substance abuse meeting in San Luis Obispo Prison full of drunks and addicts who had committed rapes and robberies and mass murders and every hideous crime you could think of while they were under the influence—a hundred lifers who don't know when they're ever getting out and fifty more guys who have thirty or forty more years to go—and I told them, "My name is Thomas and I'm an alcoholic and today I have one year of continuous sobriety, and I'm in prison, and I'm happy about this moment. This is my birthday, my sobriety birthday, and I'm happy about it." I went to two meetings a week for the entire time I was in prison.

There were even some rewards. I studied and earned a certificate that qualified me to teach the Laubach Way of Reading, a national program, and I began to lead classes in the inmate training program. I had students from twenty-one years old to fifty, career criminals who could not read or write. These men did not know their ABCs. They knew the song, could sing most of it, but they'd miss sometimes when they got to the LMNOP. I'd teach them the consonant sounds, the vowels.

At first I felt stupid saying. "This is an F," and tracing it with my finger in a primer. "This is a fish with a long fin. Say 'fish.' " But I had five students and some of them took to it. Not all of them, a couple dropped out, but I was persistent and after five months the two worst students, who I didn't figure had a prayer in hell of ever putting their names on paper, wrote the first letter of their lives. It was to their mothers. The letters were simple but the spelling was correct and they did their best at punctuation. They used little words like "love" and "miss." "I miss you. I love you. This is my first letter, Mama, I am learning how to read and write and a guy named 'Hollywood' Henderson is helping me."

I felt wonderful. I was giving something away.

I had broken off contact with Diane right before I went inside. I didn't want to drag her into my degradation. But after five months I wrote to her and we began to correspond with each other. When I got transferred to San Luis Obispo she drove five hundred miles round-trip to see me and we found that we really liked, loved, wanted and needed each other. She was an inspiration and we talked and wrote and sustained each other.

On June 3, 1985, I married Diane Marie. This dope addict, this convicted sex criminal, this condemned man had a smart, lovely, beautiful wife who loved him and was waiting for him. Diane's love and patience and understanding helped me stay sober, helped me function as a person and not as a convict. It was the most important strength she could give me.

On November 8, 1985, a year after my first sobriety birthday, at the same prison in front of the same core of people, I stood up and said, "My name is Thomas. I'm an alcoholic and I'm still among you. You know there are a lot of drugs here but today I have two years continual sobriety. I'm living in serenity in the midst of madness."

My whole life was based on sobriety. I could have a life out there if I didn't drink and didn't use drugs.

In prison I got letters from Roger Staubach and Bob Bruenig wishing me well and offering me moral support. I called my friend Jeff Cohen and talked to him. "Thomas," he told me, "I like you but I don't trust you. But hearing you talk about your sobriety you sound like a new man. Just do what you say you're going to do."

I got out of prison at 10:00 A.M. on October 15, 1986. My wife came to the prison gate and picked me up. I got in her car and did not look back. About a minute out of there I started to laugh. Not some amused chuckle, not a celebrity's smirk or some clown's giggle, this was loud hysterical guffaws coming up from somewhere deep in my chest. I laughed for ten minutes solid, it was that or break down completely.

There was a pizza place on the side of the road. "I want a pizza!" I shouted. There was a doughnut shop. "I want a doughnut!" There were the golden arches. "I want a Big Mac! And fries!" I roared. I was like a kid on a spree, I wanted everything—and I went and got it. I was overjoyed to see my wife, to be on the outside, to be free.

What I didn't do was get a drink, snort up a line, light up a bowl. Not for me. Not then, not now, not ever again.

I am building a new life with my wife, Diane. I am finally in love. I am married to a woman who loves me because I'm Thomas, not because I'm a football player or I'm famous or I'm rich—I'm none of those things. And I love her. In sobriety I understand how to give, I understand fidelity, I understand what it is to be a husband. I'm a dependent person, always have been, and I like being married now. We have a true love affair going.

Doctors tell me I am permanently disabled from having broken my neck. A doctor from the NFL told me I was a "cripple," said I was lucky I wasn't in a wheelchair. "Be careful, young man," he said, whiplash in a car crash could kill me. Normal physical labor is out of the question.

I lost five or six years of my playing career, plus a whole range of postfootball opportunities in the real world, due to an injury in a football uniform in the Orange Bowl playing for the Miami Dolphins. I can never play football again. I'll miss it. I loved to play, to hit, to feel that good adrenaline pumping inside me. And I loved all the things football brought me. I just wish I had been able to handle it better. Years ago I would have felt sorry for myself over a bunch of drinks or a bowl of cocaine. Not now. I have to let go of the past.

Even so, I would like to play one more game. I'd like to play middle linebacker against Tom Landry and the Dallas Cowboys in the Super Bowl. No, not the Super Bowl; I told Coach Landry that they wouldn't go to the Super Bowl without me. Make it the NFC Championship, fourth and goal on the one-inch line, final seconds, everything hanging in the balance. If Coach Landry loses this game he loses his job, he gets fired. They hike the ball and I come across the line, and it doesn't matter who the running back is I just nail him. The official says, "No touchdown." Time runs out.

I was lucky enough to play professional football and become famous—I loved the game—but in the midst of that success I lost the use of my free will to an obsession with drugs and chemicals. My religious beliefs were null and void. I lost complete control of my sexuality, my morals, what I really believed in, how I felt. I lost control of relationships, family ties, I lost it all. I will not forget that, I keep that memory green, but I am moving beyond it.

I've never been the perfect father but I want my daughter to know who I am and that I love her and someday I will be with her. I am proud of some of the things I have accomplished, ashamed of others, but what I'm most proud of now is that in my heart and soul I have forgiven myself and asked God to do the same. Every chance I get I try to make amends to people I've hurt along the way.

I played in three Super Bowls but now I'm in the Sober Bowl. Whenever I can talk to a drunk, or go to a rehabilitation center, or go to a meeting where people are staying sober, or talk to a newcomer who wants to get sober and tell him what it was like for me, those are big rewards.

Today I live one day at a time. My wasted years are forever gone, the days I can't recall. If I could live those days again I'd be a lot closer to God. On the other hand, there are no saints without a past nor sinners without a future.

I'm still an alcoholic and an addict and I always will be. The only difference is that I don't drink or use drugs, one day at a time. That's the deal.

These days I travel the United States sharing my experience, strength and hope at drug rehab centers, colleges, high schools, and with alcoholics and addicts who are still suffering. If education is the best deterrent, the educator must be someone who has suffered from drug addiction and alcoholism. Folks have to know *why* to say no to drugs and alcohol.

I've made a whole lot of battlefield mistakes and I know where the mines are hidden. I'm lucky to be alive. I'm not hiding anything about myself, my career, my family, or any other parts of my life that were affected by my addiction. I can tell people what it was like, what happened to me, and what it's like now. I hope that will help. I know it helped when people told it to me.

I am living one day at a time and I have been sober now for almost four years. I live in hope. As Dr. Pursch told me, "Anything is possible in sobriety. Nothing is possible if I use." Finally, for the first time, I am in control.

DON'T MISS
BRUCE NASH AND ALLAN ZULLO'S

___ **THE BASEBALL HALL OF SHAME** ....62062/$6.95

___ **THE BASEBALL HALL OF SHAME 2** ....61113/$6.95

___ **THE BASEBALL HALL OF SHAME 3** ....63386/$6.95

___ **THE SPORTS HALL OF SHAME** ....63387/$8.95

___ **BASEBALL CONFIDENTIAL** ....65832/$6.95

___ **THE MISFORYUNE 500:**
THE BUSINESS OF SHAME ....62062/$6.95

___ **THE FOOTBALL HALL OF SHAME** .....62062/$6.95

POCKET
B O O K S

Simon & Schuster, Mail Order Dept. BBB
Simon & Schuster, Mail Order Dept. BBB
200 Old Tappan Rd., Old Tappan, N.J. 07675

Please send me the books I have checked above. I am enclosing $_____ (please add 75¢ to cover postage and handling for each order. N.Y.S. and N.Y.C. residents please add appropriate sales tax). Send check or money order—no cash or C.O.D.'s please. Allow up to six weeks for delivery. For purchases over $10.00 you may use VISA: card number, expiration date and customer signature must be included.

Name _____

Address _____

City _____ State/Zip _____

VISA Card No. _____ Exp. Date _____

Signature _____ 173-06